THE GREAT LATIN AMERICAN NOVEL

:an Novel

Translated from the Spanish by Brendan Riley

DALKEY ARCHIVE PRESS

Originally published in Spanish as *La gran novela latinoamericana* by Alfaguara in 2011.

© 2011 by Carlos Fuentes
Translation © 2016 by Brendan Riley

Library of Congress Cataloging-in-Publication Data

Names: Fuentes, Carlos, author. | Riley, Brendan, translator.
Title: The great Latin American novel / by Carlos Fuentes ; translated by
    Brendan Riley.
Other titles: Gran novela latinoamericana. English
Description: 1st ed. | Victoria, TX : Dalkey Archive Press, 2016. |
    Originally published as La gran novela latinoamericana (Madrid :
    Alfaguara, c2011).
Identifiers: LCCN 2015040718 | ISBN 9781628971309 (pbk. : alk. paper)
Subjects: LCSH: Latin American fiction--History and criticism.
Classification: LCC PQ7082.N7 F78513 2016 | DDC 863/.009--dc23
LC record available at http://lccn.loc.gov/2015040718

Partially funded by a grant by the Illinois Arts Council, a state agency

This book is, in part, made possible through the generous support
of the University of Houston-Victoria.

Dalkey Archive Press
Victoria, TX / McLean, IL / Dublin
www.dalkeyarchive.com

Typesetting: Mikhail Iliatov

Printed on permanent/durable acid-free paper

For Silvia, my wife.
For Cecilia, Natasha, and Carlos, my children.

CONTENTS

1. Pre-Iberian Foreword

One of the great thinkers of our time, the Mexican comedian Mario Moreno, better known as Cantinflas, once silenced a man with whom he was arguing with this rejoinder: "Alright, enough already; the problem here is obviously your lack of ignorance!"

Cantinflas was a master of the paradox, and his comical retort contains a profound truth. Our world conceals an unwritten culture, one expressed through memory, oral transmission, and the cultivation of tradition. In order to understand it—as Cantinflas rightly believed—one needs a touch of ignorance.

In the early twentieth century, upon concluding his study of Andalusian peasants, the Spanish philosopher José Ortega y Gasset exclaimed: "These illiterate folks are actually quite cultured!" The same sort of thing might be said today about many groups of peasants and indigenous peoples in Indo-Afro-Hispanic America: Despite their illiteracy, these people are incredibly cultured!

Cantinflas was praising an "ignorance" which is perhaps synonymous with traditional, ancestral, unwritten "wisdom." What is "ignorant" for us is actually, in these oral, retentive, unrecorded cultures, "wise," and we are the ones ignorant of it.

I say this in order to establish from the outset the idea that proximity and access to words and speech is neither exclusive nor restrictive. Language is, at times, like a great flowing river, at other times barely a stream, but always the master of its channel, which is orality: "Do you remember?," "Good morning," "I love you so much," "What's for dinner?," "See you tomorrow." This whole profuse current of orality runs between two shores: memory and imagination. He who remembers, imagines. He who imagines, remembers. Language, oral or written, forms the bridge between these two shores.

I would like to consider literature in the broadest possible terms: when not being hounded and banned by political tyrannies, it is all too frequently limited and impoverished by ideological restrictions.

The various literatures of the American continent begin (and are kept alive) in the epic, ancestral, and mythic memory of its indigenous peoples. America—the name that signifies the contiguous continental geography from Canada to Tierra del Fuego: North America, Central America, and South America all together—was once uninhabited.

3

Then, descending from Asiatic or Polynesian origins, our indigenous population emerged and spoke the first words heard in this hemisphere. The Mayan *Popol Vuh* of the K'iche' kingdom recalled the creation of the world, while the *Chilam Balam* foretold its destruction. In the ages between origin and apocalypse the indigenous world resounded with beautiful songs of love and instruction as well as bellicose tones of combat and bloodshed.

These words have been perpetuated through the centuries in oral tradition, from the Pueblo Indians of the North to the Mapuche of the South. Their rhythm, their memory, and perhaps their melancholy, underlie the Spanish-language literature of America, a written literature which stands in contrast to the orality prevalent in these societies before Columbus and Vespucci.

José Luis Martínez explored the multiplicity of American cultures and languages, as well as the themes that were central to them prior to the arrival of the Europeans. He began with Alaska: Eskimos and their deep lore about the creation of the Earth and the stars, and their early, urgent questions about life and death. The Kutenai of Canada with their songs to the Sun and the Moon. The Nez Percé of Oregon and the Pawnee of Nebraska and Kansas, religions of ghostly marriages and prodigal sons. The Natchez of Louisiana and the creation of the world. The Navajo of Arizona and the tension between nomadic rootlessness and domestic rootedness. And the Cora people of Nayarit, in the place we now call Mexico, who reconfigured the rituals of Holy Week and the figure of Christ brought by the Spanish, according to their own understanding and imagination, into celebrations about the creation of the world and the Creator who existed even before the world itself. The Tarascan of Michoacán and the death of the different indigenous peoples. The Mixtec of Oaxaca and the origin of the world, a constant preoccupation of these peoples who lived so much closer to the origin of things: the Cuna of Panama remembering how man learned to cry; and in South America, the Chocó of Colombia and their memory of the universal flood; the Chachi and their legends of the dream; the Sápara people of Brazil and how they spoke with the animals of the jungle. Also in Brazil, the love and dancing of the Ñangatú. The Chilean Mapuche and the rebellion of the children of God. The Guarani of Paraguay and their memory of the first father. All of these peoples alongside the great leading cultures: the Toltecs and the Nahuatl in Central Mexico. The Olmecs, the original peoples of the Gulf Coast, who were, for a time, misclassified in the Veracruz Museum of Anthropology. The Maya in the Yucatan, and the Quechua in both Peru and the Central Altiplano of South America.

Orality and corporality, architecture and music: Enrique Florescano tells us that these ancient peoples employed these arts as a way to express their culture, preserve it, and hand it down through the ages. And if these artifacts and remnants have survived to reach us today, it is because these peoples intuited the hereditary and survivalist power of language, body, and perception.

In Mexico, out of a total population of more than one hundred twenty million inhabitants, some sixteen million are indigenous. While they are increasingly educated within the general mestizo current, the majority of them retain their original languages, which number over forty, as different from one another as Swedish is from Italian.

To travel to the lands of the Huichol people in Jalisco, or the Tarahumara in Chihuahua, the Nahuatl in Central Mexico, the Zapotecs in Oaxaca, or the Maya in the Yucatan is to discover that, even when they are illiterate, indigenous people are far from ignorant, and even when they are poor, they are not culturally impoverished. They possess an extraordinary talent for remembering or imagining dreams and nightmares, cosmic catastrophes and dazzling rebirths, as well as the minute details of daily life, a child's first words, the stupid jokes of the village idiot, the faithful family dog, favorite foods, the passing of their grandparents.

Fernando Benítez, the great chronicler of Mexico's indigenous peoples, once said that, when one person from a traditional culture dies, a whole library dies with him. And it is a fact that for a defeated people who had to become invisible in order to remain unnoticed, orality is safer than literality. To move from centuries of invisibility and orality to modern visibility and literality is a gigantic step, and a difficult one, for the indigenous cultures of the Americas. The sporadic rebellions its peoples have mounted from time to time must someday give way to a dignified, permanent, and mutually enriching relationship for all the people of the Americas, old and new.

From the first Chiapas rebellion in 1712, sparked by the miraculous vision of the young María Candelaria, to the most recent uprising in Chiapas in 1994, sparked by the equally miraculous vision that Mexico was now a first world nation, it seems interesting to note the presence—as well as the vision—of creole or mestizo leaders, Sebastián Gómez de la Gracia in 1712, and Subcomandate Marcos in 1994. Whether or not they declared themselves to be leaders of the rebellions, they are the ones who gave them a public voice, and that voice, whether we like it or not, speaks Spanish.

Today, a movement to reclaim the great oral tradition of the indigenous peoples—the Nahuatl, Aymara, Guarani, and Mapuche—extends through the ancient aboriginal lands of the Americas. The universal voice of that movement, however, the voice that links its highly respectable demands to the greater social and political community of each country, is the Castilian voice. The Guarani of Paraguay and the Maya of the Yucatan might not understand each other in their aboriginal languages but I wager that they will both recognize each other in the common language: *la castilla*, Castilian, Spanish—the Esperanto of the Americas.

Even as the indigenous peoples of Latin America strive for individual recognition and cultural autonomy, modern Spanish is the language that the vast majority of them use to speak to one another, and to the non-hispanic world beyond their borders. Spanish is the lingua franca of the Indian world in the Americas. Through Maya or Quechua translated into Spanish, the natives of America let us, the inhabitants of the continent's white and mestizo cities, understand what they desire, what they remember, what they reject. And what is our role but to listen, to pay attention, and to respect that part of our Indo-Euro-American community? It is our role to be invested in sharing the cultural wealth of the indigenous community, its ritual purity, its proximity to the sacred, its memory of what has been forgotten by urban amnesia. It is our role to respect the natives' values, without condemning them to abandonment, and to protect them from injustice.

The indigenous people of America are a part of our polycultural and multiracial community. To forget them is to condemn ourselves to being forgotten. Justice for them should be inseparable from justice for ourselves. They are the common denominator of our shared future, and we will never truly be satisfied until we share the world equally with them.

But they, in the end *a part* of us, not *all* of us, must also accept the rules of a democratic coexistence, must not use tradition as a shield to perpetuate authoritarian abuses, offenses against women, ethnic rivalries, or the parallel response to white racism, which is racism against the white or mestizo. As a Mixtec Indian said to Benítez: "They want to kill me *because* I speak Spanish."

¡Colón al paredón! "Columbus up against the wall!" This was the cry raised by a group of indigenous Mexicans gathered around the statue of the Genoese native in 1992. Fine, condemn Columbus to the firing squad—but even as the supporters of indigenous rights moved towards anti-imperialist extremism, they had to shout their demands in Spanish.

While I am certainly also concerned with the black population of America, theirs is a different history. Brought from Africa in slave ships, they surrendered their original languages and were obliged to learn those of the colonizer. My central theme in this study is fiction written in the Spanish—and sometimes Portuguese—language of the New World.

2. Discovery and Conquest

Between August 27 and September 2, 1520, at the Royal Palace in Brussels, Albrecht Dürer was the first European painter to view the works of Aztec art which the conquistador Hernán Cortés had sent to the Emperor Charles V. "I have seen the things which they have brought to the King out of the new lands of gold," wrote Dürer, "and all the days of my life, I have seen nothing that reaches my heart so much as these, for among them I have seen wonderfully artistic things and have admired the subtle ingenuity of men in foreign lands." If only the spirit of this great artist had been present in those who destroyed a large part of the pre-Columbian heritage of the Americas which they saw as the work of heathen devils.

America is both a fantasy and a nightmare, and it occupied the same dualistic role in the culture of Renaissance Europe. Which is to say: in America, Europe found lands in which to expend the excess energies of its Renaissance, a place that also allowed it to enact its vision of cleansing history and regenerating man.

The Invention of America

The Mexican historian Edmundo O'Gorman suggests that America was not discovered: it was invented. And it was invented, surely, because it was needed. In his book *The Invention of America*, O'Gorman speaks of a European man who was a prisoner of his own world. The medieval prison was built with the stones of geocentrism and scholasticism, two hierarchical visions of an archetypal universe, perfect, unchangeable although finite, because by the Middle Ages, the epicenter of European society was the ideology of the Fall of Man.

The vast natural environment of the New World confirms the Old World's hunger for new space. Having lost the stable structures of the medieval order, European man feels diminished and displaced from his age-old central position. The Earth shrinks in size within the Copernican universe. Man's passion—above all, his desires and ambitions—expand to compensate for this diminishment. Both upheavals are resolved by his desire to extend his dominion over the earth and other men: the New World is desired, the New World is invented, the New World is discovered; thus is it named.

In this way, all the dramas of Renaissance Europe come to be represented in the European colonization of America: the Machiavellian drama of power, the Erasmian drama of humanism, the utopian drama of Thomas More, as well as the drama of the new perception of the natural world. If Renaissance logic held that the natural world had finally been dominated and that man was truly the measure of all things, including nature, the New World was immediately shown to comprise a nature that is excessive, disproportionate, hyperbolic, and immeasurable. This would become a constant theme in Ibero-American culture, born from the first explorers' sense of astonishment, and persisting in the explorations of a seemingly endless natural world in books such as *Rebellion in the Backlands* by Euclides da Cunha, *Canaima* by Rómulo Gallegos, *The Lost Steps* by Alejo Carpentier, *The Devil to Pay in the Backlands* by João Guimarães Rosa, and *One Hundred Years of Solitude* by Gabriel García Márquez. Significantly, this very same amazement and fear in the face of a natural world that exceeds the limits of human control, roars above King Lear and his "cold night" on the heath, when The Fool cries out, "It will turn us all to fools and madmen."

The New World is discovered (pardon me: invented, imagined, desired, needed) in a moment of European crisis which is both confirmed by and reflected in the discovery. In Christianity, nature is proof of divine power. But it is also a temptation: it seduces us and pushes us away from our otherworldly destiny; nature tempts us to repeat the sin and pleasure of the Fall.

By contrast, the rebellious spirit of the Renaissance perceives nature as the reason for human existence. Nature is the living world celebrated by the inventors of Renaissance Humanism: the poet Petrarch, the philosopher Ficino, the painter Leonardo. The Renaissance is born, so to speak, when Petrarch casts in verse his memory of the precise day, the hour, the sublime season when, for the first time, he saw Laura—a woman of flesh and blood, not an allegory—cross the bridge over the Arno:

> Blessed be the day and the month and the year
>
> and the time and the season, the time, the spot,
>
> the beautiful country and the place where I was reunited

with two lovely eyes, which have ensnared me . . .

(*Sonnet XXIX*)

In 1535, Gonzalo Fernández de Oviedo, the Spanish conquistador and governor of the fortress of Santo Domingo, wrote his *Natural History of the Indies* and rapidly confronted the problem that lies at the heart of the relations between the Old World and the New World. As told to us by his Italian biographer, Antonello Gerbi, Oviedo's attitude toward the recently discovered lands belongs as much to the Christian world as to the Renaissance. It belongs to Christianity because Oviedo shows himself to be pessimistic about history. It belongs to the Renaissance because he shows himself to be optimistic about nature. In this way, if the world of men is absurd and sinful, nature is, itself, living evidence of God's reason. Oviedo can sing the dithyramb to the new lands because they are lands without history, lands without time. They are atemporal utopias.

America becomes Europe's Utopia. As Edmundo O'Gorman writes, it is a utopia invented by Europe but also a utopia desired by Europe and so, for that reason, a necessary utopia. But was it truly necessary?

The American utopia is a utopia projected in space, because, in the transition between the Middle Ages and the Renaissance, space is the vehicle for European imagination, desire, and necessity. The rupture in medieval unity is first manifested in space as the outer defenses of the walled cities crack, their drawbridges fall forever, and stumbling into the new, open cities—the cities of Don Juan and Faust, the city of *La Celestina*—come the epidemics of skepticism, individual pride, empirical science, and the crime against the Holy Spirit: usury. In come love and inspiration separate from God, embodied in Shakespeare's Cleopatra and Cervantes's Don Quixote.

More than time, modern history was defined by space because nothing distinguishes the old from the new with such crystal clarity as space. Columbus and Copernicus reveal a hunger for space which, in its appropriately Latin American version, ironically culminates in "The Aleph," the famous modern story by Jorge Luis Borges. The Aleph is the space which contains all others but the story's success does not depend on a minute and detailed description of all the places in space; it simply suggests a simultaneous vision of the infinite: all the spaces of the Aleph occupy the same point in a gigantic instant, "without overlap and without transparency: . . . each thing was infinite things . . . because I saw it clearly from every point in the universe. I saw the swarming sea, saw the dawn and dusk, saw the multitudes of America, saw a silver spider web in the very center of a black pyramid, I saw a cracked and broken labyrinth (it was London) . . . I saw all the mirrors on the planet and none of them reflected me . . ."

The image of the Aleph contains a double irony. On one hand, Borges is forced to enumerate his vision with simultaneity because a vision can indeed be simultaneous, but his recounting of it must be successive, because such is the nature of language. On the other hand, this space of all spaces, once seen, is totally useless unless it contains a personal history. In this case, the personal history is that of a beautiful dead woman, Beatriz Viterbo, "tall, frail" and with "a sort of graceful clumsiness, a touch of palsy" in her walk.

A personal history. And history is time.

Thus, Borges aptly begins the story with a quotation from *Hamlet* which functions almost like an exergue: "Oh God, I could be bounded in a nutshell and count myself a king of infinite space . . ."

ERASMUS IN AMERICA

The Renaissance, one of the important paths of development for the Ibero-American novel, affirmed for itself the freedom to influence reality, something traditionally associated with the political philosophy of Machiavelli, although qualified, in our time, by Antonio Gramsci's interpretation: Machiavelli is the philosopher of the active utopia, appropriate to the creation of a modern state. In opposition to this freedom, Thomas More's *Utopia* affirmed the liberty of being able to enact what should be; an ideal, in turn, qualified by the political practice of our century, which has tried to impose civic happiness through violent or subliminal methods.

A third Renaissance freedom invites us, with a smile, to consider what could be. It is the smile of Erasmus of Rotterdam which begets a vast literary progeny, beginning in Spain with Erasmus's influence on Cervantes, whose characters Don Quixote and Sancho Panza represent the two Erasmian modes: belief and doubt, the tendency to universalize and to particularize; the illusion of appearances, the duality of all truth, and the praise of folly. This will be the great antecedent to the work of Julio Cortázar.

Moriae Encomium: the praise of folly is the praise of More, friend of Erasmus; it is the ironic praise of Utopia, and of Topia as well, since both—what is and what should be—are submitted to the critique of reason; but reason, in order to be reasonable, must see itself with the eyes of an ironic folly. Erasmus proposes this relative operation at the crossing of two periods of absolutism. He criticizes the medieval absolute of Faith, but also the humanist absolute of Reason. The folly of Erasmus takes up residence in the hearts of Faith and Reason, warning both: if Reason must be reasonable, it requires a critical complement, which Erasmus calls the praise of folly, so as not to fall into the dogmatism that corrupted Faith. Irony converts what the absolutes of Faith or Reason consider "folly" into a questioning of man, by man, and of reason, by reason. Relativized by this ironical and critical folly, man is liberated from the dogmatic fatality of Faith, but does not become the absolute master of Reason.

Politically, Erasmus's ideas were translated into a call for reasonable reformism, from within society and the Christian church. The sage of Rotterdam directed his message not only to the Church of Rome, but also to the ethical culture of Christianity, to the Catholic state and to its violence. Erasmus's enormous influence in early imperial Spain, at the court of the young Charles V, is attested to by the Emperor's personal secretary, Alfonso de Valdés, a disciple of Erasmus, who calls for the coincidence of ideals and practice. Christianity cannot proclaim to uphold certain ideals and yet practice the very things it denounces. If this contradiction cannot be overcome, says Valdés, it would be better to abandon the faith once and for all and convert to Islam or animalism.

It was no small matter to make such a statement in the very moment in which Spain was, after expelling the Jews and defeating the Moors, inaugurating its immense overseas empire through the Conquest of *different* cultures. To say this as the monarchical power was solidifying into vertical structures, marked by the intolerance of Church and State, was intolerable. The Catholic Church and the Spanish State were not about to accept any theory of double truth: no reform from within, only orthodox unity; no rational faith, only militant Counter-Reformation: the Inquisition; and no specious, ironical reasoning: the Holy Office.

The popularity of Erasmus in Austrian Spain was gradually replaced, first by suspicion, then by prohibition, and in the end, by silence. However, with regards to the New World, this process was much delayed in comparison to the writer's popularity in the Americas. In *Erasmo y España* (Erasmus and Spain), French Hispanist Marcel Bataillon informs us that from the Antilles to Mexico to the River Plate, Erasmus was banned but still read. Bataillon adds that the ban itself reveals the degree to which Erasmus's works were esteemed and jealously guarded from the Inquisition. *They mattered.*

Erasmus was introduced to the culture of the Americas by men like Diego Méndez de Segura, the principal scrivener on Christopher Columbus's fourth expedition. Upon his death in Santo Domingo in 1536, he left to his children ten books, half of which were written by Erasmus. Other supporters included Cristóbal de Pedraza, cantor of the cathedral of Mexico and future bishop of Honduras, who introduced Erasmus to New Spain; and no less than Pedro de Mendoza, the founder of Buenos Aires, whose inventory of property from 1598 includes "a book by Erasmus, medium sized, bound in leather." In the final section of *Erasmo y España*, Bataillon gives a complete and enticing catalog of Erasmus's presence in America.

Erasmus was so important that we can even say that his spirit, the spirit of irony, of pluralism and relativism, has survived as one of the most demanding, although politically less fulfilled, values of Ibero-American civilization. If Governor Pedro de Mendoza was already reading Erasmus in Buenos Aires in 1538, there is no question that Julio Cortázar was reading him in the same city four centuries later.

THE GOLDEN AGE

The dissolution of medieval unity brought about by the end of geocentrism and the discovery of the New World gives rise to the responses of Machiavelli, More, and Erasmus: *This is. This must be. This can be.* But these responses from European age are answers to questions about American space. There is no real synderesis. Just as the New World lacks time, so it lacks history. We have responses to a question about the nature of the space of the New World, transforming this place into Utopia. This is the source of its contradiction, because Utopia, by definition, is the impossible place: the place that is not. Nevertheless, although there is no such place, the history of America insists that there is no *other* place. This territorial, historical, moral, intellectual, and artistic conflict remains unresolved.

The invention of America is the invention of Utopia: Europe desires a utopia, names it, and finds it in order to, in the end, destroy it.

For sixteenth century Europe, the New World represented the possibility of regenerating the Old World. Erasmus and Montaigne, Vives and More herald the century of religious wars, one of the bloodiest centuries in European history. In response they set up a utopia that finally, contradictorily, has a place: America, the space of the noble savage and the Golden Age.

In space, things are *here* or *there*. It turns out that the Golden Age and the noble savage are *there*: somewhere else: in the New World. In his letters to Queen Isabella *the Catholic*, Columbus describes an earthly paradise. Utopia's existence is confirmed, only to be, immediately, destroyed. If these natives encountered by Columbus in the Antilles are so docile, living in harmony with the ways of nature, then why does the Admiral feel obliged to enslave them and send them to Spain, bound and weighted down in chains?

These events lead Columbus to inaugurate the Golden Age, not as a time of ideal perfection but a space filled with gold, a fountain of inexhaustible riches. Columbus emphasizes the abundance of natural resources such as wood, pearls, and gold. The New World is *only* nature: it is an a-historical u-topia, ideally uninhabited or, in the long run, depopulated by genocide and repopulated through European colonization. Neither civilization nor humanity is present in this space.

But Columbus believes, after all, that he has found an ancient world: the empires of Cathay and Cipan Guó: China and Japan. By contrast, Amerigo Vespucci is the first European who says that this truly is a New World: a place deserving of his name. It is Vespucci who firmly plants the utopian root in America. Utopia is a society, the inhabitants of Utopia live in harmonious community; they scorn gold: "The peoples live in harmony with nature, and it is better that we call them Epicureans than Stoics ... No one of them possesses property but all is held in common." As they have no property, they do not need government: "They live without king and without any sovereign class, and every man is his own master."

All this greatly impressed contemporary readers of Columbus and Vespucci, explains Gerbi, because they knew that while Christopher was a feverish gypsy, a son of Genova, that port of ill repute, a man of visionary greed, and practical, stubborn passions, Amerigo was, to no less a degree, a cold, skeptical Florentine.

Therefore, when this consummately *cool* man informs his readers that the New World is new, not only as a place, but also in its substance: plants, fruits, birds and beasts; that it is truly an earthly paradise, Europeans are disposed to believe it, because this Vespucci is like Saint Thomas the Apostle. He believes only what he sees, and what he sees is that Utopia exists. He has been there, a witness to that "Golden Age and its happy estate" (*l'età dell'oro e suo stato felice*) celebrated by Dante, where "it is always spring, and the fruits abound" (*qui primavera è sempre, ed ogni frutto*). Thus America was not discovered: it was invented. All discovery comes from desire, and all desire from necessity. We invent what we discover; we discover what we imagine. Amazement is our reward.

Wondrous Reality

From Dürer to Henry Moore, by way of Shakespeare and Vivaldi, *Le Douanier* Henri Rousseau, and Antonin Artaud, America has been imagined by Europe, as much as Europe has been imagined by America.

This imagination, from the outset, acquires a fantastic character.

If the fantastic is a duel with fear, imagination is the first exorcist of the terror of the unknown. The European fantasy of America operates through bestiaries of the Indies, in which the Caribbean Sea and the Gulf of Mexico appear as the dwelling places of mermaids, seen by Columbus himself on January 9, 1493: "they came right up out of the sea." Although the Admiral admits that, "they were not as beautiful as they are painted, their faces were rather like those of men."

By contrast, Gil González, explorer of the isthmus of Panama, encounters, upon a wide stretch of dark sea, "fish that sang in harmony, the way they say mermaids do, and which make you sleepy in the same way." Diego de Rosales sees "a beast that, stretched out across the water, looks from the front to have the head, face, and breasts of a woman, with a pleasant appearance, with long mane and locks, blonde and flowing. She carried a child in her arms. And when she sped away they noticed that she had the back and tail of a fish . . ."

Perhaps the febrile imaginations of those who sailed the Caribbean and the Gulf of Mexico saw not mermaids but whales, to which they attributed, as Fernández de Oviedo writes, "two teats on their breasts [Thank goodness!] and this way give birth and suckle their young."

More problematic is the appearance of so-called "shark fish" of these coasts, described with anatomical precision by Fernández de Oviedo: "I have seen many of these sharks," he writes in his *Sumario de la natural historia de las Indias* (Summary of the Natural History of the Indies), "that have the male or generative member doubled." "What I mean," Oviedo adds, "is that each shark has two penises . . . each one the length of a large man's arm from the elbow to the furthest tip of the finger."

"I don't know," the chronicler discretely admits, "if in using them, it exercises both together . . . or each one by itself, or at diverse times . . ."

For my own part, I'm not sure whether to envy or pity these sharks of the Gulf and the Caribbean, but I do remember, along with the chronicler Pedro Gutiérrez de Santa Clara, that these beasts happen to give birth only once in their whole life, which would seem to contradict the existence of the organ and its function — the member suggests fertility and abundance, belied by the few offspring it helps produce . . .

The letters of Pedro Mártir de Anglería concerning the astonishing bestiaries of the American sea were the object of derision in pontifical Rome, until the Archbishop of Cosenza and Spanish Papal Legate, Juan Rulfo — what a beautiful coincidence that his name will also belong to one of Mexico's great twentieth century writers: Juan Rulfo, the author of *Pedro Páramo* — confirmed the accounts of Pedro Mártir, and expanded the field of wondrous reality from the Gulf and the Caribbean to include the vihuela fish, capable of sinking a ship with its incredibly strong horn; and the firefly, the lantern of the coasts, by whose light the natives "spin, weave, sew, paint, dance, and do other things by night . . ."

The gannets, which take to the air in search of sardines. The buzzards or vultures that Columbus saw on the coasts of Veragua, "abominable, repulsive, foul-smelling birds" which light upon the dead soldiers and are the "intolerable torment to those upon the earth." It is the night of the iguana, a creature about which Cieza de León, in his chronicle of Peru, cannot decide "if it is meat or fish," but which, when young, lightly crosses the surface of the water and, when old, moves slowly along the floor of the lagoons.

The wonders increase. Tortoises with shells large enough to cover a house, so fertile that they lay thousands of eggs in their enormous nests on our sandy shores. Beaches of pearls, writes Fernández de Oviedo, "black as jet, others tawny as lions, and others very yellow and resplendent like gold." And the mythical salamander, burning inside but with skin so cold, says Sebastián de Covarrubias in his *Tesoro de la Lengua Castellana* (Treasury of the Spanish Language), "that crawling over hot coals extinguishes them as if it were solid ice."

These marvels of the sea and the coasts of discovery would soon take shape in the wonders of human civilization, marvelously described by Bernal Díaz del Castillo, who accompanied the army of Hernán Cortés as it entered the Aztec capital, México-Tenochtitlán:

"On another morning we reached the wide road leading to México and we stopped and stared in wonderment, telling each other that this resembled the things and enchantments in the book of Amadís ... and even some of our soldiers said that perhaps they were seeing all of this as if in a dream."

The First Novelist

I call him our first novelist, and I say it with all the reservations appropriate to the case. Is Bernal's book not a "true chronicle," an account of events that really happened between 1519 and 1521? At the same time, it is also an account written forty-seven years later, about which Bernal, seventy-three years old and blind, writing from Guatemala and forgotten by all, decides that nothing of what occurred a half century before must be forgotten: "Now that I am writing, everything appears before my eyes as if it happened only yesterday."

Yes, but not only did it not happen yesterday or today but in another country: that of memory, the inevitable country of the novelist.

As true as he wishes his memory to be, if imagination does not lend it wings, he knows it will be no more than a mere listing of dates and events, especially when what the eyes have seen in the historical reality is comparable to what the chroniclers of the Indies have seen in the fabulation of the New World: "To see things never heard nor seen nor even dreamed, as we saw." As Francisco Rico, the penetrating critic of Spain's literary past, has observed, Bernal unites "the singular coexistence of naturalness and astonishment."

"To see things never heard nor seen nor even dreamed, as we saw," writes Bernal, giving credit to the fabulous imaginations of Fernández de Oviedo and Pedro Mártir. But did these fabulists not anticipate, perhaps, with their own imagination, Bernal Díaz del Castillo's vision of Anáhuac? Observe how our fictions are simultaneously authorized as both a legitimate fantasy and a dream come true. What lies at the heart of this apparent contradiction? Is it really more about a complementary attempt to understand? No. Behind each mermaid and each tortoise, as behind each clash of arms and imperial conquest, there is a paradox of civilization: a spent, exhausted country applies the title of Conquest to the final act of seven centuries of Reconquest. It is the final assault of El Cid Campeador, no longer facing the Moors but now the Aztecs, the Incas, and the Araucanians.

As a young law student I used to walk every morning at a quarter to eight across the Zócalo, the great central plaza of Mexico City, my terrifying and wondrous city. The collective taxi took me from my home near the Paseo de la Reforma to the corner of Madero Avenue at the Majestic Hotel. From there I would walk the width of the square into the narrow colonial quarter leading to the School of Law at the National University on San Idelfonso Street.

As I crossed the Zócalo each morning, another scene hurried violently in flight across my vision. To the south, I could see men and women in white tunics gliding on flat-bottomed canoes down a dark, flowing canal. To the north, there was a corner where the stone broke into shapes of flaming shafts, red skulls and placid butterflies; to the west, a wall of snakes beneath the twin roofs of the temples of rain and fire. To the east, another wall, of skulls. Images of both cities, ancient and modern, dissolved back and forth before my eyes.

In 1521, the conquistador Hernán Cortés razed the Aztec city—an Indian Venice—and on its ruins rose the capital of the Viceroyalty of New Spain, later the capital of the Mexican Republic. The vice-regal palace was built on the site of the temple dedicated to the god of war, Huitzilopochtli. The houses of the conquistadors rose upon sites once reserved for serpents, and the great Cathedral—the largest in Latin America—on the grounds of the former palace of the Emperor Moctezuma, a palace with courtyards filled with birds and beasts, chambers for albinos, hunchbacks, and dwarfs, and rooms replete with silver and gold.

As I walked across the enormous square of broken stone, I knew that my feet were trampling upon the graveyard of a civilization. I knew that all of these things I imagined had once existed there and were now no more. I was treading on the ashes of the capital city of Tenochtitlan, which would never be seen again.

My admiration was no less tangible than the awe experienced by Bernal Díaz del Castillo, the man who memorialized the conquest. As he and his companions entered the Aztec capital in 1519, he tells us: "We stopped and stared in wonderment, telling each other that this resembled the things and enchantments in the book of Amadís ... and even some of our soldiers said that perhaps they were seeing all of this as if in a dream."

History and fiction: as the French historian Jules Michelet wrote, a people have a right to dream their future. I would add that they have a right to dream their past. We all exist in history because the times of men and women are still unfinished. We have yet to pronounce our last word.

It is a matter of the highest political and historical importance: What do we remember? What do we forget? What are we responsible for? Who are we accountable to?

But it is not, finally, a question subject to mere political appraisals. It is part of the dynamics of culture, as the artist attempts to imagine the past and remember the future, giving a fuller version of reality than the one to be found in political controversy, statistical grayness, or factual neutrality.

Remember the future. Imagine the past. This is a way of saying that, since the past is irreversible and the future uncertain, men and women are left with only the stage of the present if they wish to represent the past and the future. The human past is called Memory. The human future is called Desire. They both occur in the present, where we remember, where we yearn.

William Faulkner, one of the creators of the collective memory of the Americas, has one of the characters in his novel *Intruder in the Dust* say: "It's all now you see. Yesterday won't be over until tomorrow and tomorrow began ten thousand years ago." And in Gabriel García Márquez's *One Hundred Years of Solitude*, the inhabitants of Macondo invent the world, learn things, and forget them, and are then forced to rename, rewrite, remember: for Márquez, memory is neither spontaneous nor gratuitous nor legitimizing: it is an act of creative survival. We must imagine the past so that the future, when it happens, can also be remembered, avoiding the death of the eternally forgotten.

To the shared memory of the writers of the Americas, let me add the name of the Spanish chronicler of the epic conquest of the Aztec Empire, Bernal Díaz del Castillo; I wish to share his memory and to share the imagination of the creation of the Americas, with its powerful deployment of courage, dream, disappointment, fatality and will; its sense of limits, dashed ambitions, shattered cosmogonies and, rising above the ruins, the profile of a new civilization.

Bernal Díaz del Castillo was born in 1495, in Medina del Campo, Valladolid, Spain, three years after Christopher Columbus's first voyage to the New World. He arrived in America in 1514, and in 1519 he joined Hernán Cortés's expedition from Cuba to Mexico.

After the Conquest, he took up residence in Guatemala, where he wrote his *True History of the Conquest of New Spain*. The book was conceived as an answer to the historian Antonio López de Gómara, who exalted the figure of the conquistador, Hernán Cortés, at the expense of the common soldiers.

Bernal finished writing his *History* in 1568, forty-seven years after the conquest, when he was seventy-three years of age. He sent his manuscript to Spain, where it was not published until 1632, 111 years after the events it describes.

Blind and exhausted, Bernal died in Guatemala in 1580 at the age of eighty-four, before he could supervise the edition of his incomplete book, which finally appeared in its complete form in Guatemala in 1904.

But in 1519, when he went ashore with Cortés in Mexico, Bernal was only twenty-four years old. He had one foot in Europe and another in America. He fills the dramatic void between the two worlds in a literary and singularly modern manner. In effect, he does what Marcel Proust did in his search for lost time. Only instead of madeleines dunked in tea, the springs of memory in Bernal are the warriors, the number of their steeds, the list of their battles:

"I declare that I will relate this history ... and who were the captains and soldiers who conquered and settled these lands ... and here I want to set down from memory all the horses and mares that came over." And so he does, soldier by soldier, horse after horse.

> A certain Martín López came over, and he was a good soldier ... And an Ojeda also came ... and had his eye broken in the battle for Mexico ... And a certain De la Serna also sailed with us ... who had a scar on his face, earned on the battlefield. I don't remember what became of him ... And so-and-so Morón also came, and he was a great musician ... And the brothers Carmona from Jerez were here. They died from their wounds.

This is a world which has disappeared by the time Bernal writes about it. He is in search of a lost time: he is our first novelist. And, as in Proust, time lost is a time that can only be recovered as a single minute liberated from the succession of time. In Bernal's book, it is the epic poet himself who becomes the searcher for the lost instant. Like Proust, Bernal has already lived what he is about to tell, but he must give us the impression that what he is telling is happening while being written and read: life was lived, but the book must be discovered. With Bernal, at the dawn of the shared memory of the Americas, we happen upon a new way of living: of re-living, certainly, but also of living, for the first time, remembered experience as written experience.

As the tale unfolds, the epic will waver. But a vacillating epic is no longer an epic: it is a novel. And a novel is a contradictory and ambiguous thing. It is the messenger of the news that we truly no longer know who we are, where we come from, or what our place in the world is. It is the messenger of freedom at the price of insecurity. It is a reflection on the price paid for material advancement at the cost of losing our moral premises and philosophical roots: it is the price paid by Prometheus. *Don Quixote* will be the greatest Spanish contribution to this drama of modernity, but Bernal Díaz prefigures it in his faltering epic. What do I mean by faltering epic? By vacillating chronicle?

Strolling Across the Zócalo

As a descendent of both Spain and Mexico, I walked upon the hidden ruins of Moctezuma's capital, and my wonder at what I could imagine in the twentieth century was no less great than the amazement of Bernal Díaz del Castillo, the chronicler of the Conquest, in the sixteenth century.

No less, either, the hesitation of my pen. For in the midst of one of the great epic adventures of all times, the Spanish soldier Bernal Díaz could say that he did not know or even imagine if he could really write about so many things "never heard nor seen nor even dreamed, as we saw."

This sense of astonishment followed by a sense of humility in the literary description of the dream finally resolves itself in the obligation to destroy the dream, transforming it into a nightmare. Bernal Díaz writes with admiration, indeed with love, of the nobility and beauty of many aspects of the Indian world. His description of the great marketplace at Tlatelolco, of the emperor's palace, and of the encounter between Cortés and Moctezuma are among the most moving pages in literature.

But Bernal's epic is also full of the distant rumor of drums and death, flaming torches and secret sacrifices: "blood and smoke." A tone of prevalent menace, impending disaster, and the fear that the courageous band of less than five hundred warriors, their retreat cut off by the decision to scuttle their ships, could be readily wiped out at any moment by the superior power of the Aztec armies. Yet as the city falls to the Spaniards in 1521 and its inhabitants mourn the death of the warrior, the blood of the child, the branding of the woman, and the fall of the Aztec Empire, the conquistador, the destroyer, joins his victims in a grand elegy for what had been, says Bernal Díaz, "fallen, strewn, and lost forever."

It is not common for the epic chronicler of the Middle Ages and of the Renaissance (indeed, Simone Weil would say, it is unusual for any epic poet after Homer) to love what he is forced to destroy. But Bernal comes quite close. On the surface, his book is an epic chronicle of events. He is writing a glorious page in history about a hardy group of men in consonance with their individual consciences and their political means and ends. They are here to carry out the will of divine providence, the salvation of the heathen and, with lesser impetus, to extend the might of the Spanish crown. In this way, all the principal currents which drive the men of Spain to the New World are present in his chronicle: the militant individualist ambition, the crusading army, the militant Church, and the militant Crown.

This coherence between the tale told and the consciousness behind the telling is common to the epic theme. But Bernal, writing the first European epic of the New World, introduces a novelty into the epic voice, perhaps because he is, in all actuality, describing novelty itself, a New World, whereas the epic, according to both the Spanish philosopher José Ortega y Gasset and the Russian critic Mikhail Bakhtin, is only concerned with what is already known.

Let me linger for one moment upon the generic problem as it affects the *True History of the Conquest of Spain*, since I believe that every great literary work, like Bernal's, contains not only a dialogue with the world, but also with itself.

Most literary theorists see the epic and the novel as opposites. So that we might properly situate Bernal's epic at the dawn of the New World, let us see what they have to say.

For José Ortega y Gasset, novel and epic are "exact opposites." The epic occupies itself with the past as fact, it speaks to us of a world that *was* and has *concluded*: the epic past flees from the present. The epic poet, says Ortega, speaks only of *what is finished*, of what his audience already knows: "Homer," he writes, "does not pretend to tell us anything new. What he knows, the audience already knows, and Homer knows that it knows." That is: by the time the epic poem appears, it tells a well-known tale, accepted and celebrated by all.

The novel, by contrast, as Mikhail Bakhtin states, is a literary operation founded on novelty. Epic, writes the Russian critic, is based on a unique and unified vision of the world, obligatory and undoubtedly true for the heroes, author, and audience. Along with Ortega, Bakhtin thinks that the epic deals with the categories and implications of a completed past, of an understood (or comprehensible) world.

But if the epic is something complete, the novel is incomplete: "it reflects the tendencies of a new world still in the making," says Bakhtin. The epic unity of the world is shattered by history and *the novel* appears in order to take its place.

Hegel assigned the epic another place in literary discourse: that of shattering the preceding world, specifically the world of myth. For Hegel, the epic was a destabilizing human act that disturbed the tranquility of existence in its mythical integrity, the dynamic that drives us from our mythical home and sends us off to war at Troy and upon the voyages of Ulysses: the chance event that damages our very essence.

For her part, the great French writer and Judeo-Christian philosopher Simone Weil attributes to the Homeric epic the exact opposite of what Ortega gives it. For Weil, *The Iliad* is an unfinished movement, whose moral message is waiting to be fulfilled in our own time. *The Iliad* is a not a poem *past* but a poem *yet to come*, when we prove ourselves capable, Weil says, of learning the lesson of Homeric Greece: "How never to admire might, or hate the enemy, or despise those who suffer."

I believe that Bernal belongs more to this epic movement, or epic-in-movement described by Hegel and Simone Weil, than to the idea of the *finished* epic evoked by Ortega and Bakhtin. But if we accept the premises of the Spanish philosopher and the Russian critic, Bernal also writes *a novel* which is *a novelty* in regards to the epic, in this case the epic medieval romances of chivalry.

Allow me to speak as a Catholic would, and say that perhaps Bernal writes an epic novel, with as much movement and novelty as the *epic* according to Hegel and Weil, and with as much novelty and dynamism as the *novel* according to Bakhtin and Ortega.

In any case, like all great literature, Bernal Díaz del Castillo's great popular chronicle transforms the facts of the past and recalls them in a continuous succession of events which is being read in the future—the future in relation to both the events being narrated and the writing of these events by the author—but which actually happen in the present, where both the work of literature and its reader always, and finally, meet.

First, as he writes in response to Gómara's biography of Cortés, Bernal denies that the Conquest was an individual epic, but rather a collective enterprise enacted by the rising middle class to which he, and Cortés, belonged. Bernal does not disparage Cortés, whom he greatly admires. But he does stake a claim against the cult of the conquistador's personality, in favor of the foot soldier, the cavalryman,

the gunner: the five hundred odd comrades who cut off their own retreat and crossed the Rubicon into the unknown empire of the Aztecs
and its rumors of death and sacrifice. This is the collective epic, not
of great heroes, kings, and knights, but of humble men out to fashion
their own destiny: the people as actors of history: a premonition of
Michelet's interpretation of the French Revolution as the passage of
"a whole people" from silence to voice.

But, in the second place, this chronicle is not recorded as the
events occur, but from the perspective of old age, almost fifty years
after the events in question. Now a resident of Guatemala, Bernal
breaks his long silence in order to do justice to the soldiers of the
Conquest. He has no literary pretensions: he writes his book for his
children and grandchildren, and indeed, leaves it behind as a sort of
testament. He did not live to see his work in print. But when he died
at the age of eighty-four, he was content to consider it the only wealth
he could bequeath to his family. This perspective gives the book its
strangely melancholy note: a yearning for a lost time, youth; a vibrant
and sad reminder of the unpolluted promise of personal courage
rewarded.

Bearing the influence of epic romance   the book is full of ref
erences to the paladin Roland, Amadís de Gaul, and the books of
chivalry—Bernal's work is written with the inclusiveness and moral
consonance proper to the epic poem. Everything must be included,
in impressive litanies: soldiers, horses, and battles, even the fruits
and vegetable in the Aztec marketplace. Yet as he approaches a more
modern novelistic strategy he will hedge and abbreviate as he writes
certain phrases: "But I will waste no more time on the subject of
idols" he says; or "Let us leave behind the subject of the treasure"; or
about the Indian interpreter Melchorejo: "Let him go, and bad luck
to him, *and we will return to our story.*"

Bernal's conformity with the ideals of Christian faith is never in
doubt, *nor* his allegiance to the Crown of Spain. Yet he is capable of
certain jarring notes, if not heretical, then wryly humorous, to be
sure. Gómara had said that the victory in battle on the Tabasco sa-
vannah was accomplished thanks to the physical apparition of the
apostles St. James and St. Peter. But Bernal comments that "As a sin-
ner, I was unworthy to see them."

What Bernal does see are the great feats of Cortés and his band of bravos. His narrative genius consists in employing the powers of memory to evoke them, while preserving for us their freshness. Novelty and astonishment are the premises of his writing: "a marvel to gaze on ... a marvelous place ... a marvelous sight ... It was all so wonderful that I do not know how to describe this first glimpse of things never heard nor seen nor even dreamed, as we saw." But *memory* is the vessel which recovers the deluge of marvels: the events seem to be *in the making* because *the memory is in the making*: "I have put down those soldiers' names from memory. But later, in the proper time and place, I will record the names of all those who took part in this expedition, in so far as I can remember them."

Bernal's memory is the modern recall of the novelist. It is marked by five profoundly novelistic traits:

1) *Love of characterization*: Bernal will have us know that he *is* referring to *plain old* Rojas, *not* Rojas the rich; to Juan de Nájera, *not* the deaf man who played ball in Mexico. These are concrete individuals, not allegorical warriors. The figures are at times as eccentric as anything in Shakespeare or Melville. We see Cervantes the Fool who precedes and warns the parade of soldiers. We see the Astrologer, Juan Millán, the old madman and soothsayer of the expedition.

2) *Love of detail* that de-sacralizes the epic figures: in Champotón, Cortés loses a sandal and lands barefoot in the mud during the first great battle in Mexico; Moctezuma and Cortés play dice to while away the hours in Mexico City, and the emperor accuses the bold captain Pedro de Alvarado of cheating.

3) *Love of gossip*. Without which, undoubtedly, there would be no modern novel or even epic narrative: from the rape of Helen of Troy to the kidnapping of Albertine, from Homer to Proust, Defoe, Dickens or Stendhal; all are, in this sense, gossipmongers. Bernal is no exception. He informs us that Cortés has just married, in Cuba, a woman called La Marcaida; it is said to be a love match; but those who have seen it in close quarters "have a great deal to say about this marriage." Having planted the seed of rumor with about as much subtlety as Henry James, Bernal withdraws from "this delicate subject."

4) There are the great *social portraits*, critical social portraits. Bernal Díaz is particularly perceptive in describing the Spanish—and later Latin American—tradition of the *hidalgo*, the gentleman, literally the *hijo-de-algo*, the son of something. Bernal gives an extraordinary por-

trait of Cortés on the island of Cuba where, as soon as he is appointed General, he begins "to adorn himself and to take much more care of his appearance than before." He wears "a plume of feathers, with a medallion and a gold chain, and a velvet cloak trimmed with loops of gold." Yet this splendid hidalgo has "nothing with which to meet these expenses, for at that time he was very poor and in debt." Finery, entertainment, prodigality: from the debt of the Spanish Armada to the debt of the IMF, the spendthrift generosity of the patrimonialist clans of Latin America and their seigniorial ambitions are already depicted by Bernal in the figure of Cortés and the conquistadors.

But these things, in the case of Hernán Cortés—here we have our fifth narrative trait—are only the outward signs of a profound love for the (5) *Theatricality and intrigue* that became essential to obtaining his political purposes. Cortés impresses the envoys of Moctezuma with the almost cinematic device of galloping horses along the beach at low tide, a deliberate display of magnificent power before people who had never before seen horses: "A horse,"—writes the Swedish poet Artur Lundkvist, as if he were describing the steeds of the conquistadors painted in a mural by José Clemente Orozco— "a horse: that powerful creature with fire in his belly and lightning in his hooves; with dark rush of heavy blood, powerful as an imprisoned waterfall." Imagine seeing this beast for the first time; from the indigenous people's perspective, only magic and myth could account for such an apparition. Cortés adores duplicity, employs doubles, and sees through the farce of the doubles Moctezuma sends in place of himself. Cortés seduces, astounds, and frightens potential enemies; for the sake of theatrical impression, he makes horses smell their mares, and angry cannons spout fire at appointed hours. But he also listens, learns, hears complaints, arrests tax collectors, frees peoples from their tribute to Moctezuma, and sees to it that the news spreads: the Spanish have come to liberate the indigenous peoples in the thrall of Aztec tyranny. Cortés has come to bear the white man's burden. In this way, Machiavellian politics transform Bernal's novel, which in itself was the transformation of Bernal's epic, into Bernal's political history. This is, finally, a story of colonization, imperialism, genocide, and greed.

From the moment at Cempoala when the Spaniards receive their first one hundred *tamemes*, or fardel bearers, to the moment when the first indigenous people are enslaved and branded, violence occupies the place of enchantment, and then *awe* is overtaken by *greed*, corruption, and the shadow of bureaucratic authoritarianism.

The description of the quarrel over Moctezuma's gold is an ugly tale of deceit, suspicion, and outright theft: the foot soldiers see nothing of these spoils.

Yet, there is a sixth facet of this tale that I wish to recall: the drama of *will* versus *fate*. Determination versus destiny. Moctezuma is ruled by fate; Cortés is ruled by will. They face each other in one of the most dramatic confrontations in history. Cortés is the great Machiavellian character of the discovery and conquest of the New World but, of course, he never read Machiavelli. *The Prince* was written in 1513 but not published until 1532, posthumously, a decade after Cortés had consummated the Conquest of Mexico and then fallen from royal favor.

Yet Cortés is the best extant proof that Machiavellianism, the figure of the Prince who has conquered his own power, was already in the wind, represented in the essential reality of the affirmation of humanism, and that it was becoming *real* not only in the figures evoked by Machiavelli in European history, but, with even more dramatic coincidence, in the startling, unprecedented figures of the conquistadors of the New World.

Machiavelli is the brother of the conquistadors. For, what is *The Prince* but a treatise in praise of will, a rejection of providence, a manual for the new man of the Renaissance who prepares to become the new statesman, freed from excessive obligations towards uncertain fortune, inheritance or high birth? The Prince wins his earthly kingdom through the right of conquest.

Faithful to his Machiavellian destiny, Hernán Cortés lives through this profound irony: all of his *virtú*, the strength of his arm and the size of his will, are not sufficient to conquer his secret failing, his fortune, his hazard, his providence. In this he resembles, finally, his victim, the emperor Moctezuma. Moctezuma is ruled by fate. In the end, in June of 1521, he is stoned to death by his own people.

The Great Voice

Moctezuma, the Great Tlatoani of Mexico, that is, the Lord of the Great Voice, the Absolute Owner of Words, was stripped of his attributes by a man of the European Renaissance, the very embodiment of the Machiavellian spirit, Hernán Cortés, and a woman who gave her native tongue to the Spaniards and, in turn, the Spanish tongue to the natives: Marina, *La Malinche*, enslaved princess, interpreter, Cortés's lover and, symbolically, mother of the first Mexican *mestizo*, the first child of both Indian and European blood.

Moctezuma hesitated between submitting to the fatality of Quetzalcoatl's return on the day foreseen by religious prophecy, or fighting these white, bearded men mounted on four-legged beasts and armed with thunder and fire. This vacillation cost him his life: his own people lost faith in him and stoned him to death. Cuauhtémoc, the last Aztec king, struggled to save the Aztec nation as a center of identification and solidarity for all the Mexican peoples. It was too late.

Cortés, the Machiavellian politician, discovered the secret weakness of the Aztec empire: the people subjected to Moctezuma hated him and joined the Spaniards against the Aztec tyrant. They lost the Aztec tyranny, but they gained the Spanish tyranny.

Written five decades after the events it describes, Bernal's account offers a lasting adventure; a memory, a resurrection of the lost kingdom. But it is not only hindsight that permits him to understand the inherent sadness and futility of all human glory. It is a deeper vision that we generally attribute to great fiction. Bernal's book resounds with omens of danger and defeat, but none is greater than the danger and defeat we carry in our own hearts.

This wisdom is implicitly projected onto the two principal figures of the tale, the Aztec emperor and the Spanish conqueror. The vertical autocracy of Moctezuma's rule was replaced by the vertical autocracy of the Spanish Hapsburgs. We are the descendants of both verticalities, and our stubborn struggles for democracy are all the more difficult and, perhaps, even admirable, for it.

Machiavelli's *The Prince* was first published in Spanish translation in 1552 and subsequently listed on the Index of Prohibited Books—the *Index Librorum Prohibitorum*—by Cardinal Gaspar de Quiroga in 1584.

But before that, in March of 1527, the Crown ordered that there should be no further printing of Cortés's letters of relation from Mexico to King Charles V of Spain. Six years after the end of the conquest, the conquistador, who had deprived Moctezuma, the Great Tlatoani, of his voice was, in turn, condemned to silence.

And in 1553, yet another royal decree forbade the exportation to the American colonies of all histories dealing with the conquest. We were not allowed to know ourselves, and so, deprived of history, we eventually had to write novels. Loaded with the rumors, silences, vacillations, and ambiguities which humanize the epic certitude of the Spanish imperial conquest of the indigenous peoples of Latin America, our first novel was written by Bernal Díaz del Castillo.

Nevertheless, his popular, collective contemplation of events necessarily tells an individual history, because if Cortés's destiny is represented by the Spanish soldiers, the destiny of the Spanish soldiers is also represented by Cortés. All of this comes together in Bernal's book. The tension that builds up in the book belongs to those novels where individual destiny crosses paths with historical destiny. But there is yet another tension in Bernal's chronicle, and this is between the utopian promise of the New World, the European certitude that paradise had been rediscovered in America, and the destruction of Utopia by the military and political necessity of the epic deeds.

Bernal thus gives us an epic in love with its utopia, its golden age, its lost garden, now destroyed by the iron and boots of the epic itself. An enormous Latin American vacuum then opens between utopian promise and epic reality.

This vacuum has been filled in many ways, through renewed utopian promises; through yet more violence, as happened in most of the newly conquered native lands; through the Baroque, an art designed to fill voids, and which, in Latin America, becomes an essential ingredient of what the Cuban writer José Lezama Lima called the Counterconquest: an absorption of European and African cultures and a maintenance of the indigenous cultures which, meeting and blending, create Latin American culture or Indo-Afro-Ibero-American culture.

Name, Memory, and Voice: What is your name? Who were your mother and father? What language do you speak? How do you speak? Who speaks for you? All these urgent, present-day questions of the

American continent are formulated, tacitly or expressly, by Bernal, and they shall become the questions of Rubén Darío and Pablo Neruda, of Alejo Carpentier and Juan Rulfo, of Gabriela Mistral and Gabriel García Márquez.

The Conquest of Mexico was not only a battle between Men and Gods, or between Myth and Firearms; it was also a conflict of voices: a struggle for language. Because the Emperor Moctezuma, the Tlatoani, He of the Great Voice, listened only to the Gods he was defeated by men. Hernán Cortés, the Conquistador, listened only to the voices of men: thus he was defeated by institutions, by Church and Crown.

Perhaps she who truly rescues the voices of all, the victorious and the defeated, native peoples, Europeans, and mestizos, is a woman: Malintzin is her birth name, a name of ill fortune. Born a princess, her parents, fearing the omens of her birth, gave her up into slavery to the *caciques*, the chieftains of Tabasco, who in turn gave her to Cortés as a trophy of war. Marina is her Spanish name, given to her on baptism. But La Malinche is her Mexican name, the name of the betrayer who gave herself to the Conquistador, who became her lover but also her interpreter *mi lengua* ("my tongue") Cortés called her—and through her words and her knowledge of the native universe, Cortés conquered Mexico.

Symbolically, she gives birth to the first Mexican, the first mestizo, Martín Cortés, who already, in the first generation after the Conquest, becomes the protagonist, along with his half-brother, also called Martín, the son of Cortés and a Spanish noblewoman, of the first fledgling movement towards Mexican independence, promptly crushed by the Spanish Crown in 1567.

A new reality is born with La Malinche and her mestizo son, both abandoned for the political and social aspirations of the father, Hernán Cortés. Her voice brought us to the brink of a deeper understanding of the Iberian conquest of the New World, and it transforms us, the descendants of natives and Europeans in the Americas, into witnesses of the terrible act of our own death and immediate resurrection.

Before our eyes, in the present day, we all experience the fact that gave birth to us.

We are the eternal witnesses of our own creation.

And we endlessly repeat the questions of that creation:

What is our place in the World?

To whom do we owe allegiance?

To our Spanish fathers?

To our Aztec, Mayan, Quechuan, Araucanian mothers?

To whom should we now speak: to the ancient gods, or to the new ones?

What tongue should we now speak, that of the conquered or that of the conquerors?

Bernal Díaz gives us the answers to these dilemmas through his epic memory translated by novelistic imagination. For besides the language of the conquered and the conqueror, Bernal gives words to a chronicle, which acknowledges and celebrates its own gestation, contemplates itself, and debates with itself. And at the center of the book is its author, Bernal, who, as he discovers the marvels and the dangers of the new world, is also discovering his own self. And in his own self hides the real enemy, but also the true savior: the loving, amatory self, the self in love with the world it describes. For there is a chink in the armor of the Christian warrior facing off against the Aztec heathens, and through it shines a heart sadly in love with its enemies.

This is the secret source of Spanish-American fiction as it faces the enigmas of the historical world. Bernal Díaz writes a mysterious lament for the opportunities lost by the men of modern Spain, in the form of a troubled epic—an essential novel—in which the victor ends up loving the defeated and recognizing himself in them.

Another voice, a new voice, sometimes hidden, silent, insulting, and bitter; at times a vulnerable and loving voice; at other times screaming with the stridency of a being that demands to be heard, to be seen, and thus to exist, ceaselessly repeating our question:

Who speaks?

To whom, to how many, does the voice of Spanish America belong? These are the questions addressed to the name, the voice, and the memory of the Americas.

Memory and Desire

We describe the marvelous, just as Bernal Díaz did when he came upon the Aztecs' city on the lake: "this resembled the enchantments in the book of Amadís . . . Some of our soldiers said that perhaps they were seeing all of this as if in a dream." We are shaped by this fantasy of America: this desire for the New World.

But all desires have their objects and these, according to Luis Buñuel, are always obscure, because we not only want to possess the object of our desire but to transform it as well. There are no innocent desires; no immaculate discoveries; there is no traveler who, secretly, does not repent leaving his land, fearing that he will never again return home.

Desire drags us away because we are not alone; one desire is the imitation of another desire that we want to share, to possess for ourselves. The voyage, the discovery, ends with the conquest: we long to hold the world in order to transform it.

In the Caribbean islands, Columbus discovers the Golden Age and the noble savage. He sends the latter, bound in chains, to Spain, and the earthly paradise is burnt, branded, and exploited. Bernal Díaz's melancholy is that of the pilgrim who discovers the vision of paradise and is then forced to kill what he loves. Astonishment becomes pain but both are saved by memory; we no longer desire to travel, discover, and conquer: we now remember in order not to go mad, and to evade insomnia.

History is the violence that, like Macbeth, murders sleep. Glory offers death and, when unmasked, appears as death itself. Bernal, the chronicler, the writer, can only remember: there, in his memory, *the discovery remains forever marvelous.* The garden is intact, the end is a new beginning, and the destruction wrought by war coexists with the appearance of a new world, one born from catastrophe.

To remember, to return. We then realize that we live surrounded by lost worlds, by vanished histories. These worlds and their histories are our responsibility: they were made by men and women. We cannot forget them without condemning ourselves to being forgotten. We must maintain history in order to have history; we are the witnesses of the past so that we might have a future.

We then understand that the past depends on our memory *here* and *now*, and the future on our desire, *here* and *now*. Memory and desire are our present imagination: this is the horizon of our constant discoveries and this is the journey we must renew each day.

For that reason we write novels.

3. Colonial Culture

1.

Jean Bodin, the author of *Six Books of the Commonwealth*, the foundational work for the theory and practice of the centralizing French monarchy, offers a typically Gallic variant to the theme of a utopia in the New World.

In 1566, he writes in order to simply question whether a utopia can have a place among the "primitive" peoples, or if these people will regenerate a corrupt Europe. It might well have been that the noble savages were also living "in an age of iron" and not in an age of gold. According to Bodin, what the New World had to offer was a vast geography, not a happy history: a future, not a past.

Before this original prophecy of America-as-future became unduly optimistic, Bodin set us all straight by means of the simple but elegant praise for reality: the New World is extraordinary for the very ordinary reason that it exists. America exists, and the world is finally complete. America is not Utopia, the place that is not. It is Topia, the place that is. It is not a wondrous place, but it is the only one we have.

Such realism, nevertheless, does not manage to extinguish the dream of the New World, the fantasy of America. Because even if America is reality, America was first a dream, a desire, an invention, a necessity. The "discovery" only proves that we never find anything except what we have first desired.

American researcher Irving Leonard holds that the conquistadors arrived to the New World armed with what he calls "the books of brave men," the epics of chivalry which taught daring and honor. To whom? Surely not to the Spanish aristocrats who read them hungrily, but to the protagonists of the Spanish epic in America: men of an emerging middle class, failed students like Hernán Cortés; new Christians with dubious connections at court, such as Gonzalo Fernández de Oviedo, alias *Valdés*; members of the Andalusian petty noble class, like Álvar Núñez Cabeza de Vaca; but also illiterate commoners like the brothers Pizarro, and nobodies like Diego de Almagro, of whom the chronicler Pedro de Cieza de León writes that his origin was so lowly, his lineage so recent, that it began and ended with him. Corsairs like Hernando de Soto, who became rich with treasure stolen from the murdered Incan emperor Atahualpa, and then lost it on his expedition to Florida. Or older ones, like Pedro de Mendoza, the founder of Buenos Aires, who financed his own enterprise on the River Plate with plunder from Charles V's sack of Rome:

Conquer the pagans

With the gold of Romans

Rich men like Alfonso de Lugo, Governor of the Canary Islands, and debtors on the run, like Diego de Nicuesa. Largely men of Andalusia and Extremadura, the shining lights of utopia and topia, of wealth and glory, they faded away in the chimera of El Dorado. Son of an alderman, reader of *Amadis of Gaul* and the other "books of brave men," Bernal Díaz del Castillo, as we have seen, is the prototype of the new man who risks himself to travel from Spain to the West Indies, impelled by dual impulses: self-interest and dream, individual effort and collective enterprise: the epic and the utopia.

The voyages of exploration and discovery are as much a cause as a reflection of a hunger for space. The discoverers and conquistadors are men of the Renaissance. Spanish historian José Antonio Maravall even describes the Discovery of America as a great feat of the Renaissance *imagination*.

These men, brimming with a confidence which made them aware of being actors in their own history, although that also signified being victims of their own passions, did not arrive alone. The Niña, the Pinta, and the Santa María were followed by the ship of fools, the *navis stultorum* of the famous woodcutting by Sebastian Brandt. Machiavelli was the watchman on this fools' voyage, while Thomas More was the pilot, and the bent, stooping, vigilant Erasmus of Rotterdam the cartographer. The slogans and standards of their ship were, respectively, *this is*, *this must be*, and *this can be*.

Machiavelli came from an Italy shattered by the conflicts between its city-states: a world of violence for which Machiavelli demanded a realist leader, earthly but also possessed of the idealism necessary for building a nation and a State. Thomas More came from an England that had lost its agrarian innocence and capitulated to the demands for land enclosure, the partition of ancient common lands given over to capitalist concentration and exploitation. Erasmus was the ironical observer of historical folly, simultaneous witness to Topia and Utopia, to reason and unreason; as much a witness to traditional faith as new realism. To both — reason and faith — Erasmus warns them to be relative. Erasmian humanism signifies the abandonment of absolutes, be they faith or reason, in favor of an irony capable of distinguishing knowing from believing, and of putting any truth in doubt, because "all human things have two aspects." The absolutes of faith and reason judge this relativist reason of humanism to be folly. In his letters, Erasmus traces a middle path between *realpolitik* and idealism, between topia and u-topia: his irony signifies a smiling compromise between faith and reason, between the feudal world and the commercial world, between orthodoxy and reform, between external rite and internal conviction, between appearance and reality. He does not wish to sacrifice any term: he is the father of Cervantes and the ironical fictions that, among us, culminate with Borges and Cortázar. Thence comes *In Praise of Folly*, whose Latin title is *Moriae Encomium*, which is also, in this way, the praise of More.

In the New World, More sought a society based on natural right and not on the disorderly expansion of capitalism. It was preferable to imagine a utopia that shared the virtues and the defects of precapitalist societies, Christian or savage.

Machiavelli's political realism and energy; Thomas More's dream of a just and honorable human society; and the Erasmian praise for the ironical position that permits men and women to survive their ideological folly. The three of them will become scales of measurement in the New World.

But it often turns out to be difficult — even impossible — for the ship of fools to reach a safe haven because it runs aground in the shallows of the stoic individualism that Spain inherits from Rome and transmits to America; or it becomes becalmed in the Sargasso Sea of medieval organicism; or it is battered by the tormented exigencies of imperial autocracy.

In spite of these accidents, Machiavelli, More, and Erasmus manage to reach the New World, arriving because they are part, not of America's Roman and medieval inheritance, but of the "invention of America."

In my home office hang reproductions of the portraits of Thomas More and Desiderius Erasmus by Holbein the Younger, each one looking at the other while I look at them. I confess my fear of having a portrait of Machiavelli near at hand. His impenetrable countenance has something of the rapacious animal, the sharp and hungry gaze which Shakespeare, in his play *Julius Caesar*, attributes to Cassius. As if describing the Florentine, Shakespeare writes: "He thinks too much. Such men are dangerous."

Erasmus and More, by contrast, both reveal a grave aspect balanced by a spark of humor in their glances, forever representing their first meeting in the summer of 1499, in Hertfordshire:

"You must be either Thomas More or nobody at all."

"And you must be Erasmus, or the Devil himself."

If Niccolò Machiavelli had joined them, what might he have added? Perhaps only this: "All the prophets who arrived armed were successful, while those prophets unarmed met their ruin."

This great Renaissance triad wrote its slender, powerful, influential volumes within the same decade: *In Praise of Folly* by Erasmus appears in 1509; Thomas More's *Utopia* in 1516; and Machiavelli finished *The Prince* in 1513, although the book was only published posthumously, in 1532. Which is to say: all three coincide with "the invention of America."

These three books make their appearance in the New World on distinct dates. As Silvio Zavala has shown us, More's *Utopia* is the favorite book of Vasco de Quiroga, bishop of Michoacán, and it serves him as a model for his utopian foundations in Santa Fe and Michoacán, in 1535. It was also read by the first bishop of Mexico, Brother Juan de Zumárraga. *In Praise of Folly* was found in the library of Hernando Colón, son of the Discoverer, in 1515. The sage of Rotterdam's most influential work in Spain, *Enchiridion* (*Handbook of a Christian Knight*), is translated in 1526 and becomes the gospel of an internalized and personal Christianity, in opposition to the purely external forms of religious ritual. *The Prince* is finally published in a Spanish translation in 1552 and included in the *Index Librorum Prohibitorum* by Cardinal Gaspar de Quiroga in 1584.

Thus do these works reach America, not *thanks to*, but *in spite of* the Spanish Empire. Like the continent itself, they are, in a certain way, invented figures, desired, needed, and named by the "New World" which was first imagined and then found by Europe.

2.

Montaigne does not have the same luck as Amerigo Vespucci. Unlike the Florentine cartographer, the French essayist has not been to Utopia but he would have liked to have had "the fortune to . . . live among those nations, of which it is said that they still live in the sweet liberty of the first and incorruptible laws of nature."

This desire is born of a desperation, perfectly expressed by Alfonso de Valdés, the Spanish Erasmian and secretary to the Emperor Charles V: "What blindness is this? We call ourselves Christians and we live worse than Turks and brute animals. If it seems to us that this Christian doctrine is some kind of witchcraft, why then don't we abandon it once and for all?"

With less emphasis but with identical persuasion, Erasmus asked Christianity to believe in itself and adapt its practice to its faith: outward Christianity should be the faithful reflection of inner Christianity. He preached, in effect, the reform of the Church *by* the Church itself. As usually happens, although such reform did not come to pass, Erasmus enjoyed the immense popularity that the sick man reserves for the doctor who assures him of his recovery. But when the surgeon showed up, scalpel in hand, to remove the tumor, the kindly critic was thrown out of the city to join that other fearful surgeon of the Church of Rome, Martin Luther. Erasmus resisted this association and maintained his fidelity to Rome, but Christianity's educator was already the heretic, the reprobate, the banned author.

Sebastian Munster's *Cosmographia* contains a portrait of Erasmus which was censured by the Spanish Inquisition: the humanist's noble features are brutally outlined in heavy ink, his eye sockets empty like a skull, his mouth gaping and bloody like a vampire. The real Erasmus is the image of ironic intelligence as painted by Holbein, just as Martin Luther is the hard, strained, plebeian image painted by Cranach and portrayed by Albert Finney in the play by John Osborne.

The first theoretician of the Reformation, Erasmus never joined Luther's practical reform, not only out of his fidelity to the Church but also out of a profound conviction about human liberty. Erasmus reproached Luther for his ideas about predestination and demanded, from the Church but for the civil capitalist society adopted by Protestantism, "a power of the human will . . . applicable in multiple senses, which we call free will ... What good would man be," muses Erasmus, "if God treated him the way the potter treats clay?"

The paradox of this debate is, clearly, that Luther's fatalistic severity would lead to societies of increasing civil liberty and economic development, while the Erasmian fidelity to free will within orthodox Christianity would witness the economic and political paralysis imposed on the Spanish world by the Council of Trent and the Counter-Reformation. Between these options, Europe sheds its own blood in the wars of religion, that terrible epoch which Brecht evokes in the figure of Mother Courage, "dressed in holes and rottenness," in which "victory or defeat" is nothing more than "a loss for all." But farewell to illusions: "War is made for commerce. Instead of butter, they sell lead. And our children die." *Dulce bellum inexpertis*, writes Erasmus: war is only sweet for those who do not suffer it.

Thomas More responded to these realities with the fantasy of Utopia. In Utopia's eccentric society, one without Christianity but with natural right, both the vices and virtues of paganism and Christianity could be seen more clearly. More writes *Utopia* as a response to the England of his time and to the economic themes which absorbed his contemporaries: the end of an ancient agrarian community and its replacement by the capitalist system of enclosure which in the sixteenth century put an end to the common lands, fencing them off and handing them over for private exploitation.

Invoking in *Utopia* a society based on natural right, More imagined the meeting between the Old World and the New World not only as an encounter between Christianity and paganism, but also as the creation of a new society which would end up sharing both the virtues as the well as the defects of Christian and aboriginal societies.

More's Utopia is not the perfect society. It abounds with the traits of cruelty and authoritarian demands. Greed, however, has been eliminated and community restored. But the negative traits constantly threaten the positive ones: *Utopia* is not a naive book, and thanks to its chiaroscuro dynamic and constant questions about social possibilities, it is a work which leaves open two interminable questions, which continue as a legitimate part of our heritage, and of our preoccupations.

The first is the question of community values and their situation with respect to individual values and the values of the State. More

places community values above individual ones and those of the
State, because he considers these last ones to be only *a part* of the
community. In this sense, *Utopia* is a continuation of Thomist philosophy which favors common good over individual good. Scholasticism, supported by the utopia, will be the school of Ibero-American
politics for the next three centuries.

The second is the question, derived from the two previous ones,
of political organization. If the community is superior to both the
individual and the State, then, More tells us, political organization
must be constantly open and disposed to renewal in order to better
reflect and serve the community. Thus, *Utopia* can be read as a democratic anticipation of the eighteenth century Enlightenment and the
political philosophy of Ibero-American independence.

These are positive utopian values and should be considered while
we shape our history and our contemporary culture. But additionally
More's modernity is found primarily in his celebration of the pleasure
of the body and the mind. Thomas More's *Utopia* is a supremely personal book. Like almost all other great books, it is the author's debate
with himself: a debate of More with More, because as William Butler
Yeats said, of our debates with others we make rhetoric but in the debate with ourselves we make poetry. It permits us to see More and his
society in the very moment of entering the secular age. In effect, what
More does in *Utopia* is to explore the possibility of the secular life for
himself and for all men. He explores the infinitely fascinating theme
of the relationship between the intellectual man and power: should a
wise man serve the king? More explores the combination of elements
which could create a good society. As he permits the inhabitants of
Utopia to live as he himself would like to live, More offers a very personal ideal of life. Utopia's disagreeable, disciplinary, and misogynis-
tic aspects are, in the end, values of Thomas More, because he would
have liked to have been a married priest who brought the cloister to
the court. But perhaps the most interesting aspect of More's book is
that he offers this image of the possibly happier world, or more possible happiness, submitting it to a critique that does not renounce ambiguity and paradox as instruments of analysis.

Let us keep these lessons in mind while we move on to consider
Thomas More's arrival in the New World, carried there by the hand
of his most fervent reader, the Dominican friar Vasco de Quiroga.

3.

The humanist friars reached the New World treading on the heels of the conquistadors. In 1524, the so-called Twelve Apostles of the Franciscan order disembarked in the Mexico of Hernán Cortés; they were followed in 1526 by the Dominicans, among them Quiroga. They arrived to make sure that the civilizing mission of Christianity—the salvation of souls—would not be lost in the flurry of political ambition and the haste of Machiavellian affirmation.

Bartolomé de las Casas was the supreme denouncer of the destruction of Utopia by those who sought it out. Vasco de Quiroga, however, did not come to denounce but to transform utopia into history. He arrives with Thomas More's book tucked firmly under his arm. His reading of More simply identifies the Dominican bishop's conviction: *Utopia* should be the Magna Carta, the constitution of the peaceful coexistence between the devastated world of the indigenous peoples and the triumphalist attitude of the white man in the New World. Quiroga, affectionately called *Tata Vasco* (Papa Vasco) by the Purépecha people, is inspired by the vision of the New World as Utopia: "since it is not in vain but with good cause and with good reason that this world here was called the New World, and so it is new, not because it was newly found but because, it is in its people and almost everything, akin the first Golden Age, which thanks to our malicious and the greedy ways has become an age of iron and even worse." (Vasco de Quiroga, quoted by Silvio Zavala.)

The influence of Thomas More and the work of Quiroga in New Spain have been the object of brilliant and exhaustive studies carried out by Silvio Zavala. I also recall that Alfonso Reyes called Quiroga one of "the leftist fathers of America." These religious men set foot on lands where angels feared to tread, but where the conquistadors had already entered, stomping and even kicking.

In one sequence of his memoirs, Pablo Neruda described them as *voracious* conquistadors: "Devouring it all, potatoes, fried eggs, idols, gold, but giving us in exchange their gold: our language, the Spanish language."

Noisy conquistadors, whose rough and resonant voices contrasted with the birdlike voices of the natives. Once I heard a Mexican man with a soft, sweet voice ask the Spanish poet León Felipe:

"Why do you Spaniards speak so loudly?"

To which León Felipe answered imperatively:

"Because we were the first to cry: *Land-ho!*"

Cruel conquistadors: the humanists, including the clergy, accused them of trampling the lands of Utopia, stamping them back into the Iron Age. Perhaps Vasco de Quiroga is the only true utopian. Knowing himself to be in the "Iron Age" of the Spanish Conquest, he tries to restore a modicum of human community among real, living human beings: the people of the conquered Purépecha kingdom.

More than anyone, Quiroga illustrates the truth that history is only worthy of mankind when man builds, upon the ruins of a previous civilization, the edifice of a new coexistence. The tracks of Alvarado, Cortés, and Nuño de Guzmán were still burning along the footpaths of the Mexican natives. Quiroga douses their fiery tracks with his wisdom, patience, and infinite respect for the conquered people. His utopia was part of a vast educative effort that, even while it included evangelization, also went beyond it. In the school at Santiago Tlatelolco, the indigenous people quickly demonstrated their aptitude for learning languages, writing, and the art of memory. They learned Spanish, Greek, and Latin. In Michoacán, they learned how to respect themselves anew in the organization of work and daily life together. The fact that both experiments failed is one of the great sorrows of Mexico. For an instant, at the dawn of New Spain, Utopia, as a *paideia* for creative power and civilized coexistence, was real.

Persistent, tireless, the utopian dream returned in the Jesuit missions in Paraguay. In the eighteenth century, the population of the missions between the Upper Paraná and the Uruguay River exceeded 100,000 souls. The Jesuit order imposed a regimen of tutelage for the Guarani population. With the suppression of the Jesuit religious order in 1767, these people were left unprotected. In his dissertation, American ethnohistorian Charles Gibson similarly cites the example of the Yaqui region in northern Mexico and their agricultural work under the Jesuit organization during the centuries following the Conquest.

4.

In 1550, during the Valladolid Debate about the rights of conquest, even Friar Bartolomé de las Casas accepted the concept of just and unjust wars. Juan Luis Vives responded that such a distinction was a trap that could justify all the principles of destruction and slavery. *Dulce bellum inexpertis*: in his *Enchiridion militis Christiani* (*Handbook of a Christian Knight*), Erasmus asks nations to remember that war is sweet only for those who do not suffer it. The aboriginal peoples suffered it to unimaginable extremes of cruelty, slavery, and extermination. Friar Antonio de Montesinos's sermon on the island of Santo Domingo on Christmas Day in 1511, Friar Bartolomé's campaign, and the drawings in both the Peruvian chronicle of Poma de Ayala and the Codex Osuna provide clamorous proof of the violence which the conquistadors exercised against the conquered peoples.

Nevertheless, and in spite of the fact that tragedy, as explained by Max Scheler, is a conflict of values condemned to mutual extinction, it was not a tragic literature which arose from these events. The Conquest spelled the mutual extermination of Utopia and Epic, both foundations of the New World. History did not find resolution in tragedy because Christian evangelization did not transmit tragic values, but instead an otherworldly optimism. The conquered world collapsed without the critical instruments necessary to save itself from crisis and fatality. The praxis of colonization only deepened these abysses. The tragic opportunity of Spanish America—that act of renewal which illuminates and transcends past existence, in order for continued existence without sacrificing any of the components; tragedy as conscience and contemplation of ourselves and the world—remained in reserve, alive but latent in the heart of our culture.

The void was filled by the sorrowful Baroque of the New World, a formal response of the nascent Latin American culture to the defeat of the utopia of an invented America and the epic of its conquest: a defeat shared by More and Machiavelli, of the duty to exist and the wish to exist, of desire and will. From the abyss between the two sides, hungry and desperate, emerges what José Lezama Lima calls

"Our Lord the Baroque." The art of the Counterconquest.

In the art of the Counterconquest, Our Lord the Baroque is the anonymous builder and decorator of the chapel of Tonantzintla in Mexico, and of the cathedral in Puno, Peru. It is, now given a name, the builder known as the Indian Kondori, sculptor of "the willful mass of stone on the edifice of La Compañía [church]" in Potosí. It is, above all, the crippled mulatto Aleijadinho, the artist who chipped away at the Baroque stone with his face hidden because, as Lezama remembers, Brazil makes progress by night, while the Brazilians sleep. Aleijadinho, the "culmination of the American Baroque," needs the dark night of the soul to sculpt the wonders of Ouro Preto in secret, disguised, in the Baroque language of abundance and parody, substitution and condensation and, finally, eroticism. Mulatto, one-handed leper, the night is his ally and the Baroque is his mirror, his health, his clarity: Aleijadinho.

It is an eroticism sustained by the Baroque intellectual voracity which also belongs to Ibero-America: to know all, to accumulate everything, to fully take advantage of the Counter-Reformation's great concession to the sensual world in order to intoxicate the senses with knowledge and scattered forms: at a precise moment in time, the Baroque comes to resemble our freedom. It was the great escape valve of the American colonial world but it also reflects the economy of His panic profligacy. The Baroque: a name for the richness of poverty. Protestantism: a name for the poverty of richness.

Baroque eroticism belongs to the history of waste; it is a million-dollar fireworks show that turns the pitiful savings of a peasant town in the Sierra Madre or the Andes mountains into sparkling embers from heaven. If Luther and Calvin condemn images, decorations, and any sort of profusion in the reformist churches, the Counter-Reformation emphasizes adornment, architectural design, abundance and exorbitant cost to the point of delirium.

The cost of the Baroque: if Protestantism is the religion of thrift and its art comprises the white church walls of Northern Europe and the bare church walls of New England, Catholicism must be the religion of extravagance, of sumptuous cost, of prodigality. A concession by the Church to the Renaissance, the American Baroque is, additionally, the Conquest's concession to the Counterconquest, and Baroque proliferation permits not only hiding idols behind altars, but also substituting languages, making room, in Spanish, for the indigenous silence and the black psalmody, for the copulation of Quetzalcoatl and Christ, of Tonantzin and Guadalupe. It is a parody of the history of the conquerors and the conquered, with smiling white masks covering sad dark countenances. It both cannibalizes and carnivalizes history, converting sorrow into celebration, creating literary forms and artistic intrusions, the one intermeshed with the other, regardless of rules or genres, as do the writings of Borges, Neruda, and Cortázar in our times. It is a literature of texts loaned, borrowed, swapped, mimicked, and parodied, like the modern examples of Manuel Puig, Luis Rafael Sánchez, or Severo Sarduy. Blank texts, astonished by the challenge of a page's space, language that speaks of language, from Sor Juana and Sandoval and Zapata to José Gorostiza and José Lezama Lima.

Born of a hunger for space, the Baroque is not the basis for narration; it is neither history nor story. Instead, being successive chronology or combinatory imagination; past as it was and past as the present; registrable fact and continuous event — it is, for all these reasons, time itself. I suspect that the old quarrel between those who favor a Baroque-as-original-chaos and those who support a Baroque-as-will-of-artifice has its origin in this testimony of the New World. The Baroque was the new territory, it was first desired and then discovered in order to satisfy the Renaissance hunger for space. History suffered the consequences of this simple expansion as boots, cannon rounds, and cavalry helmets trampled the new ground. While it was only space, it was a devastating epic of the previous, mythic world of indigenous American. The European replaced the aboriginal myth with his own myth: Utopia. This also failed to survive the epic push of the conquest. Both indigenous myth and European Utopia survived only thanks to the synthesis of the American Baroque, a response to historical chaos and the artistic desire for salvation in the face of the void. It reflects both of them. It is their word, their form. Ibero-American culture is thus constructed upon a series of contradictions.

First contradiction: Between Renaissance humanism and monarchical absolutism.

Second contradiction: Between the Protestant Reformation and the Catholic Counter-Reformation.

Third contradiction: Between the Puritanism of Northern Europe and the sensuality of Southern Europe.

Fourth contradiction: Between the European conquest of America and the Amer-Indian and Afro-American Counterconquest of Europe.

As much in Europe as in America, the art of the Baroque appears as the conciliation—abrupt at times, distilled at others—of these contradictions. The European Baroque saves Catholic southern Europe from dogmatic continence and offers it a solution of voluptuous possibilities. The American Baroque saves the conquered world from silence and offers it a solution of syncretic and sensual possibilities.

5.

The Conquest and the colonization of the Americas by Spanish arms and letters was a multiple paradox. It was a catastrophe for the aboriginal populations, notably for the great native civilizations of Mexico and Peru. But a catastrophe, María Zambrano advises us, is only catastrophic if it offers nothing that might redeem it.

From the catastrophe of the Conquest all of us, the Indo-Ibero-Americans, were born. We were, from the first, mestizos—men and women of indigenous and Spanish blood and, soon, African blood as well. We were Catholic, but our Christianity was the syncretic refuge of the indigenous and African cultures. And we speak Spanish, but we immediately gave the language American, Peruvian, and Mexican inflections.

Because of the extent to which the Spanish language embraced the peoples of the Americas, and in so far as it mixed its blood, first with the indigenous world and later the African world, it ceased to be the language of empire and became something much greater.

On the American shore, on our side of the Atlantic, it became a universal language of recognition between the European and indigenous cultures whose greatest fruits in the sixteenth and seventeenth centuries were the poetry of the Mexican nun Sor Juana Inés de la Cruz and the prose of the Peruvian historian, El Inca Garcilaso de la Vega.

Sor Juana saw her own poetry as a product of the earth. "What are these magical infusions / of the Indian herbalists / of my na-

tive land, that spill enchantment across my pages?" El Inca Garcilaso went further, refusing to see Indo-Spanish America as an eccentric
or isolated region, but rather one which connected the culture of the
New World to the vision of a world united by many cultures: as El
Inca exclaimed, "There is but one world," true for his age and for our
own.

Because from the other side of the Atlantic, Spain's own literature,
subject as it was to religious dogmas, the vigilance of the Inquisition,
and a demand for purity of blood, created a whole new realm of the
imagination. If the Church and the State imposed the rules of the
Counter-Reformation, the literature of Spain invented, by contrast, a
counter-imagination and a counter-language.

From Fernando de Rojas to Miguel de Cervantes, from Francisco Delicado to Francisco de Quevedo—described by César Vallejo
as "that instantaneous grandfather of the dynamiters"—literature expresses everything that cannot be said in any other way.

Against the difficulties imposed by censorship, against the evidence of moral and political decadence, Spain affirms, more vigorously than the rest of Europe, the right to define reality in terms of
the imagination. What we can imagine is, at the same time, both possible and true. True for Cervantes, true for Velázquez. Today we celebrate, in this way, not the language of the empire, but the language
of encounters, the language of recognitions, the language that links
Lorca and Neruda, Galdós and Gallegos, but also Juan Goytisolo in
Spain, and Juan Rulfo in Mexico.

No one represented this fact to a higher degree, during the colonial period, than Sor Juana Inés de la Cruz. Born Juana de Asbaje in
central Mexico, in 1648, she was probably an illegitimate child. When
she was seven years old, she pleaded with her mother to dress her as a
boy so that she could study at the university. Her brilliant intelligence
led her to the viceregal court as a teenager. There, she amazed the university professors with her knowledge of everything from Latin to
mathematics. She won praise and fame, but promptly saw the difficulties of being a woman writer in colonial Mexico. Not only would
she face male opposition and ecclesiastical oversight, but her time
would be undermined, and her safety threatened. She went into the
Church hoping, perhaps, to find protection in the institution that
would one day attack her. Yet her cell at the Convent of San Jerónimo

warded off any premonition of danger. There she collected over four thousand volumes, her papers, her pens and ink, her musical instruments. There, from a cell where knowledge was permitted, she could write about everything under the sun. There she could display, in both discipline and contentment, her imagination and wisdom. There, in the world of religion and letters, united for one moment in time, she would be known as Sor Juana Inés de la Cruz — Sister Juana.

There, as Roald Hoffmann writes in a beautiful poem dedicated to her, "she mixed lands," she attempted to bring together heaven and earth, but also body and soul, Europe and America, White and Native, Reason and Mystery, Life and Death. A Dream held it all together, a "First Dream," an initiatic dream, as she called one of her greatest poems. Within the dream, she seeks to see things as clearly as possible:

> Let those who with green glasses spectacled,
>
> see everything the color of their wish,
>
> follow your shadow in search of day;
>
> But I, more mindful of my destiny,
>
> hold both my eyes in both my hands,
>
> and only see what I can touch.

What she sees, with almost clinical lucidity, is the cruel game of love, no longer disguised as a mystical metaphor, but almost Proustian in its psychological acuteness:

> If an ingrate doth leave me, I seek out a new lover,
>
> But the lover who seeks me, I ungratefully leave;
>
> I constantly adore my own love's executioner,
>
> But do execute my love's constant pleader.

She has to know all things, for she has "a dark inclination towards wisdom." Especially, she must know more than any European of her time, thus creating a tradition for the Latin American writer, that of knowing as much as any European as well as something that a European does not know: the heavy obligation of the Latin American writer. We must know Descartes but also the *Popol Vuh*, the sacred book of the Maya. Her knowledge is admired in Europe, and she coyly acknowledges this in a poem:

> You have brought shame on me
>
> by giving me fame,
>
> for the light that you give me
>
> reveals more than ever more clearly my defects

But she must also know more than any man:

> Foolish men, you accuse woman without reason
>
> Since you are the reason for what you accuse . . .
>
> Whether favored or disdained
>
> I fear men are all the same:
>
> They complain if we treat them bad;
>
> They mock us if we treat them well

And yet, those clear eyes that will not be beguiled by green spectacles, know full well that everything in this life is "colorful deceit":

> a withered yearning, and in truth
>
> 'Tis corpse, and dust, and dusk, and naught . . .

Sor Juana once saw two girls spinning a top. So she had flour sprinkled on the floor, and as the top spent its force, its spiral trace could be seen. The world, after all, was not a circle, but a spiral. A few decades later, the Neapolitan philosopher, Giambattista Vico, would found modern historiography on just such a principle. History is made by men and women, it proceeds not in a straight line, not in a circle, but in a spiral of constant *corsi e ricorsi*, forwards and backwards, picking up what the past, other peoples, and different cultures, have done. In her plays and her carols, Sor Juana certainly anticipated the multicultural nature of the American World.

But more than this, she constantly proposed poetry as an alternative, as the other voice of society. And since no one was more silent in colonial society than woman, perhaps only a woman could have given a voice to that society, while lucidly admitting the divisions of her heart and mind:

> In confusion, my soul
>
> is divided in two

One, is passion's slave

the other, reason's to command.

Passion? Reason? Slavery? Where are certainty, faith, blind acceptance of religious precepts? After all, who was this presumptuous nun, admired in Europe, consorting, perhaps sexually, with the Viceroy's wife, holding court in her cell, admitting that "I suffer in loving and being loved." By whom? When? At what hours?

In the end her cloistered cell was not protection enough from authority, male and rigidly orthodox, personified in her persecutor, the Archbishop of Mexico, Aguiar y Seijas. At age forty, she was stripped of her library, her musical instruments, her pen and ink. She was driven back into silence. In 1695, at the age of forty-three, she was dead, perhaps from this burden. Speak no more, Sister Juana.

Yet she defeated her silencers. Her Baroque poetry had the capacity to hold, forever, the shapes and words of the abundance of the New World, its new names, its new geography, its flora and its fauna never before seen by European eyes. For she herself wondered if her poetry was but a product of the land, "a magical infusion brewed from herbs of the Indians of my own country."

6.

If something was needed to both deepen and amplify the transatlantic European, Indigenous, and Mestizo culture of the Americas, it was the African universe that came to us in sorrow and bondage only to give us freedom and joy. From William Faulkner's Mississippi to Alejo Carpentier's Cuba to Jean Rhys's Dominica to Derek Walcott's St. Lucia to Aimé Cesaire's Martinique to Gabriel García Márquez's Barranquilla, a stream of recognitions, black, white, and mulatto, gave yet another color to the human face of the Americas.

The Spanish Crown regulated the slave trade for its own profit. In 1518, Charles V granted a concession to introduce four thousand African slaves into the Spanish colonies. From then on, the African population in Spanish America would grow at a rate of eight thousand people a year, to thirty thousand in 1620. In Brazil, the first Africans arrived in 1538. Over the next three centuries, 3.5 million African slaves would cross the Atlantic: Portugal would import into Brazil a population of Africans several times larger than the native population. Today, the American continent has the world's largest black population outside of Africa. Men, women, and children were carried to the New World on slave ships amidst pain and suffering. Even before they embarked, many attempted to commit suicide. Once on board, they were stripped naked, branded on their chests, and chained in pairs. Sold by the yard, they now traveled in the space of a grave, tightly packed together deep in the holds, with no sanitary precautions and hardly any space in which to breathe. At times they even attempted revolts against their captors, though these generally failed. But wherever they went, the slaves were rigidly tied to the plantation economy, that is, to the intensive and extensive cultivation of tropical produce.

This rigid equation—black slaves plus plantation economy—was complicated by a great rivalry for the power to control both the slave trade from Africa and the source of products from the New World. Crushed between the demands of international politics and trade, slaves could not even appeal to the conscience of their Christian enslavers. They were hunted down for profit by the African rulers. Then they were bought by European traders who said that they were liberating them from tribal violence, while the Christian church said that they were being saved from paganism. This pompous exercise in hypocrisy and injustice failed to destroy the creative, much less the rebellious, spirit of the black slaves in the Americas. Rebels, runaways, saboteurs, they rarely managed to liberate themselves. Sometimes they did gain their freedom and became overseers, artisans, farmers, and teamsters. They toiled endlessly, not only in the fields, but also as masons and jewelers, carpenters and painters, tailors, shoemakers, cooks and bakers. There was hardly any aspect of labor and life in the New World untouched by black culture. In Brazil, they even helped to explore and conquer the lands of the interior. Black regiments under black leaders fought the Dutch, and defended Rio de Janeiro against the French. They proved vital to the conquest, settlement, and development of Brazil. They also rose up against their oppressors.

And, many times, they simply disappeared into the interiors, founding settlements known as *quilombos*. One such, at Palmares in Alagoas, Brazil, lasted well into the seventeenth century. With a population of twenty thousand, it became an African state with its own

African tradition in the heart of South America. But, as with the indigenous cultures, it was in the encounter with the European that the Black became, even more so, a denizen of the New World, a creator of a mixed culture, of a new art.

Of course, it is both important and interesting to trace, as far as possible, the African origins of the New World blacks. The reason for this is that it strengthens the sense of continuity which I find crucial to the identity of a Latin American universe that, I repeat, is Indigenous, African, and European. But even more important for us is, indeed, the new culture created by Africans in the Americas. For wherever they came from in Africa, from the moment they were thrown together in a Senegalese port of embarkation, they were forced to create new relationships, with their masters but especially with the other slaves, from all parts of the African Atlantic coastlands. A whole new set of relationships, and the culture that went with them, thus came to depend on the jobs that the slaves were to perform in the New World. And a new set of questions was expressed. For newcomers on the plantation, where did they come from? On what sort of ship did they travel? Where did they land? For the less recent arrivals, what was now their "color"? Had they intermarried or not? Were they mulattoes, children of blacks and whites, or Zambos — children of blacks and Indians? And how did the two cultures, European and indigenous, influence them all?

Language had to adapt with protean agility to these questions. If you wanted to understand and be understood by the overseers or by your fellow workers, also black, but from a region distant from yours; or, certainly, by your newlywed wife. And what language would the children speak?

The black culture of the New World flowed naturally into the Baroque. For in the same way that a Latin American Baroque came into being, from Tonantzintla in Mexico to Potosí in Upper Peru, through the encounter of the indigenous and the European, so the fusion of blacks and Portuguese created one of the greatest monuments to the New World: the Brazilian, Afro-Portuguese Baroque of Minas Gerais, the most opulent gold-producing region of the world in the eighteenth century.

There, the mulatto Antonio Francisco Lisboa, known as Aleijadinho, wrought what many consider the culmination of the Latin American Baroque. Aleijadhino was the son of a black slave woman and a white Portuguese architect. But he was shunned by his parents and by the world. The young man suffered from leprosy. So he turned his back on the society of men and women and instead looked to a Baroque society of stone. The twelve statues of the Prophets carved by Aleijadinho in the staircase leading to the church of Congonhas do Campo shun the symmetry of classical sculptures. Like Bernini's Italian figures (but how absolutely remote from them geographically!) these are three-dimensional, moving statues, rushing down toward the spectator; rebellious statues, twisted in their mystical anguish and human anger, but also liberating statues, possessed by a new assertive sense of the body and its possibilities.

The roundness of the Baroque, its refusal to grant anyone or anything a privileged point of view, its assertion of perpetual change, its conflict between the ordered world of the few and the disordered world of the many, is rendered by this mulatto architect in the Church of Our Lady del Pilar, in Ouro Preto (literally: "Black Gold"), the great mining capital of colonial Brazil. The exterior of the church is a perfect rectangle. But inside, everything is curved, polygonal, egg-shaped, like the orb of Columbus, like the discoverer's egg, indeed. For the world is circular and it can be seen from many points of view. Aleijadinho's vision thus joins that of the artists of Iberia and of the Indo-American New World. In Congonhas and Ouro Preto, our vision is reconciled, we see with both eyes, and our bodies are whole again. Paradoxically, they are joined by the vision of a shunned man, a young leper who, it was said, worked only by night, when he could not be seen. But of Brazil itself, has it not been said that the country grows by night, while the Brazilians sleep?

Working by night, hemmed in by sleep, perhaps Aleijadinho gives body to the dreams of his fellow men and women. For he has no other way of speaking to them, except through the silence of stone.

7.

All of these different social profiles—indigenous, black, Iberian, and through Iberia, Mediterranean: Spanish and Portuguese, but also Jewish and Arab, Roman and Greek—flowed into one vast mestizo culture of the Americas.

All of these factors converged in the nascent urban cultures of the New World. For if at the beginning—and for a long time—it was the hinterland that supplied subject matter and characters, space and time, at last the city became the protagonist, as much in our modern novel as in the traditional one. Buenos Aires in Roberto Arlt, Macedonio Fernández, Ernesto Sábato, Julio Cortázar, and Bioy Casares; Santiago in the Chilean novelists; Lima in Vargas Llosa and Bryce Echenique; Havana in Lezama Lima; Mexico City in Gustavo Sainz and Fernando del Paso.

The territory of colonial Latin America was dominated from the political center of the great Baroque City or, rather, the string of cities created in America by Spanish ambition with native, black, and mestizo hands, from California to the River Plate: not frontier posts, not mere settlements, but great ports—San Juan de Puerto Rico, Havana, Veracruz, Cartagena de Indias—mining towns—Guanajuato, Potosí—and superb capitals—Mexico, Guatemala, Quito, Lima—all born under the sign of the Baroque.

Bernardo de Balbuena, Spanish poet who arrived in America as a child, composed his reflections on the grandeur of Mexico City in 1604, providing us with the most precise description of a great Baroque metropolis in the New World. In his thoughts on art and entertainment alone, Balbuena speaks of "a thousand gifts and pleasures," including conversations, games, receptions, hunting and garden parties, picnics and balls, concerts, visits, races, promenades, "a new comedy every day," fashion, carriages, women's chimerical hats, and their husbands' pains and worries, and all of this in jewels, gold and silver, pearls and silks, brocades and brooches, and attended by liveried servants. Whatever whim might wish, says Balbuena, desire shall have.

These extraordinary pretensions are brought down to Earth, notably, by the chroniclers of the other viceregal capital, Lima. Mateo Rosas de Oquendo ridicules the Lima oligarchy, "a thousand poets of scarce wit, courtesans of honor erased, and more crooked cardsharps than you'd dare to count."

The viceroy, he says, is surrounded by "vagrants and duelists, gamblers and conmen," while the police are "the most learned of thieves." He calls Lima a city "of murky suns, and darky births." Simón de Ayanque, in his own description of colonial Lima, goes further into riskier territory: this is a city, lest anyone forget it, of "Indians, Zambos and mulatto women; of Chinese, mestizos and blacks." "In all occupations," writes Ayanque, "you shall see Chinese, mulattoes and blacks, but very few Spaniards" as well as "many Indians come down from the sierra, to avoid paying tribute, and to pretend that they are gentlemen."

Pretension: the pretension to be something or somebody else: if dark, white; if poor, rich; if rich, courtly and European. This seems to be one of the marks of the Colonial urban societies, torn between rich and poor, disputing ecclesiastical orders, passionate love affairs and equally passionate denials of sex and the body.

Since independence in 1821, even while striving to become cosmopolitan and industrialized, our modern cities have not completely overcome the contradictions of the colonial period with its extremes of want disguised under a veneer of opulence, or the clash between its cultural components. That is why, rather than dwelling on the spectral images of the past, I would like to choose an image from a modern Latin American novel, a contemporary symbol of the living culture of Latin America.

It comes from *Paradiso*, the novel by Lezama Lima, in which three young men, searching for their cultural and emotional identity, prowl the streets of Havana in the dark night of the soul. Suddenly, a house in the center of the city, in the heart of darkness, is brightly lit up, instantly dazzling the three youths with its luminosity and opulence.

It is the renewed light of the past, Lezama Lima seems to be saying, serving a modern function in the contemporary *polis*, the city of Latin America. This function is to recall that neither the Conquest nor the Counterconquest of Latin America are yet concluded, that we continue to oppress and suppress our fellow Latin Americans with as much cruelty—even if, at times, only the cruelty of indifference—as the Iberian conquistadors; that we must continue to offer a cultural response to the political and economic problems of our daily life. In Latin America we possess a cultural continuity that remains our greatest wealth in the face of economic and political fragmentation and disruption. And this culture was created by the civil society, by men and women who also live political and economic lives. The question in Latin America today is: can we bring the authenticity of the culture to bear on the life of the city, on our political and economic lives?

Yes, answers the inclusive, fluid thinker that is José Lezama Lima, certainly, if we realize that a culture is its imagination, that a history is its memory, and that a culture incapable of creating its own images, or a history incapable of imagining its own memory, is destined to disappear.

The past is our task.

4. From Colony to Independence: Machado de Assis

1.

The Spanish Crown prohibited the writing and circulation of novels, alleging that reading fiction was dangerous for a population recently converted to Christianity. In another sense, this constitutes praise for the novel, considering it not innocuous but dangerous.

The degree to which the poetic word could be dangerous becomes evident if we consider the case of the greatest writer of the colonial era, the Mexican nun Sor Juana Inés de la Cruz, praised, exalted, reduced and, in the end, silenced by the colonial ecclesiastical authority. Nevertheless, poetry has been the faithful companion, sometimes the shadow, other times the sun, of literature written in Spanish in the Americas. From Ercilla to Neruda in Chile, from Sor Juana to Sabines in Mexico, the muses have been no less present than the Catholic Mass. In the nineteenth century, Rubén Darío serves as proof of this fidelity. There are others, too, though the great Nicaraguan alone would suffice.

But if poetry is our oldest, most constant companion, at the beginning of the eighteenth century a rival appears to dispute the primacy of our love. This recent usurper is the politics of identity, the self-reflection of the body politic: the nations of colonial Spain were beginning to think seriously about independence. Paradoxically, modern politics becomes tremendously seductive to Latin America thanks to the modernizing spirit of Carlos III in Spain and his decision to expel the Jesuits. Although the Marqués de Croix, Viceroy of New Spain, in a private letter to his brother, called the Jesuits "absolute masters of the hearts and consciences of all the inhabitants of this vast empire," he saw himself publicly obliged to uphold the monarchy's rationale in its dealings with the colonies. "From now on the subjects of the great monarch who occupies the throne of Spain must understand that they were born to keep quiet and obey and not to offer ideas, nor opine about the high affairs of the Government."

There were two things that the viceroy's double rhetoric could not conceal. The first, as expressed by the Peruvian Jesuit Juan Pablo de Viscardo y Guzmán in 1792, upon celebrating the New World's third centennial, was Spanish America's growing sense of urgency to establish its own identity: "The New World is our native land, and it is here where we must examine our present situation, so that we may decide for ourselves to do what is necessary for the preservation of our own rights."

Viscardo y Guzmán wrote these lines while living in exile in London, illustrating the other event which accompanied the expulsion of the Jesuits: the intellectuals of the Jesuit order took revenge against the King of Spain by writing, from their exile, books which proclaimed the national identity of the countries they longed for. From Rome, Father Clavijero defines Mexican identity as proceeding from pre-Cortesian antiquity. Father Molina, also from Rome, writes a national and civil history of Chile, whose title includes those very terms: *national* and *civil*. By defining these places according to their own history, geography, and society, essentially as nations, the Jesuits strengthen Latin American national identities. This also distances these nations from Spain as well as from any possible unity: it precipitates the movements for independence and proposes to the writers of the nineteenth century, the century of independence, the obligation to set down the histories of their different homelands.

In order to transcend these dilemmas and overcome these contradictions, the Latin American intellectual class of the nineteenth century follows a sometimes torturous path that passes through various stages.

First Stage: As Carmen Iglesias tells us in her great essay *La nobleza ilustrada* (The Enlightenment Nobility), the Count of Aranda (1718-1798), minister to King Charles III, inspired by a desire to modernize and reform, clearly distinguishes between colonies and crowns. The Indies, adds Iglesias, were not *colonies* of Spain, but part of *the Spanish Crown*. To that American part of the crown correspond three appanages (Mexico, Peru and Costa Firme) in order to "witness their union with Spain in a type of *commonwealth*" (Iglesias). Thus, Aranda tried to prevent what occurred: fragmentation, vacancies of power, civil wars.

Second Stage: In 1810, the Courts of Cádiz, with equal representation from all the different countries in the Spanish American empire, adopt a liberal constitution. The kingdoms of America are considered part of Spain. Cádiz establishes such principles as the division of powers and civil equality.

Third Stage: King Ferdinand VII is a prisoner of Napoleon, Spain is occupied, and Joseph Bonaparte is placed on the throne. In the absence of a king, the kingdoms of America, from Mexico to Caracas to Buenos Aires, rebel.

Fourth Stage: Restored by Napoleon in 1813, Fernando VII declares wars against the independent states. Their response is summed up by Bolívar's declaration of "war to the death."

Fifth Stage: With independence achieved in 1821, the problem centers on the form of government. Constitutional monarchy or republic? And, if republic, what kind? Federal or centralist? Unitary state or a confederation of states?

Whichever political option was chosen, there was an underlying social reality which presented itself in the revolutions for independence as a contradiction between the "royal nation" and the "legal nation." During the colonial period, class differences rarely manifested themselves, and when they did they were rapidly repressed. In Mexico, the riot against the high price of corn (1692), preceded by the native insurrection in the mines of Topia (Durango) in 1598, presaged the black rebellion in Veracruz led by Yanga, and the founding of the town of San Lorenzo de los Negros.

The eighteenth century had seen various uprisings. The Tzeltales uprising in Chiapas (1712), and the Comuneros in Paraguay (1717), and the state of constant rebellion of the Afro-Brazilian *quilombos* who took the English name (kilombo) for their communities. Túpac Amaru headed the indigenous rebellion in Upper Peru in 1780, and the *comunas* of New Granada revolted in 1781.

The legal nation was protected by the paternalistic monarchy of the Hapsburgs and Bourbons. The royal nation was dominated by landowners, petty tyrants, and overseers. The motto of the legal nation was "the law is obeyed." But the royal nation's response was: "In reality it is disregarded."

The revolutions for independence and the appearance of new republics fostered and deepened this contradictory situation. Formally, the legal nation—modernizing, progressive, founded upon an imitation of the laws and constitutions of France, England, and the United States—was a formal juridical screen, behind which the old royal nation continued to exist. *Legal Nation*: acting as the protector of Peru, in 1821 José de San Martín legally abolished the indigenous tribute system. *Royal Nation*: nothing changed. Again and again, the legal inequality of the colonial era was substituted for the royal inequality of the independent era, now disguised as legal equality. In his speech at Bucaramanga, in 1828, Simón Bolívar denounced an aristocracy of leisure, wealth, and high status that spoke of equality, but only wanted to establish it among the upper classes, not the lower ones.

The royal nation was described by Sarmiento in his book *Facundo: Civilization and Barbarism* (1845). Argentina is two nations: city and country, each one a stranger to the other. In the countryside there is no society; its chief inhabitant, the gaucho, owes his fidelity only to his boss. The result is a world of unrestrained authority without responsibility where brute force dominates. In 1845, Sarmiento offers us, *avant la lettre*, the definition of what Max Weber would later call patrimonialism: it is the archaic form of domination, the absence of foresight and of the sense of what both the State and modern society might be, in favor of the irresponsible exercise of authority. This obedience to the boss and not to the law defines the political life which Sarmiento called "barbarism."

Nevertheless, those who break the law often invoke it; they wrap themselves in their toga and take a seat on their throne because if the local boss is the national dictator in miniature he is also a reduced version of the ontological model of power among us: the Roman Emperor who requires the written law—which cannot be ignored—in order to legitimize himself and his deeds.

The educated classes of these new societies tried to respond to these contradictions through political means in order to achieve a divergent, pluralist cultural reality. How well can ideas and words transform reality? We won't know, answered the nineteenth century, if we are ignorant of the history of the new nations. For that reason the nineteenth century belongs to historians and educators, and very marginally to the poets and novelists.

In Chile, José Victorino Lastarria opposes the colonial order and writes a new political history of the nation (1844). Francisco Bilbao forms a new party, "The Society of Equality," publishes *El Evangelio Americano* (The American Gospel) in the name of justice and liberty, and in 1857 coins the term "Latin America." Benjamín Vicuña Mackenna establishes Spanish American urban history with his books about Valparaíso and Santiago (1869).

In Mexico, José María Luis Mora writes *México y sus revoluciones* (Mexico and its Revolutions, 1836): a true account of the history of Mexico, its laws, finances, foreign policies, and ethical possibilities.

Other writers navigate between politics and letters: Fray Servando Teresa de Mier, José María Heredia, Vicente Rocafuerte, Manuel Lorenzo de Vidaurre. But perhaps the two men who stand as the most important essayists, educators, and historians are Andrés Bello and Domingo Faustino Sarmiento.

Andrés Bello, a Venezuelan, and the teacher of Simón Bolívar, moved to Chile in 1859. The author of a grammar of the Spanish language adapted for use in the Americas, he founded the National University of Chile, and was its first president. He also served as a minister of the "enlightened" oligarchy which was governed from the shadows by Diego Portales, the great organizer of Chilean institutions, during periods dominated by the dictators Antonio López de Santa Anna, in Mexico, and Juan Manuel Rosas, in Argentina.

Bello carried on a famous dispute with the other great South American statesman-writer, Sarmiento, the author of *Facundo: Civilization or Barbarism*. This book is many things: a biography of Facundo Quiroga, the tyrant from La Rioja who was capable of kicking a man to death or setting fire to his own parents' house. Besides being a history of Argentina, the book is also a geography of the country and a study of its society. It expresses Sarmiento's conviction: the past is barbarism. The present requires transcending the colonial past through modernization, something proposed by Sarmiento when he served as the seventh president of the republic between 1868 and 1874: banks, communications, European immigration, urban development . . .

Facundo is one of the two great Spanish-American books of the nineteenth century, both of which came from Argentina. The other is *Martín Fierro* by José Hernández. The novels of the nineteenth century are barely a sigh amid the winds of change. *Cecilia Valdés* (published in Havana in 1839 and, years later, in its definitive version, in New York, in 1882) by Cirilo Villaverde, Cuban romantic and practitioner of *costumbrismo*, the literature of local customs and manners; and *Martín Rivas* (1862) by the Chilean realist and liberal Alberto Blest Gana. In Mexico we find the adventurous tradition of Manuel Payno in *The Bandits from Río Frío* (serialized from 1888 to 1891), and the novella by Vicente Riva Palacio whose title is more inventive than its contents: *Monja, casada, virgen y mártir* (Nun, Wife, Virgin, and Martyr). In that order.

In addition to a fervent and audacious attempt to imbue the language with an extreme, dangerous poetic sensibility through an exploration of unrealized possibilities — the rediscovery of America — we see an affirmation through the very negation of Spanish linguistic continuity, a walk along the edge of the abyss: Modernism and Rubén Darío.

The avalanche of poetry — civic, patriotic, rhetorical, and sentimental — affected even the most serious thinkers. It was Andrés Bello — not Agustín Lara — who proclaimed: "divine poetry, you of habitual solitude." The reaction was profound, subtle, and ironic. The Nicaraguan poet Rubén Darío (1867–1916) introduced the famous techniques of poets like Whitman, Poe, Verlaine, and Lautrémont in a verse which adapted past forms in order to transcend them. He sings: "In his nation of iron lives the grand old man, lovely as a patriarch, holy and serene." Verlaine is the "celestial lyrist who lent your enchanting accent to the Olympian instrument and the wild syrinx; Panida!" On Spanish rhetoric: "Here comes the cortege! Now you can hear the clarions clear." And politics: "The Spanish lion has a thousand cubs on the loose. Be careful. Long live Spanish America!" (T. Roosevelt). And, finally, Darío himself:

Happy the tree which is barely sensitive

and more so the hard stone because it no longer feels,

as there is no greater pain than the pain of being alive

no greater nightmare than the conscious life.

(*Fatality*)

Just as Darío's renewal of poetry in Spanish (in America and Spain) leaves novelists the rich and ambitious legacy of his language, the novel itself is transformed by a Brazilian miracle: Joaquim Maria Machado de Assis.

2.

Brazil was part of the Portuguese empire in the Americas and its history differs considerably from that of Spanish America. The Napoleonic invasion of Portugal in 1807 obliged the royal family to take refuge in Brazil. In 1808, the Prince Regent, Don Juan de Portugal, brought Portuguese institutions to Brazil and, in 1816, assumed the throne as ruler of Portugal, Brazil, and Algarve. In 1821 after naming his son, Don Pedro, regent of Brazil, he returned to Lisbon. In 1822, Pedro I became emperor, and Brazil achieved its independence without the battles and bloodshed of Spanish America.

In 1831, Pedro I abdicated the throne in favor of his young son Pedro II, leaving a regency to govern Brazil until 1840, when Pedro II assumed the throne and occupied it until 1889 when he renounced his rule and went into exile. In February of the same year, Brazil became a federal republic (1889-1908).

I provide these facts in order to place Machado de Assis in a context distinct from the Spanish American one, although perhaps his national filiation is less important than his literary one. Machado de Assis does not belong to the Romantic and Realist current of nineteenth century Spanish America; instead, he revives the great tradition of La Mancha: the tradition of Cervantes-Sterne-Diderot. Better yet: Machado de Assis is a miracle. And miracles, Don Quixote tells Sancho Panza, are things that rarely happen. Nevertheless, the miracle happened, and not even God can take it away.

Aren't miracles, by definition, those rare occurrences so unlike the common events of daily life? Machado de Assis calls Romanticism and Naturalism a tired old charger, a once-proud stallion tamed, devoured by sores and maggots. What was its original name? Rocinante? Clavileño?

There is no great distance between the mediocrity of the nineteenth century Latin American novel and the absence of a Spanish novel after Cervantes and before Leopoldo Alas and Benito Pérez Galdós. The reasons for this absence would fill several pages: I only wish to register my astonishment over the fact that in the language of the modern novel founded in La Mancha by Miguel de Cervantes, in the wake of *Don Quixote*, we find only empty fields and gloomy hills.

La Regenta, and *Fortunata y Jacinta*, restore vitality to the Spanish novel in Spain, but Spanish America will have to wait longer, just as Spain waited for Clarín, Benito Pérez Galdós, Jorge Luis Borges, Miguel Ángel Asturias, Alejo Carpentier, and Juan Carlos Onetti.

By contrast—and this is the miracle—Brazil gives its nationality, its imagination, its language, to the greatest—if not the only— Ibero-American novelist of the nineteenth century, Joaquim Maria Machado de Assis. What did Machado know that other Latin American novelists did not? Why the miracle of Machado?

The miracle rests upon a paradox: Machado takes up, in Brazil, the lesson of Cervantes, the tradition of La Mancha forgotten by Latin American novelists from Mexico to Argentina, regardless of how many public and scholarly homages they rendered to *Don Quixote*.

Was this a result of a Hispanophobia which accompanied the heroic feat of achieving independence and the first years of nationality? No, I repeat, not if we focus on the formalities of the discourse. But if we focus on the generalized rejection of the independent cultural past, the answer is yes: to be black or indigenous was to be barbarian, to be Spanish was to be retrograde. To be modern, one had to be North American, French, or British, especially if the desire was to be prosperous, democratic, and civilized.

The illogical imitations of the independent era believed in a Nescafé civilization: we could be instantaneously modern by excluding the past and denying tradition. Machado's genius is based precisely on the contrary: his work is permeated with a conviction: there is no creation without tradition to nurture it, just as there will be no tradition without creation to renew it.

But Machado did not have a great novelistic tradition behind him, neither Brazilian nor Portuguese. By contrast, he was the master of the tradition that he shared with us, the Spanish speakers of the continent: he had the tradition of La Mancha. We had forgotten it; Machado recovered it. But had not post-Napoleonic Europe also forgotten it? The Europe of the great realist novel, the novel of customs, psychology, and naturalism, from Balzac to Zola, from Stendhal to Tolstoy? And was not our modernizing pretension, throughout all Ibero-America, a reflection of that realist current which I like to call the Waterloo tradition, as opposed to the tradition of La Mancha?

In *The Art of the Novel*, Milan Kundera laments, more than anyone else, the change of direction that interrupted the Cervantean tradition as carried on by his greatest heirs, the Irish writer Laurence Sterne, and the French writer Denis Diderot, in favor of the realist tradition described by Stendhal as the reflection caught by a mirror moving along a road, and confirmed by Balzac as the act of offering a vision of life that competes with the official record of events.

In a chapter entitled "The Depreciated Legacy of Cervantes" Kundera cries out for playfulness, dreams, thoughts, and time. Where did they go? The response is, if not miraculous, definitely surprising: they went to Rio de Janeiro and they were reborn through the pen of a poor Carioca mulatto, the self-educated son of a bricklayer. He learned French in a bakery at night. Like Dostoyevsky he suffered from epilepsy, like Tolstoy he was myopic, and he hid his genius within a body so frail, like that of another great Brazilian mulatto, Aleijadinho, the leper who sculpted alone, only at night, when he could not be seen. But of Brazil, I repeat, has it not been said that the country grows at night, while the Brazilians sleep? I promise not to say it again.

Not Machado. He is wide awake. His prose is as bright and clear as day. But the same is true of his mystery: a solar mystery, that of an American writer of Portuguese language and mixed race who, alone in the world of Realism, like a Baroque statue from Minas Gerais, rediscovers and reanimates the tradition of La Mancha in opposition to the tradition of Waterloo.

La Mancha and Waterloo. What do I mean by these two traditions? Historically, Cervantes inaugurates the tradition of La Mancha as a deliberate frustration to a triumphant modernity. *Don Quixote* is an eccentric novel of counter-reformist Spain, obliged to establish a different reality through imagination, language, jest, and a mix of genres. The tradition continues with Sterne's *Tristram Shandy*, which accents temporal play and the poetics of digression, and Diderot's *Jacques the Fatalist and his Master*, where the ludic and poetic adventure consists of offering, in almost every line, a repertory of possibilities, a menu of narrative alternatives.

The tradition of La Mancha is interrupted by the tradition of Waterloo, meaning, by the realist response to the saga of the French Revolution and Bonaparte's empire. The social movement and affirmation of individuality inspire Stendhal, whose character Julien Sorel secretly reads Napoleon's biography; by Balzac, whose Rastignac is a

Bonaparte of the Parisian salons; and by Dostoyevsky, whose Raskolnikov has a portrait of the great Corsican as the only decoration in
his Petersburg garret. These novels are critical, certainly, of the same
things which inspire them. Beginning with Sorel's crime, the upwardly
mobile professionals of post-Bonaparte society culminate in the false
glory of social-climber Rastignac, and end with Raskolnikov's crime
and misery.

Amid both currents, Machado de Assis revalidates the interrupted
tradition of La Mancha and allows us to contrast it, in a very general
way, with the triumphant tradition of Waterloo.

The tradition of Waterloo is affirmed as reality. The tradition of
La Mancha is known to be fiction and, what is more, is celebrated as
fiction.

This is the ludic tradition whose neglect Kundera laments but
which Machado, unexpectedly, recovers. Published in 1881, *The Posthumous Memoirs of Brás Cubas* are written from beyond the grave but
from the grave itself by a writer whose authorship can be as certain as
death itself, except that Brás Cubas converts death into an certain uncertainty and an uncertain certainty, by means of the ironic touch he
introduces, *ab initio*, which is the Cervantean theme of a fiction that
is conscious of itself being so: "I am a dead writer," says Brás Cubas,
"not in the sense of one who has written before and is now dead, but
in the sense of a writer who has died but continues writing." This
writer, for whom, "the tomb is really a new cradle," is the posthumous narrator Brás Cubas, who, upon renewing the Cervantean and,
above all, Sternean tradition of speaking directly to the reader, is fully aware that, this time, the reader has to identify less with an uncertain author like that of *Don Quixote*, or with an author anguished
over writing down his whole life's story before dying, like Tristram
Shandy, than with an author who writes from the grave, who dedicates his book "to the first worm that gnawed my flesh" (note the use
of the preterite tense) and who admits the fatality of his situation:
"We all have to die. It's the price of being alive."

In this way, Brás Cubas transfers his own living past and his own
dead present to the reader, with much of the humor of Cervantes,
Sterne and Diderot, but with an acidity and, at times, a rabid fury.
This would seem surprising coming from a character like Brás Cubas
and an author like Machado de Assis, the two of them so sweet-

tempered, but both warn us, from the first page, that these *Posthumous Memoirs* are written "with the pen of mirth and the ink of melancholy." This seems to me the essential phrase of the Cariocan novelist's Manchegan novel: to write with laughter's pen and melancholy's ink.

But laughter comes first. Tristram Shandy's admiration for Don Quixote, to which I alluded some lines above, is based on humor: "I am persuaded," we read in *Tristram Shandy*, "that the felicity of Cervantean humor is born from the simple fact of describing small, silly events with the circumstantial pomp usually reserved for great events."

Sterne stands this humor on its head, describing pompous deeds with the humor of small ones. The War of the Spanish Succession, the inheritance of Carlos the Bewitched, who once again sowed the fields of Flanders with blood, is reproduced in *Tristram Shandy* by Uncle Toby, deprived of fighting in the war thanks to a wound in his groin, now seated between two rows of cauliflowers out on the lawn that he once used for bowling. There, Uncle Toby can reproduce the Duke of Marlborough's campaigns without spilling a drop of blood.

Machado's humor goes beyond that of Cervantes and Sterne: the Brazilian narrates small events in brief chapters with a mixture of laughter and melancholy which resolves itself, on more than one occasion, in irony.

One American critic has called it an epicurean book. Another review, from New York, calls it a terrifying book, because of its implacable denunciation of the pretension and hypocrisy hidden in common, everyday people. No, corrects Susan Sontag: it is merely a radically skeptical book, which imposes itself on the reader with the force of a personal discovery.

It's true: the carnivalesque elements, the jocular laughter which Bakhtin attributes to the great comic prose of Rabelais, Cervantes, and Sterne, is also present in Machado. Suffice to recall Brás Cubas's picaresque encounters with the con artist cum philosopher Quincas Borba, the vaudeville of his encounters with his secret lover, Virgilia, the description of the way in which she uses religion: "like a secret, protective suit of red flannel underwear." Suffice to evoke the satirical portraits of Rio de Janeiro society and Brazilian bureaucracy, sharply epitomized in a splendid comic passage that reduces politics to one man's problem of how to become a governor's secretary in order to be able to accompany his lover, the governor's wife, to the interior of the country. The problem of adultery is thus resolved administratively.

To a large degree, Machado's humor determines the rhythm of his prose: not only the brevity of his chapters, but the velocity of the language. This rapidity set to match the comic humor, obvious in the accelerated movie images of Charlie Chaplin or Buster Keaton, has its musical antecedent in Rossini's *Barber of Seville*, its poetic antecedent in Pushkin's *Eugene Onegin*, and its novelistic antecedent in Diderot's *Jacques the Fatalist*, from which I extract the following example: the author meets "a woman as beautiful as an angel . . . I wish to sleep with her. I do so. We have four children."

In *Brás Cubas*, the author characterizes himself in this way: "Why deny it? I felt passion for theatricality, advertisements, and pyrotechnics." And Virgilia, the narrator's lover, is discovered and described in a few sure lines: "Pretty, spontaneous, freshly molded by nature, full of that magic, precarious but eternal, which is secretly transmitted for the sake of procreation." Nevertheless, the Rabelaisian laughter quickly freezes on the lips of Machadian melancholy. In *Tristram Shandy* the battles from the War of the Spanish Succession occur, bloodlessly, in Uncle Toby's *jardin potager*. In *Brás Cubas*, Machado emphasizes that the meeting of laughter and melancholy will not lead to violence. One illustrative paragraph indicates this. Facing the possibility of a violent encounter, the author promises that the expected violence will not occur and no blood will stain the page. The Latin American reader could encounter this sentence as an historical subtext about Brazil as the one Latin American nation that has known how to conduct its historical processes without the violence of the other countries on the continent. Perhaps the exceptions confirm the rule. In any case, in Machado's novel, the sounds of Rio de Janeiro's carnival remain outside and distant, to such an extent that the ink of melancholy outpaces the pen of mirth.

Not long ago I watched a television documentary about Carmen Miranda. It begins with the infinite melancholy of traditional Brazilian songs in the voice of this exceptional woman which Hollywood turned into the vibrant symbol of carnival, with her exuberant happiness and a fruit basket hat on her head. But to the extent that the cliché reveals the face of death, the Chica-Chica-Boom spectacle vanishes, allowing the authentic voice to return, the lost voice, the voice of melancholy. It is as if, from death, Carmen Miranda exclaimed: "Don't take away my sadness!"

That is why I believe that the most meaningful sentence in Machado's book is this one: "Written with the pen of mirth and the ink of melancholy." Well, what is *Brás Cubas* but the melancholy history of an old bachelor who must first risk the dangers of adultery and, later, those of lonely old age and ridicule? At the end of a reverie in which he discovers another unity forgotten by Aristotle—the unity of human misery—the narrator announces: "The death of a bachelor at the age of sixty-four years does not approach the level of high tragedy."

There is an almost Proustian moment when, as he departs from a dance at four o'clock in the morning, Brás Cuba asks us: "And what do you think was waiting for me in my carriage? My fifty years. There they were, uninvited, not stiff with cold or rheumatism, but exhausted and dozing, longing for home and bed." Before death, Machado tells us, it is oblivion which lies in wait for us: "The problem consists not in finding someone who remembers my parents, but in finding someone who remembers me." Brás Cubas begins by imitating death: "He doesn't like to talk because he wants everyone to believe that he's dying." But only a critical reading of this great novel can lead us to a literary question, to a question about the tradition which Machado revives and prolongs, the tradition of La Mancha, also answered, in its own way, by another great Latin American novel written from within the grave: *Pedro Páramo* by Juan Rulfo. The question is, "Is to be dead to be universal?" Or, phrased in another way, "To be universal, do we Latin Americans have to be dead?"

In her answer, Susan Sontag affirms Machado de Assis's modernity, but also warns us that our modernity is only a system of flattering allusions which permit us to selectively colonize the past. We know that we have suffered from an exclusionary, orphaned modernity in a Latin America that functions like neither Mother nor Father—and that we are determined and committed to conquering an inclusive modernity, with Dad and Mom, encompassing everything we have been: Children of La Mancha, part of the racially and culturally mixed impurity which today extends around the globe, in order to create a poly-narrative that manifests itself as a true *Weltliteratur* in the India of Salman Rushdie, the Nigeria of Wole Soyinka, the Germany of Günter Grass, the South Africa of Nadine Gordimer, the Spain of Juan Goytisolo, or the Colombia of Gabriel García Márquez. The world of La Mancha: the world of hybrid literature.

Machado does not lay claim to this world for reasons of race, history, or politics, but for reasons of imagination and language, which embrace the former reasons. How universal, but how Latin American are sentences like these from Machado! "I have complete faith in dark eyes and written constitutions." Or this one: "Only God knows the strength of an adjective, especially in new, tropical nations."

Faith in written constitutions brings Machado back to the pen of ninth, but this time within a constellation of astonishing references and premonitions, which lead us, newly, along the comical path, from the writer that we Spanish Americans did not have in the nineteenth century—Machado de Assis—to the writer that we did have in the twentieth century—Jorge Luis Borges. The Borgesian strategy of breaking the absolute idea with the comic accident is already present in Machado de Assis when Brás Cubas declares his intention of writing the book that he never wrote, a *History of the Suburbs*, whose concretion contrasts absurdly with the abstraction of the fashionable philosophy of nineteenth century Latin America: Comte's positivism, the motto of his trinitarian philosophy, *Order and Progress*, manifested on the Brazilian flag, and which the scientists during the time of Porfirio Díaz in Mexico also made their own, as opposed to the comic accident of Brás Cubas: to write a history of the suburbs and in place of order and progress offer the practical invention of a hasty poultice against melancholy.

And nevertheless, Latin American hunger, the eagerness of ending it all, of appropriating all traditions and all cultures, including all aberrations; the utopian zeal to create a new heaven, in which all spaces and times can coexist simultaneously, appears brilliantly in *The Posthumous Memoirs of Brás Cubas* as a surprising vision of the first Aleph, prior to Borges's so famous one, of which, of his own, Borges says: "Incredible as it may seem, I believe that there is, or that there was, another Aleph." Yes, it is the Aleph of Machado de Assis.

"Imagine, reader," says Machado, "imagine a procession of all the epochs, of all the races of men, all his passions, the tumult of empires, the war of appetite against appetite and hatred against hatred." This is "the monstrous spectacle" that Brás Cubas sees from the peak of a mountain, like Walter Benjamin's angel of history, contemplating the ruins of history. "The living condensation of history," says the authorial cadaver of Brás Cubas, whose mind is "a stage . . . a tumultuous confusion of things and of people in which all things could be seen with precision, from the rose of Smyrna to the plant that grows in your back patio garden to Cleopatra's magnificent litter to the corner of the beach where the beggar trembles while he sleeps." There (in the first Aleph, the Brazilian Aleph of Machado de Assis) "could be found," continues the author, "the atmosphere of the eagle and the hummingbird, but also that of the frog and the snail."

Machado's vision of the Aleph, his universal hunger, thus colors his literary passion and his way of addressing the reader, a "poorly learned reader," a reader that is "the book's defect," because the writer wants to live rapidly so as to quickly reach the end of the work which moves as slowly "as a pair of drunkards staggering through the night." It is this unloveable reader to whom Machado directs his games and threats, more grave perhaps, than those of Sterne or Diderot, although they appear formally similar:

> Reader, skip this chapter; go and read this other one; content yourself with knowing that these are merely notes for a sad and vulgar chapter that I will not write; be irritated that I oblige you to read an invisible dialogue between two lovers that your gossiping curiosity would like to know; and if this chapter seems offensive to you, remember that these are *my* memories, not yours, and from the beginning I warned you: this book is sufficient in itself. If it pleases you, excellent reader, I will feel rewarded for my effort; but if it displeases you, I will reward you with a snap of my fingers and good riddance to you.

The somewhat rude treatment which Machado reserves for the reader, it seems to me, is not far from a demand comparable to the bells at midnight heard by Falstaff. It's about waking up the reader, of pulling him out of his romantic, tropical siesta, of setting him onto more difficult tasks, and bringing him to an inclusive, passionate, hungry modernity.

Claudio Magris makes a statement about our literature which seems to me to be applicable to Machado. Latin America, writes the author of *Danube*, has dilated the space of the imagination. Western literature was threatened by incapacity. Europe assumed negativity. Latin America assumed totality. But today Europe must admit its guilty conscience in the celebration of Latin America. Today, we all must resist the temptation to read Latin America for the sake of exotic adventure. European readers (and Latin American ones as well, I would add) must learn to do their homework of seriously reading the hard, difficult, melancholy prose of Latin American writers.

In spite of the beautiful overall lightness of his writing, Magris could be describing the books of Machado de Assis. But when Machado writes the first Aleph, he is also demanding of Latin Americans that they be audacious, that they imagine everything.

Machado's models are Cervantes and Sterne, and in them the comic spirit indicates the limits of reality. In *Tristram Shandy*, the reproduction of the battlegrounds of Flanders in a kitchen garden signals not only the limits of literary and historical representation but also the limits of history itself. Because history is time, and time, Sterne tells us at the end of his beautiful novel, is fleeting:

> Time wastes too fast: every letter I trace tells me with what rapidity Life follows my pen: the days and hours of it, more precious, my dear Jenny! than the rubies about thy neck, are flying over our heads like light clouds of a windy day, never to return more . . . and every time I kiss thy hand to bid adieu, and every absence which follows it, are preludes to that eternal separation which we are shortly to make———
>
> ———Heaven have mercy upon us both!

And in *Don Quixote*, the novel's tone changes radically when the protagonist and Sancho Panza visit the Dukes who offer them, in reality, what Don Quixote previously only possessed in his imagination. The castle is a castle, but Don Quixote first needed the castle to be a simple country inn. Deprived of his imagination, he truly becomes the Knight of the Rueful Countenance and takes the road, fatally, towards death: "Long ago I was mad and now I am sane; I was Don Quixote de la Mancha and I am now . . . Alonso Quijano the Good."

Dostoyevsky was right when he called *Don Quixote* the saddest book ever written, because it is the story of disillusionment. But it is also, adds the Russian author, the triumph of fiction. In Cervantes, truth is saved by a lie.

Machado de Assis is also located between the strength of an all-inclusive fiction, like the Latin American imagination which would like to encompass everything, and the limits imposed by history. "Long live history, voluble old history, which serves every purpose," Brás Cubas exclaims from the grave, only to indicate for us that this totalizing capacity is only that of error, that, as Pascal said: "Man is only a reed . . . but he is a thinking reed." And Cubas affirms: "Each period of life is a new edition which corrects the preceding one and which will be, in turn, corrected by what follows, until the definitive edition is published, which the editor then tosses to the worms, free of charge."

The pen of mirth and the ink of melancholy are once again united to find the very origin of their tradition: the praise of folly, the Erasmian root of our Renaissance culture, the wise dose of irony which prevents reason or faith from dogmatic imposition.

I recall Julio Cortázar's love for the figure of the serene madman, which Cortázar himself consecrated in various characters in *Hopscotch*. Machado has his own wise fool, named Romualdo, and he is completely sane but for one thing: he believes himself to be Tamerlane. Just as Alonso Quijano believes himself Don Quixote; as Uncle Toby fancies himself a military strategist; and the titular character of Luigi Pirandello's *Henry IV* believes himself to be Holy Roman Emperor Henry IV. In every other way they are all reasonable people.

Machado believes that when such fixations are carried out in political action they can certainly lead to catastrophes: witness Bismarck, he tells us, and his obsession with unifying Germany; proof of history's caprice and immense irresponsibility.

For this reason, it makes sense to respect the serene madmen, to leave them alone in their space, like the Athenian evoked by Machado who believed that all the ships entering Piraeus were his; like the madman evoked by Horace and picked up by Erasmus: a fool who spent his days laughing inside a theater, applauding and having fun, because he thought that a play was being performed on the empty stage. When the theater was closed and the madman turned out into the street, he complained: "You haven't cured me of my madness, but you have destroyed my pleasure and the illusion of my happiness."

In this way, Erasmus asks us to return to the words of Saint Paul: If you think that you are wise in this age, you should become fools so that you may become wise. For the wisdom of this world is foolishness to God."

In Iberia and Ibero-America, the children of Erasmus become the children of La Mancha, the children of a stained world,[1] impure, syncretic, Baroque, and corrupt, inspired by the desire to stain in order to be, to contaminate in order to assimilate, to multiply appearances with the goal of multiplying the sense of things, as opposed to the false consolation of one single, dogmatic reading of the world. Children of La Mancha that duplicate all the truths in order to impede the installation of an orthodox world, one of faith or reason, or a pure world which excludes the various passional, cultural, sexual, political attitudes and practices of women and men.

Machado de Assis, Machado de La Mancha, miraculous Machado, is a pioneer of imagination and irony, of miscegenation and the contagion of a world threatened more each day by the henchmen of racism, xenophobia, religious fundamentalism, and another implacable fundamentalism: that of the marketplace.

With Machado and his Manchegan and Erasmian ancestry, with Machado and his Macedonian, Borgesian, Cortazarian, Nelidian, Goytlsolitarian, and Jullanøfluvlul descent, we writers of Iberia and America will continue striving to invent what the great Lezama Lima called "imaginary eras," because if a culture does not manage to create an imagination, it will turn out to be historically indecipherable.

Machado, the miraculous Brazilian, continues to decipher us because he keeps imagining us, and the true Ibero-American identity is only that of our imagination, one that is literary, political, social, artistic, individual and collective.

---

1 Translator's note: *La mancha* is Spanish for stain, spot, mark, or blemish.

5. Rómulo Gallegos:
Impersonal Nature

1.

Jorge Luis Borges's emblematic tale "The Aleph" reproduces all the world's spaces then shrinks them down and fits them into one single infinitesimal all-encompassing space. "The Garden of Forking Paths" multiplies the different times possible and available in the world, but ultimately Borges can only find room for them all in "The Library of Babel," a library that is infinite if it is encrypted within a book that is the compendium of all others. Funes the Memorious remembers everything but Pierre Menard is bound to rewrite one single book, *Don Quixote de la Mancha*, so that we, the Latin Americans, can count on, and reckon with, two different universal histories: one internal, one external.

While Borges is one author of our internal history, Rómulo Gallegos writes an external history which, upon rereading, provokes the sensation of confronting an authentic repertoire of the very themes many of our narrators must revisit, refine, advance, and, sometimes, through luck and misfortune, destroy.

Gallegos's central theme is historical violence, traditionally wielded with impunity, and the responses to it: civilization or barbarism. These responses, sometimes enacted individually, also confront the political realities of Latin America. Nonetheless, the basic foundation of Gallegos's novels is the natural world, a primary, initially silent, and necessarily impersonal nature.

My primary focus here is Gallegos's novel *Canaima* because it contains the finest example of his concept of the primacy of nature, without time, space, or name. As Gallegos writes in the novel's first chapter "The Adventurers' Guayana," it is "an immense mysterious region as yet unknown to man." The Orinoco is aloof, autonomous: "The great river flows alone." From beginning to end, despite appearances, despite different gazes — "eyes accustomed to a suspicious disbelief before the quiet green canyons"— the natural world in *Canaima* maintains its impersonal virginity, and forever, desperately, remains "The fascinating jungle from whose influence Marcos Vargas would never more be free. The abyssal world encrypting the timeless codes.

The inhuman jungle . . . a temple with millions of pillars . . . ocean of the thick, densely-woven forest beneath the wing of the wind which passes over without penetrating her . . . cemeteries of vanished people in forests now deserted."

Human life, if it ever existed here, is barely a memory: if it continues to exist, it will still be barely a memory when it fatally disappears. In short, it will always remain what Gallegos calls the "dawn of a frustrated civilization." For the Venezuelan Gallegos, the kingdom of American nature is either one of frustration or a portrait of history: "A world portrayed, an inconclusive world, Venezuela, whose discovery and colonization are both inconclusive."

And despite, or perhaps thanks to that, it is also a "promised land": open space, river, and jungle do in fact engender a time, although perhaps it will only be a time that belongs to nature: "A disquieting landscape, over which still reigns the primeval shock of the first morning in the world."

2.

Connections and contrasts alike exist between the theme of nature as explored by Rómulo Gallegos in the twentieth century and Gonzalo Fernández de Oviedo in the sixteenth century. It is one of multiple direct meetings between the founding chronicles of colonization and the contemporary fiction which interests me here. According to Gerbi's interpretation in *The Dispute of the New World*, Oviedo's treatment of American nature reveals his thinking to be equal parts Christian and Renaissance. Christian because of his pessimism for history, Renaissance because of his optimism about nature. Where the world of men is patently absurd or sinful, nature stands as evidence of God's own reason; this permits Oviedo to exalt the greatness of the new lands because they are lands without human time or history: atemporal utopias.

Four centuries after Oviedo, *Canaima* is a novel that explores the humanization of that nature which affirmed its health in atemporality, in the contradiction of wanting to be a pure Utopia of space, a material object, philologically impossible: Utopia is the place that is no place, *U-Topos*. But it is also the time that *can* be. The conflict provides fertile ground for an understanding that, with luck, we can only truly create ourselves in contravention to our founding illusions.

Gallegos understands this directly when, in the first chapter, he speaks to us about the *different* nature of the gazes that watch nature. Nature is a point of view, and man not only sees but *sees himself* distinctly depending on how he looks at nature: Marcos Vargas, as spectacle; Gabriel Ureña, as spectator.

Which history is Rómulo Gallegos relating in *Canaima*? How do we humanize a nature that is inhuman to begin with and which will, naturally, inevitably, return to its primarily inhuman state again? As he writes in *The Vortex*: "The jungle swallowed them up." What is this terrible interval that is the human lifespan, the illusory time of men and women, spent upon this earth, amid the natural world? How does this life acquire, albeit *intermediately*, a history, and move from existing in space to living through time, although it also ends up wasting time?

Mythic Land: Gallegos writes about "the old myths of the world reborn in America." *Utopian Land*, because it is a "promised" land, but also a *historic land* because no Utopia has been created; the land has been violated by crime, attacked with impunity. Therein we locate the notion of unfinished history, and the origin of *Canaima*.

Historical violence slices open the pages of the novel right down the middle, and takes its place, bleeding and weeping, in the very center of the text. The historic heart of *Canaima* is a date in time, one night when "the machetes lit up Vichada": the night of Cholo Parima's bloody crime: Parima murdered Marcos Vargas's brother, the waters ran red with blood, and human violence increased the natural, flowing violence of a river that Gallegos describes as born from sacrifice: "An immense land is squeezed and wrung out so that the Orinoco might be wide."

On this level, Gallegos touches the classic problem of the origin of civilization: how to answer the challenge of nature, to remain in touch with her but also be, inevitably, different from her? How we choose to answer this question shapes the position we grant to human beings dwelling amid nature itself; without nature no human group or individual can subsist. When man arrogantly calls himself "the master of Creation" he imposes religion on a historic event: man, master of nature. Within nature? Hölderlin points out that Nature will devour us. Outside nature? Freud tells us that we will feel exiled, expelled, orphaned. Outside, but determined to be reconciled with her? Adorno considers such an enterprise impossible. We have damaged nature beyond recuperation and, in the process, distorted ourselves beyond recognition. But, perhaps, if we recognize this double injury, we may achieve a point of view relative to nature. According to Adorno, human society cannot, by necessity, stop exploiting nature. Intellectually we deny nature's point of view; we deny its voice because doing so would demonstrate the sheer feebleness of our own. The loss of a clear differentiation between nature and man would be catastrophe rather than liberation, no less catastrophic in our mind than a sudden inability to distinguish between subject and object. It would authorize a totalitarian absolutism in order to impose reconciliation as the supreme good. Adorno sees clearly the dangers of a forced model of reconciliation and mistrusts the Romantic impulses that would like to recover unity. He is right to declare that unity is not being. And to be undifferentiated implies a lack of unity. We have no other option, perhaps, than to find value in heterogenous difference; what Max Weber calls the polytheism of values.

The Ibero-American novel of the early twentieth century, which provides an almost constant flow of information about the natural world, first confronts nature in its ravenous extreme. As José Eustacio Rivera exclaims in *The Vortex*, in realization of the catastrophe feared by Hölderlin: "The jungle devoured them." In Lezama Lima's writing, we later face the creation of anti-nature, whose self-sufficient artifice, the Baroque, recalls the metallic garden invented by one of Goethe's dramatic characters: it tries to prove anew that humankind is the master of Creation. We can *create* an *artificial* nature. Lezama clearly favors a Baroque movement that divests statuary fixity of its artificial perfection, distancing it from immobile perfection by first subjecting it to movement, then to incarnation. Standing as both our great Catholic novelist and pagan, neo-Platonic poet, Lezama locates man's problematic relationship with nature in flux between two ideals: proximity to God, which is non-nature, and surrender to man, which is erotic passion, a part of nature but distinct from it, neither devoured nor exiled. Finally, Julio Cortázar will say better than anyone, that as we are caught between a natural world that devours us and a history that exiles us, our only response is art: specifically the art of storytelling.

Gallegos responds to this question simply and directly. *Canaima* is the story of Marcos Vargas, a man who is first caught between nature and himself, and then struggles to be one with nature without being devoured by it. Gallegos vigorously personifies this dilemma but also simplifies it even as he moves beyond it, reducing it to a dichotomy between barbarism and civilization, good and evil, virtue and sin, nature and man. In the end, he transcends it, verbally creating a hermetic, self-sufficient space, permitting us to listen to the magnificent and terrifying silence of a natural world supremely indifferent to man, and giving Marcos Vargas, in exchange, nothing but a text, *Canaima*, the fugitive and enduring embodiment of verbal possibility, the only reality by which Vargas can be one with nature without being devoured by it. It is his book, just as Camus's *The Stranger* is Mersault's book.

In order to reach this conclusion, Gallegos must pass through the debate about our modernity and its avatars of progress. History is the first recourse of the humanization of nature. First history was Utopia—space—violated by the "violence *impune*" that transformed the Golden Age into the age of iron. But if inhuman nature could achieve a Golden Age, a human utopia, it can also progress from the Iron Age to the age of civilization, the age of laws and progress. Barbarism—the violence *impune* of the Iron Age—can only be superseded by the authority of law.

The story of *Canaima* unfolds in a barbarous world dominated by petty tyrants: the Ardavines, known in the pseudo-epic style as *The Yurarí Tigers*, and their *guaruras* (bodyguards) and relatives: Apolonio, Sute Cúpira, Cholo Parima: the despotic and patrimonial army has usurped legal and political functions in Latin America. The forces of civilization stand, ineffectively, opposed to them. These forces are embodied by honest merchants such as Marcos Vargas's father, decent farmers and ranchers like Manuel Ladera, young intellectuals like Gabriel Ureña, the telegraph operator, and Marcos Vargas himself when he goes to work with Ladera. We observe what, in Mexico, Molina Enríquez with great expectations called "the ample middle classes," protagonists of the positive aspect of the disjuncture between civilization and barbarism. They are the forces of a new Golden Age, the promise of a more just, more civilized city, standing in opposition to the age of iron, the reality of an unjust and barbarous city, bathed in blood.

3.

Barbarism: we witness the world of petty tyrants, rural political bosses who stand as miniature figurines of the national tyrants who govern under the purported aegis of law for the sole purpose of violating
that law all the more completely, indulging their whims in a permanent, deliberate confusion of public and private functions.

This is the very definition of patrimonialism which Max Weber
considers in *Economy and Society* under the category of "Traditional
Forms of Domination" and which, according to the interpretation of
North American historians Richard Morse and Bradford Burns, truly
constitutes the tradition of government and the most prolonged exercise of power in Spanish America. This tradition has long persist-
ed since the ages of the most highly organized indigenous empires,
during the three centuries of Iberian and republican colonization,
through all forms of domination, from enlightened tyrants like Dr.
Francia and Guzmán Blanco to executioners like Pinochet and the
Argentine juntas. It has also arisen within the progressive, institutional forms of modernizing authoritarianism the most balanced,
polished example of which, until recently, was the PRI regime in
Mexico. It is worth noting that this merely describes the common
ground of a long list of literary despots and tyrants: Asturias's Señor Presidente, Valle-Inclán's Tirano Banderas, Carpentier's Primer
Magistrado, García Marquez's Patriarch, Rulfo's Pedro Páramo and
Gallegos's Ardavines, Roa Bastos's El Supremo, Mariano Azuela's
dwarfish Don Mónico, and Vargas Llosa's Benefactor Trujillo.

As Max Weber explains, the administrative framework of patrimonial power is not composed of functionaries but of underlings,
subservient to their bosses, who feel no objective obligation towards
legal statues or the posts they occupy, but mere personal loyalty towards the boss, whose orders, however capricious and arbitrary, they
carry out as legitimate.

At the parochial level is Don Mónico in Azuela's *The Underdogs*.
He brings the Federation crashing down on top of Demetrio Macías
precisely because the farmer spat in the cacique's face and refused to
submit to patrimonial law. Weber points out that patrimonial bureaucracy is comprised of the boss's family, his relatives, his favorites,
and his clients. In Gallegos: the Ardavines, the boss Apolonio, and

Sute Cúpira. In Rulfo: Fulgor Sedano. They occupy and then undermine the place reserved for professional competition, the hierarchy of reason, and the objective norms of public function and well-regulated promotions and appointments.

Surrounded by clients, relatives, and favorites, the patrimonial boss also requires a patrimonial army, composed of either mercenaries, *guaruras* (bodyguards), *halcones* ("hawks"), "white guards," or the Triple "A"—the Argentine Anticommunist Alliance. For the boss and his syndicate, patrimonial domination seeks to treat public, economic, and political rights as private rights: namely, as prospects that can and should be appropriated for the benefit of the boss and his extended ruling family.

According to Weber, the economic consequences of such organizations reveal a disastrous absence of rationality. Because no formal administrative structure exists, the economy cannot be based on predictable factors. The caprice of the governing group creates too wide a margin of discretion, too open to bribery, favoritism, and the buying and selling of positions. This "traditional form of domination" affects the exercise of power at all levels in Latin America. But the distance between each of these levels is immense, and the boss's self-reserved function is that of the "power moderator" between the distant national powers and those who imitate too closely his own despotic interpretation of power.

Spain's "Indian monarchy" in America was characterized by a physical, as well as political, distance between the metropolis and the colony, and within the colony, between its multiple and varied social and political strata. New England was founded upon local self-government and never stopped practicing it; which means that when revolution came in the late eighteenth century the transition from colony to republic was practically a natural one. By contrast, the "Indian monarchy" was founded on a persistent quarrel between the distant royal power and the local noble power. Madrid never admitted the noble privileges claimed by the new "aristocracies" of the young nations of Spanish America because these fledgling governments chafed at the centralist, authoritarian, and ecumenical restoration of the Hapsburgs in Old Spain. From the outset, Charles V's scornful opinion of assemblies, town hall governments, or American courts is clear: "They offer scant profit and cause great harm."

There was distance between royal centralist power and local noble power, but also enormous distance between the Latin Creole republic and the Indian republic, not to mention the marginalized and
incarcerated republic of black and indigenous slaves. Since the colonial era, Spanish America has experienced the contradiction of a
central authority *de jure* which obstructs the development of multiple *de facto* local authorities. The result was the deformation of both,
the shrinking of absent authority and the enlargement of the present
authority modeled on the former. As one noted Mexican politician
imperiously told me the only time I broached the subject with him:
"The tyrant establishes order where the central law does not reach."

Despotic order reproduces the imperial system of authoritarian
delegations and absences either on a regional scale or in the local village. José Francisco Ardavín commits crimes but he does so under
orders from his brother Miguel, who reserves for himself the role of
father protector of his own victims and can thus pacify any repercus-
sive rage. The hidden tyrant, like nature, the horizon, and the Venezuelan plains, is a "man lost to sight."

Gallegos denounces the calamity of political tyrants, who are "the
plague of this land," and who want to reserve all productive enterprises for themselves. Nicaragua was the private estate of Somoza and
his people, while the island of Santo Domingo belonged to Trujillo. Their chain of power is based on a chain of corruption: the small
time despot Apolonio robs the rancher Manuelote of his mare, with
impunity; the Ardavines, greater despots, steal it from Apolonio. Nobody squeals. The living word dies. Injustice and barbarism are common and widespread:

> Coarse, lanky women with yellow, sagging flesh, looking out from
> the doorways as the travelers pass by; naked children with bloat-
> ed bellies and skeletal pustular legs swarming with flies sucking
> at their open sores; scrawny, shriveled old men, barely dressed
> in filthy aprons. Dumb, sickly human beings whose brutish
> faces seemed to wear a mummified expression of anxiety. Guaya-
> na, hunger lying side by side with gold.

Barbarism and injustice are commonplace and systematic:

> Bank accounts were liquidated. The peasants, with nothing but

debts to their name, lowered their heads in silence and scratched
at their matted, lice-infested hair; the ones who had been more
laborious and prudent, or luckier, got some cash; from there they
went out on the town to squander their money drinking and later they returned to their shacks, shrugging their shoulders and
telling themselves that next year they would harvest more rubber, they would earn more money and would not fritter it away.
But all of them, one way or another, were already dragging the
chain of "advances" on their pay, the other end held fast by the
company's claws.

Injustice and barbarism are, nevertheless, also individual. Patrimonialism is a sociologically elegant name for caprice, and caprice bestows
death, an absurd, gratuitous death like the one Don Manuel Ladera
suffers at the hands of Cholo Parima. A chain of deaths is set in motion, an eye for an eye, a tooth for a tooth, culminating with the simple slap upon the table with which Marcos Vargas, to avenge all the
deaths, closes the circle and destroys, out of pure fear, the despot José
Francisco Ardavín, revealing his condition: he was exhausted but nobody had dared try to move against him. The tyrant dies in the circular confrontation with his own self.

But *Canaima*, a decalogue of barbarism, also aspires to be the text
of civilization, the repertoire of civilized history's answers. For Gallegos this is inseparable from the process of growing personalization,
of the loss of human anonymity amid the natural world.

4.

Civilization: Name and Voice; Memory and Desire. For Gallegos, the
first step in escaping anonymity is to baptize nature itself, to name it.
Here, the author fulfills a primary function which prolongs that of the
discoverers and introduces the function of those narrators conscious
of the creative power of names. Here Gallegos baptizes, with the
same urgency and power of a Columbus, a Vespucci, or an Oviedo:

> *Amanadoma, Yavita, Pimichín, el Casiquiare, Atabapo, Guainía!*
> ... those men were not describing the landscape, nor revealing
> the total mystery which they had penetrated; they limited them-
> selves to mentioning the places where their adventures had hap-

pened, but all the tremendous, fascinating jungle was quivering with the suggestive value of those names.

In the following chapter, the first thing that Marcos Vargas discovers about the natives in the jungle is that they do not, for anything in the world, say their names aloud, because "they believe that if they give their true name they surrender something of themselves." In a kind of symmetrical resonance, this also becomes the last detail we learn about Marcos Vargas: by entering the world of the natives he has forsaken his name.

Nomination, the act of naming, is the minimal response to barbarism. Protocol, courtesy, respect for ways of doing things, also have the purpose of exorcizing violence, as in the encounter between Manuel Ladera and Marcos Vargas:

"I've already had the pleasure of meeting your father."

"Well, here you're looking at the son."

"I've also had the honor of meeting Miss Herminia, your saintly mother."

"Saintly is perhaps an understatement, Don Manuel. But your compliment about my mother has already won me over."

"For me, a good son is already halfway to a friend."

"I don't know if I have the right. My mother made sacrifices for my upbringing, but it didn't bear the fruit she expected."

"Please allow me to be your friend."

"It's good to have friends in high places."

All these circumlocutions are meant to anathematize caprice, to postpone the use of force, choosing civilization instead, in order to allow it to offer its maximum response: ideological salvation through fidelity to the ideas of the Enlightenment, specifically, the philosophy of progress. This is the weakest aspect of Rómulo Gallegos's writing, in which he assumes the role of a D'Alembert of the interior plains, dispensing good advice for reaching happiness through progress, as in these words from Ureña to Marcos Vargas: "Read a little, cultivate yourself, civilize that barbarous strength you've got inside, study the problems of this land and assume the attitude to which you're obliged. When life gives you skills, and I tell you again that you've got them, it also gives you responsibilities." Up to this point, Gallegos echoes the eighteenth century Enlightenment ideal; but immediately, in the same conversation with the same character, the discourse takes a surprisingly Ibero-American turn: "This whole town is waiting for a man—what they call these days *el Hombre Macho*—and you, why not you? You can be that Messiah."

This singular mix of the capitalist philosophy of the self-made man and the authoritarian philosophy of the providential ruler, reveals a knowledge of Marcos Vargas's psyche that is lost on the pure progressive Don Manuel Ladera, who praises labor and capital, and condemns the illusory dreams of gold and rubber and the slave system which serves that illusion: "What the peasant finds on the mountain is practically slavery, thanks to the debt he owes for pay advances, with no way of escaping from businessman, nor any authority to protect him from it . . . Slavery, which sometimes his children inherit along with the debt." Marcos Vargas does not agree with all this. His response is that of the Spanish *hidalgo*—the man of honor—the one descended not from the philosopher Rousseau but from the conquistador Pizarro: "It was possible that from a practical point of view Ladera was right; but the adventure of seeking gold and rubber had another side: the adventure itself, a passionate endeavor: the risk taken, the fear overcome. A fierce measure of manhood!"

Gallegos assumes the consequences of his contradiction, which are the consequences of our Latin American tradition. In spite of himself, perhaps, he tells us the story of a man gifted with every possibility but who lacks faith in progress, who could be the Boss, *el Hombre Macho*, of an enlightened patrimonialism, the most distinguished individual of the group, who, nevertheless, will inevitably end up lost in the jungle, becoming acculturated with the natives, anonymous in the midst of nature, swallowed alive. Marcos Vargas's destiny seems a strange one, although in reality it is not, because that other individual, macho destiny which Ureña designs for him is an ersatz myth standing in contradiction to the collective nature of the authentic myth. Marcos Vargas asks constantly—and one recalls Jorge Negrete playing this role in a Mexican film from the 1940s: "*¿Se es o no se es?*"[2] The astonishing thing about *Canaima* is that the macho man's brash question conceals the secret affirmation of the true

---

2 Translator's note: While translator Will Kirkland claims this palindrome to be untranslatable, others read it as a variant of Hamlet's timeless question, "To be or not to be." A literal English equivalent would be "Is it or is it not?"

myth. Marcos Vargas enters the mythological world of the natives and there he ceases to be the macho, virile male, the very picture of the boss, the enlightened despot which Ureña dreamed him to be. Marcos Vargas *is* because *he is no longer*.

Count Giaffano, one of the eccentric characters in *Canaima*, best expresses the individualized response to barbarism. Giaffano is an Italian expatriate who has gone to the Venezuelan jungle with the goal of "purifying himself of human filth." Only there in the jungle does he cultivate friendship, love, and the mystery of the self: stoic qualities and "hermetic intimacy" which for him is the only response to the jungle, the only "escape valve" from nature. To confess this intimacy, says Giaffano, is to lose it, which means losing "the integral sensation of self." The European Giaffano is what Ureña and Vargas can never be: an individualist without a temptation or weakness for power or showmanship, a private being. To recall the words of the Mexican dramatist Rodolfo Usigli, in society Ureña and Vargas are, simply, *gesticulators*.

Among the criticism, contradiction, and mere insufficiency, what remains to Rómulo Gallegos in his strange and fascinating palimpsest of Ibero-American being and transience? A supreme paradox for one who has so sharply required the masked role of written equality. What remains behind the masks of appearance and power is, once again, the written word. The first level of civilization's final response is the naming of places, spaces, and people that are to be assimilated within it: rivers named according to the sound of their waters, men named according to the sound of their actions: the Yurarí Tigers, Cholo Parima, Sute Cúpira, Juan Solito, Aymará, the Indian woman Arecuna.

But the second level, also inseparable from the third, is this: the dramatization of the force of the written word. The deceased despot José Gregorio Ardavín is married, in full *rigor mortis*, by the boss Apolonio, to the native woman Rosa Arecuna. With the marriage consummated in writing, Apolonio exclaims: "Look what papers can do, Marcos Vargas!" Would men like Emiliano Zapata, and Rubén Jaramillo, all of our rebel farmers and peasants, armed more with property deeds and papers than with rifles, say otherwise?

But would those powerful men armed with colonial laws, republican constitutions, and transnational contracts also have something else to say? The written law is a double-edged sword, and it will be Gabriel García Márquez, in *The Autumn of the Patriarch*, who with greater lucidity but more implicit means, explores the dualities of writing: literature and law, word and power. But in this scene from *Canaima*, Gallegos sets out, for the first time, the theme in the Latin American novel and that allows him to very quickly reach, at the very heart of his literary work, the only possible solution to this level of conflict which both he and Sarmiento before him tried to resolve. Both men sought this accomplishment through political action, because both were presidents of their respective nations, although Sarmiento was more fortunate in Argentina than Gallegos in Venezuela.

Finally, the third level of civilization's response to barbarism is nothing less than this, that of Rómulo Gallegos writing his novel about the struggle between civilization and barbarism, demonstrating, in the process, that he possesses no other way of dramatically transcending the conflict. Beyond didacticism and sermonizing, however, how does he manage to resolve the conflict at the level of writing?

Literature's most elemental right is that of naming. Imagining also signifies naming. And if literature creates both authors and readers alike, it also names all three: which is to say, it also names itself. In the act of naming is found the heart of that ambiguity which makes the novel, according to Milan Kundera, "one of humanity's great conquests." Kundera goes on to say that this game of naming characters can be considered antiquated but it might also be the best game ever invented, a permanent invitation to escape from oneself (from our own truth and our own certainty) and understand the other.

When Pascal's God slowly departed the throne from whence he had directed the universe and its order of values, says Kundera, Don Quixote also departed his own house and found himself no longer quite capable of comprehending the world. Until then transparent, the world had become confused, and man with it, confused as well. Since that moment, the novel has accompanied man on his adventure throughout a world suddenly subject to relativity.

The novel is a crossroads of individual and collective destiny expressed through language. It is a reintroduction of man into history and of the subject into its destiny, and thus the novel becomes an instrument of liberation. There is no novel without history; but if it introduces us to history the novel also allows us to seek a way out of history so that we might gaze upon the face of history and thus become truly historical. The opposite, to be immersed and lost in history without the possibility of finding a way out, so that we might understand history and make it *better* or simply *different*, is to be nothing more than history's victims.

In his time, Gallegos faithfully served all these demands of the narrative art. Without him, such books as *One Hundred Years of Solitude*, *The Green House*, or *The Lost Steps* would never have been written. But Gallegos's value lies not only in being a precursor, a venerated first father, later detested and, finally, understood. I maintain that Gallegos was always faithful to the art of the novel because, like Don Quixote, like Pip, like Mitya Karamazov, like Anna Karenina, his characters went forth into the world and, failing to understand it, they suffered the defeat of their illusions but gained the experience of a great adventure: the realization of relative truth.

Gallegos uses literature to resolve the conflict between civilization and barbarism by assimilating his character Marcos Vargas, a creature of the written word, to a dialectic, to a movement of relative germination and contradiction. This first offers us a vision of Nature, followed by a vision of History as its opposing face—the Janus of Utopia and Power—and upon this dual cranium Gallegos places the crown of authentic human vision, one that is neither totally natural nor totally historical, but simply verbal and imaginative. Between the voracious natural world and the void of historical exile, the art of the novel creates space and time that are human, relative, livable, and convivial.

Rómulo Gallegos is a true writer: he defeats himself. He defeats his thesis, creating the conflicts of Marcos Vargas caught between the demands of nature and history; and those conflicts, unexpectedly, give the character a different profile. Marcos Vargas, conquistador, man of honor, *el hombre macho*, and frustrated messiah, first acquires an awareness of injustice, and this is the rational element within him: "From Guarampín to Río Negro they were all doing the same thing, he among the oppressors against the oppressed, and this was life in the fascinating jungle, so beautifully dreamed." In the course of this reflection, Marcos Vargas realizes that conquering a personality means no less than contending with nature itself, knowing full well that one belongs to that nature. As in Meursault's encounter with the violent Algerian sun in *The Stranger*, as in Ishmael's encounter with the raging and beneficent sea in *Moby-Dick*, this tension is resolved in *Canaima* through an extraordinary epiphany.

Marcos Vargas is alone in the jungle, caught in the middle of a tropical storm, and it is there that he discovers himself in nature, a part of nature, but different from it, mortally threatened by it, and suffering equally in both situations. His macho cry, *¿se es o no se es?* is swallowed up by the storm, which does not hear him but carries off his words; they fly away on the wind, they become the wind, they nourish it. After this trembling windstorm (the highest descriptive moment in Gallegos's novel) Marcos Vargas will end up—better yet, he will be discovered—naked, soaking wet, trembling, and clutching a small howler monkey which takes shelter in his arms, trembling and crying the same as the man.

Marcos Vargas goes to live with the natives. He marries a native woman, Aymará; he fathers a mestizo son with her, the new Marcos Vargas, who, at the age of ten, returns to "civilization." There, Marcos's fiancé, Aracelis Vellorini, the youngest daughter of her family, has by this time married an English engineer. Ureña is married to the beautiful Maigualida, daughter of Manuel Ladera, and has become a respected merchant. He receives Marcos Vargas's son at his home. The cycle begins again. The second opportunity shows itself. Tensions persist, however, tensions between Myth and Law, between Nature and Personality, between Remaining and Returning, between Civilization and Barbarism. They are not resolved, they must not be resolved: amid these opposing forces, *Canaima*'s most conspicuous fact is the destiny of destinies. This is a novel of sudden, hasty destinies, immediately fulfilled on either extreme by the honest, upright Ladera and the criminal Parima—or, by contrast, of destinies forever abandoned, statically located in counterpoint to the novel's main concern, which is that of fleeting destiny.

In this way, Marcos Vargas's fortune becomes a symbol of the speed of destiny as it assumes the faces of disappearance, oblivion, death, and of destiny forsaken as it assumes, contrarily, the savage persistence of nature and power. In both cases, destiny comes to resemble history as a blind, inescapable force, while also resembling nature as an untouched, virginal absence. Marcos Vargas stretches out his hand to touch a destiny that is neither overwhelmingly abrupt nor overwhelmingly absent; he enters the aboriginal world of myth, whose postulation is simultaneity, the eternal present.

Thanks to its mythical eminence, *Canaima* manages to simultaneously reunite and dissolve the contradictory worlds of Latin American nature and power. Inside and outside of history, we can see the terrible world of Cholo Parima and the Ardavines as our own world, and know, at the same time, that its violence is no longer exclusive to Spanish America, no longer only our own, not after what we have lived through in our own times.

Rómulo Gallegos, the regionalist writer, enters the history of twentieth century violence. And that violence, as a way to move towards a conclusion, is perhaps the only passport to universality in the closing years of our time. Rómulo Gallgos, primary and primordial novelist of Spanish-America, Afro-America, and Indio-America, offers us, simultaneously, a way out of nature without sacrificing it, and a way into history, without turning us into its victims.

Following the path of radical exception to the most successful modern philosophy of progress and pragmatism — that of the United States of America — William Faulkner reached the threshold of tragedy: the recognition of the value of defeat and our fraternity with disaster, which is the rule, not the exception, of human experience. His exemplary literary experience and achievement does not, however, replace our Ibero-American experience and our attempts to blindly hack a way out of the primary, impersonal nature described by Gallegos.

For this reason Gallegos is important. We know that there is something more important, perhaps, than his writing, which turns out to be paltry, simplistic, and sentimental in comparison to Faulkner's. But that writing is also irreplaceable, as irreplaceable as one's own father. If we must come to a place of tragic awareness, the truest freedom human beings are capable of finding and maintaining, we will have to do so through our father Gallegos and the miseries which the Venezuelan novelist communicates to us with so much Latin *verecundia* — so much paternal reverence. Our Father who art Gallegos. By your path one reaches *Paradiso*, Lezama Lima's contradictory, erotic and mystical, pagan and Christian novel: our own tragic threshold so far from Gallegos's impersonal nature, the "immense mysterious regions where man has not yet penetrated."

6. The Mexican Revolution

1.

The twentieth-century Mexican novel was dominated by the main event of the twentieth century in Mexico: the social, political, and cultural revolution which took place from 1910 to 1920. *The Underdogs* by Mariano Azuela; *Let's Go with Pancho Villa* by Rafael Muñoz; and *La sombra del caudillo* (The Shadow of the Dictator) by Martín Luiz Guzmán all bore witness to these events and reflected them with their aesthetic realism, as well as works by Francisco L. Urquizo: *Tropa vieja* (The Old Guard) and Nellie Campobello, while the Catholic counterrevolution — the Cristero War — was novelized by J. Guadalupe de Anda in *Los bragados* (The Brigands). The efforts by the group known as "The Contemporaries" (Torres Bodet, Salvador Novo, Gilberto Owen) to compose intimist novels were minimized, if not replaced, by a growing and exclusivist national rhetoric ("Whoever reads Proust, prostitutes himself") and an anguish over political dreams and losses (José Revueltas). Finally, two works, *Al filo del agua* (At the Water's Edge) by Agustín Yáñez and *Pedro Páramo* by Juan Rulfo, bring the cycle of the Revolution and the agrarian world to a brilliant close. The urban novel went on to occupy a central place in fiction and with it there appeared a very thematically diversified literature.

2. The Barefoot *Iliad*: Mariano Azuela

I wonder, to what degree is the impossibility of fully following the path from myth to epic to tragedy inherent to the frustrations of our history? To what degree is a barely pallid reflection of the modern decision — Judeo-Christian first, bureaucratic-industrial second — to banish tragedy, unacceptable for a vision of constant perfectibility and final happiness for humans and their institutions?

I choose Mariano Azuela's novel *The Underdogs* to attempt a response which, if approximately valid, will doubtless set in motion a new constellation of questions. But if we approach the first hypothesis — the story of Mexico and Latin America as the brave new world — *The Underdogs* offers an opportunity for understanding the relationship between nation and narration. With its amphibious nature —

an epic corrupted by the novel, a novel corrupted by chronicle—it
is an ambiguous and uneasy text which swims the waters of many
genres and proposes a Latin American reading of the possibilities and
impossibilities of the same. Bernal wrote a vacillating epic; Azuela
writes a degraded epic. Between both, the nation aspires to be narration. In Gallegos or in Rulfo, a myth germinates from the delimi-
tation of narrative reality. In Gallegos, this is preceded by nature; in
Rulfo, by death. The myth that can be born from Azuela is more disquieting, because it arises from the failure of an epic.

Nation and narration: in the same way that the absence of the
Spanish novel from the time between Cervantes and Clarín stems
from a lack of verbal response to the decadence which rules during
the reigns of Felipe IV and Carlos the Bewitched, both the Latin
American novel and, especially, the Mexican novel are absent until
The Mangy Parrot: The Life and Times of Periquillo Sarniento by José
Fernández de Lizardi, when the nation begins to discover controversy and offers fiction an opportunity. We participated in the nation's
Romantic, sentimental, Rousseauan illusion, derived from reading
Rousseau's *Julie, or the New Heloise*, although with less lachrymose inspiration than other writers such as the Colombian Jorge Isaacs and
the Argentine José Mármol. Our best moment in nineteenth century
fiction is found in the adventure novels of Payno and Inclán: preludes
to the Mexican Revolution, as were *Facundo* and *Martín Fierro* for Argentina. But a new prestige, seen as a duty, again obscured the national narrative behind the screen of Zolaesque Naturalism. In the novel
María Luisa, Mariano Azuela takes part in this terrible combination
of sentimentality and clinical observation. It shows a world objecti-
fied and predestined, in which the stones have no history, and fatality
no grandeur: it was a dramatic pretext to inspire progress, not a totalizing vision of the past and its common obstacles and facilities for
achieving true development, which also implies and involves the
presence of the past.

More than any other novelist of the Mexican Revolution, Mariano Azuela lifts the heavy stone of history to see *what lies beneath*.
What he finds is the history of colonial Mexico that no one before
him had ever really narrated using imagination. Whoever focuses on
the simple relationship of "present" events in Azuela, without understanding the contextual richness of his work, will have not read him.

Nor will they have read the nation as narration, which is Azuela's contribution to Latin American literature; we are what we are because we are what we were.

But when I say, "the history of colonial Mexico," I should say, "the tale of two colonies": because Azuela is our Dickens. Stanley and Barbara Stein, historians of colonial Mexico at Princeton University, distinguish various constants: the hacienda, the plantation, and the social structures linked to the system of latifundium or large private estates; the mining enclaves; the exportation syndrome; elitism, nepotism, and clientelism. But what is notable about these elements is not only that they reveal the reality of the colonized country, but that they are also reflected as vices of the colonizing country itself, Spain.

A tale of two colonies. A colonial nation colonizes a colonial continent. "Let us now sell manufactured goods to the Spaniards," ordered Louis XIV, "and receive from them gold and silver." In *Criticón*, Gracián exclaimed: "Spain is the Indies of France." He could have said: Spain is the Indies of Europe. And Spanish America was the colony of a colony posing as an empire.

Exportation of wool, importation of textiles, and a flight of precious metal into northern Europe to pay off the Iberian debt, to import luxuries from the Orient for the Iberian aristocracy, to pay for the counter-reformist crusades and the mortifying monuments to Phillip II and his successors, defenders of the faith. In his *Memorial de la política necesaria y útil restauración a la república de España y estados de ella, y desempeño universal de estos reinos* (Petition for the Politically Necessary and Useful Restoration of Spain and her States, and the Universal Redemption of These Kingdoms), written in 1600, the economist González de Cellorigo, as cited by John Elliott in *Imperial Spain*, says that because Spain had money, gold, and silver, it had nothing; and if Spain were poor, it was due to being rich. Cellorigo concluded that, regarding Spain, it was thus possible to say two things that were simultaneously contradictory and true.

I fear that Spain's colonies did not escape Cellorigo's ironic conclusion either. After all, what was the tradition of the Spanish Empire if not a vast chaotic patrimonialism, by virtue of which Spain's dynastic riches increased exorbitantly, but not the riches of the Spaniards? If England, as Stanley and Barbara Stein write, eliminated all restrictions on economic development (royal, corporate, or class privileges; monopolies; prohibitions) Spain multiplied them. The American empire of the Hapsburgs was conceived as a series of kingdoms added to the crown of Castile. The other Spanish kingdoms were legally incapacitated from participating directly in the exploitation and administration of the New World.

Like Pedro Páramo's fictional Comala, the Ardavín family's Guarari, and the tyrant Don Mónico's Limón in Zacatecas, America was the personal patrimony of the King of Castile.

Spain did not grow, the royal patrimony grew. The aristocracy grew, the Church grew, and the bureaucracy grew to the extent that in 1650 there were 400,000 active edicts relating to the New World: Kafka with a powdered wig. Both the military and ecclesiastical militancy passed, uninterrupted, from the Reconquest of Spain to the Conquest and colonization of America. On the peninsula there remained a weak aristocracy, a centralized bureaucracy, and an army composed of rogues, thieves, and beggars. Cortés was in Mexico, while Calisto, Lazarillo de Tormes, and Cervantes's Lawyer of Glass remained in Spain. But Cortés, new man of the middle class from Extremadura, active embodiment of Niccolò Machiavelli's politics *for the purpose of* conquest, *for* newness, *for* the self-made Prince who needs inherit nothing, is defeated by the imperium of the Spanish Hapsburgs, the absolutism imposed on Spain, first, by the defeated rebellion of the Castilian townships in 1521 and, second, by the defeat of Catholic Reform at the Council of Trent from 1545–1563.

Spanish America had to accept what European modernity would judge intolerable: privilege as the norm, a militant Church, insolent, ostentatious wealth, and private use of public resources and powers. As Barbara and Stanley Stein tell us, it took Spain eighty years to occupy its American empire and two centuries to establish the colonial economy upon three pillars: the mining centers of Mexico and Peru; the farming and ranching centers on the peripheries of the mines; and the system of commerce oriented towards the exportation of metals to Spain to pay for imported goods from the rest of Europe.

The mines paid the administrative costs of the Spanish Empire but were also primarily responsible for colonial genocide, the death of the population that, between 1492 and 1550 was reduced, in Mexico and the Caribbean, from 25 million to 1 million, and in the Andean regions, between 1530 and 1750, from 6 million to 0.5 million. In the midst of this demographic disaster, mining, the central pillar of the Empire, contributed to the catastrophe, intensifying and perpetuating it through forced labor, a form of slavery known as *la mita* (a tax paid to landlords), perhaps the most brutal form of a colonization which first destroyed indigenous agriculture and then sent the dispossessed to mining concentration camps because they could not pay their debts (Stanley and Barbara Stein, *The Colonial Legacy of Latin America*).

3. THE STONE OF HISTORY

Brave New World: in the aftermath, what could remain of the utopian dream of a New World regenerated from European corruption, inhabited by the Noble Savage, destined to restore the Golden Age? Erasmus, More, Vitoria, and Vives flow away, swallowed up in the dark tunnels of a mine in Potosí or Guanajuato. Spain's Golden Age turned out to be the hacienda, the paradoxical refuge of the dispossessed and those condemned to forced labor in the mines. Spanish American history seems to be written according to *malmenorismo*, the Jesuits's troubling practical law of choosing a lesser evil; comparatively, the large landowners grant themselves the right to play this multifaceted role of protector, patriarch, judge, and benevolent jailer, one that paternalistically demands and obtains the labor and loyalty of the peasant who receives from the patriarch, in uneven exchange, rations, religious consolation, and sorrowfully relative security. The patriarch's name is Pedro Páramo, Don Mónico, José Gregorio Ardavín.

Azuela's characters stagger under this impossible burden, beneath the heavy stone slab that has been laid upon their lives: they are the victims of all the dreams and all the nightmares of the New World. Should we be surprised that, as they struggle to crawl out from beneath the heavy slab, they seem at times to be insects, blind scorpions, dazzled by the sun, turning circles, disoriented after many centuries of darkness and oppression beneath the monoliths of Aztec, Iberian, and Republican power? They emerge from that darkness: they cannot see the world clearly; they travel, move, emigrate, fight, they go to the Revolution. They fulfill the requirements of the original, age-old epic even as they also, significantly, degrade and frustrate them.

As such, *The Underdogs* is an epic chronicle that seeks to establish the way events—not myths—occur because myths do not feed the immediate textuality of *The Underdogs*. It is, however, a novelistic chronicle as well, one that not only recounts events but also scrutinizes them, both critically and imaginatively. The description of general events is at times synthetic:

> The federal troops in Zacatecas had fortified the hills of El Grillo and La Bufa. Rumor had it that this was Huerta's final stronghold, but everybody predicted that the town would be taken. Families fled towards the South; the trains were choked with people; there was a shortage of carriages and wagons, and along the highways, many refugees, overcome by panic, trudged along carrying their belongings on their backs.

At times Azuela's prose juxtaposes velocity and sluggishness:

> Demetrio's horse seemed to have eagle's claws instead of hooves, and it climbed right up the craggy hills. "Up! Move up!," shouted his men, following behind like wild deer, scrambling up over the rocks, men and beasts moving up together as one. Only one boy went off the trail, slipped and tumbled down into the canyon; suddenly the others appeared on the peak, overrunning trenches and cutting down the enemy. Demetrio lassoed the machine guns, pulling them down, dragging them like wild bulls. It couldn't last. The Federal troops had greater numbers and could have wiped out Demetrio's men faster than they could reach the top. But we took advantage of the momentary confusion, and with dizzying speed rushed their position and cleared them out of there. That chief of yours is a mighty fine soldier!

Other passages show the panorama rendered directly and curiously present in the foreground:

> From the top of the hill they could see one flank of La Bufa hill, with its high crest like the plumed head of a proud Aztec king. Six hundred meters high, the slope was covered with dead men, their hair thickly matted, their filthy clothes caked with blood and dirt. A crowd of ragged women ranged among the still warm bodies like a pack of famished coyotes, searching, looting, and stripping the corpses of clothes and possessions.

Azuela's repetitive, enunciative, declamatory characterization of heroic qualities is also epic: in the same way that Achilles is brave and Ulysses is shrewd, and Álvar Fáñez girded his sword in a brave hour, and Don Quixote is the Knight of the Rueful Countenance, here, Demetrio Macías becomes the hero of Zacatecas, and Pancho Villa is named the "Mexican Napoleon ... the Aztec eagle who nailed his steel beak into the head of the viper Victoriano Huerta."

But it is right here, at the epic, patronymic level of naming, where Azuela begins his devaluation of the Mexican revolutionary epic. Does Demetrio Macías deserve his fame? Is he a hero? Did he really defeat someone in Zacatecas? Did he spend the night before the attack drinking? Did he wake up in the morning lying next to an old whore with a bullet in her guts and two recruits with holes in their heads? This novelistic doubt begins to seem like a different epic, not the unwavering epic of Hector and Achilles, of Roland, or the Arthurian cycle, but the Spanish epic of El Cid Campeador: the only one which begins with the hero cheating two men, the Jewish merchants Raquel and Vidas, and culminates with a malicious humiliation: the count García Ordóñez having his beard ripped out. Not a feat of war, but a personal insult, vengeance.

Demetrio Macías's rebellion also begins with a barbed and bearded incident—the beard in this case belongs to *el Güero* Margarito, tyrant of Moyahua—and Macías's most violent companion. He does not pluck petals from wildflowers but the hairs of his own beard: "I've got a really bad temper, and when there's nobody for me to take it out on, I tear out my beard until the mood passes. I swear, General, if I didn't do that, I'd perish from sheer anger!"

This is not the wrath of Achilles, but rather his degraded, vacillating, Latin American counterpart. The schemes of El Cid are reproduced by Hernán Cortés, who confesses to having procured, like a "genteel corsair," the necessary supplies for his Mexican expedition from his neighbors on the Cuban coast; and they explode dizzyingly in the barefoot *Iliad* which is *The Underdogs*.

It is an epic tainted by a history enacted before our very eyes, although Azuela takes our knowledge of that history for granted, not only in the sense that the events are known to the public, but also in the sense that what is known is repetitive and fatal. Nevertheless, unlike the familiar high epic style, *The Underdogs* lacks a common language for its two principal characters. The comrades at Troy understand each other, as do Charlemagne's paladins, and the sixty knights of El Cid. But Demetrio Macías and "el Curro" Luis Cervantes do not: and in this they are deeply novelistic characters. This is because the novel's language is one of astonishment in the face of a world no longer comprehensible. It calls to mind Don Quixote venturing forth into a world which does not seem like itself, but also the incomprehension borne by the characters that have missed the analogies of the discourse. Don Quixote and Sancho do not understand each other; nor do the members of the Shandy family; nor Heathcliff the gypsy and the decent English family of the Lintons; nor Emma Bovary and her husband; nor Anna Karenina and hers.

In the end, what connects Macías and Cervantes? Rapine, the common language of plunder, as in the famous scene in which each thief, pretending to be asleep, sees the other rob a strongbox, knowing that the other is watching him, thus sealing a pact of silence between the thieves. The government's pact has also been formed and confirmed: it's a kleptocracy. The events are fatal: Valderrama offers a peroration: "Juchipila, cradle of the Revolution of 1910, a blessed land, watered with the blood of martyrs, with the blood of dreamers . . . the only good men!" And a former Federal officer riding by, brutally completes the sentence: "Only because they had no time to be bad." And the events are deliberately, meaningfully repetitive:

> "You just takes whatever you wants. You don't ask no permission," says La Pintada. "If not, who wuz the Revolution for? For all the fat cats? Well, we're the fat cats now."

> ⋆

> "*My general*," Cervantes said to Macías, after some minutes of silence and reflection.

> *

> "*We're* the fat cats now," brags La Pintada.

4. THE EPIC OF DISENCHANTMENT

The Underdogs is a strange epic of disenchantment; and between these two exclamations the novel outlines its true historical spectrum. The internal dialectic of Mariano Azuela's work abounds in two verbal extremes: bitterness engendering fatality and fatality engendering bitterness. The disenchanted Solís believes that the protagonist of the Revolution is "an unredeemed race" but confesses being unable to separate himself from it because "the Revolution is a hurricane." The psychology of "our race"—continues Solís—"is reduced to two words: steal, kill . . . How beautiful is the Revolution, even at its most barbarous." And he concludes, famously: "What a failure it would be, my friend, if those of us who give all our spirit, even our very lives, for the sake of overthrowing a miserable murdering tyrant, end up working to build an enormous pedestal where they could raise up a hundred or two hundred thousand monsters of the same kind!"

If *The Underdogs* had resigned itself to being no more than a simple diversion, vacillating between two extremes that feed into one another, it would lack authentic narrative tension; its unity would be false because of the binomial disillusion and resignation that soon exhaust each other, and end up reflecting each other; like an ape making faces at itself in the mirror. For obvious reasons, criticism has lingered too long on these more obvious aspects of Azuela's work, overlooking the nucleus of a tension that grants these two extremes their active distance in the narrative discourse.

Azuela refuses an epic that is satisfied with reflecting, much less with justifying: he is a novelist dealing with epic material in order to make it vulnerable, to damage it, to affect it with the act that breaks the simple unity. Thus, in a certain way, Azuela completes the cycle opened by Bernal Díaz, he raises the heavy stone slab of conquest and asks us to look at the beings crushed by the pyramids and churches, by *la mita* and the haciendas, by local despotism and national dictatorship. The stone is also that stone that never stops tumbling and falling; in this light, the tempestuous, volcanic revolution ceases to be associated with fatality in order to take shape as that human, novelistic act that breaks the previous epic model which celebrates all of our historic feats and constantly threatens us with the soporific norm of self-praise.

Consequently, what would seem in Azuela to be, at first glance, resignation or repetition, is a critique of the historical spectrum which is built upon his group of characters.

In the midst of a different revolutionary hurricane, Saint-Just wonders how to wrest power from the law of inertia which constantly drives it towards isolation, repression, and cruelty: "All the arts," said the young French revolutionary, "have produced wonders. The art of government has only produced monsters."

Saint-Just reaches this pessimistic conclusion once he has drawn a distinction between the historic moment of the revolution and the revolution itself, while he remains steadfastly opposed to his adversaries, destroys the monarchy, and defends himself from foreign invasion: this is the epic order of the revolution. But then the revolution turns against itself; and this would be the tragic order of the revolution. Trotsky wrote that socialist art would revive tragedy. He stated this from the epic point of view, predicting a tragedy no longer of fatality or the individual, but rather one of class conflict and, finally, of collectivity. He did not know then that he would be one of the protagonists of the tragedy of socialism, and that this would occur in history, not literature.

Azuela knows perfectly well the limits of his literary and historical experience, and his warning is only this: the epic order of *this* revolution, the Mexican one, can be translated into a reproduction of the previous despotism because — and this is the true richness of his work as a novelist — the political, familial, sexual, intellectual, and moral matrices of the old colonial and patrimonial order have not been deeply transformed. The temblor in Azuela's writing is a ghostly premonition: Demetrio Macías can be only one chapter more of destiny, that old enemy, as Hegel calls it. And why not? The microcosmos needed to replace Don Mónico is already present, in the band of Demetrio and his followers, clients, and favorites: el Güerro Margarito, el Curro, Cervantes, Solís, la Pintada, and la Cordoniz soon confound and appropriate public rights in order to serve the Chief's whim and their own private appetites.

Mariano Azuela saves Demetrio Macías from his enemy destiny thanks to a reiteration of the action that, behind its fatalist appearance, resembles Hegel's epic action. The epic is a distancing of man's action in the face of divine action. But Azuela, the novelist, permits his vision, in turn, to transcend the degraded epic and acquire, in the end, the resonance of myth. And this is the myth of the return home.

Like Ulysses, el Cid, and Don Quixote, Demetrio Macías left his land, saw the world, recognized it, and failed to recognize it, and was also recognized and unrecognized by it. Now, in accord with the laws of myth, he returns to his lair:

> Demetrio slowly headed for the camp.
>
> He was thinking about his oxen: two sturdy young beasts. He'd been working them for slightly less than two years so far on his two corn fields, well-tended and fertilized. He thought of his young wife, saw her face clearly in his mind: sweet and gentle when she smiled on her husband, proud and haughty towards strangers. But although he struggled to recall the face of his son, it was no use: he had forgotten him.
>
> He reached the camp. Alongside their horses with their heads bowed and eyes closed, the soldiers lay sleeping, stretched out in the furrows of the field.
>
> "The horses are really worn out, Anastasio: it would be good if we stayed to rest, at least a day."
>
> "Well, Compadre Demetrio, I'm eager to reach the mountains! If you could see them . . . you might not believe me . . . there's really nothing about this place that makes me want to stop . . . I'm not really sure what it is, but I feel sad . . . lost . . ."
>
> "How many hours' ride from here to Limón?"
>
> "Not hours; it's three long days of hard riding, Demetrio."

Before dawn they set out for Tepatitlán. Their silhouettes wavered indistinctly across the highway and plowed fields with the slow, steady plodding of the horses, then dissolved in the pearly light of the waning moon that bathed the whole valley.

> Dogs barked in the distance.
>
> "By noon today we'll get to Tepatitlán, tomorrow Cuquío, and then . . . the mountains," said Demetrio.

But Ithaca is a ruin: history has killed it, too:

> Like the other towns they'd seen since Tepic, passing through Jalisco, Aguascalientes and Zacatecas, Juchipila was a ruin. The black print of the fires could be seen in the now roofless houses, in the burnt eaves and balconies. The houses were shuttered; the few stores that remained open seemed like a cruel joke, the bare

shelves recalling the white skeletons of horses they saw along all the highways. The frightened look of hunger was now on the terrified faces of the people, and when they stared at the soldiers the bright flame in their eyes burned with hatred.

Revolutionary history robs the epic of its mythic support: *The Underdogs* is the journey from one origin to another, but without myth. And the novel immediately robs the revolutionary history of its epic basis. This is our deep debt to Mariano Azuela. Thanks to him we have been able to write modern novels in Mexico; he prevented revolutionary history from imposing itself upon us as a purely epic celebration, despite its enormous efforts to that effect. The home that we abandoned was destroyed and we need to build a new one. The struggle is not over. Azuela has reminded us of this since 1916; it is possible that the bricks we might use today are different from those a century ago, but the powerful whiplash, the stinging urgency, remain the same. Azuela the novelist tells us not to fool ourselves, even at the price of bitterness. It is better to be sad than to be stupid.

In the end, criticism and humor save the revolutionaries from the excesses of a solemn authoritarianism. Azuela gave us the weapons of criticism, while the Revolution itself provided us with the weapons of humor. There is an inherent humor in a revolution whose anthem, "La cucaracha," mocks President Huerta, calling him a cockroach who can't walk straight because he's got no marijuana to smoke.

5. Martín Luis Guzmán: A Match in the Night

Demetrio Macías, the hero of *The Underdogs*, is an invisible man, one of countless anonymous souls that helped spark the Mexican Revolution and then died fighting it. The protagonist of Martín Luis Guzmán's novel *La sombra del caudillo* (Shadow of the Dictator) is another invisible man, the supreme leader whose corruption helped bring about the Revolution and who profits from it.

In Mexico we like to say that one day the Revolution dismounted from its horse and stepped into a Cadillac. Guzmán's novel portrays a political society halfway between the horse and the Cadillac. What was called the "armed phase" of the Revolution has ended: the fight against the dictatorship of Victoriano Huerta and the subsequent war between revolutionary factions: Carranza against Zapata and Villa, Obregón against Carranza, Huerta's faction against Obregón. The consolidation of the Obregón-Calles regime after 1921 did not prevent the revolts of ambitious or dissatisfied military officers like Francisco Serrano, Pablo González, and Arnulfo R. Gómez.

With one foot in the stirrup and the other on the gas pedal, Guzman's tyrant is always, as the title indicates, in the shadows. His power is manifest in the characters who act, whether for him or against him, also in his shadow. The dictator manipulates, frustrates, lays traps, foments rivalries, in the end obliging the opposition to act publicly, showing themselves in the light of day as targets, while the dictator, like any puppeteer, operates from the shadows. Outside the shadow, the dictator implies, there is no safety. In broad daylight there is a wall and a firing squad. Or worse: there is the vicious hunting down of the opposition forces, like animals.

Guzmán portrays a political power that is still insecure, moving from change to permanence, from "the hubbub" to "the institution." Calles did not tolerate the opposition, and ordered his enemies to be killed. But he also absorbed the opposition, creating a party of parties that would add factions in favor of a single, presidential, centralist power: *el Partido Nacional Revolucionario* (PNR). And in the end, and eternally, *el Partido Revolucionario Institucional* (PRI), which would govern Mexico for seven decades.

In *La sombra del caudillo* this initial transition is baptized in a blood bath of violence and betrayal, virtues contrasted by Guzmán's limpid prose. Together with Alfonso Reyes, Guzmán had written film criticism in Madrid under the pseudonym "Fósforo," ("Match")[3] and this experience shows in the eminently clear Spanish prose style of his books, *La sombra del caudillo*, and *The Eagle and the Serpent* (both from 1928). It is as if the opacity of their themes required the luminosity of his prose. His work demonstrates a notable visual perception which, nevertheless, in its very *perfection* gives these works an academic dimension. Guzmán's diaphanous prose is the crown on the head of the turbulent histories he recounts. There is nothing else, no contradiction between form and depth, because such dark matter could only be written in this luminous way. The apparent contradiction is overcome by the prioritization of style. Guzmán aspires, classically, to reconcile form and depth. He writes—and very well—to

---

3 *Fósforo*: a match; in Mexico, a coffee laced with brandy; in Central America, a hothead.

achieve a kind of linguistic timelessness.

A change of direction was necessary, to explore new forms for old themes and new themes for old forms, to transcend history in order to reencounter history with previously unseen weapons of imagination and language. The universal form of the national theme had to be found. Society had to be understood beyond what society is, what it imagines, and how we imagine society to be.

6. Agustín Yáñez and the Future of the Past

Al filo del agua (At the Water's Edge, 1947) by Agustín Yáñez signals the end of the so-called "Novel of the Revolution" narrating, without paradox, the beginning of the Revolution. Yáñez breaks with the habitual styles of realism (Azuela, Guzmán, Muñoz) introducing, from the outset, a plundered chorus of verbal adornments. The author calls it a "preparatory act" and its voice is that of a chorus whose first, celebrated declaration is: "a village of women in mourning" followed by—still the chorus speaking—"village without fiestas . . . dry village, without trees or gardens . . . town in the sun, bone dry."

A choral novel from the start, *Al filo del agua* establishes its internal continuity by using the tragic chorus as an introductory device. This chorus is, traditionally, a liturgy which precedes and represents the tragic action, and which can be as varied and dissimilar from the choral voice as necessary, but without it the action itself cannot occur. This is vital for an understanding of both the newness and the importance of *Al filo del agua*. Before Yáñez, the Mexican novel (the novels of Azuela and Guzmán) had narrated events in a direct and chronological way, as the norms of realism demanded. Yáñez presents, not a "new" realism but rather a rupture of what is real: the novel foresees the historical event but subjects it to the very thing which preceded it: ignorance of things to come. Yáñez thus achieves a newness in our literature. He reveals to us the secret of the unknown.

The great chorus which begins *Al filo del agua*—the preparatory act—would seem to be the calm before the storm. A deceptive calm. The choral stasis contains all that is yet to come: the action, which ceases being a temporal succession in order to become, through the art of the chorus, a simultaneity of times. Yáñez's art consists of telling us what history confirms. Between 1909 to 1910: the looming revolution has begun—in such a way that history is unaware. This is, in effect, what happens: history has no crystal ball to predict the future; history has no other mirror than the past; but the past evoked by a novel is unknown as such because it is pure present narrative.

The chorus of *Al filo del agua* is, thus, falsely static. It contains the action yet to come, yet "the action" in this work occurs not only *outside* but also *within* the characters. Outside, there is a village, as the priest Don Dionisio murmurs, "in the hands of God." Rituals are performed predictably and emptily. Lives unfold: sin, pardon, sorrow, death, all dictated by the mortifying calendars which forbid fiestas.

Yáñez appeals to modern narrative techniques to get inside the mute, afflicted minds of the "town of women in mourning." The interior monologue here serves a double purpose. It breaks the silence of a doomed town and gives voice to a silent people. Desire, guilt, fear, and silence acquire a strange sonority, moving from internal monologue to rebellion against the silence. They break superstitions just as the howling dog disrupts prayers, denies the centuries-old obedience, and watches those who try to leave, believing that escape from the "town of mourning women" is possible. Workers from the North arrive. Victoria, "who stirs up the neighbors" departs and returns. The country rises up and the tranquility is shattered. In the end the revolutionaries arrive and the only one who remains in the town is Gabriel, the bell ringer, named for the archangel, who has celebrated so many occasions and emotions, silent loves, and that eternal secret of the unknown. Gabriel also departs. Don Dioniso winds up exhausted. Religion without festivity has been conquered by the fiesta of the revolution. Agustín Yáñez thus conquers the linearity of history through the diversity of literary voices.

7. Juan Rulfo: End and Beginning

Emerging from "the hegemony of one, unique and unifying language"—that of the Spanish Counter-Reformation—which for three centuries blocked the importation, writing, printing, or circulation of novels, our first national fiction coincides with the triumph of the battles for independence: it is *The Mangy Parrot: The Life and Times of Periquillo Sarniento* by José Fernández de Lizardi, in 1816, which inaugurates the Spanish-American novel, celebrating the city and the contradictions of the city. But in 1816 we were still not prepared to plumb the depths of Lizardi's conflictive discovery and his hero Pedro Sarmiento, who is neither native nor Spanish, but mestizo; neither dogmatic Catholic nor Romantic liberal, but both things.

We had to pass through a great deal of Romanticism, Realism, Naturalism, and Psychologism, before Pedro Sarmiento would lend his hand to Pedro Páramo.

But the Mexican novel is only a chapter in the greater literary enterprise of the Spanish language, to which we, *nos-otros* ("us-others"), and you, *ustedes*, all belong, and this is a literature born of the myths of indigenous cultures, from the epics of the Conquest and the utopias of the Renaissance. All together we emerged from this common ground—this *terra nostra*—we were nourished by it, we forgot it, we rediscovered it, and we let it fly away in the force of a recovered language, which was first that of our great shining poets, Rubén Darío and Pablo Neruda, Leopoldo Lugones and Luis Palés Matos, César Vallejo and Gabriela Mistral. Thanks to them, we novelists had a language with which to work on the unfinished task of the Counterconquest of Spanish America.

This Counterconquest passes through a chapter of national identity perfectly represented by the novel of the Mexican Revolution: the chronicle of Martín Luis Guzmán; the enormous comedy of Mariano Azuela—an account that goes from *Andrés Pérez, Maderista* to *El camarada Pantoja* (Comrade Pantoja), by way of the renowned *The Underdogs*—Rafael Muñoz's dramatic anecdotes of Pancho Villa; the acidic Cristero writings of Guadalupe de Anda; and the genre's formal renovation by Agustín Yáñez, all of which permit us, as Mexicans, to discover ourselves. There is no self-knowledge without self-criticism.

Juan Rulfo engages this whole tradition. Stripping it bare, he plucks out all the spines from the cactus and nails them like a rosary into our breast, he brings down the highest cross from the mountain and shows us that it is a dead tree from whose boughs, nevertheless, hang the sombre, golden fruits of the word.

Within these pages I've called Bernal Díaz our first novelist: the author of a faltering epic, uncertain of his material, of its affects and of the memory, the sole instrument upon which Bernal, as much as Proust, relies. Juan Rulfo is a conclusive novelist, not only in the sense that, with *Pedro Páramo*, he concludes, consecrates, and assimilates various traditional genres of Mexican literature—the rural novel, the novel of the Revolution—but Rulfo also initiates an alternate narrative modernity in which he is, simultaneously, agonist and protagonist.

To imagine America, to relate the story of the New World, not only as an expansion but as history. To say that the world remains unfinished because it is *not only* a limited space, but rather a time without limit. The creation of this American *chronotopia*—time and space—has been the very province of Spanish language narrative in our hemisphere. *The transformation of space into time*: transformation of the jungle in *The Vortex* into the story of *The Lost Steps* and *One Hundred Years of Solitude*. It is the time of the space that contains all things in *The Aleph* and the space of urban time in *Hopscotch*; virgin nature in Rómulo Gallegos, the reflected book and library of Jorge Luis Borges, the aural and impassable city of Luis Rafael Sánchez. For Juan Rulfo, the American chronotopia, the meeting of time and space, is neither river nor jungle, neither city nor mirror: it is a tomb. And there, from the grave, Juan Rulfo actively regenerates and contemporizes the categories of our American foundation: myth and epic.

Juan Rulfo's novel, *Pedro Páramo*, is presented ritually with a classic element of the myth: the search for the father. Juan Preciado, the son of Pedro Páramo, arrives in Comala like Telemachus searching for Odysseus. He is guided by a muleteer named Abundio, who represents Charon, and the River Styx of their crossing is a river of dust. Abundio reveals himself as the son of Pedro Páramo then abandons Juan Preciado at the gates of the hell that is Comala. Juan Preciado takes up the Orphic myth: he will sing and tell his tale while he descends into hell, on the condition that he not look back. He is guided by the voice of his mother, Doloritas, the humiliated Penelope to Pedro Páramo's muddy Odysseus. But that voice becomes increasingly tenuous: Orpheus cannot look back and this time he does not recognize Eurydice. Nor does he find her in the succession of women who supplant the mother, and who seem more like a series of Virgils in skirts: Eduviges, Damiana, and *la Cuarraca* Dorotea with her muffler rolled up like a baby, pretending it is her child.

They all introduce Juan Preciado to Pedro Páramo's past: an adjacent, continuous past like the one imagined by Coleridge: not behind, but rather to the side, beyond that door, when you open that window. Thus when Juan meets with Eduviges in her tiny hovel in Comala, there is the boy Pedro Páramo, in the outhouse, remembering a certain Susana. We don't know that he is dead; we suppose that he is a boy dreaming of the woman who will be his great love.

Eduviges stays with the young Juan throughout the story of the young Pedro: she reveals to him that she was going to be his mother and she hears the horse of Miguel, another son of Pedro Páramo, who is coming to relate to us his own death. But alongside the story of this death, another is present: the death of the father of Pedro Páramo. On page twenty-seven, Eduviges asks Juan:

> "Have you ever heard the groans of a dying man?"
>
> "No, Doña Eduviges."
>
> "Better for you" [answers the old woman].

These words return on page thirty-six: "Better for you, child. Better for you."

But between Eduviges's two dialogues which represent the same dialogue in the same instant—words identical to themselves and their time, mirror words—Pedro Páramo's father has died, and Pedro Páramo's son Miguel has died, Father Rentería has refused to bless Miguel's body, and Miguel's ghost has visited his lover Ana, the priest's niece who is suffering pangs of conscience that keep her from sleeping. And more: the very woman speaking, Eduviges Dyada, in the act of speaking, and while all this occurs contiguously, is revealed to be a soul in purgatory, and Juan Preciado is recognized by his new substitute mother, the nursemaid Damiana Cisneros.

We thus have two principal orders of literary structure in *Pedro Páramo*: a given reality and the shifting of that reality. The segments of reality I have mentioned—Rentería refuses to bury Miguel, the child Pedro dreams of Susana while he sits inside the outhouse, Pedro's father dies, Juan Preciado comes to Comala, Eduviges disappears and Damiana takes her place—only have reality in the narrative movement, in how they make contact with what follows or precedes them, in the juxtaposition of each segment's time with the times of the other segments. When the words—*better for you child, better for you*—return nine pages after first being pronounced, we understand that those words are not separated by time: they are instantaneous and only instantaneous; nothing has occurred between page twenty-seven and page thirty-six. Or rather: what has occurred has occurred simultaneously. Which is to say, it has occurred in the eternal present of myth.

The second time that I read *Pedro Páramo* and I understood that the novel's times are simultaneous, I began to retroactively accumulate and juxtapose this contiguity of the moments I was getting to know. Rulfo invites us to enter various times which, even if they are finally resolved in myth, in their narrative origin resist mythification. As in Sterne's *Tristram Shandy*, or Eliot's *Four Quartets*—to consider a broader range of works—the temporal, epic sequence, which at least since Lessing is attributed to literature, is in the end replaced by a simultaneous, not successive, presence in the mental space, which is in this case a mythic space.

Pedro Páramo's story, as recounted to Juan by his successive mothers, is a "realistic," linear, political and psychological story. Pedro Páramo is the Jaliscan version of the patrimonial tyrant whose portrait is evoked in the novels of Valle Inclán, Gallegos, and Asturias: the mini-Caesar who manipulates all the political forces but at the same time must make concessions to them; a kind of agrarian Machiavellian Prince.

A descendant of the conquistadors of New Galicia, a ferocious emulator of Nuño de Guzmán, Pedro Páramo accumulates all of Machiavelli's great lessons, save one. Like the Florentine, the Jaliscan knows that a wise prince must feed some of the animosities against him, with the goal of enhancing his greatness when he conquers them; he knows that it is far safer to be feared than to be loved. In the amusing segments in which Rulfo narrates Pedro Páramo's dealings with the revolutionary forces, the tyrant of Comala follows Machiavelli's advice and Cortés's example: unite the less powerful enemies of your powerful enemy; then destroy them all, then usurp the places of all, friends and enemies, and never loosen your grip on them. Machiavelli, Cortés, Pedro Páramo: it is important to speak virtuously but also possess a mind capable of changing rapidly. Pedro Páramo, the Conquistador, the Prince: he sows destruction among his enemies in one fell swoop; he distributes his benefits one by one.

Nevertheless, this hero of New World patrimonial Machiavellianism, lord of the dagger and the gallows, master of lives and haciendas, owner of a desire that prevails over the destiny of others and appropriates for his private legacy everything that belongs to the public trust, this armed prophet of unpunished caprice and cruelty, surrounded by his bands of bloody overseers, did not learn Machiavelli's other lesson, which is that it is not enough to impose one's will. One must avoid the vagaries of luck; the Prince who depends on Lady Luck will be ruined by her.

Pedro Páramo is not Cortés, nor is he the Machiavellian Prince because he is ultimately only a fictional character. He has a secret flaw, a loophole through which he uselessly bleeds the prescriptions of power. Pedro Páramo's destiny is a woman, Susana San Juan, of whom he dreamed when he was a boy, in the outhouse, with whom he flew kites and swam in the river, when he was a boy.

What is Susana San Juan's role in the novel? If we return from Eduviges Dyada's repeated phrase to the reason for the novel's technique, and if we connect it to the tremendous political and social acidity of the rural tyrant that Rulfo ends up offering us, her first function is to be dreamed by a boy and to open, in that boy who will grow up to become the tyrant Páramo, the psychological window that will end up destroying him. If, by the end of the novel, Pedro Páramo crumbles like a pile of stones, it is because the fissure in his soul was opened by his childhood dream of Susana: through the dream, Pedro was pulled towards his political, Machiavellian, patrimonial history before living it, before being it. Nevertheless, as a child he entered the myth, and the simultaneity of times that rule the world of his novel. That simultaneous time will be his downfall because, in order to be the total tyrant, Pedro Páramo could not admit wounds in his logical, successive, linear time: the future-making time of epic power.

Once this window into his soul is opened by Susana San Juan, Pedro Páramo is pulled out of his purely "historical," political, and Machiavellian history, in the very same moment in which he is living it. His passion for Susana San Juan places Pedro on the margin of a mythic reality that does not deny historical reality, but instead brings to it contrasting tones of color and relief. At times Rulfo resembles Goya and Orozco, the masters of black and white, who, in fact, allow us to *better* understand historical truth.

Giambattista Vico, who first located the origin of society in language and the origin of language in mythic development, saw in myths the "imaginative universality" of the origins of humanity: the imagination of *ab-original* peoples. Rulfo's voice reaches down to this root. It is, at the same time, silence and language; and, in order not to sacrifice, even for a moment, its two components, it is, above all, rumor. In *Structural Anthropology*, Claude Lévi-Strauss tells us that the function of myths consists of incorporating and exhibiting the oppositions present in the structure of the society in which the myth is born. The myth is the manner by which a society understands and ignores its own structure; it reveals a presence, but also a shortcoming. This is due to the fact that myth assimilates cultural and social events: the biological fact of giving birth becomes, mythically, a social event. The play between sexual reality and erotic theatricality in Dolores Preciado, Eduviges Dyada, Damiana Cisneros and *la Cuarraca* Dorotea around the "child" narrator Juan Preciado, is part of this circulation between biology and society across the myth-bridge.

There is more: Lévi-Strauss indicates that each myth reflects not only its own poetics (meaning the manner in which the myth is retold in a determined moment or society) but rather that it also makes room for all the unspoken variants, of which this particular version is only one variant more. In *Morphology of the Folktale*, Vladimir Propp distinguishes some twenty-odd functions of Russian fairy tales. The order of the elements themselves may vary; there is no story that does not include, in one form or another, some various combination of them. Are there new myths, born out of new circumstances? Harry Levin reminds us that Emerson called for an industrial mythology for Manchester, and Dickens delivered it. Trotsky asked for a revolutionary art that would be capable of reflecting all the contradictions of the revolutionary social system, but Stalin denied it to him. Today's audience for soap operas and light or "entertaining" novels is unaware that it is actually watching and reading combinations of the most ancient myths. Nevertheless, only the criticism of underdevelopment continues to support the Romantic myth of originality, precisely because our societies have yet to fulfill the sentimental promises of the nineteenth century's middle classes. Every great writer, every great critic, every great reader knows that no book is an orphan: there is no text that does not descend from other texts.

Myth explains this mimetic and genealogical reality of literature: as Lévi-Strauss explains, no myth has a single definitive version, of which all others would be copies or distortions. Every version of the truth belongs to myth. Which is to say, each version of myth is part of the myth and this is its power. The same myth—Oedipus, for example—can be told anonymously, or by Socrates, Shakespeare, Racine, Hölderlin, Freud, Cocteau, Pasolini, and in a thousand dreams and fairy tales. The variations reflect the power of myth. By contrast, try to retell a novel by Sidney Sheldon or Jackie Collins more than once.

As it contains all these aspects, the myth also establishes multiple relationships with society's invisible or unspoken language. In this sense, the myth is the expression of the potential language of the society in which it is manifested. Given that language and myth are responses to primal terror in the face of imminent natural catastrophe, this is equally true in the ancient worlds of the Mediterranean and Meso-America. We first speak in order to create a myth that permits us to comprehend the world, and myth requires a language in order to manifest itself. Myth and language appear at the same time, and myths, writes Vico, are the point of ingress into the vast imagination of the first men. The language of myth allows us to hear the mental voices of the first men: gods, family, heroes, authority, sacrifices, laws, conquest, bravery, fame, land, love, life and death: these are the primary themes of the myth, and the gods are the *first* actors of myth. Man remembers the stories of the gods and, before dying, communicates them to his children and family.

But man abandons his home, he travels to Troy, obliging the gods to accompany him; he fights, transforms the myth into epic and epic battle—the historical struggle—he discovers his personal rift, his heroic flaw: from being an epic hero, he becomes a tragic hero. He returns home, he communicates the tragedy to the city, and the city, in its catharsis, joins the sorrow of the fallen hero and reestablishes, in its sympathy, the values of the community.

This is the circle of fire of Mediterranean antiquity—Myth, Epic, and Tragedy—excluded first by Christianity and later by modern secularity because both believe in future redemption, in the eternal life or in a secular utopia, in the city of god or in the city of man. The western novel does not return to tragedy: it rests on the preceding epic, degrading it and parodying it (*Don Quixote*) but it experiences an intense nostalgia for the myth which is the origin of the material of which literature is made: *language*.

Pedro Páramo is no exception to this rule: it confirms it with incomparable brilliance, telling the epic story of the protagonist, but this story is violated by the mythic history of the language. To deny myth would be to deny language. This is the true drama of Rulfo's novel. Language is in the origin of myth, myth is in the origin of language: both are a response to the terrifying silence of the world before man: the mute universe into which the narrator of Alejandro Carpentier's *The Lost Steps* travels, stopping himself at the edge of the abyss.

For these reasons, it is significant that at the very center of *Pedro Páramo* we hear the vast silence of an approaching storm—and this silence is broken by the lowing of cattle. Fulgor Sedano, the tyrant's dangerous right-hand man, orders the cowboys to move Enmedio's herd beyond what was then Estagua, and to run the herd at Estagua up to the hills at Vilmayo: "'And hurry,' he concluded, 'the rains are upon us!'"

Hardly has the last man set out for the rainy fields, when the tyrant's pampered son, Miguel Páramo, enters the scene at full gallop. He slides off his horse right under Fulgor's nose, and lets the animal wander to its stall. "Where you coming from at this hour, kid?" Sedano asks him. "I been milking" Miguel answers, and then in the kitchen, while Damiana is cooking his eggs, he tells her that he's come "from over yonder, visiting some of the mothers around here." And he asks her, while she cooks his food, to also give some morsels to a woman "who's right outside the door," with a ball of wool rolled up in her shawl, "saying that it's her baby boy. Seems like she had some bad luck in times past; but, she never tells, and nobody knows what happened to her. She lives by begging."

The silence is broken by the voices that we don't understand, the mute voices of the lowing herd, of the milk cow, of the woman giving birth, of the child that is born, of the inanimate ball of wool that a beggar woman rolls up in her muffler.

This silence is that of the very etymology of the word "myth": *mu*, Erich Kahler tells us, is the root of myth, the imitation of the eternal sound: cows, thunder, groaning, muttering, murmuring, mumbling, silence. From the same root comes the Greek word *muein*: to close, to shut one's eyes: from which the words *mystery* and *mystic* are derived.

As many know, *Pedro Páramo* was originally called *Los murmul-*

los (Murmurs), and Juan Preciado, as he radically violates the norms of his own narrative presentation in order to enter the dead world of Comala, says:

> "The murmurs killed me."

The silence killed him. Mystery killed him. Death killed him. He was killed by the myth of death. Juan Preciado enters Comala and, in doing so, enters the myth incarnating the linguistic process described by Kahler, which consists of giving, in a word, the opposite meaning: like the Latin *mutus*, "mute," becomes the French *mot*, "word," the onomatopoeic *mu*. The inarticulate sound, the groan, becomes *mythos*, the very definition of the word.

Pedro Páramo is an extraordinary novel because, among other things, as a mythic novel, it is self-generating, in the same way that myth is verbally generated: from the silence of nothing to the identification with the word, from *mu* to *mythos* and within the collective process which is indispensable to the mythic gestation, which is never an individual development. As Hegel explains, the act is the epic. The character Pedro Páramo is an epic character, but his novel, which bears his name, is a myth that strips that character of his epic quality.

When Juan Preciado is conquered by the murmurs, the narration ceases speaking in first person and assumes a collective third person: from there onward, it is the *nosotros* —the "we"—which speaks, which reclaims the *mythos* of the work.

In Antiquity, the myth nourishes both epic and tragedy, meaning that it precedes them in time, as well as in language, given that myth historically illustrates the movement from silence—*mutus*—to the word—*mythos*.

Myth's precedence in time, as well as its collective nature, are both explained by Carl Jung when he tells us in *The Archetypes and the Collective Unconscious* that myths are the original revelations of the preconscious psyche, involuntary declarations about disquieting psychic events. Jung also stresses that myths possess a vital meaning. They not only represent life: they *are* the psychic life of the tribe, which immediately decays or shatters to pieces when it loses its mythological inheritance, like a man who has lost his soul.

I recall two modern narratives which, in an exemplary way, assume this vital collective function, by virtue of which the myth is not invented, but rather lived by all people: William Faulkner's story, "A Rose for Emily," and Juan Rulfo's novel *Pedro Páramo*. In these two tales, myth is time's collective incarnation, the inheritance of everything which must be maintained, pathetically, by all people, because as Vico wrote, *we* make history, *we* create time, and if this is true, if history is the work of *our* will and desire, and not the whim of the gods or simply the course of nature, then it is our obligation to maintain history: to maintain the memory of time. It is part of our duty in life: to be able to sustain ourselves.

Pedro Páramo also contains its happy *past*: Comala as described by the disembodied voice of Doloritas, the mother's murmur: "A town that smells like spilled honey." But this town with its luxuriant foliage which guards our memories like a strongbox that can only be recovered in memory; it is López Velarde's "subverted Eden," a historical creation of memory but also a myth created by memory.

But, who in Comala can remember, who can create history or myth from memory? In other words, who has the right to language in Comala? Who possesses it? Who does not? In a brilliant study of *Pedro Páramo*, Stephen Boldy, critic and Dean of Emmanuel College, Cambridge, responds that the father is the master of the language; those dispossessed of the language are the others, those who lack paternal authority.

The lush, shady town of Comala has been destroyed by a man who refuses collective responsibility and lives in the isolated world of individual physical power, material strength, and Machiavellian strategies which are needed to oppress and objectify the people. How does this occur? Why does Juan Preciado come to this dead town in search of his father?

This is the story behind the epic: Pedro Páramo loves Susana San Juan, a woman who does not belong to the epic sphere. Instead, she belongs to the mythic world of madness, infancy, eroticism, and death. How can he possess this woman? How can he reach her?

Pedro Páramo is used to possessing everything he desires. He forms part of a world where the master of the verbal sphere is the master of all those who speak, like the emperor Moctezuma, who bore the title *Tlatoani*, the "Lord of the Great Voice," the monopolist of language. A character from Rulfo's story "Talpa" has to shout while he prays, "only" to know that he is praying and, perhaps, to believe that

God or the Tlatoani can hear him. Pedro Páramo is the father that dominates Rulfo's novel. He is the Tlatoani.

Michel Foucault has written that the father is the fundamental element of symbolization in each individual's life. And his function—the most powerful of all functions—is *to pronounce* the law and unite the law with language. The essential oration, of course, is invoked "in the name of the Father," and what the father does, in our name and in his, is to separate us from our mother so that incest does not occur. He does this by naming us: he gives his name and, by extension, as Professor Boldy reminds us, his being.

To name and *to exist*, for the *father*, are the same thing, and in *Pedro Páramo* the tyrant's power is expressed in these terms when Pedro says to Fulgor: "From now on, we are going to make the law." The application of this law demands the negation of others: in Spanish *los demás*, or *los de-más*, meaning the extra ones, those who *are not* Pedro Páramo: "Those people don't exist."

But he—the Father, the Lord—exists only in the measure of those who fear him, and as they fear him, they recognize him and hate him, but they need him in order to have a name, a law, and a voice. Comala has died because the Father decided to fold his arms and let the town starve to death. "And so it did."

His pretext is that Comala turned Susana San Juan's death into a carnival. The truth is different: Pedro Páramo could not possess the woman he loved because he could not objectify her within his own verbal sphere. Because Pedro Páramo condemns Comala to silence, he condemns it to death—he condemns it to the point of origin, before language—but Comala, Susana and, finally, Juan Preciado, see what Pedro Páramo ignores: death is found in the origin, it begins with death, life is the child of death, and language proceeds from silence.

Pedro Páramo believes he condemns a town and its people to death because death for him is in the future, death is the work of Pedro Páramo's hand, the same as silence. For all others—for that chorus of old nursemaids and abandoned young women, for witches, beggars, and their ghostly pupils, for the children of Pedro Páramo, Miguel, Abundio, and, finally, Juan Preciado—the first thing that we must remember is death: our origin, and silence: *Mu*, myth, and groan, the first word born of the emptiness and terror of death and silence. For them all, death is in the origin, it begins with death, and perhaps this is what finally unites Juan Preciado and Susana San Juan, Pedro Páramo's son and his beloved: the murmurs, the incipient language, born of silence and death.

Pedro Páramo's dilemma is how to approach Susana. The problem his children have, including Juan Preciado, is how to approach Pedro Páramo; this is also a problem of the verbal sphere. What can bring us closer to the father? The very *language* that the father first tried to give us and then take away from us: language, which is the father's power but, when he loses it, his impotence.

Rulfo opts for something better than vengeance against the father: he adds it to an effort to maintain language by means of myth, and Rulfo's myth is the myth of death through the search for the father and language.

Pedro Páramo is a certain kind of Telemachia, the saga of the search for, and reunion with, the father, but as the father is dead — he was murdered by one of his children, the muleteer Abundio — searching for him and rejoining him is to search for death and be reunited with it. This novel is the story of Juan Preciado's entrance to the kingdom of death, not because he found his own death, but because death found him. It made itself part of his upbringing, it taught him how to speak and he identified death as a voice, or rather, death as a verbal longing, for a word like the one which Xavier Villaurrutia accurately called nostalgia for death.

Juan Preciado says that the murmurs killed him: meaning, the words of silence. "My head became filled with sounds and voices. Yes, with voices. And there, where the air was thin, you could hear them better. They stayed inside you, heavy, worrisome." Death is that reality which with deeper gravity, trembling, and tenderness demands language as proof of its existence. Myths have always been told alongside tombs: Rulfo goes further: he goes inside the tombs, side by side, in dialogue with the dead.

"I feel as if someone were walking above us."

"Stop being scared now . . . You must think of pleasant things because we are going to be buried for a long time."

The land of the dead is Juan Rulfo's kingdom, and in it this author creates and encounters his narrative archetype, one intimately linked to the dualities of father and mother, silence and voice.

For Jung, the archetype reflects the collective unconsciousness, and is manifested in two movements: flowing from the mother, the matrix which gives it shape, and from the father, the bearer of the archetype, its *mitóforos* (mythophors). From this window we can see Rulfo's novel as a visit to the land of the dead which makes use of the ultimate mythical movement, the regression to the uterus, to the mother that is recipient of the myth, fertilized by the myth: Doloritas and the surrogate mothers, Eduviges, Damiana, Dorotea.

In what direction do the mothers, along with Juan Preciado, send us? Towards Pedro Páramo, the bearer of the myth, the father of the tribe, the cursed ancestor, the founder of the New World, the raper of mothers, the father of every last one of *los hijos de la chingada*, the children of Malinche, the violated woman, the sons of Mexico. This father, however, refuses to carry the myth, and in doing so he betrays his children and descendants; he cannot take charge of "the words of the tribe."

As Jung points out in *Symbols of Transformation*, the myth is what is always believed, everywhere and by everyone, for which reason the man who believes that he can live outside of the myth, or without it, is an exception. He is like a rootless being, lacking a connection to the past, or the ancestral life that lives on inside of him, which includes contemporary human society.

Like Pedro Páramo in his last years, old and immobile in a wicker chair next to the big door at Media Luna, waiting for Susana San Juan (like Heathcliff waited for Catherine Earnshaw in *Wuthering Heights*), but radically separated from her because Susana belongs to the mythic world of madness, infancy, eroticism, and death, while Pedro belongs to the historic world of power, the physical conquest of things, and the Machiavellian strategy for subjugating and objectifying people.

This man outside of myth, says Jung, does not live in a house like other men, rather he lives his own peculiar life, sunk in the subjective mania of his own making, which he considers a newly discovered truth. Pedro Páramo's newly discovered truth is death, his desire to be reunited with Susana. "Not long now. Not long. This is my death. I'm going that way. I'm going now."

He dies once he has abandoned Comala, because Comala turned

the death of Susana San Juan into a carnival. "I will fold my arms and Comala will starve to death." And so he did. As he condemns Comala to death from his wicker chair where he awaits his own, Pedro Páramo appears like that man without myth of whom Jung speaks: for all that he has suffered and for all that he has given, he is a newcomer to the kingdom of death, which is part of the psyche's reality.

The father's power is damaged because he does not believe in the myth—he does not believe in language—and when he discovers them, it is in the dream of a woman who will not share his dream—which is to say, his myth—with him. Susana San Juan, by contrast, is the protagonist of various intertwining myths: the myth of incest, with her father Bartolomé, and the myth of the idyllic couple, with her lover Florencio. But, in the end, she is the bearer of the myth that contains all the others: the myth of the eternal presence of death. In order to possess his daughter, Bartolomé, the other father, kills Florencio.

Deprived of her lover, Susana decides to deprive her father as well. Pedro Páramo murders Bartolomé San Juan in order to recover Susana, his beloved, thirty years later, but in doing so he loses her, because for Susana the loss of her father signifies precisely what the father's presence signifies for the town of Comala: *law: protection: language*.

Upon losing her father, Susana loses law, protection, and language: she sinks down into silence, she goes mad, and her only communication is transmitted via her own closed oral monologue. She first denies her own father, then denies her religious father, Padre Rentería, and finally denies God the Father. How then can Susana San Juan ever recognize the usurper of paternal authority, Pedro Páramo, if she has ceased to recognize God, the fountain of patriarchal authority?

This is the reality that Pedro Páramo cannot penetrate or possess; he cannot even be recognized by Susana because he can never enter her verbal universe, a world of silence which Pedro's power over the word cannot penetrate: "But which was the world of Susana San Juan? That was one of the things that Pedro Páramo never managed to learn." For once, the all-powerful patriarch, the father, the conquistador, is excluded. In the same way that he crosses his arms and lets Comala starve to death: Susana San Juan escapes from him, even in death, through death itself.

Buried alive, an inhabitant of a world that gnashes its teeth, im-

prisoned in a "sepulcher of bedsheets," Susana makes no distinction
between what Pedro Páramo would call life and what he would call
death: if her "mouth is filled with dirt" it is, at the same time, because
"my mouth is filled with you, with your mouth, Florencio."

Susana San Juan loves a dead man: a dead woman loves a dead
man. And this is the door by which Susana escapes Pedro Páramo's
dominion. Because although the tyrant has dominions, she has demons. Mad love, André Breton would call it; Pedro Páramo's mad
love for Susana San Juan and Susana San Juan's mad love for Florencio. But no mad love for Susana and Pedro.

In climate and mood, *Pedro Páramo* is similar to Emily Brontë's
Wuthering Heights. It is interesting to compare them because a foolish battle has swirled around Rulfo's novel, a dichotomy that insists
on judging it, either as a kind of poetic writing or a kind of political writing, without understanding that the novel's tension hangs between both poles, the myth and the epic, and between two periods of
time: the time of passion and the time of interest.

This is also true in Emily Brontë's work, where Heathcliff and
Cathy belong, simultaneously and in tension, to the passional duration of the recovery of childhood's erotic paradise and the self-in-
terested duration of its social *position* and its monetary *possession*.
Georges Bataille sees in *Wuthering Heights* the story of a rupture of
a poetic unity followed by the story of a rebellion of those expelled
from the original kingdom, a rebellion of the damned possessed by
the desire to recreate paradise. By contrast, the Marxist critic Arnold
Kettle sees it as the story of a revolutionary transgression of bourgeois moral values using bourgeois weapons. By manipulating money, landed property, and dowry, Heathcliff humiliates and ruins the
Linton family. Both readings are accurate with respect to Brontë, just
as they would be to Rulfo. These are not reducible novels. The difference between the two is more intense and secret. Heathcliff and
Cathy are united by a passion which recognizes itself to be destined
for death. Heathcliff's gloomy grandeur is found in the fact that he
knows no matter how much he degrades Cathy's family by manipulating his old masters to the point of financial ruin, the time of childhood shared with Cathy—that wonderful instantaneousness—will
not return; Cathy also knows it and for that reason, because she *is*
Heathcliff, she moves forward to the only possible resemblance with

the lost land of the past moment in time; the land of death. Cathy dies in order to tell Heathcliff: this is our true home; come here and be reunited with me.

Susana San Juan makes this journey alone, and for that reason her destiny is more terrible than Catherine Earnshaw's. With Pedro Páramo she shares neither childhood, nor eroticism, nor passion, nor interest. Pedro Páramo loves a woman who is radically separated from him, a ghost who, like Cathy with respect to Heathcliff in *Wuthering Heights*, precedes him to the grave but only because Susana was already dead and Pedro did not know it. Nevertheless, Pedro loved her. Pedro dreamed of her. And because he dreamed of her and loved her he is a vulnerable, fragile being, deserving of love, and not the evil tyrant, the Mexican movie villain, that he could have been. Pedro owes his wound to Susana; Susana invites him to recognize himself in death.

Death, says Bataille about *Wuthering Heights*, is our origin in disguise. Given that the return to the instantaneous time of childhood is impossible, mad love can only be consummated in the eternal, static time of death: an endless present instant. The absolute end embraces all the possibilities of the past, present, and future. Infancy and death are the signs of this endless instant. And being instantaneous, they alone have the power to reject devious, calculating self-interest.

Retrospectively, the totality of *Pedro Páramo* happens in death. Hence the parallel and contiguous structure of the stories; each one of them is like a tomb; rather, it *is* a tomb, damp, crumbling, contiguous to all the others. Here, his earthly education completed, his education of death and terror, perhaps Juan Preciado stretches out his hand and finds, yes, he finally finds his own passion, his own love, his own recognition. Perhaps Juan Preciado, in the cemetery of Comala, lying next to her, with her, knows and loves Susana San Juan and is loved by her, like her father wanted to be but could not. And perhaps that is why Juan Preciado becomes a ghost: to know and love Susana San Juan in the grave. To penetrate in death the woman that his father could not possess. To experience eroticism as an affirmation of life until death.

Reading Juan Rulfo is like remembering our own death. Thanks to the novelist, we have been present at our death, which thus forms part of our memory and makes us better prepared to understand that the duality between life *and* death does not exist, nor the option of life *or* death, but rather that death *is part of* life: everything *is* life.

Upon situating death in life, in the present and, simultaneously, at the point of origin, Rulfo makes a powerful contribution to creating a modern Latin American novel, one that is open and inconclusive, which refuses an ending — a technical, inclusive ending — which would deprive it of its last vestige of hope, its grave, its Eros and Thanatos.

Literally, each word should be final. But this is only its appearance: in fact, there is never a last word, because the novel exists thanks to a plurality of truths: the novel's truth is always relative. Its home, writes Mikhail Bakhtin, is individual conscience, which is, by definition, partial. Its glory, recalls Milan Kundera, is that of being the transitory paradise in which each and every one of us has the right to speak and be heard.

The novel is the instrument of dialogue in this deep sense: not only dialogue between characters, as understood by social and psychological realism, but rather the dialogue between genres, between social forces, between languages, and between historical times, contiguous or separated, which is how it was understood by those innovative writers who helped to create and advance the novel: Cervantes, Sterne, and Diderot yesterday; and in our time Joyce, Kafka, Woolf, Broch, and Faulkner. And Juan Rulfo.

7. Borges: Silver from the River Plate

When I read Borges for the first time, in Buenos Aires when I was only fifteen years old, it made me feel that writing in Spanish was a greater adventure, and also a greater risk, than writing in English. The reason is that the English language possesses an uninterrupted tradition, while Spanish suffers an immense hiatus between the last great poet of Spain's Age of Gold, who was a seventeenth century Mexican nun, Sor Juana Inés de la Cruz, and the next great poet, who was a restless Nicaraguan of the late nineteenth century, Rubén Darío; and a still greater interruption between its greatest novel, the founding novel of Western literature, *Don Quixote*, and its next great novelists, Galdós and Clarín in the nineteenth century.

Borges abolished the barriers of communication between literatures. He enriched our Spanish linguistic home with all the imaginable treasuries of the Orient and the broader Western literature, and permitted us to move forward with a feeling of possessing more than what we had written, which is to say, all that we had read, from Homer to Milton to Joyce. Perhaps all of them, together with Borges, were the same blind seer.

Borges attempted a superior narrative synthesis. In his stories, literary imagination appropriated all cultural traditions in order to give us the most complete portrait of everything we are, thanks to the present memory of how much we have said. The legacy of Muslim and Jewish Spain, mutilated by monarchical absolutism and its dual legitimization based on Christian faith and purity of blood, reappear, marvelously fresh and vital, in Borges's stories. Without stories like "Averroës's Search," "The Zahir," and "The Approach to Al-Mu'tasim," I certainly would never have experienced the fraternal and temporal revelation of my own Hebrew and Arabic inheritance.

I also decided that I would never meet Borges in person. I chose to blind myself to his physical presence because I wanted to maintain, throughout my life, the pristine sensation of reading him as a writer, not as a contemporary, although we were born forty years apart. Four decades, which are nothing in literature, are a great deal in life. How would Borges age? As well as some, or as badly as others? I only wanted to read Borges in his books, to view him only through the invisibility of the written page, a blank page which would become visible and alive only when I read Borges and I became Borges . . .

And my subsequent decision was that, one day, I would confess my difficulty at having to choose only one or two facets of the most multi-faceted of writers, conscious of the fact that as I limit myself to a few aspects of his work, I will be forced to sacrifice others which, perhaps, are more important. Although we might be comforted by Jacob Bronowski's reflection on chess: the moves that we imagine mentally, and then reject, are an integral part of the game, as much as the moves that we actually carry out. I believe that this is also true in reading Borges.

Because in truth, the Borgesian repertoire of possibilities and impossibilities is so vast, that one could give not one but multiple readings of each possibility or impossibility from his canon. *Borges the writer of detective literature*, in which the true enigma is the mental work of the detective against himself, as if Poirot were to investigate Poirot, or Sherlock Holmes discovered that he himself was Dr. Moriarty. But we may simultaneously encounter *Borges the author of fantasy stories*, illuminated by his celebrated opinion that theology is a branch of fantastic literature. This, moreover, has four possible themes: the work within the work; time travel; the double; and dreams invading reality. Which leads me to a Borges divided among four:

Borges the dreamer who wakes up and realizes that he has been dreamed by another.

Borges the philosopher who creates his own personal metaphysic which never degenerates into a mere system.

Borges the poet who is incessantly astonished in the face of the mysteries of the world, but, ironically, is dedicated to inverting the mysterious (as one might a glove or a balloon), in accordance with Quevedian tradition: "Nothing astonishes me. The world has bewitched me."

Borges the author of the work within the work is the author of Pierre Menard who is the author of Don Quixote who is the author of Cervantes who is the author of Borges who is the author of . . .

The journey through time: not one, but multiple times, the garden of forking paths, "an infinite series of times, a growing, dizzying web of divergent, convergent, and parallel times. That fabric of times that approach one another, fork, are snipped off, or are simply unknown for centuries, contains *all* possibilities. In most of those times, we do not exist; in some, you exist but I do not; in others, I do and you do not, in others still, we both do."

And finally, *the double.* "Years ago," writes Borges, and perhaps I write as well, "I tried to free myself from him and I moved on from the mythologies of the slums and suburbs of the city to games with time and infinity, but those games belong to Borges now, and I shall have to conjure up other things," he writes, I write, and we write together, Borges and I, infinitely: "I am unsure which one of us is writing this page." It is true: when Borges writes this celebrated page, "Borges and I," the other Borges is another author—the third person, him—but it is also another reader—the first person, I—and the passionate product of this sometimes sacred, sometimes profane, union: You, *Lector y Elector,* the reader who chooses.

From this immensely rich genealogy of Borges as poet, dreamer, metaphysic, double, time traveler, and poet, I will now elect the humblest theme of the book, the poor relation to this princely mansion: Borges the Argentine writer, the Latin American writer, the urban Latin American writer. I neither betray nor reduce him. I am well aware that other aspects of his writing are perhaps more important than the question of knowing if, in effect, he is an Argentine writer and, being so, how, and why.

But in so far as dealing with a theme that concerned Borges himself (witness his famous lecture on "The Argentine Writer and Tradition") I would like to, in passing, more closely examine Borges today, when the most virulent lines of literary nationalism have been eliminated from the literary field of Latin America, through words that he wrote some fifty years ago: "Everything we Argentine writers do felicitously will belong to Argentine tradition."

In Argentina, surrounded by the flat, endless plains, the writer can only evoke the solitary ombú tree. Borges invents a space for it, the Aleph, where one can see, without confusion, "all the places of the world, seen from every angle." I can do the same in the Indo-Baroque chapel of Tonantzintla, without needing to write a single line. Borges must invent the garden of forking paths, where time is an infinite series of times. I can gaze forever at the Aztec calendar in the Museum of Anthropology in Mexico City until I become one with time itself—literature, however, does not provide the same experience.

And nevertheless, in spite of these noticeable differences which, *prima facie,* exempt me from imagining Tlön, Uqbar, or Orbis Tertius but which impose the imagination of absence on an Argentine writer like Borges, the two of us, Mexican and Argentine, certainly share a language, as well as a divided being: a double within each nation or, to paraphrase Disraeli, the two nations within each Latin American nation and within Latin American society as a whole, from Río Bravo to the Straits of Magellan.

Two nations, urban and agrarian, but also royal and legal. And between both, astride the royal nation and the legal nation, the city, which thus participates in both the urban and agrarian cultures. Our cities, with ever more problems in common, but trying to resolve them with a supremely varied literary imagination, from Gonzalo Celorio in Mexico to Nélida Piñón in Brazil, from José Donoso in Chile to Juan Carlos Onetti in Uruguay.

Nevertheless, let us consider that perhaps all the projects of salvation of the agrarian interior—the second nation—have proceeded from the first nation and its urban writers, from Sarmiento in Argentina, da Cunha in Brazil, and Gallegos in Venezuela. On the other hand, when such projects have emerged, as authentic alternatives, from deep within the second nation, the answer from the first, centralist nation has been bloodshed and murder, from the response to Túpac Amaru in Upper Peru in the eighteenth century to the response to Emiliano Zapata in Morelos in the twentieth century.

Let us consider, then, Borges as an urban writer, more particularly as a writer from Buenos Aires, inscribed in the tradition of Argentine literature. Between two vast solitudes—the pampas and the ocean—the silence threatens Buenos Aires and the city hurls forth its exclamation: "Please, verbalize me!" And Borges does indeed verbalize Buenos Aires in a short tale, "Death and the Compass," where, in a few pages, the author manages to deliver us to a city of dreams and death, of violence and absence, of crime and disappearance, of language and silence . . . How does he accomplish this? Borges has described death as the opportunity to rediscover all the moments of our lives and recombine them freely like dreams. We can achieve this, he adds, with the help of God, our friends, and William Shakespeare.

If the dream is what, in the end, defeats death by giving form to all the moments of life, liberated by death itself, Borges naturally employs the oneiric in order to offer us his own, most profound vision, of his city: Buenos Aires. Nevertheless, in "Death and the Compass,"

Buenos Aires is never mentioned. But—again, nevertheless—it is his greatest and most poetic vision of his own city, much more poetic than any of his stories which approach naturalism, such as "Man on Pink Corner."

Borges himself explains that "Death and the Compass" is a kind of succubus in which elements of Buenos Aires are found, but deformed by nightmare. "In spite of the story's German or Scandinavian names, it takes place in a Buenos Aires of dreams: the swerving Rue de Toulon is el Paseo de Colón." Borges thinks about the country houses in Androgué and calls them Triste-le-Roy. When the story was published, his friends told him that they found it to contain the flavor of the Buenos Aires suburbs. That flavor was there, says Borges, because he did not plan to include it, in the same way that The Koran is an Arab book although not one single camel appears in it. Borges gives himself over to the dream. In doing so, he tells us, he manages to achieve what he had been seeking in vain for years. Buenos Aires is what he had been looking for, and his first book of poems tells us *how* he had searched for it, fervently: "Fervor de Buenos Aires." But, in the end, the reality of Buenos Aires has only been made present through a dream, which is to say, through the imagination.

At a very young age, I also searched that city and, like Borges, I only found its essence in these words from "Death and the Compass": "The train halted on a silent loading platform. He got off. It was one of those deserted evenings that seem like the dawn." When I read this metaphor, it became the legend of my own relationship with Buenos Aires: the delicate and fugitive instant, as Joyce would say, the sudden spiritual reality that appears in the midst of our most normal or most memorable days. Always fragile, always passing: the epiphany. I seek refuge in the metaphor, even while I reasonably say to you that through these Argentine authors, A for Aira, B for Bianco, Bioy, and Borges—the three B's, though not the three bees—and C for Cortázar, I understand that the presence might well be a dream, the dream a fiction, and the fiction a renewable history which begins with absence.

Argentine fiction is, as a whole, the richest in Spanish America, owing, perhaps, to the clamor about verbalization that I mentioned above. But as they make such fervent demands on their language, the writers of the River Plate create a second history, equally valid, perhaps more so, than the first. This is what Jorge Luis Borges achieves in "Death and the Compass," obliging us to venture deeper and deeper into his work.

How does Borges proceed to invent a second history, converting it into a past just as indispensable as that of true history? An immediate response would be the following: the writer is not interested in epic history, which is to say, the finished history. Instead, his interest lies with the inconclusive, novelistic history of our possibilities, and this is the history of our imaginations.

The Argentine essayist Beatriz Sarlo suggests this seductive theory: beginning with the pampas, his ancestral land, Borges has appropriated numerous zones of legitimization, only in order to leave them behind: "My grandfathers made friends / with this great expanse / and conquered the privacy of the pampas," followed by the city of Buenos Aires: "I am a man of the city, neighborhood, and street . . . The streets of Buenos Aires run deep in my soul," to culminate with the invention of *las orillas* (shores; riverbanks), as a border between the urban and the rural which I mentioned before. This permits Borges, eternal shore dweller, to place himself on the margins, not only of Argentine history, but of European and Asiatic histories as well. This is the final legitimization of Borgesian writing.

But if this movement from pampas to city, from rural to urban is true in a critical sense, in another way it produces a perfectly coherent result with regards to Borges's militant presence among the modernist vanguard of his youth: the project of abandoning mimetic realism, folklore, and naturalism. Let's not forget that it was Borges who opened the closed windows in the chambers of flat realism to show us a wide horizon, no longer one of clinical characters, but one of prospective figures. This is one of his gifts to Latin American literature. Beyond exhausted psychologisms and constrictive mimesis, Borges grants the role of protagonist to the mirror and the labyrinth, to the garden and the book, to times and spaces. He reminds us all that our culture is wider that any reductivist theory, literary or political. And that this is so because reality is wider than any one of its definitions.

Beyond his obvious and numerous debts to the fantastic literature of Felisberto Hernández or the linguistic liberty achieved by Macedonio Fernández, Borges was the first Spanish language narrator in the Americas (Machado de Assis had already, miraculously, achieved this in the Portuguese language in Brazil) who truly liberated us from naturalism and redefined the real in literary terms, which is to say, imaginative terms. Borges confirmed for us that in literature, reality is what is imagined. This is what I have called, numerous times, the Borgesian Constitution: a confusion of all genres, a rescue of all traditions, a creation of a new landscape upon which to build the houses of irony, humor, and play, but also a profound revolution which identifies liberty with the imagination and which, following from this identification, proposes a new language.

Borges taught us to understand, in the first place, the relativist yet inclusive, reality of modern time and space. There can be no closed, self-sufficient systems of knowledge, because each observer will describe any given event from a different perspective, and to do this, the observer needs make use of a language. For that reason, time and space are elements of language needed for the observer to describe his environment (his Orteguian "circumstance").

Space and time are language.

Space and time constitute an open and relative descriptive system.

If this is true, language can accommodate diverse times and spaces, precisely the "divergent, convergent, and parallel times" of "The Garden of Forking Paths," or the spaces of "The Aleph," where all places are found and can be seen simultaneously.

In Borges's stories time and space become characters, with the same titular eminence as Tom Jones or Anna Karenina in realist literature. But when it comes to Borges, we are assailed by doubt: is it all time and all space — inclusive — or is it our time and our space — relative?

Borges, writes André Maurois, was attracted to the metaphysical, but he does not accept the truth of any system. This relativism sets him apart from the European proponents of a universal and invariable human nature which turns out to be nothing more than how those same powerful Europeans — generally members of the enlightened middle class — see themselves. On the other hand, Borges offers a variety of spaces and a multiplication of themes, each one distinct, each one the bearer of values that are the product of unique cultural experiences but in communication with others. Because in Europe or in America—Borges and Alfonso Reyes understood it immediately in our century, to our collective benefit—an isolated culture is a culture condemned to disappear.

In other words: Borges makes it very clear that we live in a diversity of times and spaces, which in turn explicitly reveals a diversity of cultures. I maintain that he is not alone in contributing this idea to our literature, not only because of his forerunners, from Vico to Alberdi, nor for his eminent and fraternal fellow citizen in spirit, Reyes, nor for the other novelists of his generation or those close to it. Borges does not allude to the indigenous or African components of our culture: Miguel Ángel Asturias or Alejo Carpentier take charge of that. But perhaps only an Argentine—a desperate verbalizer of absences—could shoulder the cultural totality of the Western world with the goal of demonstrating, perhaps in spite of himself, the partiality of a Eurocentrism formerly accepted by our republics in earlier times, but which today has been denied and refused by modern cultural awareness.

But even when Borges does not refer thematically to this or that Latin American matter, he offers us at every moment the instruments to reorganize, amplify, and move forward in our perception of a changing world whose centers of power—without respite—shift, decay, and renew themselves. What a pity that these new worlds rarely agree with the tender Borgesian aspiration: "A secret and benevolent society . . . arose to invent a country."

Meanwhile, enigmatic, desperate, and enlivening, Argentina is part of Spanish America. Its literature belongs to the universe of the Spanish language: the realm of Cervantes. But Latin American literature is also part of world literature, to which it contributes, and from which it receives. Borges gathers together all these threads. When I affirm that the Argentine narrative is part of Latin American and world literature, I only want to recall that it is part of an incomplete form, the narrative form that by definition never *is*, but always *is being* in an arena where distant histories and conflictive languages can meet, transcending the orthodoxy of one single language, one single faith or one single vision of the world. In our particular case, this means dealing with languages and visions of the indigenous theocracies, of the Spanish Counter-Reformation, of the rationalist beatitude of the Enlightenment, or of the current, industrial, and even post-industrial Creso-hedonisms.

All this leads me to the final part of what I want to say: the fittingly literary act, the event of Jorge Luis Borges writing his stories. The Russian critic Mikhail Bakhtin, perhaps the twentieth century's greatest theorist of the novel, points out that the process of assimilation between the novel and history necessarily includes a definition of time and space. Bakhtin calls this definition the chronotope: *chronos* (time) and *topos* (space). In the chronotope, narrative events are organized actively. The chronotope makes time in the novel visible in the space of the novel, upon which depend the narrative's form and communicability.

From there, once more, comes Borges's decisive importance in Latin American fiction. His economy and his highly praised rhetorical nakedness are not, for me, virtues in and of themselves. At times, they only occur at the expense of density and complexity, sacrificing the Augustinian right to error. But this brevity, this nakedness, do make the architecture of time and space visible. With the reader's leave, they establish the chronotope as a star in the narrative firmament.

In "The Aleph," and "Tlön, Uqbar, Orbis Tertius," space is the protagonist, with as many virtues as the hero or heroine of a realist novel. In "Funes the Memorious," "The Immortal," and "The Garden of Forking Paths," this role is occupied by time. In all these stories, Borges observes a total time and space that, at first glance, could only be approximated through total knowledge. Nevertheless, Borges is not a Platonist, but rather a perverse sort of Neoplatonist. First he postulates a totality. Then he demonstrates its impossibility.

To examine one obvious example, in "The Library of Babel" Borges introduces us to a total library that would, by nature, need to contain a book which contains all knowledge. In the first place, it makes us feel that the world of the book is not subject to the demands of chronology or the contingencies of space. In a library all authors and all books are present, here and now, each book and each author contemporaneous in and among themselves, not only within the space thus created—"The Aleph" and "The Library of Babel"—but also within time: the volumes of Dante and Diderot support each other mutually, and Cervantes exists side by side with Borges. The library is the place and the time where a man is all men and where all men who repeat a line of Shakespeare *are* Shakespeare.

Can we then affirm that the totality of time and space exists here, within a library that ideally should contain one single book that is all books, read by one single reader who is all readers? The response would depend on another question: Who perceives this? Who can, simultaneously, have a book by Cervantes in one hand, a book by Borges in the other, and recite, at the same time, a line of Shakespeare? Who possesses this freedom? Who is not only one but many? When the poem, as Shelley said, is one and universal, who is the reader of it? Who is always diverse, even when, as Emerson said, the author is the only author of all books ever written? Who, after all, reads them: the book and the author? The response, of course is: *You*, the reader. Or *We*, the readers.

In such a way, Borges offers a book, a time, a space, a library, a universe, all unique and total, but seen and read and lived by many readers, reading in many places and in multiple times. And thus, the total book, the book of books, a metaphysical justification of the total library and total knowledge, of absolute time and space, are all impossible because the condition for the unity of time and space in any literary work is the plurality of the readings, present or future: in every case, potential readings.

The reader is the wound in the book he reads: through his reading he bleeds all ideal, totalizing possibility from the library in which he reads, from the book he reads, including the possibility of one single reader who is all readers. The reader is the wound of Babel, the fissure in the tower of the absolute.

Borges creates hermetic totalities as the initial, and ironic, themes of several of his stories. In doing so, he evokes one of humanity's most profound aspirations: nostalgia for unity, at the beginning and the end of all times. But he immediately betrays this idyllic nostalgia, this totalitarian aspiration, and he does so, in exemplary fashion, through the comic incident, through the particular, private accident. "Funes the Memorious" is the victim of a hermetic totality. He remembers everything. For example, he always knows what time it is, without needing to consult the clock. His problem, in order not to turn into a small, unwitting god, consists of reducing his memories to a manageable number: let's say, fifty or sixty thousand articles of memory. But

this means that Funes must choose and indicate. In doing so, however, he demonstrates aesthetically that there can be no absolute or
closed systems of knowledge. There can only be relative perspectives
in the search for a language that expresses variable times and spaces.
The truth is that all the simultaneous spaces of "The Aleph" are not
worth one glimpse of the dead beauty Beatriz Viterbo, a woman in
whose walk there was "a sort of graceful clumsiness, a hint of palsy,"
although she also possessed an "almost implacable clear-sightedness,"
compensated for by "distractions, disdain, real cruelty."

Borges: The search for absolute time and space occurs by means
of a repertory of possibilities which make the absolute impossible or,
if one prefers, relative. In the universe of Tlön, for example, everything is negated: "the present is indefinite . . . the future has no reality
other than as a present hope . . . the past has no reality other than as
a present memory." But doesn't this negation of a traditional time—
past, present, future—give a supreme value to the *present* as a time
that not only contains, but also gives its most intense presence, that
of life, to the remembered *past* here and now, to the *future* desired today? The repertoire is inexhaustible.

In "The Circular Ruins," past, present, and future are affirmed as
a simultaneity while, returning to Tlön, others declare that all time
has already occurred and that our lives are only "the crepuscular, and
undoubtedly falsified and mutilated, memory or reflection of an un-
recoverable process." We are in the Borgesian universe of creative criticism, where only what is written is real, but what is written perhaps
has been invented by Borges. For that reason, it turns out to be reas-
suring that a footnote recalls Bertrand Russell's hypothesis, according
to which the universe was created just a few minutes ago and provided with a humanity that "remembers" an illusory past.

Nevertheless, I think that the most Borgesian theory of all is the
following: "The history of the universe . . . is the scripture produced
by a subordinate god in order to communicate with a demon." All of
which means, in the final instance, that each one of us, like Funes,
like Borges, you and I, his readers, must turn ourselves into artists: we
choose, we relativize, we elect: we are *Lectors y Electors*, Readers and
Deciders. The absolute chronotope, the almost Platonic essence that
Borges invokes again and again in his tales becomes relative thanks to
reading. Reading makes faces in front of the mirror of the Absolute,

it tickles the ribs of the Abstract, it forces Eternity to smile. Borges teaches us that each story is something changeable and susceptible to fatigue, simply because it is constantly being read. History, the story, the account, changes, it moves, it becomes one of its successive possibilities, in the same way that a man can be a hero in one version of the battle, and a traitor in the next.

In "The Garden of Forking Paths," the narrator conceives each possibility of time, but feels obliged to reflect that "everything happens to a man precisely, precisely now. Centuries upon centuries and only in the present do things happen."

We only read history in the present moment. And even when history presents itself as the only true version of events, we, the readers, immediately subvert any such singular attempt at unity. The narrator of "The Garden ..." for example, reads, within history, two versions "of the same epic chapter." Meaning: he reads not only the first version, the orthodox one, but also a second heterodox version. He chooses "his" epic or coexistent chapter, if he thus desires it, with both, or with many, histories. In terms of Latin American history, this means that the reader of Borges not only reads the Conquest but also the Counterconquest, not only the Reformation but also the Counter-Reformation and certainly, in even more Borgesian terms, he reads not only the Revolution but also the Counter-Revolution.

In truth, the narrator of *The Garden of Forking Paths* does nothing more than define the novel as being in the process of distinguishing itself from the epic. Because the novel could be defined, of course, as the *second* reading of the epic chapter. According to Ortega y Gasset, the epic is what is already known. The novel is the next voyage of Odysseus, the voyage towards what is unknown and ignored. And if the epic, as Bakhtin tells us, is the story of a concluded world, the novel is the hazardous reading of a nascent world: the renovation of Genesis by means of the renovation of the genre.

Through all these impulses, the novel is a mirror that reflects the reader's face. And like Janus, the reader of novels has two faces. One looks toward the future, the other toward the past. Obviously, the reader looks toward the future. The novel's material is essentially what is uncertain, unfinished, the search for a new world in the process of becoming. It is the world of Napoleon Bonaparte and his children, Julien Sorel, Rastignac, Becky Sharp. They are the children of

Waterloo. But through the novel, the reader also incarnates the past, and is invited to discover the newness of the past, the novelty of Don Quixote and his descendants: we are the children of La Mancha. The tradition of La Mancha is the novel's other tradition, the hidden tradition, in which the novel celebrates its own genesis thanks to the marriage of tradition and creativity. Cervantes officiates at the very beginning of this ceremonial narrative, which reaches one of its contemporary peaks in the work of Jorge Luis Borges, thanks to the well-known conviction and practice of his fiction, in which each writer creates his own ancestors.

When, in one of Borges's famous stories, Pierre Menard decides to write *Don Quixote*, he is telling us that in literature the work that we are reading becomes our own creation. As we read it, we become Cervantes's inspiration. But through us, the readers, Cervantes (or, in his case, Borges) become our contemporaries, as well as contemporaries with each other. In the story "Pierre Menard, Author of the Quixote," Borges suggests that the new reader of any text is also the new writer of that same text, which now exists on that shelf alongside everything that occurred between its first and its subsequent readers.

Far from the petrified stories that with fists full of archival dust hurl anathemas against literature, Borges's story offers his readers the opportunity to reinvent, and relive, the past, with the goal of continuing to invent the present. Because literature moves not only towards a mysterious future, but rather toward an equally enigmatic past. The enigma of the past demands that we reread it constantly. The future of the past depends upon it.

Along with Borges, I believe that the meaning of books lies not behind us in our past. On the contrary: it faces us from the future. And you, the reader, are the author of *Don Quixote* because each reader creates their own book, translating the finite act of writing into the infinite act of reading.

8. Upriver: Alejo Carpentier

1. The Century of Lights

Some works of art provide what Henry James called "the sense of visitation": open works that do not evade contamination so that they might assure correspondence, the "visit" from a ghost of the same work. I have never hidden my scarce interest in those closed works of pretended self-sufficiency and sure reduction. They are the blood clots — a warning of death — that block cultural circulation. By contrast, I am delighted, enlivened, by the idea of reading a story by Julio Cortázar as if it were a film by Alain Jessua or a saxophone solo by Coleman Hawkins.

Reading Alejo Carpentier has always provoked in me a ghostly visitation from Edgar Varèse — to the degree that I can read the words of the one while hearing the music of the other. Often and justly interpreted as the summit of magical realism and Latin American Baroque, Carpentier's work is not only the peak but also the slopes of the mountain. Like all authentic literature, the great Cuban novelist's work closes and opens, culminates and inaugurates, is a gateway from one field to another: what he says matters as much as what he predicts. But as Carpentier is one of our first professional novelists, this realization is not purely intuitive. He obeys a structure that is not in the least accidental in which, like in Varèse's "Deserts," one would have to distinguish between two elements: the instrumental group (piano, wind, brass, percussion) and the soundtrack or "brute sounds."

In Carpentier's fiction, the "orchestra" would be those traditional elements that he develops to their clear culmination. The piano is a lightly modulated intrigue, a thread that leads us, within a circular time, in the search for an origin that can be an ending: the argument as investigation, which is to wander about and pick up the trail again. The brasses are that sensual presence of nature, the victim and executioner of wandering pilgrims and a watery mirror of their hungers, coral forests and seas of grass, cities that are "gigantic Baroque candelabra," hotels converted into caves, and forests transformed into cathedrals, Haiti, Cuba, Santo Domingo, Venezuela, Guadalupe. I use the word "nature," but Carpentier's brasses are locations, the Caribbean oasis, the last rattling gasp of Mediterranean culture which perhaps, in its American upswell, chooses to transform itself into a bird, like the sorcerer Ti Noel in Carpentier's *The Kingdom of This World*. In Carpentier's oeuvre, nature and culture are joined only to be transfigured and revealed in a mythic elaboration of the lost landscape between chaos and cosmos. The wind instruments are those characters, atavistic women and alienated intellectuals, solitary cousins, exemplary cadavers, loyal mothers and dubious fathers, harried terrorists, allegorical liberators, drummers of the conquest, witch doctors and courtesans, black slaves and monarchs, merchants and revolutionaries, soldiers from the "war of time" who, sustained and *localized* in the brasses of nature, are carried away, captured by the drum beats of history: discovery and conquest, tyranny and resistance, revolution: forms of hunger and suffering, from inconclusive pilgrimages, from aspiration, in the end integrated in a grand dramatic vision of the Latin American novel.

Where there had only been—Gallegos, Güiraldes, Rivera, Icaza—the isolated perception of those elements, there is from now on, in Carpentier's works: *The Kingdom of This World*; *The Lost Steps*; *The Chase*; *War of Time*; and *Explosion in a Cathedral*, an orchestrated integration of the enormous Latin American facticity, and the appetites for justice and life of those men who are unsatisfied with simply living—rootless and dispossessed—upon the American land, demands of both a dialectical movement and a tragic awareness, no longer from an outraged sentimental declaration. Carpentier's novels are dialectical because they are tragic, in the sense that Lucien Goldman attributes to Pascal: "the tragic dialectic simultaneously answers *yes* and *no* to all the problems proposed by man's life and his relationships with other men and the universe."

Yes and no. Or rather, yes with no. At first glance, Carpentier's narrative structures would seem to stretch from one genesis to another. From a lost love to a love found. From a broken promise to a new annunciation. In *The Lost Steps*, the narrator abandons his wife and his lover for a dark, unconscious encounter with a primitive woman, Rosario, an androgynous mirror of the Tellus Mater—Mother Nature, the earth goddess—capable of solitary self-begetting. In *Explosion in a Cathedral*, Sofia abandons Esteban, an incarnation of the pure demands of the revolutionary ideal, in order to be with Victor Hughes, the pragmatist who, amid contradictions, embodies a minimum part of that ideal.

Yes and no. Each genesis, barely ceasing to be the motionless act, the *fiat* of pure creation, barely taking form in movement, summons a specter that points out the path of history. The apocalypse is the squire of creation. Victor Hughes, herald of the French Revolution, disembarks in the New World with two weapons: the Decree of Pluviôse of the Year II of the Republic which dictates freedom for slaves, and the sharp, naked blade of the guillotine: genesis and apocalypse. "Displaying all the distinctive marks of his Authority, immobile, stone-like, with his right hand resting on the uprights of the Machine, Victor Hughes had suddenly transformed into an allegory. With liberty came the first guillotine in the New World." The character of *The Lost Steps* goes up the Orinoco towards its paradisiacal headwaters, only to confirm that each year, when the flood waters rise, the way to Eden disappears and, with it, all trace of humans, all human memory prior to each specific catastrophe. The traveler searches for the original Golden Age, but this already recalls his own lost Golden Age. And nevertheless, this cancellation of time by time is repeatable because it is mythic, because it is exemplary, because it is eminently presentable. Primordial time prefigures all time. Like Elena Garro's excellent book, Carpentier's entire novel could be titled *Memories of the Future*. And Carpentier's entire oeuvre is a double divination: simultaneously a memory of the future and a prediction of the past.

The main character in *The Lost Steps* travels upriver toward the roots of life, but he cannot find them—says Carpentier—"because he has lost the doorway to his authentic existence." This reference points us to a third kind of time. Alejo Carpentier has said that art belongs, not to genesis, or to its twin, apocalypse, but to revelation. Revelation is the time of conscious human history which, at the same time, possesses a solar center of aspirations: revolution. Yes and no: a third ambiguous time, like gestation or catastrophe, no longer inevitable. The revolution is Victor Hughes, the cynical opportunist, a man of action and also a sensualist who, in some way, even more terrible, would like to give shape to his ideals. The revolution is Esteban, the young dreamer of eighteenth-century Havana—the Century of Lights—for whom the ideal, born of his secret readings of Voltaire and Rousseau, is a tree of air, a sea of lights. For Esteban, all incarnation is inferior to expectation.

> Esteban felt disconcerted in the face of the incredible servitude of a vigorous and energetic mind, but one so absolutely politicized that it refused the critical examination of the facts, refusing to see the most flagrant contradictions: faithful to the point of fanaticism ... to the dictates of the man who had invested him with powers.
>
> "The Revolution," said Victor slowly ... "the Revolution had given my existence an object."
>
> "Contradictions and more contradictions," murmured Esteban. "I dreamed of such a different revolution."
>
> "And who orders you to believe in what was not?" asked Victor. "A Revolution is not debated: is it made."

Facing Victor's blind certainty, Esteban represents critical ambiguity, as when Victor accepts that France, by virtue of its democratic principles, cannot exercise the slave trade, but that it can, in Dutch ports, sell slaves that have been seized from the English. Immediately disposed to abandon the betrayed Revolution and Victor Hughes, Esteban goes out to fulfill this assignment in the Dutch colony of Suriname. His mission is to secretly distribute the Pluviose Decree of the Year II of the Revolution among the subjects of the King of Holland. He decides to throw the printed copies, tied fast to large stones, to the bottom of the river. But first, in the hospital at Paramaribo, he witnesses a ceremony of punishment as various slaves from the colony, convicted of trying to escape, have their legs deliberately mutilated. A prisoner of his own nausea and fright, Esteban goes out to distribute the Decree of Freedom among the blacks: "Read this," he shouts to them. "And if you don't know how to read, find someone to read it to you."

Defeated, Esteban returns to Havana: "Let's be careful about too pretty words; of those Better Worlds created by words. Our time succumbs to an excess of words. There is no other Promised Land than what a man can find within himself." And now it is Sofía—knowledge, "blithe knowledge"—who abandons Esteban to go back to Victor Hughes, named by Bonaparte as an agent in Cayenne. But in reality she does not abandon him: she goes to witness, in the name of Esteban, for the love of Esteban, the tragic downfall of Victor Hughes. Out of love for Esteban, for whom the revolutionary dream is twin to the dream of love for his cousin, Sofía goes to be Victor Hughes's lover. Yes and no: Sofía, wisdom of the revolution, nucleus of revelation, lover and nurse, will be the one who manages to show the true Victor Hughes — not only the mason, anti-mason, Jacobin, military hero, Agent of the Directorate, Agent of the Consulate, but rather a man who, behind the titles, is Ormuz and Arimán — that the same man could just as well reign over the darkness as the light. Victor has opened the doors of Cayenne to the priests and applies the new decree, the Law of 30 Floreal in the Year X, which reestablishes slavery in the French colonies of America. But, amid the persecutions of the blacks, he falls, slain by the fever brought to Cayenne with the slaves captured by Napoleon in the battle of Egypt:

> the doctor used a new remedy that in Paris had worked wonders, curing eyes afflicted by the Egyptian Sickness: laying on thin strips of fresh, bloody beef. "You look like a parricide from ancient tragedy," said Sofía, seeing that new person who, emerging from the room where they had just finished treating him, made her think of Oedipus. For her, the times of mercy had ended.

Witness to glory, to the contradictions and the defeat of Victor Hughes, Sofía only renounces pity when tragedy is fulfilled in death. But she does not renounce knowledge. Victor Hughes has lived to attest to the tragic abyss between the absolute annihilation of justice and the concrete use of force, in the same way that Esteban — now a reader of Chateaubriand — suffers in the military prison of Ceuta the tragic destiny of the men lost in the abyss between human hope and the human condition. Napoleon Bonaparte has drawn the curtain across the Century of Lights with a few words: "We have finished the romance of the Revolution; now we must begin its history and reflect upon only what is real and practicable in the application of its principles." Notwithstanding, Sofía — the conciliating knowledge, the fraternity of opposites — was right: "Everything became clear . . . Victor's presence was the beginning of something that would be expressed in vast charges of riders on the plains, navigations on fabulous rivers, crossing enormous mountain ranges. An epoch was born which would fulfill, in these lands, what in the European fall had been badly managed. This time it would mean the massacre of generals, bishops, magistrates, and viceroys."

Yes: in spite of everything, Victor Hughes brought the Revolution to America, and if this Revolution failed, the movement would continue, contradictory, often absurd, but in the end human, just as Sofía's final exclamation is human, renewed, hoped for, wise, and lacking in rancor or defeat when she and Esteban leave their confinement in the Palacio de Arcos in Madrid to join the multitude in the May uprisings against the French: "Let us go there! Let us go to fight ... for the sake of those who took to the streets! We've got to do something! ... Something!"

I wish to emphasize that *Explosion in a Cathedral* is not an allegory which illustrates the destiny of revolutions. We know that in a revolutionary process only one phase or stage of the events is susceptible to being reduced to *technique*: the manner of taking power. But the transformation of a society has never been nor ever will be codified: each revolution is irreversible and unrepeatable and the men who make it, illuminated and enlightened by a nocturnal sun, must invent it all over again. If *Explosion in a Cathedral* is taken as a historical chronicle, it can only refer to the French Revolution. But if not, it is an allegory—the mere illustration of known truths—it does contain a symbology—a real search for new truths. And that symbology speaks to us about a conciliation between justice and tragedy. Yes and no: revolution now, and again, and once again: liberty is identical to a permanent aspiration, that of men who live in ambiguity and do not accept it, but rather maintain the exigency of absolute human values while knowing that reality denies them or impedes them. The Revolution is the Revelation, it is Divination that recalls the sacred origin of time and formulates its human destiny. Historical revolution is literary divination when the writing, as in Carpentier's work, is radically poetic: only poetry can simultaneously propose multiple antagonistic truths, a truly dialectical vision of life.

We can now revisit Varèse's music. Because Carpentier's prophetic vision depends not only on the orchestration which the writer uses to provide American aphonia with tone and seriality, rhythm and chronochromie (time-color)—in short, resonance—but also on those prerecorded tapes of "brute sounds" which, played against the grain of traditional instrumentation, integrate a totally new narrative in which fiction creates itself by means of a language that is a reflection on language. Without these recordings, Carpentier's fictions might have been the chronicles and messages of the previous chapter of our novel.

But it would be unjust to limit this distinction to the narrow range of Spanish language literature in America. By full right, Carpentier's novels belong to the universal movement of the narrative, a movement of renewal which substitutes the crucial convention of characters and argument (similar to the vertical-horizontal crux of melody and harmony in music) for a *fusion* in which characters and intrigue dislodge the center in order to become a form of resistance to a language that develops, from out of itself, in all the directions of *what is real.* While music has also earned the right to be total sound, or painting a pure visual impression, the novel claims the evident necessity of being, first and foremost, literature, a connection of language with all levels and orientations, not of "reality," but rather of "what is real."

Carpentier is the first Spanish language novelist who intuits this radicalization and its corollary: all language supposes a representation, but the language of literature is a representation which represents itself. For example, in *Doña Bárbara*, language, to the degree in which it is conscious of itself, aspires to directly represent reality: the plains truly mean to be the plains, and Santos Luzardo really believes that he is Santos Luzardo. But the retrospective cadaver of *Viaje a la semilla* (Journey to the Seed)—I deliberately choose this novella by Carpentier—lacks that primary ingenuity: it knows that it only represents an earlier representation. And it knows that its actual representation does not exist outside of literature. As in Cervantes, in Carpentier's work the word is the foundation of the artifice: exigency and unevenness confront the reader who would like to nod off with the easy assurance of reading reality; exigency and a challenge that obliges the reader to penetrate the levels of what is real, that which quotidian reality denies or veils from sight.

Thanks to this representation of representation, Carpentier revolutionizes narrative technique in the Spanish language: we move from the *a priori* fabricated novel to the novel that makes itself in its own writing. Carpentier's musical formation is not alien to this realization of the real. Let us remember that *The Chase* develops in accord with an external rhythm—the performance of Beethoven's *Eroica*—

which reorients us to an internal symphony—that of the troubled character—still unfulfilled, still in the process of being written or being read. While the traditional orchestra religiously follows the set musical score, the pre-recorded sound tape opposes to it, at the identical time, the unpredictable development of a destiny formulated by, and within, a language.

At a complete remove from improvisation—recall his aforementioned professionalism—or gratuitousness—Carpentier believes that cultural revolutions are not enigmas of social revolutions, but rather that both complement and illuminate one another—the language of these novels also fulfills the author's obsession: to denominate the anonymous world of America, to give name to the bird, the mountain, the tree and the Madrepore coral. In Carpentier, the verb's function is, once more, attribution, while the name creates foundation.

It would be fitting to go further. Rousseau asserted that a history of freedom and slavery could be made based on the study of languages. A similar project would deserve to be carried out in Latin America, a fertile zone, like few others, for projecting onto the screen of language the images of a profound divorce between reality and its signifiers. In *Explosion in a Cathedral* there is a quotation on a portico which says: "Words are not pronounced in vain." Not even vain words. Like that of many contemporary musicians, Carpentier's work—an immense metamorphosis of the roots and crystallizations of our language—makes use of melody to transcend melody: Carpentier takes advantage of rhetoric in order to transcend rhetoric. In one single movement, which at times seems like a suspended animation, the novelist consecrates that which he profanes, and profanes that which consecrates. The discourse and the poem, the clamorous lie and true silence, are united in one single language: that of the tension between nostalgia and hope.

What does it really mean that the same language has given us Cortés's *Letters from Mexico*, the nocturnal, pyramidal poetry of Sor Juana, the monstrous decrees of Rosas, the lucid humanism of Lastarria, the chaotic demagoguery of Perón, and the cold logic of Borges? What unites all these dissimilar expressions but the unfulfilled utopian foundation, degraded by a bastardized epic that would happily assume the utopian promise if its progress were not impeded by the imagination that transforms nostalgia into desire? Everything in

Latin America is language: power and liberty, domination and hope. But if the language of barbarism desires to subject us to the linear determinism of time, the language of the imagination desires to break that fatality, liberating the simultaneous spaces of the real. Has the moment arrived, perhaps, to exchange Sarmiento's dilemma— civilization or barbarism?—for that of Carpentier, and with him the best artists from our part of the world, who seem to ask instead: imagination or barbarism?

2. The Search for Utopia

Art has traveled a long road in search of the happy land of its origin, from Nausicaa's island in Homer, to Luis Buñuel's ironic visit to an island of skeletons and excrement in his film *L'Age d'Or*, wandering through Hesiod's idyllic lands of Arcady, the age of truth and faith in Ovid, the Christian springtime of Dante, the age of rivers of milk in Tasso, and, finally, to John Donne's sour outpouring in his poem: "The golden laws of nature are repeal'd," and the disenchanted recollection in Cervantes:

> Happy centuries and whole ages so fortunate that the men of ancient times called them golden, and not because gold itself, held in such high esteem in this our Iron Age, was easily procured then but because the people of those times neither knew nor used these two words *yours* and *mine*. All things in that holy age were held in common; and all one had to do in order to procure his daily sustenance was to reach out his hand and pluck from the robust oak trees which freely offered him their sweet, delicious fruit. In magnificent abundance, the clear fountains and rushing rivers offered them their flavorful and transparent waters . . . all was peace then, all friendship, all harmony . . .

Cervantes's evocation is voiced by the Bishop Quiroga: and both, at the same time, belong to Ovid in *The Metamorphoses*:

> In the beginning was the Golden Age, when men, by their own will, without laws and without fear of punishment, worked honestly and in good faith . . . The earth . . . produced all things freely . . . It was the season of eternal spring . . . The rivers flowed with milk and nectar . . . but then came the Iron Age and with it

all manner of crimes; modesty, truth, and loyalty fled, usurped by treason and treachery; deceit; violence and criminal greed.

They all speak of a time, not a place, *U-Topos* means: *there is no such place*. But the search for Utopia is always presented as the search for a place and not a time: the same idea of Utopia in America seems marked by the hunger for space which belongs to the Renaissance.

The New World thus becomes a living contradiction: America is the place where you can find the place that does not exist. America is the utopian promise of the New Golden Age, the space reserved for the renovation of European history. But how can the place that is no place have any space at all?

The indigenous world, the world of myth, has answered this question since before being conquered. Utopia can only have time. A nonexistent place cannot have territory. It can only have history and culture, which are the ways of conjugating time. The origin of the gods and man; exhausted times, new times; auguries; time's responses to a threatening nature, to an imminent natural cataclysm.

Thomas More describes the irony of this truth when he sends his utopian traveler, Raphael Hythloday, back to Europe. But, More tells us, Hythloday might not have returned, nor the reader either: "You should have been with me in Utopia with me, and seen with your own eyes their manners and customs as I did—for I lived there for more than five years, and would never have left, if it had not been to make that new world known to others."

In his novel *The Lost Steps*, Alejo Carpentier conceives of his fiction as a journey in space, up the Orinoco River, to the headwaters of the river, but also as a trip through time. The novel's movement is a conquest of space but also a reconquest of time. Unlike Hytholoday, Carpentier's traveler goes from modern cities to the rivers of conquest to the jungles before the Discovery to "the night of times," where "all times are come together in the same space."

Traveling backwards, towards "the rhythms of Genesis," Carpentier's narrator stops at the edge of atemporality and only there finds Utopia: a *tempo* where *all times* coexist, while Borges found the Aleph to be the *space* where *all spaces* coexist. His narrator, like More's, has been in Utopia and has lived his perfect time, an eternal instant, a Golden Age which does not need to be remembered or foreseen.

As much as Carpentier, More would like to remain in Utopia. But both succumb to the rationalization of their modern cultures: they must go back and tell about Utopia, with the purpose, says More, of "making known the discovery of that new world to the Europeans"; in order, says Carpentier more than four centuries later, to communicate Utopia's existence to "a young person somewhere" who "perhaps awaited my message, in order to discover in himself, upon encountering my voice, the liberating path."

Because if utopia is the *recollection* of some happy time and the desire of reencountering it, it is also the *desire* for the happy time and the will to construct it. "No return" is the verb of the utopia of the original golden age. "Return" is the verb of the utopia of the new city where justice will rule.

The narrators in Thomas More and Alejo Carpentier are divided by this double utopia: they debate with themselves between finding what is lost and conserving it, or returning, communicating, reforming, and liberating. In the end, the protagonist of *The Lost Steps* commits "the irreparable mistake of retracing the path already walked, believing that what is exceptional can be so twice."

3. Utopia: Spaces and Times

Alejo Carpentier's *The Lost Steps* repeats the most ancient voyage of the men of the Old World in search of the New World, the pilgrimage "to the vast country of the permissible Utopias, of the possible Icarias." It is also the discovery that Utopia consists of "shuffling notions of past, present, and future." Beginning with a displacement in space, the utopian voyage terminates with a disappointment and also with wisdom. *U-Topos* is the place that is not; but if it is not space, it is time. The European purity of a utopian conception on a minimal spatial scale, with the continent at hand, so to speak, is spoiled and distorted by the immensity of the American space. This is the paradox: the time of the Utopia can only be won after surveying an immense space which denies it; to survey, traverse and conquer, neutralize, and eliminate. In *Canaima*, Utopia is seen as space but it must convert Gallegos's scenes set along the river and in the jungle into time.

That is difficult because American space seems indomitable. Europe converts nature into landscape. Among ourselves, it spoils the astonishment of Manuel José Othón's great poem, aptly entitled, "Savage Idyll." Although the poet speaks of "landscape," a painting by Poussin or Constable would be devoured by "the savage desert," the "horrendous cut" of this "accursed steppe" of blocks wrenched by earthquake, a "sparse, dry bowl of dead ocean." In this "killing field," sorrow and fear seem to be the only human elements drawn among the pure extension of the space. But the predominant note is, once again, that of a wild, untamed nature, which dominates us with its greatness:

Look at the landscape: immensity below,

immensity, immensity reaching upwards . . .

The landscape in Latin American literature is strange; gardens, artificial evocations of marble. In *A House in the Country* (1978), the civilized spirit of José Donoso converts the landscape into a character. Nevertheless, it deals with a new kind of savage idyll: a monstrous, fabricated landscape in which tamed nature becomes suffocating. Nature is now an artificial garden from which the oxygen has fled, and the dialogue is spoken by equally artificial children: willful, voluntary robots, Midwich Cuckoos of the Chilean countryside. An echo of Rugendas's landscapist wisdom and Monvoisin's portraitist wisdom, Donoso's wisdom, like Goethe's garden, is savagely artificial. It is a nostalgia of the primitive, untouched world of the first dawn. The fact that it is populated by children, also artificial, prolongs the sensation of impossible innocence: in *A House in the Country*, David Copperfield has arrived to the desert isle of *Lord of the Flies* without any more defense than his good English education. He has excellent table manners when he dines with his peers.

Perhaps the great Mexican landscape artist, José María Velasco, has a literary equivalent in the transparent prose of Alfonso Reyes. But in our novels, from Payno to Altamirano to Azuela to Rulfo (Othón's "most bitter and brackish prairie . . . the poor, rocky forsaken hilltop" seem written for *The Burning Plain* and *Pedro Páramo*), nature is not landscape: it is augury or nostalgia for something untamable. From Clausel's impenetrable forests to Dr. Atl's volcanoes to Orozco's flaming skies and Siqueiros's rocky topographies, Mexican painting abounds in nature, not in landscape. But if in its secondary iteration, "Savage Idyll" implies an impersonal nature, inhuman space, a *selva selvaggia* (wild jungle) which leads to hell, it also announces the idyll that rescues a time that is lost, past, and, perhaps, happy.

In *The Lost Steps*, the search for this earlier, happy place, Utopia, creates its own time, and this is revealed to be something more than just ordinary time. Or rather: not the linear time of progressive logic. Carpentier identifies the utopian enterprise with the narrative enterprise: both attempt to conflate ideas about time and to transcend the successive discretion belonging to language and the times of positive reasoning. To conquer space—the monster of pure immensity—and create time.

Clock time, the first anticipation of this intention in *The Lost Steps*, the first of many symmetries to which Carpentier recurs in order to enrich our impoverished reality is, classically, the representation within the representation: the Chinese box or Russian doll, the narrative onion which permits Shakespeare in *Hamlet,* and Cervantes with Master Pedro's puppet show, and Julio Cortázar in his story "Instructions for John Howell," to introduce the representation within the representation so that the poem, drama, or fiction contemplates itself, if it is worth doing so. The spectator / reader is invited to do the same, even at the cost of experiencing a sublime illumination, similar to that of those comical characters in Luis Buñuel's *The Discreet Charm of the Bourgeoisie,* frustrated in their supreme French effort to sit down and enjoy a good meal. When it finally comes, and they are just beginning to spoon their soup, they see the curtain rise before their eyes and realize that they are on stage, facing a packed theatre and a public expecting clever, possibly racy, conversations, while they pretend to eat their cardboard chicken. The terror of knowing themselves to be represented—and ours of knowing them to be represented—spoils our alimentary digestion but facilitates mental digestion.

In *The Lost Steps*, the goal of the "play within a play" is that of "making our lives coincide." Carpentier here refers to two lives, those of an unhappy couple, the narrator and his wife, the actress Ruth. If her life acting in a play about the American Civil War is more real to her than her narrator musicologist husband, then how can their times be effectively made to coincide? What's more, the play is a long-running hit in which "the actors are slowly annihilated, growing old in the public eye inside their unchangeable clothes."

As the narrator cannot make his time coincide with Ruth's, he departs for South America with his French lover, Mouche, who does share the narrator's time or interests. Suffice to say that this is an illusion and that the relationship between the narrator and Ruth is only a premonition of the novel's central erotic/utopian question and relationship, which presents itself in the Orinoco, when the narrator meets Rosario. What was a banal question in New York becomes an essential question in a place which the maps of utopian memory call Santa Mónica de los Venados: how can the times of the narrator and Rosario be made to coincide?

The narrator arrives to a Latin American city that can only be Caracas. In the Hispanic New World "Rousseau and the Holy Office, the Virgin and *The Capital* all coexist," but when an armed uprising isolates the hotel where the narrator is staying, cutting off the lights and water, spiders, ants, centipedes, lice, and other vermin come swarming up out of the sewers and cellars.

The narrator wants to go further. He has not come looking for some caricatured extension of North American modernity in modern Latin America, but an *ab-original* reality: the threnody, the most basic unit of music. It is worth saying: he seeks the myth of myths, the word of words, the sound from which, in a ritual lament—the threnody—all others are born. But that sonorous myth is hidden in the heart of darkness, in the entrails of a dense, impenetrable nature. The narrator ignores the overall extent of space; more than an obstacle, this is an invitation which identifies him with the first discoverers of the New World. It permits him to relapse into his astonishment—that of Columbus and Bernal, Solís and Balboa—and acquire a different sense of proportion. The mountains grow, human prestige ceases, and the human beings, tiny and silent, feel that they no longer move among things on their scale. "We were upon the backbone of the fabulous Indies, upon one of its vertebrae."

We are already familiar with nature as an impersonal force: it is the nature of *Canaima*. But Carpentier will allow nature to reveal itself as time and strip itself of its sheer size. The Cuban novelist was also a musicologist, and his writing is comparable to certain great modern musical works—I think of Varèse, Stravinsky, Debussy's *The Martyrdom of Saint Sebastian*—which seem to identify themselves as an extension in space that seeks only to unite a time. Similarly, in *The Lost Steps*, at the extremes of nature, among the dark rushing rivers, beasts and flora, the jungle comes to be revealed as *a hidden nation*.

Accompanied by his dog Gavilán, a small man with bushy eye-brows known as *el Adelantado* (the Forerunner) holds forth to the Narrator in a tavern in Puerto Anunciación, the rural town where they leave the horse lands behind and enter the lands of the dog:

> Covering immense territories—he explained to me—, enclos-ing mountains, chasms, treasures, nomad peoples, the last traces of lost civilizations, the jungle was, nevertheless, a world com-pact, complete, which fed its fauna and its men, formed its own clouds, powered its own storms, caused its own rainfall: a hidden nation, a coded map, a vast vegetable realm with very few gate-ways . . . In order to penetrate that world, el Adelantado had had to obtain the keys to its secret entrances: he alone knew of a cer-tain pass between two trees, the only one for fifty leagues, which led to a steep, narrow rocky staircase by which one could descend to the vast mystery of the immense telluric Baroques below.

El Adelantado is, without the least pejorative intention (quite the contrary), *el Retrosado* (the one going backwards): he knows how to go forward into the past because he has been there before, and per-haps in the company of Raphael Hythloday, Thomas More's utopian traveler. In 1517, More advises us that entering Utopia requires mak-ing a dangerous passage through channels "known only to the Uto-pians, so that foreigners can only enter this bay guided by a Utopian pilot. Even the inhabitants themselves would be unable to enter safe-ly were it not for certain landmarks along the coast."

I do not mean to marginalize Carpentier's narrative charm: the novel has a magical, childlike element, worthy of Stevenson and Verne, because to return to Treasure Island or to the center of the earth also requires a secret knowledge, a map, a memory. Utopia lies in the memory and it is necessary to remember in order to return to a land that does not exist in space but in time. The keys to unlock-ing *U-Topos* must be keys found in time, and the memory of time is called myth, "the living recollection of certain myths," as Carpentier writes.

The catalyst of this mythic world, of this memory, is a wom-an: Rosario. A stupefied woman, seated on a stone by the riverside, wrapped in a blue poncho, her umbrella lying on the ground, with

a vague, misty gaze and trembling lips, a woman reclaimed from
the shadows, resuscitated, who seems to have returned from very far
away. She looks at the narrator "as if she knew my face," gives a cry
and clutches him, imploring him to "not let her die again."

One of the common denizens of many fictional lands is an ancient sorceress: she inhabits the isle of Circe in Homer; Thessaly in
The Golden Ass by Apuleius; the Scottish moors in Shakespeare's *Macbeth*; and the Spanish streets of Rojas's *La Celestina* (The Tragicomedy
of Calisto and Melibea), but also the astonishing wedding salons of
Dickens, where Miss Havisham awaits death among the relics of torn
veils and a wedding cake devoured by rats, and in the Venetian pala-
zzos of Henry James where she, the ancient sorceress, guards the secrets of the word and of history: this woman—the woman—is "the
conduit towards the first rites of man." The sorceress is mistress of the
esoteric codes. Rosario belongs to this lineage. And esoteric—*eso-
theiros*—means to introduce, to enter into. The "esotericism," in this
case, appears to be the entry into the jungle, into nature; but in reality—as in More—it is the entry to Utopia, the place that does not
exist in space but which, perhaps, has *a place* in *time*. In order "to enter," passing from space to time, from *topos* to *chronos*, one must van-
quish the walls which the senses call "reality."

In parallel fashion to the encounter with sorcery, Carpentier insists, for these reasons, on a process of derealization of nature which
leads to the fight between nature and naturalism and its final consequences:

> After sailing for some time along that secret channel, one began
> to experience something very much like what mountaineers feel
> when lost in the snow: there was a kind of disorientation, a diz-
> ziness of the eyes, and the sense of verticality was lost. One could
> no longer tell where the tree ended and the reflection of the tree
> began. Did the light come from above or below? Was the sky wa-
> ter or was the water the earth? Were the tangled spaces between
> the trees and foliage pools of light in the flood? The trees, branch-
> es, and lianas were reflected at every angle, creating the illusion
> of channels, passages, and banks. With all appearances twist-
> ed into an endless array of minuscule mirages at arm's length, I
> began to feel confused, then totally lost and unspeakably over-
> whelmed. It was as if I were being spun round and round upon

myself to deliberately disorient me, before bringing me to the threshold of some secret dwelling place.

Nevertheless, this feeling of strangeness and displacement is accompanied by another sensation of constant assimilation: what most astonishes the traveling narrator is "the inexhaustible mimicry of virgin nature. Everything here was something else, creating of itself a world of appearances which concealed reality, casting doubt on many truths."

From Christopher Columbus to José Eustasio Rivera, from Amerigo Vespucci to Rómulo Gallegos, however powerful and uncommon it might be, American nature, for being nature, resembles itself. After Carpentier, nature no longer looks like nature. It is pure, timeless, space. It deceives, it is a mirage. But behind the vast deception of space hides a vast aperture of time. The naturalistic derealization allows Carpentier (the inventor of "magic realism") to fulfill his aesthetic objective by imposing time on space, thanks to those recovered steps: the movement from "naturalistic" nature to "alienated" nature to purely metaphorical, mimetic nature.

Time's intrusion in *The Lost Steps* occurs in Section XXI, when the missionary Fray Pedro seems to speak of the "power of moving backward and forward through time." This is not a mirage: it is simply the reality of another culture, a distinct culture: the natives "in their setting, in their own environment, seemed to me absolute masters of their culture. Nothing was further from their reality than the absurd concept of being savages. The fact that they were unaware of things which were for me essential and necessary, was a far cry from seeing them as primitive beings."

This other culture is the other time. And as there are many cultures, there must be many times. As possibilities, certainly; but only on the condition of recognizing them in their origin, of not deforming them *ad usum ideologicum* in order to serve the progressive time of the Western world, but rather to enrich occidental time with the variety of civilizations in time (as foreseen by Carpentier, Vico, Lévi-Strauss, Marcel Mauss, Nietzsche), in which their configurations emerge from the shadows and offer themselves as protagonists of history.

That is why in *The Lost Steps*, no sooner is time discovered than it begins to recede with the speed of a waterfall ascending to its source:

Time has rolled back four centuries. This is a Mass of the Discoverers ... Perhaps it is the year 1540 ... The years fall away, dissolve, vanish in the haze, in a vertiginous backwards flight of time ... until we reach the time in which man, weary of wandering across the face of the earth, invented agriculture ... and, needing greater music ... invented the organ by blowing into a hollow reed and mourned his dead by making a clay amphora moan. We are in the Paleolithic Era ... We are intruders ... in a city born at the dawn of History. If the fire those women were fanning suddenly went out, we would be unable to rekindle it with nothing more than our own hands.

This is the narrative system that Carpentier employs in one of the finest short stories in Latin American fiction, "Journey to the Seed," in which the candles at a vigil, instead of burning down, begin to grow taller until they are whole again and go out, while the man being awakened sits up in his coffin and his life begins again in retrospective, regressing to youth, childhood and the womb. The story is thus a counting: a countdown for a space launch, ten-nine-eight-seven ... until zero. But this is a launch into time; and if in *Viaje* ... it is the narration itself which tells the story backwards, in *The Lost Steps* the conduit of this reverse movement, of this countdown or *conto alla rovescia*, is Rosario, who, immersed in time and absent in space, does not recognize remoteness: "She doesn't care where we are going, and she doesn't seem worried whether there are towns near or far. Rosario has no sense of some place *being far away*."

This is because Rosario lives in time: "This living in the present, without possessing anything, without dragging yesterday along behind you, without thinking about tomorrow, astonishes me." And it astonishes the reader. The narrator's effort to go backwards in time and join past, present, and future is for him both private and necessary because he wishes *to reach* Utopia. But for Rosario, who *is already in* Utopia, yesterday and tomorrow are unnecessary. The narrator triumphs over profane, consecutive time. Rosario is already installed in mythic, simultaneous, and sacred time.

The encounter between the narrator and Rosario creates a double movement in the novel: the narrator's retrograde motion, which is the very rhythm of the novel, "moving backwards towards the rhythms of Genesis"; and Rosario's movement, which, although for both reader and Narrator, it is a backwards movement, towards an original past, for Rosario herself it is nothing but an immobile eternal present. The narrator has to be moving, if not towards the future, then towards the past. Rosario does not need to move. She already is as she is. The narrator encounters Rosario and believes that she will accompany him on his journey to the source, to the beginning of things. He does not know that Rosario *is already there* and cannot abandon her primeval state or (like H. Rider Haggard's Ayesha or the Tibetan woman in James Hilton's *Lost Horizon*, and other heroines from popular novels) the sorrowful punishment of turning to dust that comes with crossing the threshold from her sacred time and entering the common, everyday Newtonian, sublunar time.

This double movement, before splitting up again, melts in a single movement into "the night of ages." Here, all times meet in the same space that is canceled by the actual abundance of the time that occupies it completely. In that instant, before the seed, before the fire, where dogs exist before dogs, and captives are held by other captives, "there is a clay shape fired in the sun": "A kind of jar without handles, with two holes opposite each other . . . and a navel drawn on the convex bulge . . . This is God. More than gods it is the Mother of God. It is the primordial mother . . . the secret prologue."

Nature converted into culture is far more terrifying than nature portrayed, as "naturalistic" or "verisimilar." In Lezama Lima we see how the Baroque, carried to extremes, converts artifice into a different kind of nature, more natural than the artifice of nature, which is, according to the author of *Paradiso*, "born substituting." Carpentier's concern, if this is indeed so, is "the world that is revealed to our eyes as it was before man." If what we want is virgin nature, frozen here in all its terrible loneliness; not the complacent, naturalistic picture of a nature that startles and frightens us because we are, at any rate, capable of seeing it, of being in it, but rather a radically lonely nature, without human witnesses, and for that reason, possible.

> Here . . . although the bee works in the caverns, living creatures seem unknown. We are in the world of Genesis, at the end of the Fourth Day of Creation. If we were to go back a little further, we would reach the place where the terrible loneliness of the Creator begins—the sidereal sadness of the times without incense

or songs of praise, when the earth was without order and empty, and darkness was upon the face of the deep.

Taken to this extreme, the novel's movement begins to split into two. Carpentier has just shown us the abyss; there is nowhere further back left to go. Now, will we remain forever on the edge of dawn, at the myth of creation, or will we imbue the origin with a different set of contents and turn it into history? But, can the creation myth survive if it becomes history, in movement toward the future? Such is the dilemma of every utopia: whether to remain at the happy origin of the past, or advance towards the happy city of the future.

4. The Golden Age

The novel's movement breaks down into two utopias. The most important utopian temporal activity is the foundation of the city; but this primacy is disputed by another contrasting activity: the search for the Golden Age. The contradiction is evident: the foundation of the utopian city introduces history, and its development introduces politics, just as the Golden Age, like its feminine incarnation, Rosario, is a living myth in an absolute and immobile present.

The Modern Age resolves Utopia's eternal contradiction through a temporal inversion. If the Golden Age was previously found at the point of origin, and mythic acts tended to recall and reestablish that privileged moment of vital health, Christianity, as it introduces the divinity into history through a promise of surrender, situates Paradise in the future. The Renaissance initiates the process of secularizing the Golden Age in the New World, and the Century of Lights confirms it as the standard of modernity: Voltaire informs us that the past is, by definition, barbarous, and the future is the only escape.

But like Thomas More's utopian traveler, the narrator of *The Lost Steps* has been in Utopia and has experienced, in its perfect time, an eternal instant, a Golden Age that does not need to be recalled or foreseen. First, he elects to remain in the Golden Age, making the "great decision to not return to civilization." However, his cultural rationalizations immediately come to impose themselves on him and he decides to return: "A young man, somewhere, perhaps awaited my message, to discover in himself, upon encountering my voice, the liberating path," says Carpentier's narrator. More than four centuries earlier, Thomas More's narrator said the same thing, and upon reaching the kingdom of Michoacán tucked under the arm of Bishop Vasco de Quiroga, he repeated it: "You should have been with me in Utopia and seen with your own eyes their manners and customs as I did—for I lived there for more than five years, and would never have left, if it had not been to make that new world known to others." (*Utopia*, Book I).

Our persuasive, ideological, Promethean culture cannot be tranquil if it does not catechize to someone: More's traveler and Carpentier's narrator return to persuade, sermonize, and transform their colleagues. These will, doubtless, listen to them and return to Utopia, to colonize it if they are on the right, or to make revolutionary tourism, if they are leftists. "No return" is the keyword of the utopia of the original Golden Age. "Return" is the keyword of the utopia of the New City.

The narrator of *The Lost Steps* is divided by the double utopia: between finding what is lost, and returning, communicating, reforming, and liberating. In the end, he commits "the irreparable mistake of retracing the path already walked, believing that what is exceptional can be so twice."

Through his novel, Alejo Carpentier recognizes both the hope and sadness of a community valued above the individual and the State, because it contains and perfects the values of both.

The Lost Steps is a novel that J. B. Priestly said he would like to have written and one which Edith Sitwell considered perfect: she said that it neither lacks nor overdoes anything. For my part, I dislike the word perfection. It eliminates the risk of creation and an allowance for true re-creation, the creator's error, which our reading can pathetically assume and supply. Instead, I would speak of totality. Not a monolithic totality—a false political and literary totality—but rather a fleeting totality of complex, dissimilar, and sometimes contradictory levels. The most evident levels of *The Lost Steps* are the erotic, the linguistic, the musical and the mythic-utopian.

The eroticism is that of the body, not in its natural state—unlike many modern novelists, Carpentier eschews anatomy lessons—but rather in its representation and, even, in its representation of a representation. This is the "concerted ferocity" of the lovers:

This time we corrected the clumsy haste of our first meetings, and began to master the syntax of our bodies. Our limbs discovered a better fit; our arms sought more comfortable positions. We felt our way, with amazed, tentative touches, choosing and settling on positions that would shape the rhythm and manner of our future couplings. With the mutual apprenticeship implied by a couple forging itself, we gave birth to our own secret language. A flood of intimate words surged from our delight, words unknown to others, which would be our nocturnal language, an invention for two voices embracing terms of possession, thanksgiving, sex declensions, words conjured by the skin, pet names— yesterday unknown and unforeseeable—which we will now use when nobody can hear us.

Today, for the first time, Rosario called me by my name, repeating it over and over, as if its syllables had to be reshaped, and my name in her mouth acquired such a strange, unexpected sonority, that it felt I were hearing it for the first time, newly coined, as if the word most familiar to me became some magic, curative charm. We experienced the unparalleled joy of a thirst shared and quenched, and when we once again became aware of the world around us, it seemed that we were remembering a country of new tastes and fragrances.

This type of archetypal copulation characterizes another erotic aspect of *The Lost Steps*: its intertextual coupling, the introduction of one text into another. The chronicles of Castillejos and Fernández de Oviedo, the diaries of Columbus and Vespucci, the letters of Cortés and the ship's log of Pigafetta are like the verbal lovers of Carpentier's novel, and the fruit of this union, the textual offspring of the other texts, could be a simple sensual phrase, an instant in which a cloud passes over the protagonists and "it began to rain butterflies upon the rooftops, in the jars, upon our shoulders." That rain of butterflies from a cloud is a descendant of the erotic wonderment shared by the chroniclers and discoverers: their contemporary intertextuality extends through the work of Malcolm Lowry and Gabriel García Márquez.

From the erotic level follows the linguistic one, because, as is well known, Carpentier proposes an immediate intertextual rescue operation of our language and its lost riches. But this operation is inseparable from the nominative function of his text because Carpentier, like Columbus and Oviedo, claims for himself the task of "Adam naming things." In the textual construction of *The Lost Steps*, this Adamic naming of the breads, trees, rivers, and fish of the New World, which we have already noted in Gallegos's work, is presented in the midst of a silence "come from afar" in which the word is an obligatory creation. Thus, the virgin silence of the abysmal nature on the Fourth Day of Creation gives the word a musical resonance, in music, silence is seen as a primary value: silence is the matrix of sound.

At the musical level of the novel, the total silence is broken by a "terrifying cry over a corpse surrounded by silent dogs." For the narrator, the cry is horrible, until he realizes that the ceremony's terrible fascination only reveals that, when confronted with Death's stubborn refusal to surrender its prisoner, the Word loses heart and yields to the minimal, unitary musical expression: incantation, death rattle, convulsion: the Threnody. Alongside the narrator, we have just witnessed the birth of Music. And Music is born when the Word dies because it does not know what to say to Death.

Here we find a prodigious assimilation of the novel's various verbal levels. If the threnody, which the narrator so dramatically discovers, is the cell word transformed into music from the need for a greater vocal intonation—something more purely a note—to achieve this form, according to Lévi-Strauss, the limit and function of the myth formed are no different from *mythemes* which are those minimal mythological elements arising from the order of language but transcending it with *something more*. In language, the phrase; in music, the threnody. The limit and function of verbal language itself are no different, formed by raising lesser minimal units to higher ones which complete the previous units.

The unity of verbal, musical, and mythic function in *The Lost Steps* is marvelously illustrated by this encounter with the birth of music, with the threnody which creates music with the purpose of bringing a dead man back to life. Nevertheless, the association of the philosophical discourse in *The Lost Steps* with its linguistic and mythic processes would be incomplete without one of their fundamental identities added to this other reality: music's intention to interrupt linear succession and simple causality, placing the listener at the center of an inexhaustible web of sonorous relationships. The listener then appears as the builder of a new, multidirectional world of liberated sonorous elements, in which all perspectives are equally valid.

The authentic utopia of Alejo Carpentier's *The Lost Steps* lies in this possibility, offered to us through its linguistic, erotic, musical and mythic substance. It builds a history and a destiny through diverse free readings. It is a means of defining art that is simultaneously superior and radical.

That said, I return again to the narrative experience of *The Lost Steps*, sharing it with its explicit but not unique narrator: each step, we know, brings him closer to both the physical and historical origins of the jungle and river. Nevertheless, there is a very powerful sensation of separation, as if traversing physical space were a waste of time, but gaining the steps of time means, in the end, accepting the loss of nature's steps. Thanks to a triple construction of time in myth, utopia, and history, the narrator wagers that recovering the steps lost in time does not entail the loss of space. But this total encounter, with no steps lost either in the realm of Topos or the dominions of Chronos, turns out to be impossible. History exploits and denies nature; myth demands a constant presence; and Utopia is a perverse myth which does not content itself with the eternal present where it originates, preferring "to have its cake and eat it, too": its vital past resides in the Golden Age, but its dynamic future dwells in the happy human city yet to be built here on Earth.

In reality, Alejo Carpentier's *The Lost Steps* is an encounter with the true re-linking element (re-linking in the pristine sense of re-ligious, from the Latin *religare*, "to bind") which allows the presence of all these human spiritual realities; memory, imagination, and desire. This re-linking is the religion of the words: language. Travel in time, travel in space; the one threatens to cancel out the other and only language prevents it.

Thus we see the novel's verbal construction, in three movements that are three pairs of verbs: Seek and Find; Find and Found; Remain or Return. The first two series are a continuum; the third pair, a divorce, an option. The first verbal series (Seek and Find) takes the narrator from the city of Topia to the city of Utopia, from the fixed and civilized space to the indivisible city. It is a trip through the wilderness of *Canaima*, an immense space which must be surveyed, colonized, neutralized, and eliminated, as the case may be, in order to transform Canaima into a place and a moment in which space and time coincide. But, how can nature be transformed into time, without devastating the former and corrupting the latter? This is the problem proposed by Rómulo Gallegos: Will time, this time, be Utopia, or only a new chapter in the history of unpunished violence? Only the narrator's pilgrimage—Seek and Find—will sketch out the answer.

The jungle through which the narrator travels reveals itself to have a history, only that this is a hidden history, a history waiting to be discovered. It is no longer about the utopian discovery of the temporal, or chronicler Fernández de Oviedo's utopia without a history. Nor is it about this auroral nature's fatal corruption through violence, as described by Gallegos. The narrator enters the hidden nation accompanied by an erotic set of partners from his verbal pairing: he *seeks* with Mouche, his young lover and the companion on his active, curious search of the West; he *finds* with Rosario, the woman of the eternal present, who is already there, who has been waiting for him, since forever, as it appears. Rosario possesses the keys to Utopia; they are the keys of myth. The narrator could not share Rosario's time—the discovery of myth, the imminent return to Utopia—with his modern-day French lover. He needs the woman who liberates the mythic imagination: Rosario. He finds her by writing her, as Dante encounters Virgil, evoked by the word, in the dark forest, in the middle of life's path.

Accompanied by Rosario, the narrator enters another time. But entering another time turns out to be a move synonymous with entering another culture. With Rosario, the narrator moves toward the initial rites of humanity. In all Carpentier's works, the awareness that different cultures correspond to different times is absolutely clear. *The Lost Steps* states this clearly:

> I had always seen those Indians through more or less fantastic tales, considering them beings situated on the margin of true human existence. In their setting, in their own environment, they seemed to me absolute masters of their culture. Nothing was further from their reality than the absurd concept of being savages. The fact that they were unaware of things which were for me essential and necessary, was a far cry from seeing them as primitive beings.

Modernity is a civilization, a group of techniques which can be lost or be surpassed. But there also exists a cultural modernity, and this is contemporary to the diverse times of the human being. One can live in a "thirteenth century" of Western technological civilization which is, nevertheless, the fullest, least dispossessed actuality, for those who live it. Carpentier wrote the first Latin American novels in which this comprehensive (and generous) modernity is made explicit. In *The Lost Steps*, this occurs in the instant in which the narrator divests himself of Occidental linear time, leaving Mouche behind and departing with Rosario to discover the plurality of times. Rosario is immersed in time and absent in space: she does not recognize distance; she lives in the fullest possible present; she demands, doubtless, too much from the narrator: she demands that he be Other, that which he is not. The novel's own narrative beauty, its accelerated forward movement, directs the text which we read in successive, linear fashion (as another narrator, in Borges's *The Aleph*, desperately notes), in tension with its regressive movement. As it moves back through space in search of original time, it becomes the past. For Rosario, this movement has no meaning, except perhaps that of representing the motionless center of movement, the most dangerous equilibrium. Rosario is at the center of a dynamic narration; the narrator should renounce narrating in order to fully accompany her, to be her constant carnal partner. But if he stops narrating, the narrator will cease to be.

That is why, upon moving to the second verbal series of *The Lost Steps*, the narrator, in love with Rosario and the eternal present, proposes an activity which joins his movement with his lover's stasis. He *has found*; now he *goes forth to find and to found*. *Finding* the eternal present of the myth; and *founding* upon it the city of Utopia, the new city of man. The narrator arrives to the very dawn of time and there finds the temporal activity that identifies time and history: the foundation of the city. The verb *to seek* melds into, and finds foundation with, the verb *to find*. With time found, we found time: we found the city as a space in time. Except that, having reached the origin of time, the narrator continues carrying a double movement. If this double meaning existed in the first verbal series of the composition (Seek and Find, progression in space, regression in time) so it does in the third and final series. The second, to Find and Found, is the nearest that the narrator comes to Rosario's symbolic mythical unity. His Faustian burden immediately becomes an option, a disjunctive, an exercise in liberty: Remain or Return. Like Prometheus, the narrator of *The Lost Steps* is man enough to know that liberty not exercised is liberty lost; the burden of liberty is to use it; and the philosopher wonders: would I have been more free if I had not used it?

This is the dilemma of Carpentier's narrator and, as we have seen, the Utopian dilemma. The perfect city is the place that is not: it has no place in space. Can it have one in time? The narrator hopes so. He hopes to capture Utopia in Time, to freeze it, along with his discovery of music, language, and his passionate love with Rosario. But no one is granted that much. Prometheus knew that hard truth all along; it cost Faust his soul to learn it. Time does not obey the narrator; Time does not halt obsequiously; Time moves, it escapes into the urban plan; it dashes headlong through genesis and, before genesis, in a nameless "world," without city, without Rosario, even without God: "the sidereal sadness of the times without incense or songs of praise, when the earth was without order and empty, and darkness was upon the face of the deep."

Having thus found the ideal community, the narrator cannot keep it. If he moves one more step backwards, he disappears into prehistory, into the absolute past. If he moves one step forward, he disappears into history, into the absolute future which is, by definition, always further, never reachable. And in both cases he loses the woman, he loses Rosario.

Utopia appears then as time, yes, but only an instant in time, a dazzling possibility of the imagination. *U-Topos*, the impossible space, turns out to be an equally impossible time, a lost double step: the two times of Utopia are mutually exclusive, the foundation city of origin cannot be the city of the future; never the twain shall meet. The Golden Age cannot exist at two different times, the remote past and the distant future. We are not going to recover lost time; we are going to live with the conflictive, heterogeneous values of liberty, never to be united again. It is better to know it. Better to accept it, not with resignation, but as a challenge . . .

Having to choose between remaining or returning, Carpentier's narrator freely chooses the return trip. But he doesn't return empty-handed. He has discovered the origin of music, he has heard the limitless possibilities of the human imagination and the capacity for knowledge. We exist in history. We live in the *polis*. We are historical and political beings but only valorous when we know ourselves, each one of us, to be the unique, irreplaceable bearers of a memory and a desire, united by language and by love.

5. NOVEL AND MUSIC

Alejo Carpentier brought many of these human and intellectual values to the Latin American novel. Like his narrator in *The Lost Steps*, he was a musicologist. He authored a history of Cuban music and a delicious fantasia, *Baroque Concert*. In it, an expatriate returned from Mexico, lost amid the carnival in seventeenth century Venice, attends a concert conducted by Vivaldi with nuns who play their eponymous instruments—Sor Rebekah (rebek), Sor Laúd (lute)—and whose carnival night culminates with him seated on Stravinsky's tomb on San Michele island watching Richard Wagner's funeral cortege glide past in a gondola. Above all, however, Carpentier is the author of a brief, masterful work of fiction, *The Chase*. It narrates a Cuban revolutionary's pursuit at the hands of the dictator Machado's police, in a Havana theatre, during the time it takes to perform Beethoven's *Fifth Symphony*. The novel coincides with the musical movements and culminates, inside the theatre itself, when silence reigns: when language dies, inside and outside the text.

The formal beauty and narrative tension of *The Lost Steps* also obey, in great measure, the musical movement I have observed in the three verbal series that arm, move, and give their conflict to the book. Carpentier was a man extraordinarily alert to movements in contemporary art and science, and his novels should not only be read taking into account the historical past so forcefully evoked in *The Lost Steps*, *The Kingdom of this World*, *Explosion in a Cathedral*, or *The War of Time* but also in light of contemporary works of poetry and music. In this way, in Carpentier's work, there occurs a cultural encounter of primary importance in itself and for Spanish language literature in the Americas. The vitality of time in Carpentier is equal to the vitality of language, and in that way the Cuban novelist shares the vision of Giambattista Vico: understanding that the past is impossible without understanding its myths, given that these form the basis of social life. For Vico, myth was a systematic way of seeing the world, comprehending it, and acting in it. Mythologies are the civil histories of the first men, all of whom were poets. Myths were the natural forms of expression for men and women who one day felt and spoke in ways which we can now only recover through an effort of the imagination. Thus Carpentier's efforts in *The Lost Steps* echo the Neapolitan philosopher's conviction: we are the authors of our history, beginning with our myths, and in consequence we are responsible for the past that we made in order to be responsible for a future we can call our own.

Musicologist and novelist, Carpentier actualizes history as our creation through narrations in which the reader's freedom is comparable to the freedom of a person listening to a serial musical composition, situated in the middle of a network of inexhaustible sonorous relationships, which give the listener the freedom to choose multiple ways of approaching the work, making use of a scale of references as wide as either the author or the listener wants them to be. This does not, therefore, create the center: it *is* the center, which is not imposed by the author, who limits himself to offer a repertory of suggestions. The result can be a writing and a reading, a composition and a listening as revolutionary as, let us say, the development from sequential computing operations originated by Von Neumann in the 1940s, to the simultaneous and concurrent operations predicted for the fifth generation of computers. Comparably, in both serial music and the threnody discovered by the Narrator of *The Lost Steps*, there is no tonal center which permits us to predict the successive moments of the discourse. Julio Cortázar (in whose work cinema has a greater presence, and whose clearest musical frame of reference must be jazz) will take this multi-directional narrative in which the auditor / reader / spectator can create his own system of relations with and within the work to its highest point of experimentation.

But it must have been Alejo Carpentier who first brought this spirit and these perspectives to the Latin American novel, enriching it beyond measure. When reading Carpentier, we do well to remember that with him our novel entered the world of contemporary culture not in any ancillary fashion or renouncing any of its own rights, but rather by fully collaborating in the creation of contemporary culture—modern and ancient, a culture of many times, among other things, thanks to novels like those of Carpentier. The cultural lag which was our nineteenth century debate—our tardy arrival to the banquets of Western culture, lamented by Alfonso Reyes—was not a problem for Carpentier or for the novelists who followed him. If there was a cultural delay, it was not fulfilled through declarations of love for France, hatred of Spain, or affiliations with one camp or another in the Cold War, but rather in the only positive way, by creating works of art of international validity.

Alejo Carpentier's narrative constructions, his uses of the simultaneity of planes, together with his fusion of languages in multiple spaces and times, offering readers the opportunity of construction, are an indissoluble part of the transitory universality that we are living.

In *Topia and Utopia*, a book that truly deserves to be reprinted in a new edition, Eugenio Ímaz, one of the great intellectuals in the Spanish Republican emigration to Mexico, reminds us that *U-Topia* is the place that is not because in time there is no place. Therefore, the author concludes, Utopia, the no-place, can only exist in a concrete present. Because if Utopia has no place in the world, it has all the time in the world. Carpentier would say: all the *times* in the world, and Spanish America, more than an immense space, is a superimposition of living times, which cannot be sacrificed. Saying this, and saying it with the literary beauty of the great Cuban novelist, is precisely what should be said when we enter a new century, a period of time whose development depends upon how we understand the multiplicity of human history.

In the world of Latin American novels, it is Alejo Carpentier who says, for the first time, that the utopia of the present lies in recognizing the time of others: their presence. In *The Lost Steps*, *The Kingdom of this World*, *Explosion in a Cathedral*, *The War of Time*, *Baroque Concert*, *The Harp and the Shadow*, *The Chase*, and *Reasons of State*, Carpentier offers us the path towards the plurality of times which is the true time of Spanish America: a condition of its history, a mirror of its self-recognition, and the pathetic promise of its struggle for a future of justice.

Between the search for the Golden Age and the promise of the New City of mankind, the literature of Alejo Carpentier stretches out like a verbal bridge which permits us to join that past and this future in a present: at least while reading his marvelous novels, the founders of our narrative present.

9. Onetti

I here take a biographical pause to remember Juan Carlos Onetti in Montevideo. He was wearing pajamas and a bathrobe. He lived with his wife. He had a sleepy, absent look on his face but his speech was lively and focused. His wife, however, was getting mad at him.

"Stop drinking that whiskey. Get to work."

Without relaxing his grip on the glass, Onetti indicated to me that we should go out. I accompanied him. With bathrobe, pajamas, and glass we reached another house situated a block and a half from the first. Onetti's mistress lived here.

He told his life's story. He'd been a porter, waiter, ticket vendor for sporting events. Later he sold fake Picassos. Many people thought that he was Irish, that his name was "O'Netty." He let them think what they liked . . .

"Put down your whiskey," his mistress said, and together we returned to Onetti's house, a block and a half away.

I met him again in New York at a famous meeting at the PEN Club arranged by Arthur Miller. The guest star there was Pablo Neruda, admitted into the U.S. thanks to Miller's help working against "blacklists" fabricated by the government in Washington, lists which also included partisans from a "second front" against Hitler in the Second World War. Some Latin American writers resented Neruda's stardom. Not Onetti: he went everywhere, had his picture taken with Neruda, taking it all in stride, he went to conferences and shook up the forgetful or mistaken lecturer with a sudden shout.

"What about Shakespeare?"

I tell all this in order to situate Onetti in a very particular kingdom of humor, which belongs to the River Plate. I speak here of Borges and Bioy, of Bianco and Cortázar. Belonging to this family, Onetti is mostly of the house of Roberto Arlt, to the degree to which both writers are, declaredly, *porteños*—people from Buenos Aires, and Buenos Aires is a unique city. It resembles no other place because it draws its influences and inspirations from everywhere else. Buenos Aires is a Spanish city but also an Italian city. It is a Jewish, Russian, and Polish city. It is a city of French whores and the pimps who shadow them. It is the city of the tango, and the tango resembles nothing but itself. And not only is the tango "a sad thought that can be danced" (Borges), it is also a coarse melodrama in which happiness does not show its face, a dance in which "one seeks, full of hope." Except that hope dies "sad, worn out and broken down" in the pre-dawn cabarets. An admirable effort by the great Tita Merello to give some humor to the tango. It only makes it stranger.

Onetti transcends these "influences" because, like all the novelists I discuss in this book, he neither influences nor is he influential. *He creates*, and in doing so continues and extends a *tradition*. The writer belongs to a tradition and enriches it with a new creation. This is owing to the tradition as much as the tradition owes to the creator. In this way, we see that the question of "influences" really has more to do with storytelling skill.

Then Céline makes himself present: the prose of imminent danger, the threat postponed, crime and transfiguration. Truculence. What is not found in Onetti is Céline's antisemitism: Onetti has too much humor to be a racist ideologue. Instead, he admits Arlt's previously cited *porteño* tradition, except that, in a magisterial manner, he broadens the former, limited register and unfolds a true symphony of the River Plate on its two banks, Buenos Aires and Montevideo. Except the music is almost not heard because Onetti's metropolis is a river town, the modest Santa María, as modest as Faulkner's Yoknapatawpha or García Márquez's Macondo. Because its placement at the lowest level permits a maximum expansion, Onetti creates a "saga of Santa María" which includes novels like *A Brief Life* (1950), *The Shipyard* (1961), and *Body Snatcher* (1965).

I limit myself to *A Brief Life* because it is not only the beginning of the saga, but also because here Onetti unleashes his whole narrative imagination in a single work, which if it is not the baptismal font of urban narrative in Latin America (Lizardi, Machado de Assis, *La Sombra del Caudillo*, other River Plate writers like Mallea and Marechal, Chileans like Manuel Rojas), it is reoriented far from the peasant agri-culture to an urban *agria-* (embittered) culture where the traditional thematic, still alive in Carpentier, García Márquez and Vargas Llosa, has been *ex-isled*, neither by naturalism nor realism, but rather by reality. And in Onetti, the reality is something more than itself. Not only is it the visible reality, but rather the in-visible. And not only the invisibility of the unexpressed subjective, but rather the *other* vision of the oneiric world.

The dream is the protagonist of *A Brief Life*, thanks to the fact that daily life and the imagination also play this role. In Onetti, the dream is dreamed because there is everyday life and there is a vigil of the imagination. The characters come and go, they work, travel, love, hate, and speak. They also imagine: they are themselves and they are, more than that, what they could be or what they would like to be according to their imagination. Then they sleep and dream. Where lies the frontier between daily life, imagination, and the dream? This is Onetti's question. To answer it he appeals to daily life, the imagination, and the dream to a degree, if not superior, then distinct to that of the other River Plate writers cited here.

He is less a naturalist than Arlt. More a realist than Borges. He gives dreams and nightmares to the world of Arlt. He gives streets, bars, apartments to the world of Borges.

The polyglot lumpenproletariat is the meat of the Arlt-Onetti prose, the lettered class of Franco-Britannic ascendency, its spirit. Onetti condenses the River Plate flesh and spirit to write a prose in which the speech of the street serves the language of dreams; this, in turn, serves the vocabulary of the imagination.

The "saga" of Santa María tells the stories of three characters. The first, Brausen, belongs to a very humble class of ancillary workers. The second, Arce, aspires to a kind of purity through crime. The third, Díaz-Grey, is a doctor with a practice in Santa María. Díaz-Grey seems perturbed by the intrusion of a woman, Elena. She visits him on medical pretexts but insinuates that she might readily offer him her body. Little by little, Arce becomes involved in the life of his neighbor, La Queca, a noisy, restless, alcoholic, bisexual woman. Brausen is married to a woman who was young and beautiful but has now lost her figure. Díaz-Grey must tolerate the appearance of Elena's husband, whose sexual permissiveness towards his wife has to be ambiguously hidden from the doctor, causing his finely controlled sexual appetite and curiosity to begin to crack wide open and end up crumbling.

Arce is increasingly committed to the fateful, ominous world of La Queca, where temptation must prevail over promiscuity, curiosity over obvious facts, and romantic anxiety over unabashed vulgarity. Brausen occasionally works for a film producer, Stein, whose artistic fantasies are no match for his business interests. Brausen fol-

lows Stein to restaurants and cabarets while the producer's wife, La
Mimi, evokes an imaginary life in Paris, sings *chansons d'amour*, plays
cards, and counts on the nostalgic indifference of Stein, who knew
and loved her, not when she was old and fat but young and slender like in the songs. Díaz-Grey is taken beyond schedules and obligations to a world where coincidence and nonsense are joined in an
enormous empty yawn of indifference: neither professional rigor nor
sexual pleasure any longer mean anything to him. Elena and her husband observe him like a couple of ghosts.

Arce does not know whether to enter the fleeting, senseless world
of La Queca. He is incited by the woman's physical and moral avail-
ability but also by her inaccessibility. Is there a mystery in La Queca's
lubricious transparency? Brausen lets his wife go to visit her family in
the country, take taxis, see Stein, and feels his life slipping between his
fingers. How can he recover his existence? How can he save himself
from the routine, from being fed up, from the self-pity which stalks
him? A wall separates him from La Queca. A river separates him from
Díaz-Grey. A city, Buenos Aires, separates him from himself. Brausen is a puritan without alcohol, tobacco or sex. Brausen is the man
in denial. Arce, by contrast, is a pure physical affirmation. He wants
to beat La Queca to death. Díaz-Grey, however, begins to feel that
he is no longer the master of his own desire.

Arce and Díaz-Grey feel themselves *created*, without autonomy.
Who, then, is the creator? Who communicates to them the conta-
gious energy which allows them to exist, speak, and move in *A Brief
Life*? Díaz-Grey begins to take the place of the unknown creator.
Through Elena and her husband he enters a territory that is not theirs
in order to be liberated from them.

Arce decides to kill La Queca in order to test his own autonomy but La Queca's fierce, grim young lover, Ernesto, beats him to
it; he kills the woman and frees Arce from the obligation, for whom
killing La Queca was an act of self-purification. Having missed his
chance, Arce is stripped of his action. In the end he is revealed as a
passive man, as passive as Brausen; both of them, Brausen and Arce,
are abandoned to a kind of fictive camaraderie. Each recognizes himself in the other. They recognize a shared territory, and realize that
they live parallel lives, simultaneous existences. Brausen has invented
a double called Arce; together Brausen and Arce enter a world which

both is and is not their own, a world where Díaz-Grey awaits them, revealed at last when he walks to the meeting with Brausen and Arce, as the third face of the same person: Brausen, inventor of Arce and Díaz-Grey, to the degree that each one feels that he awakes from a dream which includes the dreamed dream, and in which Brausen-Arce-Díaz-Grey had dreamed that he was dreaming the dream of the novel called *A Brief Life*, written by an author who signs his name Onetti but who could just as well be O'Netty. Just as Cervantes is also Saavedra and both of them are Cide Hamete and the author of *Don Quixote* is an unknown person who dropped the manuscript in a rubbish heap . . . Onetti can be O'Netty.

Onetti-O'Netty also belongs, in this way, to the Cervantean tradition of the indeterminate, multiple, or unknown author, and to the genre of genres, the novel: picaresque and epic, urban and no longer pastoral, migrant and not only Moorish, but forever Byzantine. The novel that knows itself to be a novel because it reads itself and knows itself to be read by readers. In short, a novel dreamed. In this chapter on Onetti's influences, I must be careful to not overlook two of the great oneiric works of literature. One of them is *Life is a Dream* by Calderón de la Barca, where Segismundo is condemned to dream. But, is the dream the equivalent of life? Since when does Segismundo dream? Since always? Since a few minutes ago? And until when? Condemned to dream, Segismundo cannot possess anything, save the dream in which he lives. The other work is *The Prince of Hamburg* by Heinrich von Kleist, where the dramatic action leads to the final dream which redeems and renews it. As Marcel Brion explains, the Prince of Hamburg's "somnambulism" authorizes a lucid and active "awakening." Is this because the awakening is another, unexpected, form of the dream? Do we move, do we speak, like sleepwalkers in "daily life"? And how much of our lives do we live sleeping?

The reader understands that these are the questions within literature's universal question. What are the limits between the real and the fictive? Between what is fiction and what is dreamed? Between what is dreamed and what is imagined? The works of Juan Carlos Onetti revive these questions about creation for us all, the Latin American writers and readers of today and tomorrow.

10. Julio Cortázar and the Smile of Erasmus

1.

The work of Julio Cortázar is filled with what the Argentine author himself liked to call "serene madmen." This is nothing less than the Erasmian bloodline. Men, writes Erasmus in *In Praise of Folly*, are beings who exceed their limits. "All other animals are content with their natural limitations. Only man tries to take one step further." For that reason, man is mad. As mad as Don Quixote trying to live out exactly what he has read, or Pierre Menard, in Borges's story, trying to rewrite Cervantes's text with perfect fidelity. As mad as the Buendía family reinventing alchemy in *One Hundred Years of Solitude*, or like Talita and Traveler as they step out onto their precarious plank-bridges at the asylum in Cortázar's *Hopscotch*.

There are many kinds of madness and not all of them are bad. I have mentioned the serene madness of a Greek man evoked by Horace in one of his epistles and by Erasmus in *Moriae Encomium*. This man was so crazy that he spent his days inside a theatre, laughing, applauding, and enjoying himself, because he believed that a play was being performed on the empty stage. When the theatre was closed and the madman turned out, he exclaimed: "You haven't cured me of my madness; but you have destroyed my pleasure and the illusion of my happiness." One madman laughs at another, says Erasmus, and each one gives the other pleasure. But if we observe closely, we will see that the craziest man is the one who laughs the most. And perhaps, he who laughs last.

The children of Erasmus reach from Cervantes's *Don Quixote* to Borges's *Pierre Menard, Author of the Quixote*. Along the way, we recognize other victims of a fascinating madness who end up deceiving a fascinated world. In Laurence Sterne's novel, *Tristram Shandy*, Uncle Toby reenacts the Duke of Marlborough's campaigns in his vegetable garden, as if only the miniature scale of the two rows of cauliflower could contain a political and military madness, which would be unbearable in another form. Determined to visit the hostelries of France and unable to begin or end a story, Diderot's fatalistic Jacques, along with his Master, are condemned to offer both themselves and us a repertoire of infinite possibilities for every event they summon up, and for this reason they are freer than the awareness of their fatality. We meet Don Quixote's granddaughters, Jane Austen's Catherine Morland, and Gustave Flaubert's Emma Bovary, condemned, like Don Quixote, to believe what they read: novels of chivalry in La Mancha, gothic novels in Bath, romantic novels in Yonville. We recognize Dickens's Mr. Micawber, who confuses his great expectations with the realities of his spendthrift life; Dostoyevsky's Prince Myshkin, an idiot because he believes in human goodness; and Perez Galdos's itinerant priest, Nazarín, crazy because he believes that each human being can be Christ in his daily life and that he is really St. Paul's madman: "If any man among you thinks that he is wise in this age, he must become foolish, so that he may become wise," says the apostle in one of his letters to the Corinthians. "Because the folly of God is wiser than all the wisdom of men." Is God the fool who laughs longest and laughs last?

In Spain and Spanish America, the children of Erasmus become the children of La Mancha, the children of a world that is syncretic, Baroque, and corrupt. They find inspiration and raison d'être in tainting what is pure, they assimilate by infecting, they multiply appearances and realities, they duplicate truths and impede the establishment of an orthodox world based on faith or reason, or a pure world which excludes cultural or national variety. The weapons of irony, humor and the imagination were, are, and will be those of Erasmus, in counterpoint to the mythic, epic and utopian world of Latin American tradition.

2.

Duality of truth, illusion of appearances, praise for folly. In the novelistic tradition of Europe, this Renaissance corrective to the orthodoxy of faith and the unity of language, as well as to the dictatorship of reason and its logical language, contributed to maintain the values of the critical humanism of Erasmus of Rotterdam. But this humanist criticism naturally coincided with an apogee of affirmation for novelistic characters: Dickens describes them right down to the last detail; Flaubert explores them to their very innards; Balzac to their last bank check, and Zola down to the dregs of their last drink. The fundamental problem to be considered after Kafka is the death of the traditional novelistic character, exhausted by sociology, naturalism, psychology and other realist virulences. But exhausted, above all, by the history of our time: a history of crimes committed in the name of happiness and progress, which drained the promises of Renaissance humanism, of eighteenth century Enlightenment optimism, and of the material progress of the industrial and post-industrial centuries.

Dickens knows Micawber down to the last detail. Flaubert knows that he himself is Madame Bovary, and we suppose that Emma Bovary doesn't really realize that she is Flaubert. But all that Gregor Samsa knows is that one morning he awoke transformed into a beetle. Kafka's man sees himself in the mirror and discovers that he has lost his face. Nobody remembers him. But because he is unknown he can be executed: because he is different, he is other. He is the victim of the dialectic of happiness, of perfectibility and progress, which was modernity's *raison d'être*.

From the heart of European modernity, the Czechoslovakian Milan Kundera, a great post-Kafka novelist, lucidly assumes the legacy of his compatriot, wondering: "What possibilities remain for man in a world in which external determinations have become so crushing that interior motivations have stopped having any weight?" According to Kundera, Proust tries to provide "maximum information about a character," knowing his past and granting him "a total independence with respect to the author." After Kafka none of this is valid. In *The Castle* or *The Trial*, the world no longer resembles any known reality; it is only "an extreme and unrealized possibility of the human world"; this is what matters, not the past, the physical characteristics, or the psychological motivations of the multiple K's of Kafka, lacking all the attributes of the realistic novel of the past.

Nevertheless, Kundera's *Art of the Novel* offers a particularly noteworthy phrase, in which he tells us that "Don Quixote is almost unimaginable as a living being." Nonetheless, asks Kundera, is there any person more alive than Don Quixote? He's right to ask. What has happened is that, with time, the figure of Don Quixote became an archetype; a bearer, in the Jungian sense, of tribal memory and imagination; an imaginary incarnation of the collective subconscious. But this was not always so. Kundera asks: what was Don Quixote before turning into an archetype? An unimaginable being. He was a figure, similar to Kafka's antiheroes or Beckett's non-characters today; he was a surprised study in abandonment, an enterprise, a possibility. Beckett calls such figures *unnameables*. Novalis previously called them *figures*: "Men travel by distinct paths. Whoever follows them and compares their great diversity will see marvelous figures appear; figures that seem to belong to the great Manuscript of Design."

We get the feeling of having exhausted the novelistic persona as a psychological and descriptive character. We long for new archetypes for our world that has lost the highest illusions of progress, stuck on the condemnation of crime, although without the salvation of tragedy. And in all the arts we face what we have forgotten or would still not know how to name; the figures of that "great Manuscript of Design," which no one has fully read: the reverse of the theme, the figure—Henry James—in the carpet.

This sense of the mysterious, unfinished figure, born from the rupture of the traditional character and its signs; this figure in a state of genesis or metamorphosis is one of the realities of contemporary literature. I am going to limit myself to observe it in the work of the Latin American writer who, in the most explicit manner, joins his work to the exploration of the exhausted character and the evasive figure. I refer to Julio Cortázar, in whose fictions we constantly observe the manner in which archetypes translate into figures through new forms of memory and imagination.

3.

Among all the marvelous stories by Julio Cortázar—where houses are slowly but inexorably taken over by inanimate or forgotten figures; where people forget their destiny as soon as they step up to buy their tickets at the railway station; where, like a two way street, a shopping mall in Buenos Aires leads to a shopping mall in Paris; where a character suffers an automobile accident in a European city and immediately finds himself atop an operating table which is really a sacrificial stone altar in Mexico; and where a victim of the Aztecs discovers himself to be like a new character in an unimaginable white space surrounded by masked men with shining scalpels—among all these stories, I'm captivated most by "Instructions for John Howell."

In this story an innocent spectator in London discovers that there is no such thing as an innocent spectator. Howell is compelled to join in the play he is watching because the heroine of the work murmurs to him secretly: "Help me, they're going to kill me." Howell understands these words as a plea for help to enter the woman's life. But this is only possible if he steps onto the woman's stage. In this way, her plea becomes an instruction, a stage direction which decides the life and death of John Howell.

I choose this story because it seems to me the most precise counterpart to the story of the madman in the theatre told by Horace and picked up again by Erasmus. But in these times, nobody would dare to call John Howell "crazy." Forgotten, separated, outside the traditional text; abandoned, yes: a nascent figure, a new, unfinished character, an unassimilated archetype. Like all of Julio Cortázar's characters he informs us, the same as Erasmus on the threshold of his modernity, about the insufficiencies, dangers, and humor of what is *our own.*

Frank Loveland, professor of American literature, has commented that, ironically, plans and projects for the Ibero-American natural world—the rural world, the pampas, the forest and jungle, the mountain—have come from the city. They have been imposed on a rural world by the modern urban world which sees nature as a primitive universe. This is true of the writer-statesman Domingo F. Sarmiento, but also of contemporary novelists like Rómulo Gallegos, Alejo Carpentier and Mariano Azuela. All of them, confident like the Venezuelan, skeptical like the Cuban, desolate like the Mexican, are bearers of modernizing projects. As I said about Gallegos, they are all, nonetheless, writers—not only ideologues—who admit the dialogical operation by which their theses are defeated. This is even truer for Rulfo and García Márquez, given that their "interior" visions were born of poetic empathy. In Cortázar, however, there is no need to establish any distance, because he is a fully urban writer, criticizing, from within, our modern societies.

What Cortázar shares with all the writers I have just mentioned, is the necessity of naming and of giving voice. It is a necessity that begins with the relationship between power and language, with the necessity of wrenching the word from male power (from el Tlatoani, the Lord of the Great Voice: Moctezuma) and granting it to woman, to the mother of his children (Malinche and her descendants). It is a necessity imposed by the limits with which the epic (bearer of power) besieges myth (bearer of language). In the colonial era, the Baroque poems of Sor Juana and the chronicles of El Inca Garcilaso recover voices from the silence. But the revolution in modern literature, especially in the twentieth century novel, also permitted the writers of Spanish and Portuguese America to discover and apply linguistic techniques which accelerated the process of giving greater name and voice to the largely silent and anonymous continent. Obviously, far from being a gratuitous imitation of contemporary fiction, these techniques explore something more than just time, culture, and an underlying myth in Europe and the United States. They discovered what the peoples of Ibero-America always knew, but which their writers, oriented (Westernized) to the forms of narrative realism, had not discovered as our universal reality: myth, epic, Baroque, irony, humor, and the Erasmian smile in the face of human possibility. Multiple cultures, the bearers of different times. Among Latin American novelists this modern critical imagination has no better representative than the Argentine Julio Cortázar.

The conjunction of traditional texts (pre-Hispanic myths, Indian chronicles) and new Western post-realist techniques (Joyce, Faulkner, Kafka, Broch, Woolf) has permitted an unprecedented empowerment of the Ibero-American narrative discourse, making space for its past, its present, its aspirations, its multitude of traditions, its heteroglossia: the continent's languages in conflict: Europeans, indigenous peoples, blacks, mestizos. All of that permitted us to expand and bring to light a multitude of realities which did not fit within the narrow tunnel of realism, and to insert them into a historic vision inseparable from the uses of language. The Western novel passed from the linear narrative told in the first person, aiming for and shooting towards the future (the novel as chronicle of the self and, even, the Ego: Stendhal; and not only of *el Nombre* (the Name) but rather *el Re-Nombre* (the Re-Name and the Renown): Montaigne; the narrative of the personal Confession: from Saint Augustine to Rousseau), to a more collective, pluralistic perspective by way of James Joyce and his recovery of Vico's philosophy in *Ulysses* and *Finnegans Wake,* with Vico's ample vision of language as a popular, common enterprise, which originates with civilizations themselves. Before all else, civilization signifies language, and language is a social creation.

By the very nature of its physical hyperbole and historic responsibility, the modern Ibero-American novel includes the single, unique voice but also transcends it constantly. The *conflation* of voices is a constant process in García Márquez and Vargas Llosa. In many of Rulfo's stories and novels the collective dimensions of memory and death are the true protagonists. In Lezama Lima's *Paradiso* the characters' cultural dimension is essential, as is the epic, historical force in Azuela's writing, or the vast impersonality of the jungle and the river in a whole range of novelists from Rivera to Gallegos to Carpentier.

But the two Argentines, Borges and Cortázar, are those who best signal the universality of the dilemma. Borges transcends it by giving his tales the faces of entire civilizations, vast *summas* of knowledge and instantaneous passages through time and space. But Cortázar gives his a more human and dynamic dimension. Cortázar is perfectly aware that realism's psyche-persona has died, but he refuses to kill off the faceless character that we now contemplate with a mixture of horror and pity. Cortázar manages figures, neither characters nor archetypes, but to these figures he gives his true power, which is the power of becoming, of being, of not ending. This is the very definition of the figure, being, becoming, metamorphosing, deprived of its traditional shape. But Cortázar, unlike any other contemporary narrator in our language, breathes life into his figures with an incomparable veneration, what fragile sprouts in a garden require to grow.

In Cortázar's mythic narrations, houses are taken over; staircases are used exclusively for ascending, others for only going down; windows for only looking outside, others for looking in. In a Cortázar story we can watch our own face in an aquarium, possessed anew by nature, laughing at ourselves, or we can attend a London theatre, watch the first act seated in the audience, stroll about during the intermission and come in free and easy for the second act, wondering what the words of our dialogue will be.

For all this to be narrated requires an extraordinarily creative and flexible language. Cortázar is aware of this, as he demonstrates in *Hopscotch*, the novel that is perhaps the most critical and provocative repertory in the urban modernity of Spanish America, because it is founded on the necessity of inventing a language for our actual lives. A language that can be faithful to the Cortázarian premise, as Lezama Lima articulates it in his great essay about *Hopscotch*: man is incessantly created and is incessantly the creator.

4.

The literary structure of *Hopscotch*—divided between a *there*: Paris; and a *here*: Buenos Aires—designs a game of utopias which hearkens back to the origin of our culture. If, in the sixteenth century, America was the utopia of the European, in the nineteenth century America returned the favor, converting Europe into our utopia. Not just any Europe, however, but the progressive, democratic, liberal Europe that already was, according to our illusions and dreams, what we were going to be after Independence. This, as was made explicitly clear by Domingo Faustino Sarmiento, Esteban Echeverría, and Victorino Lastarria, excluded Spain, the representative of an obscurantist past. Modern Europe, however, is the utopia which many Ibero-Americans set up in opposition to the peasant "barbarism" (Sarmiento) or the colonial "black winter" (Lastarria). And although the repudiation of the Spanish, Indian, and agrarian past extended from Mexico to Buenos Aires, Argentina is the nation which most fervently embraced the saving identification with the European utopia.

Similarly, in the Southern Cone the independent republican governments denied their burden of responsibility to the indigenous people even as they nurtured European Immigration. The campaigns of General Bulnes in Chile and General Roca in Argentina were intended to isolate or exterminate the native peoples, analogous to the campaigns against the Native Americans of the North American Far West. As the liberal Argentine ideologue Juan Bautista Alberdi famously stated, "To govern is to populate." But first they had to depopulate the indigenous regions, opening them up, by contrast, for white immigration. In 1869, the population of Argentina was barely two million inhabitants. Between 1880 and 1905, almost three million immigrants came to the country.

These comings and goings between the American and European utopias constitute the humorous backdrop of *Hopscotch*. Two movements are found in its pages, each commenting ironically on the other. One is the novel's movement defined as a displacement, an abandonment of the home, a mythic orphanhood, an epic venturing forth into the world, and a tragic return home. As observed, the commentary and undertones surrounding this classic voyage are the modern novel's inevitable trajectory, in search of a lost circularity, rebelling against assimilation to progressive modernity, forever hurtling forward in time: a kind of regressive bedwetting. From Ulysses to *Ulysses*, from *Don Quixote* to *Lolita*, the novel shifts, changes location, moves in search of something else: from Jason's golden fleece to the "pubic floss" of Nabokov's nymphet. The novel is dissatisfaction, the search for what is not there (gold in Stevenson and Dumas; society and fame in Stendhal; the absolute in Balzac; time in Proust; recognition in Kafka; spaces in Borges; the novel in Faulkner; language in Joyce). In order to satisfy the search, the novel works every imaginable twist and turn into its displacement: distortion, changing the object of desire, a regrouping of material, a substitution of satisfying comforts, disguising the erotic dream as a social dream, a triumph of the replaced allusion, the translation from immediacy to mediacy. Displacement: leave town, move away from home, in search of another reality: the invention of America by Europe but also of Europe by America.

Hopscotch takes particular pleasure in destroying the very tradition from which it comes. It is an epic dedicated to mocking impossible tragic circularity by replacing it with comic circularity. A burlesque epic of a handful of Argentines who seek their utopia in Europe, the circularity in *Hopscotch* is designed as a childlike game, a search for the ludic heaven. Beyond the game, however, without abandoning it, is the search for a utopia: the last Isle, the Kibbutz of Desire, as Cortázar calls it. A woman, La Maga, is mistress of the game. But she herself is an absence, which the novel begins by questioning: "Would I find La Maga?" In her presence and absence, she is the guiding character, the desired woman, both sought after and absent, who justifies both novelistic and erotic pilgrimage. La Maga (being present) guides the spirit of literal and metaphoric displacement, across the bridges of the Seine or (absent) across the planks between two windows in a Buenos Aires insane asylum. Lezama Lima has noted that in *Hopscotch*, Cortázar makes visible the manner in which two characters, without meeting one another, can establish the counterpoint, the dynamic, of a novel. This dynamic is a series of comings and goings, acted out by two sets of expatriates: Oliveira and La Maga, Argentine exiles in Paris, and, in Buenos Aires, Talita and Traveler (who hates his name because he has never traveled), caretakers of an insane asylum, interior exiles and doubles of a couple they do not know, Oliveira and La Maga. But, when they do meet, they rebel against the novel which contains them: they refuse to be part of it.

This rebellion following the coincidence of characters is, in a certain way, a celebration of their previous *ignorance*; but also a *recognition* of their belonging to a verbal universe and their rejection of the same. The cultural, social, historical essence of *Hopscotch*, so to speak, is the story of a failure. Neither Oliveira and La Maga in Paris, nor Traveler and Talita in Buenos Aires, are going to find utopia, the heaven of Hopscotch.

In Buenos Aires, the immigrant's utopia, the paradox revealed by literature is that Argentina's authenticity is its lack of authenticity; Argentina's reality is a fiction and its national essence is its imitation of Europe. But if Europe is the utopia then, in Cortázar, the Western world appears like a secondhand assortment of used ideas; European reason is a brothel of virgins, as if this were possible. European society is "a blind alley at the service of the Great-Idealist-Realist-Spiritualist-Materialist-Infatuation of the West, Inc." Of history, Oliveira *says* that perhaps there is a millenary kingdom, but if we ever reach it, we will no longer be able to call it that; concerning intelligence, he *says* that the simple fact of *speaking* about something instead of *doing* it demonstrates that it's wrong; Oliveira *says* that love cannot be lived because it must be *named*.

History, reason, intelligence, and love, are all not only realities but verbal realities, spoken, in the first place, by Oliveira, the novel's protagonist. Who would care to join him in such a pitiless denial of reality, a denial which is impossible because it also requires language to be manifested? To make visible, *in another way*: this might be the intention of displacement in *Hopscotch*, but its author is caught within the same vicious circle he denounces, in the same blind alley of language corresponding to a broken civilization. What can the narrator of *Hopscotch* do but declare himself, as he does, to be "at war with words, at war, doing everything necessary even though intelligence might have to be renounced . . ."?

He first renounces the dustbin of words in favor of action. But writing is also an action, is it not? Would stopping writing mean to stop being Oliveira, an inaction? As Italo Calvino *writes*, isn't the cult of action, in the very first place, a very old literary myth? Granted: Oliveira will have to write in order for his actions to be described.

But he takes his *de-scribing* to great lengths to convert it into *dis-inscription*. If he cannot renounce the said and the unsaid of speaking, at least he will do so by *dis-inscribing*, before our eyes, a new novel which might be the bearer of a counter-language and a counter-utopia. How? By taking language beyond psychological characters, realism, psychological verism, historic accuracy, and all the other conventions of an exhausted tradition, of the reality denounced in *Hopscotch*. How? By allowing that in a novel, instead of counting on all the satisfying details of social realism and compensatory psychologism, we see ourselves in the radical distress of characters in the process of becoming.

Let us then return to the initial point of my argument, the brilliant formal division of *Hopscotch*. In the novel's first part, "From the Other Side," Paris is the true homeland, the original model, *¡ay!*, but without the defects of the Argentine original; in the second part, "From This Side," Buenos Aires is the false homeland, *¡ay!*, but without the perfections of the French original. Between the bridge's two shores, between the asylum's two windows shakily connected by Oliveira's precarious plank bridge, there is a point of exile, the exclusion of both space and times. A brief stay in Europe, where so much time has passed. All the time in the world in Argentina, that has so little history and is instead rich in "generous schedules, open houses, time to kill, all the time and days to come, all of it, voof, voof, voof . . ."

To have all the time in the world is the poorest kind of richness; but not having time because we already spent it, we already wasted it, is also a state of distress and exile. In this double exile, which is also a doubly inopportune time, the unknown figures of *Hopscotch* begin to be drawn. Their presence in the novel accumulates according to how much they have been and what they have said. But in the end, as Cortázar wishes, Oliveira, La Maga, Talita, and Traveler will only become visible by realizing that, apart from our destinies, we form part of figures we still don't know. In the words of Lezama Lima, Cortázar destroys a space to build a space; he decapitates time so that time may reappear with a different head. Having done so, he has perhaps played his part and can incite his two couples, the one here and the one there, to enter the novel on the condition that they not be traditional characters, but rather part of those figures "that we still don't know."

How do we become part of these unknown, still gestating figures while we remain captives of history, reason, love, action and passivity, the language of the two sick utopias? How, hostages, from this side or that one, here or there? How, as we remain joined, in the end, to our exile—this is the tragic conscience of *Hopscotch*'s comedy—in that same history, that same reason, that love . . . ? How?

Cortázar proposes two paths. The first is sadder than the other, because it is the verbal path: the recognition that only with language, mocked, critiqued, insufficient, and lying, will we be able to create a *different* language, an anti-language, a counter-language. Citing Lezama, I have spoken about the creative meeting of the two shores, that side and this side, Europe and America, which followed the conquest. Lezama calls it the Counterconquest. Regarding *Hopscotch*, the Cuban writer, so close to Cortázar, also makes us see that the novel is shot through with "an ancestral language, with the tribal chief's babbling." This tribal language solemnizes, *elderizes*, belongs to the other family, the one which squeezes the toothpaste tube from the bottom up. But Lezama's intuition is that this language of tradition, consecrated, honored, perhaps adhering closely to the marble-like perfection which Lezama himself invokes in order to identify perfection, fixity, immobility, and death must, as in *Paradiso*, dive headlong into the pool of life and reveal itself to be a mere "babbler" in the face of the other language, that of the new family, which realizes its frightening philological abandonment and responds to the laws of the tribe with chilling mockery and grotesque language, desacralizing any situation or dialogue.

Two verbal families, the solemn and the mocking, the ancestral and the expectant. Lezama is right to say that Cortázar possesses the necessary rhythm to regulate the conversations in the two languages, "between the chief of the tribe and the shipwrecked admiral." Like Alberti, a sailor on dry land, but this time an entirely unique land: the pampas, a portrait of the horizon, a countenance without a face, an absence of features, a space in continuous recession from the gaze, the Tantalus-space of Argentina. There, Horacio Oliveira, the Buster Keaton of the pampas, Columbus without an ocean, falls flat on his big wooden poker face, facedown upon the flattest land of all, a serene fool in the Erasmian tradition. What does the serene fool think there? How would we praise his folly, here at the start of the new millennium?

Perhaps Oliveira, bearer of the first language that left him rowing on dry land, now inundates the pampas with the verbal ocean of the second language. His drama is that he cannot renounce words even when he is disposed to *de-scribe*, and to be a *de-scriber*. He is not the first "writer" in such a predicament. In his famous essay about Rabelais, Bakhtin describes the *second* language as a comic, parodic, carnivalesque language, a form of verbal masquerade, a comic reprocessing of all levels of language. But the appearance of this second comic language would require, as Viktor Shklovsky wrote about Sterne's *Tristram Shandy*, that his own artifice might be revealed, that the same technique, the framework, skeleton, or machinery of the novel, become evident. Upon displaying the same technique in the novel, against all the good advice of the little literary grannies, the novelist abandons his text: he reveals it as an unsheltered text, exposed to the elements as much as its characters or its babbling language: "Shipwrecked admirals." But in the end, only from such a radical abandonment can new figures emerge, with their new language and new text.

Shklovsky's lesson is the same as Cortázar's in *Hopscotch*. His language of rhythms, onomatopoeias, puns, neologisms and radical heteroglossia, opposes all forms of literary "good taste." It is motivated by a pulsating, multi-faceted hunger. Cortázar believed that in order to challenge society, he first had to challenge reality. And this could only be done by revealing the unauthorized dissatisfactions, projecting unspoken desires, admitting the most scandalous jokes, withdrawing the planks, rewriting and reordering the world, reintroducing it in its skeletal function, showing off his indifference to the *elderizing* fiction of well-turned phrases, hidden plots, and enchanting narration. To the Sara García of grandmotherly good taste, Cortázar unleashes a fascinating, naked Scheherazade, narrating desperately to save herself from death. In *Christopher Unborn*, I called her the first novelist and public storyteller. Scheherazade is La Maga, and in *Hopscotch* she finds Oliveira, her *cash-strapped* caliph, her stranded admiral. Between the two, to save herself from the death that stalks them both, from that life that "crouches down to be caressed like a beast with interminable flanks" (Lezama), from that crocodile which upon waking *is still there*, as in Augusto Monterroso's short story, they invent this novel and offer it, naked and abandoned, to the world, the material of multiple readings, not only one: a text that can be read, as indicated by its table of instructions, in a thousand ways.

Abandoned, being there and here, Oliveira earns his text by revealing that he is a text, a fiction, the verbal warp from which, perhaps, new figures are born, stretching out his hand to touch emotions and words as yet unregistered. But all in collaboration with the reader. The elliptical quality of Cortázar's fiction is a way of indicating that we are in charge of history's possible revision, inviting the reader, like the actress in "Instructions for John Howell," to enter the story, to create it, to share responsibility for the story. To finally enter time, to invite others to enter my time. Entering another person's time, more than space, is the best manner of really getting to know them. Perhaps the house is taken over; but outside of it, unsheltered, we can share time together. Only by knowing each other can we all, Europeans and Ibero-Americans, finally know ourselves. We can be ourselves only with others. Thus we win the game of *Hopscotch*, we conquer Utopia.

If *Hopscotch* is an invitation to recreate the language of our modernity, behind its text, nevertheless, floats the specter of how much we have been. A text of the counter-language of Spanish America, it descends from the Counterconquest, that simultaneous response to the Conquest from the first American generation, with architects, painters, poets, artisans, amanuenses and utopians; cooks, dancers, singers, lovers . . .

In a way, by creating this counter-language capable of writing, rewriting, and even de-scribing our history, Cortázar finalizes the project of the Counterconquest. His ferociously demanding concept of an Ibero-American modernity is based on language because we were founded and then corrupted by the language of the sixteenth century—America is first a utopia without time or place, then immediately a plantation, an hacienda, a country estate, forcing us to expand our language, to liberate it from orthodoxies and convert it into the time and space of an inclusive metaphor, which admits all verbal forms: like Don Quixote, we don't know *where* to find *the truth*.

But if this modernizing enterprise is to be, at last, *more authentic* than previous enterprises in our history, it will only be possible if we manage to keep the Erasmian tradition alive in its heart, so as to prevent this modernizing project from becoming a new absolute, a rightist or leftist totalitarianism, a sanctimony of State or enterprise, or a servile model of some "great potential," and foster, instead, a source of relativism attentive to the presence of multiple cultures in a new multipolar world.

5.

In many senses, Erasmus continues to be the intellectual father of Spanish and Latin American democracy. He is the link between More's idealism and Machiavelli's realism. He admits, with Machiavelli, that the real and ideal rarely coincide; instead they differ constantly. For a utopia, this divergence is untenable. But Erasmus is no utopian. He accepts divergence, only wanting to narrow it slightly so life might be more livable. Writers understand Erasmus well. It is impossible to achieve a total identity between words and things. Such identity might not even be desirable but the effort is worth the trouble. Even when it fails, the attempt to reunite words and things creates a new and marvelous reality in the world: the literary work.

That is why I place Julio Cortázar within the third great founding tradition of our culture: that of Erasmus of Rotterdam. Lezama immediately notes the divorce that Cortázar makes his own: the "grotesque and irreparable division between what is said and what one tried to say, between the spirit breathed into the word and its visible configuration." This is the difference between Machiavelli and More, between Topia and Utopia. In order to avoid the traps of absolutes — this *is*, this *must be* — Cortázar introduces us to a witness of his intellectual operation: the serene madman, an ironic narrator, the observer of the madness of Topia and Utopia, but he himself is seen as a madman by both. Erasmus / Cortázar invites the reader, as Lezama says, to mount the author, forming a new centaur. "Punished and favored by two gods at the same time," the reader "goes blind, but is granted prophetic vision." Cortázar's narrators (and narrations), the most radically modern in Spanish America, are nevertheless connected, by the Erasmian shortcut, to the prose works of our foundation. Unlike the epic, they participate in and enrich that "prophetic vision" which was expressed, from the start, as a "bestiary of the Indies." *Bestiario* also happens to be the title of one of Cortazar's lovely books of stories in which we find the latest descendants of what was seen, heard, or dreamed by Fernández de Oviedo, Pedro Mártir, Juan de

Cárdenas, Gutiérrez de Santa Clara, López de Gómara and other chroniclers of the Indies: leviathans and sirens, sea wolves, manatees with a woman's breasts and sharks with double penises.

Cortázar's fantastic bestiary includes little white bunnies vomited up at inconvenient moments; axolotls who stare at us with our own face from inside the municipal aquarium; even strange bestial life forms like a sweater that can never be removed; or some unmentionable companion that might be a person, a thing, or an animal. What is most notable about this bestiary is that we know that it is watching us. It observes us, like the most significant presences in the Cortázarian narrative: the serene madmen of Erasmian lineage, questioning all the projects of reason and history and, especially, of language, barely satisfied with themselves and driven by the desire to impose themselves on others as the truth.

The lawyer Juan Cuevas, the celebrated Uruguayan orator Mr. Ceferino Piris, the prudish nymphomaniac pianist Berthe Trépat, that fearful old man who caressed a dove on the way down to the morgue ... All these serene, lonely mad people observe the adventures of logic and its bearer, language, and respond with warnings. They interrupt the action, they multiply it with their ironic unreason, their praise of folly and madness, their permanent dissatisfaction, their search for what is not there, leading us to *Hopscotch*'s apparent denouement: Oliveira's odyssey in search of La Maga, and his encounter with Talita, La Maga's double, the sedentary Traveler, who only moved from Argentina "to cross over to Montevideo." The figures who did not know each other before become acquainted and thwart the very existence of the book that contains them: *Hopscotch*. Unaware of themselves, they promoted the novel's initial dynamic. Gaining self-awareness, they threaten to rush headlong towards what refuses it: the conclusion, unacceptable for the open novel that Cortázar is writing before our very eyes. Encountering his double, Oliveira has to *act*: his options are either murder or madness. In another way, he might have to accept that our life, in not being singular, lacks value and sense; that another person, who is me, thinks, loves, and dies for me and perhaps I am the double of my double and only live his life.

Oliveira attempts murder through terror. Not a true murder, because killing your double would be suicide, but rather an attempt to open the doors of madness. Or, at least, to make others believe that one went mad and, for that reason, be excused from all action, including writing, that disguised action. Dead to others, we cease to be the double of anybody or to have any duplication. Madness, to the degree to which it is a dis-appearance, an in-visibility, also kills the double, as it is deprived of its model. There, in the madhouse, one can believe that the serene madmen, Juan Cuevas or Ceferino Piris, are as worthy of intellectual attention as Aristotle or Heidegger: in the end, what do they do but multiply reality, inventing what seems to them to be missing in the world? And what has the novel done? And what has the novelist done that the novel has done that Oliveira has done to his double who has made a madman out of Oliveira?

Would I find La Maga? Would he? Convinced that "a casual encounter is apt to be just the opposite," Oliveira has decided to make this immense journey, from Paris to Buenos Aires, from one hopscotch to another, in search of what he calls, in the end, a "materialized nebula": La Maga. The material nebula is, clearly, the novel itself, *la niebla*, the fog, mist, nimbus, Miguel de Unamuno's *nivola* or *nubela*:[4] "Would I find La Maga?": the magic of the cloud, La Maga of the nebula, is the search for La Maga, or rather, the search for the novel. Incapable of finding closure because he has not found La Maga (there is no novel without La Maga), from inside his River Plate madhouse Oliveira directs us to the novel's "table of instructions," which simultaneously provides a re-initiation of the novel, a search, a multiplication of reality and perpetual dissatisfaction, by the shortcut via Chapter 62 where Cortázar's alter ego, Morelli, theorizes about the novel and opens two paths: one, forever accompanying Oliveira on his search for La Maga; the other, writing the following open novel: *62: A Model Kit.*

And in between, a few moments of light tenderness, listening to a jazz record with eyes closed, hearing "the din of the moon resting against his ear the palm of a small hand a little damp from love or from a cup of tea." *Il faut tenter de vivre.*

Julio Cortázar and *Hopscotch* place the Latin American novel on the very threshold of the potential novel: the future novel from a culturally diverse and unsatisfied world.

---

4 Unamuno's coinage for a modern, non-realistic novel; the name invokes the Spanish words *nube* (cloud) and *nivel* (level).

11. José Lezama Lima:
Body and Word of the Baroque

O that this too too solid flesh would melt,
Thaw, and resolve itself into a dew . . .
Hamlet, I.ii.129

1. Imaginary Eras

The Cuban poet and novelist José Lezama Lima represents a different line of force from our cultural history: the Baroque, which I have described as a contraction between the lost utopia and the perverse epic of the New World, insofar as both, in their American postulation, rest on the idea of space, the hunger for space and the liberation from the same, which Edmundo O'Gorman proposes as stimuli for the invention of America.

In our time, however, the figure of the Baroque only becomes plainly identifiable and comprehensible thanks to its inclusion within the concept of imaginary eras which Lezama Lima proposed in *The American Expression*. Nobody has seen more clearly than he, that if our political history can be properly considered a series of fragments, cultural history presents a noticeable continuity. Even when political clashes, in themselves fragmentary, try to project their own rupture onto cultural life (a negation of the indigenous world by the Spanish; a negation of the Spanish, indigenous, and Mestizo worlds by independent modernity), the concept of imaginary eras gives us the opportunity to restore continuity. Often disguised, feigning death, and mimicking others with silence, continuity has always survived through that same mimetic silence and its apparitions, here phantasmal, there clamorous, in the syncretism of the Baroque and the constancy of popular culture: music, gestures, furniture, crafts, cooking, eroticism, language, clothing, beliefs, images, customary rights . . . In short, what Lezama Lima calls the Counterconquest of what is purely European by the Indo-Afro-Ibero-American, and what Vico, before anyone else, called the civil society, history made and maintained by men and women.

Lezama's imaginary eras have the same magnitude. It is his way of saying that cultures are his imagination, not his archives. "If a culture does not manage to create a kind of imagination," he writes, it will become historically indecipherable "insofar as it suffers the accumulated burden of the millennia." For Lezama, true history consists of knowing when imagination imposed itself as history. A humanity "divided by eras corresponding to its potential for creating images" would allow memory to acquire the plenitude of the form. This plenitude doubtless includes tragedy; restoring it among ourselves has to be the result of imagination.

Applied to the eras of American life, this imagination permits Lezama to link our life to the continuity of indigenous and European myths; including the Conquest and Counterconquest; the Baroque and Utopia; the Romantic desert (Miranda and Fray Servando) and the well-established landowners (Hudson and Güiraldes), before opening ourselves again to the wandering *charro* and *gaucho*, celebrated far and wide in story and song, bearers of a popular life that subsumes and continues all the previous manifestations, until fixing them in that circumstantial *form*, that *imagination* of the event, which is contemporary art after José Guadalupe Posada.

Perhaps our most conflictive imaginary era continues to be the one which includes the conquest. In it, the tragic episode is eliminated in favor of the utopian dream and epic energy, both of them, in turn, canceled by colonial exploitation and Christian evangelization. The absence of tragic opportunity in Latin American culture leads to a Manichaeism which tries to justify the conquistador or the conquered, obviating the conflict of values and permitting us to convert the cultural conflict into a political masquerade. Creoles and Mestizos have concluded the work of the Spanish conquistadors, subjecting the indigenous people to even worse exploitation than during the Colonial Era. Liberalism and successive modernization despoiled indigenous communities of their legal shelter and of the minimum protections defended by the crown. But these same Creoles and Mestizos—we ourselves—have been the most strident denouncers of Spain's work in America as well as the most hypocritical defenders of an indigenous culture whose monuments will always stand as a recrimination if the only justice ever served these living men and women are our offensive acts and defensive words.

In the chapter dedicated to Bernal Díaz, I cited María Zambrano. It is time to remember her again, when she writes that the conflict does not assume tragic proportions if it only involves destruction, if nothing comes from the destruction which rescues and surpasses it. Without this, what seems tragic would be nothing more than the tale of a catastrophe. From the catastrophe of the Conquest we were born, the Indo-Afro-Ibero-Americans, and we created the culture which Lezama Lima calls the Counterconquest. That culture, for all the reasons and facts I have evoked, excluded the tragic dimension capable of giving us the conscience and the desire which both Lezama and Zambrano propose for us to be complete. One day, perhaps, we will learn how to see our history as a conflict of values in which nothing is destroyed by its opposite but instead, tragically, each one is resolved in the other. The tragedy would then be the definition of our miscegenation.

Both Scheler and Zambrano tell us that this process requires time so that catastrophe can be transformed into knowledge, and experience into destiny. Lezama Lima tries to accelerate this movement: to restore tragic vision in the American imagination, and for that, he knows only one true path: poetic knowledge.

2. POETIC KNOWLEDGE

The modern Latin American novel is inseparable from a poetic labor that has continued uninterrupted at least since the sixteenth century. Prior to the second half of the nineteenth century there are no true narrative camps in Spanish America; by contrast, we have never lacked a poetic tradition, and today could affirm that behind each Latin American novelist there are many Latin American poets from yesterday and today.

The novelist José Lezama Lima is his own poet, appropriate for a writer who creates his own form and tries to offer us a novel that is a myth which creates its own myth. (Franz Kafka's discovery was no different: in search of hidden myths, he invented a new myth which is that of Kafka searching for hidden myths.)

Lezama's poetics is a Baroque conjunction of time, the word, and the body incarnate. Poetry is the collective name for those three *superabundances*. And in Lezama, poetry is knowledge. Not a method of acquiring knowledge, nor something like knowledge, but knowledge itself. How does one reach it? Not without admitting that in the heart of all knowing, one confronts the relation of cause and effect, and the realities that are exempt from causality.

"With red, tired eyes they contemplate causality and the unconditioned," writes Lezama in *The Imaginary Eras*. "They contemplate irreconcilables and they close ranks along the two enemy riverbanks." Schopenhauer speaks of the man who is overwhelmed when he begins to doubt the purely causal modes of experience. Nietzsche bases "the essence of Dionysian intoxication" on this suspension of the law of causality. If therein lies the origin of tragedy, its death occurs when, through the Euripidean mask, the Socratic demon clashes with and conquers the Dionysian demon. Socrates battles tragedy because he perceives it to contain a philosophically irrational and absurd absence of the principle of causality. He is right: moral, empirical law does not tolerate a circular or recurrent experience which denies individuation because such an experience subjects individuation to a constant process of reintegration with all things. Tragedy, Nietzsche explains to us, transforms the previous epic culture without stripping away its validity and grants to the myths which historically precede the epic and tragedy their most expressive form: far from canceling them, it leads them to a kind of perfection. The three realities succeed and sustain one other historically as an actualized promise of unity. This is the circle of fire—myth, epic, tragedy and renewal through the myth—to which I have so often referred in this book.

But when religion requires historical and rational foundations to justify and impose itself dogmatically, myths die, along with their tragic culmination. I suspect that the reason for this unreason is that, as summed up by a phrase from Aeschylus's *Prometheus*, for tragedy, existence is simultaneously just and unjust and, in both cases, equally *justified*. This is intolerable for a religion—or a State—which creates its own form of justice based on a need to accuse the guilty in order to make the world believe in its own goodness and innocence.

The subsequent sacrifice is that of a poetic knowledge which Lezama Lima would like to resuscitate through verbal forms, to breathe life into the mute and frozen bodies of the statues. For Lezama, true history is the image of the world that we know through myth. Not the visible chronology, but the invisible one. The sum of myths creates the *imaginary eras* where the other reality has a place, the hidden history. Lezama clearly bets in favor of the underdog of history, the Cinderella of logic, and the Faustian desire in the Western world: non-rational and intuitive forms of consciousness.

In effect, the Venezuelan poet Guillermo Sucre has called Lezama's aesthetic "an aesthetic of intuition" which discards the causal in order to attempt creative synthesis, but which, to approach the second reality, bases itself upon the most concrete thing in the world: *the body*. Lezama identifies verbal images, metaphors and analogies *with* the body. It is the corporeal manifestation which overwhelms and shatters the gates of causality.

Additionally, says Sucre, the body in Lezama's writing is "a body that knows itself to be image." As Lezama himself explains in *Analecta of the Clock*: "In every metaphor there is something like a supreme intention of achieving an analogy, of establishing a network of semblances, in order to specify each moment of similarity." In this way, the metaphor, which is the meeting of two images — of two verbal carnalities that recognize each other as such — tends, in turn, toward analogy; casting its nets in order to find the similarity of things, which is to say, their true identity. In metaphor, language and reality lose their incomplete or fragmentary character, becoming not only language and reality *per se*, but also all that they evoke or provoke. In the metaphor, the world of immediate reality, without ceasing to be so, can become the world of the imagination.

For Proust, truth begins when the writer takes two different objects and proposes for them an analogous relationship in a metaphor. "The beauty of one thing lies in another," he tells us in *Remembrance of Things Past*. "Noontime in Combray is in the sound of its bells." Proust's path is Lezama's, the only novelist in the Spanish language who has approached, in his own work, the deeper concern of *Remembrance of Things Past*.

The modern novel is born when Don Quixote ventures forth from his village and clashes with the world at large; in his readings back home all is familiar but on the wide open roads of the world nothing is what it seems. From then on, the novelist shoulders the uneasy task of restoring similitude without sacrificing difference. For Proust, this work hidden behind the small pleasures of daily life proceeds, in turn, from the resolution of the metaphor in epiphany, which is the next step in poetic consciousness and, perhaps, its apogee. The instances are famous. They begin with the epiphanies about the madeleine, the steeples of Martinville, the mother's voice reading George Sand, apple trees in blossom, the hawthorns. Finally, as the work comes to a conclusion so do the previous details culminate in the triple metaphor of the patio tiles in Guermantes, the sound of the teaspoons, and the whiteness of the napkins. Metaphor is encounter: the final images of *Remembrance of Things Past* cast their analogical nets back towards the initial images: Venice, the trees, the beach at Balbec, recovering past time to open up to the final epiphany (epiphany: manifestation, apparition) of the single minute liberated from the order of time. Which is to say, everything culminates when time and its language, ceasing to be subjected to causal succession, are manifest and appear as the identity of knowledge and poetry.

Literary epiphany thus reveals to us that poetry is knowledge and that this is, as Vico would say, an "auroral knowledge." Poetry is the original identity of language and history, when both were, as Benedetto Croce tells us about *The Iliad*, "the same document." Now history and language are separated and only their auroral apparition — poetry — can reunite us, as in a beginning. Is this possible in a world *too damaged*, as Adorno calls it? In *Paradiso*, Lezama Lima attempts this heroic reunion, moving through all the operations which constitute the poetic arsenal: image and analogy, metaphor and epiphany.

In order to discuss Lezama and *Paradiso*, I ascribe the same value to the epiphany as James Joyce in *Stephen Hero*:

> By an epiphany he meant a sudden spiritual manifestation, whether in the vulgarity of speech or of gesture or in a memorable phrase of the mind itself. He believed that it was for the man of letters to record these epiphanies with extreme care, seeing that they themselves are the most delicate and evanescent of moments.

Lezama's poetic movement in *Paradiso*, largely analogous to that of the soul bound to material things in the philosophy of Plotinus, first tries to animate matter through language, transforming statues into living bodies and finding the equivalence of that ideal body, a matter that aspires toward God, in three solid, individualized, speaking bodies, within the world of a novel. They are the bodies of his three principal characters. Foción: chaos; Fronesis: order; Cemí: the illumination which guides the three of them, surpassing as much the chaos as the order, to the epiphany of *Paradiso*. This is the final image of the house in glowing embers in Havana, bathing the bodies in light for an instant—the single minute outside of causality, imaginary time—before being dispersed into matter, everyday life, and death.

I would like to closely follow the complex movement that, in order to reach the paradisiacal epiphany, is verbally manifest in Lezama's novel: I believe that no American novel written in Spanish has yet demonstrated higher complexity or greater linguistic and spiritual beauty.

3. COUNTERCONQUEST AND BAROQUE

The epiphanies in *Paradiso* occur by means of a departure for the distant world of the "realist" stage, a direct transit from the order of causality to the order of what is hidden, latent, possible or forgotten, that aesthetic of intuition of which Guillermo Sucre speaks. It is a poetic path, arduous at times, but one which obeys the writer's profound conviction: cultures are his imagination. Lezama Lima suggests that we divert the emphasis placed on the history of cultures in favor of "imaginary eras." What is understood by this? "If a culture," he writes in *The Bewitched Quantity*, "does not manage to create some kind of imagination," it will become, with the passage of time, "brutally indecipherable." For that reason, he proposes a history of humanity "divided by eras corresponding to their potential to create images."

In *The American Expression*—one of the great explorations of our continent's culture, along with those written by Sarmiento, Reyes, Martínez Estrada, and Mariátegui—Lezama imagines the times of Ibero-Indo-African America following their incarnation in the Pre-Hispanic myths, the "double astonishment" of the Conquest, the colonial Baroque, the "calaboose" of independence and the popular culture of the nineteenth century. As I have mentioned, Lezama observes a succession from the indigenous storyteller to the Spanish chronicler, and from this the Baroque señor, the exiled romantic and the master of the landed estate. But the nineteenth century fixation on this last element is set in motion once again by popular culture: the Mexican *charro*, the Argentine *gaucho*: chattered and gossiped about, celebrated in story and song, in *corridos*—popular ballads—

that are *recorrido*—sung and told over and over again, far and wide—
culminating in a new image: the work of José Guadalupe Posada,
who in turn announces another new movement, still without name,
because it is ours, the name for what we are now.

Julio Ortega is correct when he calls Lezama "the least trauma-
tized theorist of Latin American culture, which he understood as a
solution of continuities, always as a realization, never as a problem."
But Lezama's sense of continuity is quite distinct from remoteness or
a non-definition. Quite the contrary; it means an effective, corporeal,
dynamic approach to each phase of the cultural continuity or "imaginary eras" of our lands. But these same adjectives already indicate to
us that, among all these moments of the imagination, Lezama is most
addicted to one, the Baroque, and he employs it not only as an intellectual preference but more precisely as a form of his artistic creation.

In the end, both reference and form are reunited because Lezama
is also a Catholic writer, and if his Baroque aesthetic demands an artistic incarnation, it simultaneously demands moral, philosophical,
and spiritual reason. Immersed in the Catholic civilization of Spanish America (Counter-Reformist and closed to modernity), Lezama
searches with lucid desperation for a way out, closer than the insipi-
dity of pious Catholicism and holy cards, beyond our contemporary identification of modernity with Protestant capitalism, even as
we cover ourselves, nonetheless, with a cape of prudish Saint Sulpician piety for sporadic consumption and to remain on good terms,
as it says in some page by Emmanuel Mounier, with our reputations,
more than with our consciences.

Lezama's Catholicism is radical and committed because it chal-
lenges and denies in equal measure. Its denial is, essentially, an act
of affirmation and revelation, showing Catholicism to be part of our
"imaginary eras."

As Julio Ortega says, Lezama searches for continuities. He writes,
for example, that the Spanish Renaissance finds fulfillment in America. "Quevedian stoicism and Góngoran sparkle have popular roots
in American culture." One should not see Latin American culture as
a copy but as a mimesis implying neither sloth nor inferiority. America is a center of incorporations and, in this way, a continuation of
Spain. I believe that it carries on the potential, too, because Spain itself was, in the long run, the greatest "center of incorporations" in

Western Europe: Iberia was formed by Celts, Phoenicians, Romans, Jews, Goths, Arabs, Gypsies . . .

The Renaissance receives the chaos of the crumbling theological world and thinks anew of Arcadia: The Golden Age, Utopia, the noble savage . . . Not an idle consideration. It validates the testimony that "to the very populated European stage in the years of the Counter-Reformation, the Conquest and colonization offer a way out of the European chaos that was beginning to dissolve into bloodshed."

Europe shed its own blood in the wars of religion. And it shed the blood of the indigenous world of America. But on the incorporation of Indigenous America into the Western world, I cite Mexican novelist and essayist Hector Aguilar Camín: "Despite its cruelty and terrible demographic consequences, it inevitably yielded the symbiosis of the conquistador and the previous civilizations." What Aguilar Camín says about Mexico can be applied to all of Ibero-America: "The colonial settlement of New Spain was not propagated upon a territory whose ancient inhabitants were exterminated." This reality contrasts with the colonization of Anglo-America, above all with the United States' expansion toward the Pacific, based on the extermination of the Indians. "The formula for colonization in the United States was to exterminate in order to establish, to wipe out so as to occupy." No Indo-Anglo-American civilization was born of this experience; nor do any traces remain, in the Caribbean of an Indo-American civilization. Slavery, in both cases, brought death. In the Caribbean, Afro-American culture—or the "imaginary cra"—is born. In response to the unbearable historical voids the Baroque is also born, a charter of the foundation of the Caribbean and the fraternity of its spirits, whether they write in Spanish, French, or English. The Baroque is like a current of identification which flows from the mouths of the Orinoco, by the "islands in the stream," as Hemingway called them, to the Mississippi delta. The fish that swim in this water are recognizable by their Baroque coloring: Alejo Carpentier, Gabriel García Márquez, Luis Palés Matos, Jean Rhys, Jacques Roumain, Édouard Glissant, Aimé Césaire, William Faulkner . . . From the southern states of Anglo-America to the northern limits of the Bolivarian frontier.

But in the Southern United States, the Baroque takes a very long time to manifest itself as the awareness of a syncretic culture, in fraternity with disaster, in solidarity with defeat, an exception to the seamless triumphalism of the North American *polis*. The name of this Baroque is that of a great writer, William Faulkner, pejoratively accused by the critic Allen Tate of incurring a kind of "Southern Góngorism." Lezama was right; in *Absalom, Absalom!*, and *The Sound and the Fury*, the "Góngoran sparkle" puts down a Baroque root in the North American South.

In Latin America, by contrast, the ascent of "Our Lord the Baroque" is rapid and dazzling. It is identified with what Lezama calls the Counterconquest: the creation of an Indo-Afro-Ibero-American culture, which does not cancel but rather extends and empowers the culture of the Western Mediterranean in America. It is a sorrowful Baroque: offering itself as a syncretic cancelation, the refuge of the ancient gods, the repository of aboriginal times. The tortured anguish of the Ibero-African statues of Aleijadinho in Congonhas do Campo, the indigenous paradises contained in the Christian spaces of Quito and Oaxaca, the balconies that hang like cages in Lima and Havana, were all made by black, native, and mestizo artisans who could only express themselves with clay and color. The work of Sor Juana Inés de la Cruz further enlarges this idea: the Baroque was also a refuge for woman and, for being so for *this* woman, it was identified with the protection of the word, with the very *nomination* that I have indicated as one of the centers of Latin American narrative. Nevertheless, it is a Baroque that is mature and complete, not "degenerative." As Lezama writes, it represents:

> as much in Spain as in Spanish America, acquisitions of language, perhaps unique in the world, furniture for the home, forms of life and curiosity, a mysticism which follows new modes of praying, ways of tasting and preparing delicacies, which exhale a way of living that is complete, refined and mysterious, theocratic and self-absorbed, formally errant and deeply rooted in its essences.

The Indo-Iberian Baroque of Tonantzintla; the Chapel of the Rosary in Puebla; the churches of the indigenous architect Kondori in Peru and Bolivia; the *Royal Commentaries* of El Inca Garcilaso de la Vega. Ibero-African Baroque: the architecture and statuary of Aleijadinho in Ouro Preto. Mestizo Baroque: the poetry of Sor Juana, the synthetic and voracious curiosity of Carlos de Sigüenza y Góngora and, in the end, the narration of national history (Indigenous, Creole, Mestizo) in Chile by Molina, and in Mexico by Clavijero. Creole Baroque: painting, etiquette, furniture making, architecture, and, perhaps, even the eroticism of the Viceroyalty, evoked by Fernando Benítez in *Los demonios en el convento*. The Counterconquest is rapidly manifest through the culture of the Baroque, at all levels. It is not, as in the North American South, slow to arrive. This is the imaginary era which follows that of the indigenous cosmos, destroyed or buried. It is the contraction of the utopia conquered by the epic.

In one of his poems from *Enemigo rumor* (Enemy Rumor), Lezama Lima exclaims:

Ah, may you escape in the very instant

in which you had reached your best definition . . .

This is an extreme, sorrowful paradox which will illuminate the entire narrative density and reach of Lezama's novel *Paradiso*. In the previously-cited poem Lezama says to the woman who is a fugitive from the instant:

Ah, my friend, if in the pure marble of the goodbyes

you had abandoned the statue that could accompany us.

But in the novel this desire is fulfilled only to require   as life requires death — the movement that makes us lose what we desired. Imaginary era, the sum of indigenous, African, and European traditions in the New World, the Counterconquest's response to the Conquest; for Lezama the American Baroque would be distinct and superior to the European Baroque. As such, it is the art of displacement and corporeal nature: movement and incarnation, plurality and disorder, change and encounter. But the difference of the American Baroque is not only historic — a contraction of epic and Utopia, filling a void particular to ourselves — but intrinsic. Lezama sees in the European Baroque an accumulation without tension; a disputable affirmation, of course. But in the American Baroque he finds what he calls a "plutonism," an original fire which first breaks down the fragments and then unifies them. In his examination of the Baroque architecture of Kondori, the indigenous builder, Lezama clearly sees the meeting of American jungle leaves with Greek clover, the sound of Peruvian guitars mingling with viols, the Incan crescent moon and the Corinthian acanthus. Despised or invisible, the only mission of the Spanish polyculture, we have said, was to recompose and reincorporate what has been broken. The fact that this mission—interrupted by the expulsion of the Jews and the Moors from the Iberian Peninsula—has been recovered and extended in America by our Baroque certainly represents a distinctive causality.

Once that virtue is established, it is important to know how it takes shape, how it acquires a body. Precisely because it reunites opposites in movement and fills intolerable voids, there is no Baroque that does not require a corporeal nature which gives form to movement and a face to what before had none or was merely a gaze, forward, iconic, and lifeless.

But the body is the seat of Eros. How then does it coexist with a spiritual, Catholic culture which identifies nature and the body with temptation and the fall of man? Lezama opposes the fallen body with the resurrected body, the promise of Christianity. And upon this tension he constructs his great novel, *Paradiso*: an erotic, Baroque Catholic novel, which would be none of these things without a body or without the bodies which incarnate movement, tension, and the paradox of being, simultaneously, matter and spirit, corruption and resurrection.

4. The Body of the Baroque

Reading Lezama's novel permits us to realize that fully half the work joins the immediate reality of the text to an approach to the problems of the body. Above all, Lezama wants us to understand that there would be no literature without the body. But he also asks us, with hope, if there can ultimately be, without literature, a living body, conscious of itself? The body first appears as a statue frozen in space, and the book's initial narrative consists of observing the statue's movement—perfection, "a better definition"—into fluidity and incarnation. From the space occupied by the statue to the time lived by the body, the mediation is word and image, poetry and painting.

Like the fugitive in Lezama's poem, the body reaches, for a moment, its highest definition in the statue, but only at the expense of its sculptural fixity. Lezama's Baroque defines its beauty in this perfect death that is its negation. The poet defines it as "a whirlpool of coincidences which come to rest in the sculpture." This desire to suspend the typical Baroque abundance in the statue's frozen time leads him to conceive of the group at a Baroque concert as a still life: "As they danced the couples turned into frosted trees ... The light whitened the couples so excessively that even the sashes of black cloth were frozen votive candles."

The body's internal Baroque is also like a sculpture, a "bronchial tree"; even the shadow is Baroque, its best quality sculptural; and if architecture has a face, like the stone staircase of Lezama's poem "La universidad," man has a sculptural architecture, as when Alberto Olaya pauses indifferently on a noisy bustling street corner, "like a statue," says Lezama, like a "welded block of sand," brushed by the coastal fog.

Lezama provides the dominant word in this rocky vein of *Paradiso* on page ninety of the Era edition, when he conjugates the English verb to freeze: *freeze, froze, frozen*. But the frozen fixity convokes the metamorphosis, because if what we have read is an "as if," it is the simile's comparison, not the metaphor's identity. Lezama delays the war cry of the Baroque until after the novel's midway point, "he rejects the *horror vacui*," because he fears, and convinces us of it, that the horror of the void might not be the origin of the Baroque, but only one of its chapters. After sculptural fixity, Lezama's primary reality of perfection, comes the spectator's obligatory circling around the statue in a manner that pretends to create its movement. Historically, the Baroque was no different: first architecture, followed by sculpture and, only afterwards, painting, and architectonic and sculptural painting. Ortega y Gasset calls Velázquez the painter who liberates painting from sculpture. Foucault goes further when he notes that in *Las Meninas*, Velázquez achieves a mutual, two-way incorporation of spectator and painting. The painter of *Las Meninas* watches us only because we occupy the space of his model. His gaze simultaneously greets and dismisses us. But staring into the void, he also accepts as many models as spectators exist. Subject and object, says Foucault, invert their functions toward infinity. There is no greater aperture for the unfinished character of the Baroque, which possesses a unique quality capable of admitting a plurality of readings as well as the continual syncretism of elements which compose the discourse — read or observed — and the exercise of substitution and permanent condensation of what is insecure and unfinished. In the case of Velázquez, Foucault calls it pure reciprocity. The same could be said of Lezama, because in *Paradiso*, as in painting, all lines and gazes converge outside of the painting (and book), focused on something inaccessible but reflected in the depth of each gaze (and each word). If the world is first seen as a statue then, like statues, the world is being seen by characters gifted with reciprocity: they see, they see themselves, they are seen. This multiple vision is what animates statues, but for Lezama the full incorporation of diverse points of view has to occur in a dynamic way, as if in a painting. On the scale from inanimate matter to matter infused with spirit, Lezama introduces us first, then makes us move, from sculpture to painting, like stepping from a stone into the water.

Grandmother Munda appears on the staircase, the author tells us, like a "pure Velázquian composition." All the characters in *Paradiso* begin to seem like retouched portraits, Holbein retouched by Murillo, beggars whose smiles are touched by the light of Rembrandt. Lezama invokes examples of the unfinished and reciprocal in order to provide for the characters, who previously had a stony architecture of a pictorial nature. That is, the novel describes how the characters occupy a spatial place and a temporal instant, thus fashioning a chronotopic narration, not a psychological or descriptive one:

> Time, like a liquid substance, spreads out, covering the faces of the most remote ancestors like a mask, or, in pure inversion, that same time crawls along, nearly surrendering to the absorption of earthly games, and now a figure emerges, expanding, acquiring the texture of a Desmoulins or a Marat with burled fists beating on the variants, the echoes, or the tedium of a Thermidor assembly. After such imprecations they seem about to slide beneath the sea, or finally freeze reacting like the drops of blood that outlive them, smacking a heavy slap upon the star reflected in the bathroom mirror. Nothing more than moments of faux abundance. Very soon we see them anchored in a style, clutching for the support of a cane caddy; they stumble into a case of colored pencils, their eyes, like portals burst open by a smiling Aeolus, focus on a china cabinet, pull back, fearing that the breath of air opening the door for them will blow on the crystal, and they are resting

on a carnival Circassian hat, rimed with frost and feathers. Was that the lone expression of those long lives that found relief? Or, on the contrary, the time's caustic turpentine, was thinning them out, shrinking them, until dropping them into that one expression, as if it were an open cage waiting to catch a flighty bird. Faces preserved only in a ceremony of greeting.

Time, for Lezama, is a "caustic turpentine" which reduces, shrinks, and imprisons in fixed space. Time is the prisoner of space and appears first in *Paradiso* as an insertion into that incarcerating space; the "satanic spawn of a Baroque jailer," says Lezama, as if his turpentine belonged to Piranesi, the dramatic engraver of prison scenes. And even though time is described at the beginning of the novel, as if in some humanist slip by Lezama, "time now made for man," the phrase does not ring true. The time of *Paradiso* is too much a part of what Lezama calls "the monster of extension," and demands specific content to give value to movement, in order to oppose the statue's immobile materialization as something more than another description of movement, once again, in space, and to understand it instead as a movement in time.

How to transcend the frozen, sculptural, architectonic space of consummate entropy: a dead, inanimate world? How to resuscitate it? What is needed to give movement to time? What direction for the open, unfinished image of the "Velázquian" painting?

Lezama's response is erotic and contradictory. On the one hand, only Eros can kiss the statue's body and give it life; and the statue dissolves into movement, especially when it speaks. In Eros, body and word are indissociable. In *Paradiso*, as in Foucault's analysis of *Las Meninas*, Lezama establishes pure reciprocity through the very fact of making the bodies' animation, playfulness, and fluidity appear like a verbal deed, with no more confirmation than the poet's words. The statues are animated but they are also animalized. A pestiferous cloud escapes from beneath the armpit of a London policeman and settles like a divinity on the body of Doctor Copek, the Cuban-Danish civilian doctor in Colonel Cemí's entourage. The imprisoned princes who recall the colonel's martial mind were "stuffed into some long saurian skin sacks." This image of the body wrapped in leather, its dead homologue, prepares us for the transitional image in which the

colonel remembers one of the nights of Scheherazade—the first storyteller—on which a king from the Black Isles confesses "he was a
man from his head to his waist, and his other half was black marble."

For the colonel, it will be a sensual rumor, of water, which replaces the visual impression of the bodies: a kind of palpitant, sexual
infinity engendered "by the memory of an impossible touch." The
leather prison, the marble phallus, are the inexactitudes of one who
blindly reconstructs bodies, touching the water and listening to "the
sound of cascades filtered through the walls of a jail."

Image, metaphor, and analogy are Lezama's instruments for assimilating the body to the fluid, igneous, anti-stone elements: all those
things which are not the body and can thus animate it because the
body does not refuse a verbal comparison with things unlike itself. For
example, the boy Cemí in the scene at the pool where both the water
and his asthma, liquid and air, threaten to drown him; a dangerous
destiny if we forget that statues do not breathe. Nor do they speak.
As if to convince us that the statue has become a body, the word is
as necessary as movement. The word—poetic discourse—gives time
to the body.

Body and Word: Plotinus said that matter alone is comprehensible
in terms of unreality and negativity. Why? Because a strict interpretation of God can only say *what he is not*. And, says the philosopher
of *The Enneads*, if God can be negatively defined, so then with greater reason can the body and matter. The body, in particular, is the
prison of the soul: again Piranesi, again metaphorical prisons, again
O'Gorman, again the dungeon as symbol of the struggle for independence: the dungeons of Francisco Miranda, Fray Servando Teresa de
Mier, evoked by Lezama in *The American Expression*; and Plato's cave,
where shadow is reality; and Segismundo's tower, a prison where life
is dream. Bodies trapped within the cave, the tower, the dungeon,
the sacred host . . . in order to return to God, the body must be liberated from the body, its host and prison. The Eucharistic sacrament
is the symbol of this paradox. An imprisoned body sympathetically
communes with another body contained in an enclosed form to participate in mutual liberation. Does our saliva liberate Christ from his
Eucharistic prison, as much as the divine body liberates our imprisoned soul from a fallen body, announcing its own surrender?

A chaotic novelist, Lezama is supremely sensible to the mystery of the divinity's insertion into history through the Body of Christ. He proposes animating the flesh because if, as the Manichaeans say, its movement is the seat of the evil God (if the body is sin and proof of man's fallen nature), it is also the promise of man's resurrection is his body. And if this is not true, Christ is not true.

Moving from this notion to identifying the flesh with the word is but a single step, and if, at the beginning, José Eugenio Cemí sees his neighbors' house like a polyhedron, the geometric figure soon recedes before the unfinished picture of "a plane of massaged and divided light." At last, these realities, transformed into words, transform what is real through phrases that are seen "walking like a centipede, a serpent-head tail, a head with crenellated key-teeth, of the key to a code" to "deliver him to the labyrinths of … Chronos." The word grants the picture the gift of time. Time grants the body the gift of the word.

Body and Time: there we find the elements which the word will animatedly arrange in *Paradiso*, negating the absolutely monstrous sense of space originally found in Baroque freedom. Renaissance man liberated space then shrank it, making for himself a new, second prison, larger than the first: humanism, which opened for him the doors of modern, un-walled cities. Monster of absolute extension, prison of stony architecture, fugitive perfection of the statue, unfinished movement of the gazes, bodies emitting phrases so their heads can turn the key of the doors forever locked: those of times past or yet to come.

Being: José Eugenio Cemí, the colonel, has died and his mother thinks of "a word that will revive his frozen body." The implied question is: can she reincarnate the dead body? Can the word ensure resurrection? Can the word animate the inert body?

Out of an obligation to multiply the points of view about the objects revolving around them, Lezama departs from his own experience of the Baroque, stripping things of their absolute frontal value, as icons. One must walk around a Bernini statue in order for the statue *to be*. Frontally, it lacks true *being*. But does that being include the movement from inanimate to animate? Does it truly include the statue's incarnation?

Paradiso is, in the first place, a novel where the statues pathetically turn and come alive. The novel's first chapter is nothing if not a spectral evocation of the body in space, in place of the home, and its hunger for something more than just a place: narrating a time, the time lived as one's own true *house*, a thing of one's own.

We see a sick body, the boy Cemí, lividly swollen and wrinkled, frightened of the crosses painted on his skin, scared that nobody wants to kiss him, his body covered with stains and its elemental functions: Cemí urinates orange water, almost bloody, and the angels squeeze the sponge of his kidney until they leave him exhausted.

We discover an inexhaustible Cuban kitchen in Havana, where endless custards, flans, sweets, and apricots lift the house "toward the supreme essence," which is that of feeding, nourishing, and restoring the body.

We observe Nana Baldoviana's fundamental decision: she must, mysteriously, take responsibility for the body. And from this responsibility for his body, for his hunger and feeding, his sickness and health, a relationship can be forged — a life — "which opens interminably" and designs "disembarkations in countries not situated in time or space."

But in order to liberate the body and give times and spaces as landing ports, it is necessary to rip open the straitjacket of "the brute, elemental law of symmetry." To causality and pure size, symmetry is now added as a prison of the body, time, and the word. How to transcend it? Lezama proposes for us a textual journey.

5. WORD AND BODY

Peruse the body: this is Lezama's primary verbal function, and *Paradiso* offers countless examples from which I choose a single one. In order to set the mood during a family evening, Uncle Demetrio removes from his wallet a letter sent him by Alberto Olaya when he was still on Isla de Pinos. Alberto is present, and is bothered by the reading of something he considers "some silly prattle to cheer up an absent uncle." But Uncle Demetrio tells the boy Cemí to join him and listen carefully to Uncle Alberto's letter so that he can know him better, guess his happiness and hear, for the first time, "the language made into nature, with all its artifice of allusions and loving pedantry."

Lezama's self-definition is not gratuitous: it enables Cemí to feel that something "very fundamental had happened and come to him."

So close at hand, so diabolical, so present, Uncle Alberto, nonetheless, had another presence, contiguous but just as vibrant as his
present one. Neither *döppelganger* nor specter, but an identical neigh-
boring presence: his *word*. Alberto Olaya is always two: himself and
his word. In the end, he is a representative of history within history:
he indicates the position duplicated by all characters in the novel. In
a work of fiction, there are no real beings without the reality of the
word. Benveniste concludes that the character is only a name, his action a word. Beyond exhausted psychological characterization, Julio
Cortázar tries to divine a figure: the announcement of a new possible character. It is no coincidence that Cortázar, as much as Lezama,
forces us to ask: which one is the specter, which the double: the character, of the word: or the word, of the character? In every case, naturalism—flat realism—is the true novelistic illusion, the *lie* of *fiction*.
In *Paradiso*, the characters always have a double, which is their word;
but the word is, also, the *nature* of the character.

Thus, the multiplication of the character "Alberto Olaya" is not
only a romantic procedure: it is a Baroque necessity, intimately linked
to Lezama's concept of time and space, and the position of the individual, the American man within in it.

These provisional certainties come from my reading of *The American Expression*. I remember the marvelous human being that Lezama
was, the very fat Lezama Lima, seated like a tropical Buddha in a beer
garden in Havana's Almendares Park, ordering those signature Cuban
desserts which abound in *Paradiso*: *tocinillo de cielo* ("Heaven's Bacon," a rich egg custard), and *cascos de guayaba con queso* (guava shells
with cheese), discussing these things with me even as he seemed to be
awaiting an Ephebian palanquin to bear him home to his very narrow house on Calle Trocadero. But the litter never appeared, so Lezama steered his corpulent body as best he could through Old Havana's
Baroque labyrinths all the while quoting Plotinus. Entering his book-
lined house, he squeezed himself sideways between the shelves, repeating the words of the philosopher of the enemy body: "The spirit's
characteristic is movement of one thing to another; unlike the mind,
the spirit does not possess the being as a totality, but rather by parts;
and its continuous movement from one to the other produces time,
which is the life of the spirit in movement."

Through Plotinus's sensual, philosophical aperture, *Paradiso* begins to fill itself up, a primary text on the perfection of the immobile statue, with premonitory figures of movement and change: time and history. Time and history are manifest in *Paradiso* as the essential metamorphosis, and their officiants are manifest as witch doctors, typical of an art of syncretic secrets whose historicity, according to Lezama, lies in being the art of the Counterconquest, the art of native priests and black sorcerers disguised within the Christian church. Sisters Rialta and Leticia, José Cemí's mother and aunt, are compared to "the witches of Thessaly," a source of the Latin novel *The Golden Ass* by Apuleius. The nana-witch, Mamita, is a mytho-magical figure who expresses her terror with words sprung from "the fear that petrifies her." We also see a beggar seated in front of a church in Cuernavaca, crying out for help "for the love of God" whether or not anyone walks by him: "Entering the church, he was surprised that sometimes the beggar's plea coincided with a potential almsgiver passing by. Other times he seemed to be seated there to measure the time of another eternity by a different rhythm."

The Time of Another Eternity. Because he settles neither for an empty space nor a natural body that is not animated by verbal fiction, Lezama rejects unique, absolute, positivist, Newtonian time, "flowing uniformly from itself and by itself" (*Principia*, 1687). But he also rejects the language of this time, which is the propositional language which carries us, in the end, to the silence of Wittgenstein. The Viennese philosopher reminds us that beyond silence lies a language irreducible to reason, that of poetry and myth. A multiple language of a multiple time and space as well, which Lezama conceives in order to share it with the modern Latin American novel, following the Baroque—"Our Lord the Baroque," the "first American who rises dominating what is abundant."

Times, spaces, multiple languages. Two times, multiple times, simultaneous times, uniquely capable of making room for the American expression, for that "superabundance" which Lezama, beneath the sign of the Baroque, will oppose to the simple causality of the rational world, the surest instance of his erotic humiliation on the threshold of the tragic sensibility latent in our culture, the prisoner of a utopia forever lacking tragedy.

The time of another eternity, double, multiple, simultaneous, is manifest in the marvelous opening of Chapter VI of *Paradiso*, where the old grandmother Mela stretches out "like a Gorgon along the nodules of time" and, at ninety-four years old, knows and communicates to us an immense time which is errancy evaporated now replaced by the flesh in the mirror. Time which escapes from its own succession in order to be situated on "favorite, tyrannical" planes, upon which "the shades and the living were at the height they had reached in the previous century." A time of genealogy and memory; time disguised, like Latin American carnival dancers in Havana and Huejotzingo, Rio and Panama, where momentary joy is not enough, where, instead, the mask carries and represents the mystery of the past.

Following the appearance of this time which is, ultimately, the time of *Paradiso*, it becomes impossible to distinguish it, or to distinguish the word and body incarnate, from the text itself which is a space occupied by a verbal body. From occupation, Lezama moves to the appropriation of times by the word-space body. But from this operation is finally born the name of *something else*. The sum is not unity and the verbal body incorporates time and space only in order to attain something different. As in Plotinus and his desire for unity-in-diversity, ideally shared with classic antiquity, that passion in Lezama is the hunger for unity, the One. For both philosopher and novelist the passion is manifested through double movement. The first is multiplication, the superabundance which distances us from unity, but which is its product. The second movement is a return to unity. The passion for the lost unity does not refuse the material universe which, as we have just seen, forms in itself a unity in which good and evil coexist. Nevertheless, evil is only an attribute of the material world because purely spiritual evil is inconceivable. However, the material world does not, for that reason, cease to be the best possible image of the spirit world *at the level* of the material. This is not meant as a tautology in disguise. It is the declaration of the total reality that cannot be so if it does not consider external evil and suffering as necessary elements of oneness. *Paradiso* is a novel which deserves to be read with *The Enneads* by Plotinus in one hand and Nietzsche's *The Birth of Tragedy* in the other. Matter ceases to be evil as soon as it is illuminated by form, and the form of matter cannot be separated from its movement towards God which, Plotinus tells us, is eroticism. For Nietzsche, reason explains all, save what is inexplicable. Art's job is not to explain but to affirm the totality of what is real, including the inexplicable-real.

From the start we have seen that for Lezama, poetry is knowledge itself. It comes to him through images, the metaphor which reunites them, and the epiphany which resolves knowledge in experience: the highest is indistinguishable from what is known and what is felt. Similarly, in Proust, we have seen that in order to reach an epiphany, one must reach "a single minute set free" from language and time's causal succession. Finally, we recall that in *Paradiso* the epiphanies also occur thanks to a departure for the distant world of the "realistic" stage, a direct movement from the order of causality to the order of what is hidden, latent, possible or forgotten. Only in this way can we understand what, in traditional terms, passes for an "argument" in *Paradiso*.

6. Families: Near and Far

As in the work of Proust, *Paradiso* is a family chronicle. Colonel Cemí thinks that the "immediate family," was "the only path to reach the other family, distant, supernatural." In order to move from one tale to another within the first, Lezama appeals more than once to the technique of the byzantine novel, so often employed in the films of Luis Buñuel and the novels of Juan Goytisolo. These tales within tales prefigure the epiphanies of travel. Uncle Alberto Olaya enters a cinema and transcends the space of the theatre, seats, and screen, in order to create a new time, a secret and unsuspected relationship with a temporal landscape of lights, mice, and doors that open onto ancient forgotten kingdoms.

The young Cemí repeats his uncle's experience. Years later he enters a cinema to watch Jean Cocteau's version of the myth of Tristan and Isolde under the title *The Eternal Return*. Without leaving the cinema he returns to the couple Lucía and Fronesis in a park. But it is also perfectly possible that the couple, without leaving the park, has entered the cinema where Cemí is watching them. The two realities are welded together. The reader is not accustomed to taking such a moral leap. He ceases to be the passive reader; he creates what he reads; he believes in what he reads.

Behind each reality there is another one, and many realities, closer, truly closer — death, and the dead. The mode, but also the reality of this metaphorical reunion, is what Lezama Lima defines as *supernatura-*

lity. He defines it through José Cemí's experience: "That visibility of absence, that dominion of absence, was Cemí's strongest trait. In him, what wasn't there, was there: the invisible occupied the first plane in the visible, converting itself into a visible one with dizzying possibility."

The supernatural leads to a *superabundance* whose name is God. But its paradox is that the path from the first to the second passes through sin and death. The body is the seat of the fall and the homeland of death. But it is an object of ceremony and homage. Why? Because it is going to rise again. And if this is not true, God does not exist.

Lezama's argument runs like a vein towards the heart of *Paradiso* (as noted by one of our best critics, Ramón Xirau) carrying the word of faith. One need not believe in what is true because it is possible. Similarly, God exists because he is absurd, because he is incredible, because he inscribes death into all destinies but promises a final resurrection so that all people will be assimilated into the destiny of Christ.

The riddle of the resurrection is the game—all games—of the body in *Paradiso*: bodies imitate the resurrection, they rehearse it through fiesta, carnival, political rebellion, and verbal rhapsody. An individual and collective rehearsal, premonitory and memorable, a riddle of the resurrection but a memory of death. Only a concurrent, simultaneous, and successive vision, like that of the man who goes out to give himself to death (because it awaits him and does not yet have him) can perceive its reality.

This dangerous epiphany, a transfiguration of the individual in the festival and in death, is decisive in order to set José Cemí, the boy, the young man, in motion. José Cemí says to his mother Rialta:

> Listen to what I'm going to tell you: Don't reject danger and always try what is most difficult. There's a danger that confronts us in the form of substitution, there's also a danger that sick people seek out, a sterile danger, the danger without epiphany. But when a man throughout his days of life has tested what is most difficult, he knows that he has lived in danger, and even though its existence has been silent, even though the succession of its waves has been peaceful, he knows that a day has been assigned to him in which he will be transfigured, and he will not see the

fish inside the current but the fish in the starry basket of eternity. . . . Your father's death was a profound event, I know that my
children and I will give it depth while we are alive, because it left
me with a dream that one of us would be a witness to our transfiguration in order to fill that absence.

And Lezama the narrator concludes: "I know that those are the most
beautiful words that Cemí ever heard in his life after the ones he read
in the Gospels and that he will never hear any others that will so decisively set him in motion."

How extraordinary that the epiphany, being the most profound
event, is also the most instantaneous, the most fleeting: "When he
squeezed the cricket with the two fingers of his right hand, he saw
that what had escaped was his dream." If eternity and the instant are
the same time, and Lezama's time as well, patience and the instant
can also certainly be adapted to the identity of the present being. In
Chapter IX of *Paradiso* we read about "the joy of knowing that a person in our circle, a friend, has also earned his time, and made an alliance with time, which strengthens and polishes him, like the tide
churning over the coral branches."

In Lezama, gaining time is recognizing that the instant is the temporal aspect of the metaphor, that the metaphor is the analogy of an
instant and that in it, two terms are literally conjoined, but also,
temporally, two dissimilar times. Swan's instant will be his patience,
and the patience of Job his instant; Julien Sorel's life will be his death,
and Sydney Carton's death his life; the sin of Saint Augustine is his
salvation, and Raskolnikov's salvation his sin; the madness of Don
Quixote will be his reason, and the reason of Ivan Karamazov his
madness. To escape from the evil nature of matter, to begin the ascent
back towards unity, to move through this identity of contraries, and
this rejection of black and white moral simplicity.

Once the bodies and their immediate text are animated by the
Baroque, the sense of the trio's activity which composes the immediate text—Paradiso's second textual reality—is no different: the literary and human activity of Cemí, Fronesis, and Foción. These three
young Havanans are the actors of a rebellious suffering that seeks the
metacausal totality. This fact is stated in plain terms, through mutual
losses and gains, and beneath an enormous question mark of destiny:

Do we resemble God?

Will our bodies be resurrected?

Are we mortal because we will be immortal?

As they fashion their destinies, the three young protagonists are attended by a juvenescence which burns the hands and by a no-less-fiery intelligence. But these characters are only comprehensible if, behind the verism of their adolescent Havana world, we recognize, on the one hand, the collective, Baroque voice in which the vast *we* of the intellectual palimpsest and the linguistic synthesis of the Counterconquest speaks with them. On the other hand, we must also recognize the sum of the *imaginary* eras which accompany all individuation and which permit it, as it desires, to exceed causality for the sake of tragic poetry, "the source," says Lezama Lima, "where there is neither purity nor impurity."

Foción is *the chaos* which feeds *the order of Fronesis*. *Cemí* is "dominion of absence," "*visibility of absence*." The three young characters return us to the Baroque order / disorder of the beginning but with a new sense, full of time, never again the "pure monster of extension." Foción, Fronesis and Cemí—chaos, order, and visibility of the *other* reality—follow the paths of Ecclesiastes: paths which seem straight and finite, with rectitude and purpose, but which do not lead them away from death towards salvation. Instead, like torturous paths, they lead them to the same death. This is known in the simultaneously stupid and lucid instant of adolescence, and the only possible rebellion offers an express passion for some, a tacit one for others. It is about seeking "a succession of the creature beyond all causality of the blood and even spirit, the creation of something made by man, as yet completely unknown even by the species."

Vain illusion, stubborn hope, because if artwork is the name of that creation, how then to reconcile its radical novelty with the conviction that "what is only so much newness is extinguished in elemental forms"? Between Foción and Fronesis, between chaos and lucidity, youthful rebellion suffers because it cannot be translated into a work that repeats—the verb itself is contradictory—the creative attributes of God. If the work of art is the creature possessed of neither cause nor effect, its price is one which God did not pay: suffering. It is the price of Prometheus. The frontier of Plotinus.

Nietzsche maintained that there is no suffering in rebellion because suffering is for slaves. Fronesis disagrees, telling us that Nietzsche only knew the Renaissance and the Classic World as imagined
by the Renaissance. Lezama places himself in the medieval, Christian perspective, and perceives rebellion as suffering: "Suffering—
says Fronesis—is Promethean . . . man suffers because he cannot be
a god, because he is not immutable. The fulfillment of all destinies is
suffering."

The adolescent artist can believe that the only response to man's
mutability and difference is to create a work of art that "embraces
the totality of man's conduct." But the rebellion necessary to make
such art brings suffering, because the rebel cannot resemble God—
i.e. "I failed to create something unknown by the species,"—and has
to succumb to tradition, to pay the price of history, which is a recognition of the vast "we" that, seen with the eyes of this suffering, of
this debt, is the true bearer of the "word" which is, in turn, the "supernatural which fertilizes the city."

Aesthetic plenitude is thus seen by Cemí and Fronesis in the "sym-
pathetic profundity between the wait and the call." In other words,
the two youths must await an "annunciation" which tells them: you
are nature, but nature that "has to achieve super-nature and counter-
nature and must advance receding and recede advancing." Between
the genesis and death of all that is in nature, including them, the adolescent artists have no other remedy but "to be always listening, caressing and saying goodbye." Waiting, caressing, and separation are
part of their creation. This is the "recognizable surface" of art and
life. As a rule, it blinds us to the fullest human activity which, between the caresses of waiting and farewell, recognizes the nearness of
sin and memory, of body and art. Lezama's Augustinian sensibility in
these passages is very intense. *Paradiso*'s great erotic chapter is pleas-
antly sterile, like the plateresque foliage of a colonial church. But our
senses are always alive, not just in the exceptional act of carnal coupling, and if we suffer our senses as a sin even though we do not employ them (or do not employ them more), it is because the health of
the senses depends upon the conjunction—not the solitude—of the
individuated body with other bodies.

Fronesis speaks of the eleven sensory organs, including the unmentionable orifices. His words would like to persuade Foción that

the multiplication of the senses is the multiplication of sin. In this way, he would like to induce order in his friend's chaos. Between the two—reductivist order from one, proliferating disorder from the other—Cemí, bearer of the visible absence, eliminates the sin of sensual acts because the only sin would be memory of the sin, not a present sensory act: "The memory of an act"—says Cemí—"is its culpability, because every act has to be pure, without reminiscence, without becoming, unless it happens in the pernicious night."

The pure act is called love. This is what Cemí sees, from *chaos* or from *order*, before Foción or Fronesis can see it, qualifying it, stripping it of the pure potential of being an erotic act leading to the re-union with God. But if love is not sinful, adds Cemí, this is not only because it is directed towards God, an intention which can or cannot be fulfilled, but rather because it invariably sows itself in death. I understand that Lezama tells us that we are divided, we have lost unity, not only with God, but also with ourselves, with our mixed sexuality, previous to sexual dualism. We have lost androgyny, forgotten the sexual One capable of fertilizing itself, seeing ourselves obliged to choose between the sin which is the memory of what we have lived, and the love which permits us to be what we were, but which also promises us, fatefully, death. We have killed "what we have been" in order to become "what we were not."

Cemí saves himself from this vertigo, similar to Foción's chaos, with a reflection that is, in turn, like Froensis's order. He recalls that St. Thomas spoke of two sins against the Holy Spirit: "The envy of fraternal grace and the intemperate fear of death."

The protagonist of *Paradiso* comprehends that fraternal grace—first, what unites him to his two friends and the three of them to each other—will be combined and perhaps conquered by the intemperate fear of death. In the darkest but truest heart of his youth, he admits that only the temperate acceptance of death abolishes the contradictions of the spirit, overcomes the repetition of sin, and permits participation in fraternal grace. If this is possible, neither love nor death are sin, in any of its forms. Knowing this is the first condition required to "not let himself be walled up in a minor labyrinth" as Cemí fears, but instead discover the category of second realities, of superabundance.

In Lezama Lima, the beings privileged to enter that labyrinth and know that total reality which is the labyrinth itself but also all its contradictions, all its oppositions, all its latencies, are our old friends, the grandchildren of Erasmus, the children of Don Quixote, the brothers of Oliveira and Pierre Menard: madmen, enthusiasts, poets, children, and people in love.

Foción's father, Doctor Foción, is an innocent madman who receives a nonexistent clientele gathered together in his empty office by his wife Celia, transformed for the occasion into the ephemeral "Eudoxia," his well-spoken Dulcinea. His son, "surrounded by madness, grew up without original sin." He loses his innocence: temptation appears in the form of a "clandestine harangue," "larvas," "skeletons in the desert," "a rain of sands." Foción's temptation is the chaos which distances him from his father's innocent madness, but it brings him closer to the lucidity of Fronesis, an *orderly madman* capable of receiving Foción's chaos and transforming it into an image, semblance, likeness, or poetic gift.

Nearly infected by what Foción ceased to be, Fronesis enters the ranks of enlightened enthusiasts—once again, Erasmus, Don Quixote, and Lear's Fool—but with an even more conflictive, demoniac, and angelic heritage; that of fearsome couples. Heathcliff and Micawber, Alyosha and Myshkin, Captain Ahab and the boy Pip, Bringas and Nazarín, the innumerable Ks of Kafka; Miss Rosa and the idiot Benjy. Buster Keaton, the innocent madman, the sad clown, the invincible enthusiast. Thus do the Erasmian worlds of Lezama and Cortázar adjoin one another.

The whole problem for Fronesis consists in knowing if, nourished by the chaos born of Foción's temptation converted into Froensis's receptive enthusiasm and demented lucidity, he will be capable of passing these things on to Cemí. Because he who is capable of superabundance, and is receptive to a second reality, is the only one prepared to procreate the plurality without sacrificing unity. Man has one face, says Lezama Lima, but each man's face is different.

7. THE TRAGIC THRESHOLD

Through these extremely complex movements of the word, time, and the body, Lezama does three things in *Paradiso*.

First, he reintegrates Latin American Catholicism with art, wrenching it away from its degenerate Saint Sulpician piety and church calendar illustrations. This is not the naive, infantile Catholicism of little Saint Teresa of the Baby Jesus (Thérèse of Lisieux), but an in-depth introduction to the problem of Catholic culture, its contradiction between faith and practice, its fatal relationship with the political and economic enemies of the Holy Spirit, its assimilation into the ideologies which secularize it by negating tragedy and truncating optimism about the future. For Lezama, all of this hides the true problem of faith: *visible* must once again become *invisible* or there is no faith.

Tertulian's saying "It is true because it is impossible" is the true believer's motto, and Lezama also converts it into the poet's phrase: outside of positivist rationalism in any of its forms, the poet associates faith with the analogous poetic operation, which consists of discovering the relationship between invisible, hidden realities, which compose the true reality.

The poem is true although it is not realistic.

And the invisible is not the unreal.

Second, Lezama converts the Latin American novel into a poetic movement with its own laws, a movement nourished by a voracity which includes the protean, syncretic, fortunate, mutant, and always unfinished forms of the Baroque (body, space, time, word) manipulating figures, repositioning them, feeling a bit like Copernicus: "I am going to formulate the laws of things lost or submerged by a dark fate."

Third, in search of this historic restoration of all that has been lost or submerged by a dark fate, Lezama places our novel, for the first time, on the very threshold of tragedy. An intense restoration of all things forgotten, Lezama's work implies a decision to know ourselves, but not only in the Socratic individuation where Nietzsche saw the death of tragedy, but rather in the collective totality, the sum of the imaginary eras which are nothing but that "ode, elegy, epitaph emerging from a bitter reservoir of un-defeat" of which Faulkner writes.

Tragic knowledge does not evade those contradictions intolerable to logic. Logic is interested in being right; tragedy, that we realize our destiny. We must know, as Hegel wishes, that self-knowledge is knowledge of the enemy self. According to Max Scheler, tragic nature lies in the conflict between positive value and the very subject that possesses it. This conflict and recognition culminate in a reconciliation of the values in conflict. In tragedy, says Hegel, necessity is a mediation. Not the enemy of freedom, but rather its mediator.

Conflict is suffering, all action is suffering. In the *Oresteia*, Clytemnestra exclaims: "If we could put an end to suffering, what happiness! The spirit's hard brutal hoof has trampled our heart. Can you accept the truth?" This is the truth which Ivan Karamazov will refuse to accept: that the truth can pass for suffering. That is why he prefers justice to truth and opens the way for modern tragedy, whose names he dare not pronounce: nihilism and totalitarianism.

Lezama is not Dostoyevsky, nor is he, any longer, Columbus, nor Copernicus to whom he is compared, nor Locke in the tropics, nor Rousseau on the plains, nor Comte in the highlands, nor Marx on the pampas. His contradictory conflict between Christian faith and pagan sensuality, between visible and invisible history, between what we know and what we forget, between nature and the supernatural and counter nature, is a conflict of values which is determined at the high tragic level of two just, though opposed, necessities. Tragedy is the mediation between two values in conflict, with the goal of restoring a reality, a more free and harmonious collective, which does not sacrifice any of its parts. Lezama's conflict here is not, certainly, the elemental conflict between good and evil, progress and delay, or justice and injustice. Nor does it resolve them if it leaves them behind: as in the tragedy as analyzed by Nietzsche, it contains and integrates in a new and superior form all the forms that we have studied here but without canceling them out.

In *Paradiso*, the poet who speaks is *a* we; there is *one* we who speaks who is the poet. The contradictory consciousness of our tragic, Christian selves which Lezama opposes to our utopian persistence and our faith in modernity in order to integrate them with our historic continuity, occurs within the concrete reality of a culture: a way of speaking, a way of walking, a kitchen, a bed. *Paradiso* is also a Latin American and Havanan life of depth and extension: a true painting, not a realistic painting. And a sad painting.

Friendship is lost. The promise of youth dissipates. The Fronesis-Foción-Cemí trinity drifts apart. Cemí, the novel's hero, will become one more intellectual bureaucrat of the patrimonial administrations built by Machiavelli's descendants in America. The novel's symbolic culmination occurs on page 393 (Era Edition) when Foción, in a great Baroque pavane— *la pavana de La Habana para los tres infantes difuntos* ("the Havanan pavane for three deceased infants") Guillermo Cabrera Infante would call it— g o e s spinning, orbiting round a tree which is Fronesis, forever missing.

Cemí knows this because he is the master of absence.

The trinity's dispersion is St. John's dark night of the soul, through which the three separated friends move. But suddenly, at the novel's conclusion, in the center of dark Havana, a house is illuminated. Dazzled, Cemí is surprised by the totality of that illumination. It is illuminated by the supernatural. It is illuminated by tragic fire: this is a house whose unity is assured by a universal sympathy in which all evil and suffering occupy their places as necessary elements of the great chaos and order of the universe. It is illuminated by Cassandra's wailing cry over the absent, invisible bodies, of the three friends, their fraternal grace and their mortal destiny:

"We will die," says the visionary sister in the *Oresteia*.

"We will die but not without some honor from the Gods."

8. PARADISO: RETURN AND SUMMARY

If we hold Plotinus's book in one hand, and Nietzsche's in the other, then how do we hold Lezama's book? Surely it rests upon some sumptuous Baroque reading stand, its pages moved by the wind of those double, multiple, simultaneous times, whose hands stained with gold and clay leave a fingerprint on each paragraph: the print of "the first American," which rises "dominating what is abundant," known as Our Lord the Baroque.

Paradiso participates in all this vast transport, although perhaps nobody, like the Cuban novelist, has carried the American Baroque dialect to more certain, terrible, and contradictory conclusions. A devouring art, desperate in its natural virginity, its utopian dream, its epic corruption through knowing everything, by saying of itself *I am time and history, not only extension and violence*, Lezama's art is like that of Sor Juana, whom he describes in *The American Expression*:

> The five hundred polemical volumes which Sor Juana has in her cell ... many "precious and exquisite mathematical and musi-

cal instruments," her application of "First Dream" from the fifth part of *Discourse on the Method*: her knowledge of Kircher's *Ars Magna* (1671), where she returns to the ancient summae of the knowledge of an age, all that leads her Baroque nature to a thirst for universal knowledge.

But this universality is united to another form of abundance and proliferation: Baroque eroticism, a wastefulness opposed to productive economy, a prodigal but sterile pleasure that Lezama sums up in the exclamation: "One angel more! What useless work!"

In *Paradiso*'s celebrated Chapter VIII, all the forms of pleasure and sexual coupling which Lezama accumulates are nonproductive. Semen spills out as abundantly as the fruit pouring from the golden cornucopias of a colonial church, like the languid, serpentine Farraluque in a scene of unconsummated homosexuality, spilling his "liquor" upon the chest of young Adolfito, who ends up "smeared with a sap that had no final use."

Erotic fertility is shown immediately, unable to wait nine months. A negation of capitalist frugality and Protestant simplicity, the Baroque is an eternal instant, a drop of semen detained midway between *el oro* (gold) and *el orín* (urine), running through a virile member that Lezama, in a delirium of Baroque substitution unsurpassed even by Faulkner, calls "the leptosomatic macrogenitosomial stinger."

I know of no more perfect summary of Latin American culture than the scene in Chapter VIII of *Paradiso* where the peasant boy Leregas, possessed of the most "thunderous generative attribute" in his class, balances two large octavo volumes on the tip of his carnal cylinder: a whole encyclopedia, all the accumulated knowledge of the world, suspended like a tightrope artist upon the phallic potency of a Cuban peasant. Symbolically, there is little more to be said about Latin America.

12. García Márquez: Second Reading

1.

Liberation, by means of imagination and through the simultaneous spaces of reality strikes me as the central fact of Gabriel García Márquez's great novel, *One Hundred Years of Solitude*. If this novel's enormous Latin American success could simply be explained as an immediate recognition of self-reflection, its comparable international success makes us suspect something that goes well beyond the pleasant discovery of an identity, even various identities: Who has not, climbing up the Macondo family tree, come face to face with their dear grandma, girlfriend, brother, or nanny? Without a doubt, one of the most enjoyable and entertaining books ever written in Latin America, the amusement and recognition one experiences upon first reading *One Hundred Years of Solitude* certainly do not exhaust the book's meanings. Instead, these things demand a second reading which becomes equivalent to the true reading. That exigency is the essential, fundamental secret of this mystical and simultaneous novel. *One Hundred Years of Solitude* presumes two readings because it posits two writings. The first reading coincides with a writing we suppose to be true: a writer named Gabriel García Márquez is writing down, in linear, chronological fashion by means of Biblical and Rabelasian hyperbole, the genealogy of Macondo: Aurealiano, son of José Arcadio, son of Aureliano, son of José Arcadio. The second reading begins the moment we finish the first: the chronicle of Macondo already inscribed in the papers of Melquíades, a gypsy thaumaturge whose appearance as a character, one hundred years earlier, turns out to be identical to his revelation as a narrator, one hundred years later. In that moment, two things happen: the narrative begins all over again, but this time the chronological story has been revealed as a mythical, simultaneous historicity. I emphasize historicity and myth because in both a real and fantastic way the second reading of *One Hundred Years of Solitude* fuses the order of events (the chronicle) with the probable order (imagination) so that the fatality of the former is liberated by the desire of the latter. Each historical act of the Buendía family in Macondo is like a spinning axis around which revolve all the possibilities unknown to the external chronicle which remains just as real as the dreams, fears, madness, and imaginations of the characters in the story.

In my previous comments on Alejo Carpentier, I referred to the movement from a foundational utopia to a bastardized epic which degrades it if the mythic imagination does not intervene to interrupt fatality and recover liberty. One noteworthy aspect of García Márquez's novel is that its structure corresponds to that profound Spanish American historicity: the tension between Utopia, Epic, and Myth. The New World was conceived as Utopia. At the same moment Copernicus shattered Europe's geocentric illusion, he created the need to establish a new space to confirm the size of the known world. Giuseppe Cocchiara has suggested that America and its indigenous peoples were actually invented even before being discovered. Which is to say, they were both desired and needed. America is, above all, the renewed possibility of an Arcadia, of a new beginning for a history whose ancient presuppositions had been destroyed by the Copernican revolution. Thomas More's *Utopia* received a credible, tangible incarnation in the Christian missions founded in California and Paraguay. But this dream, at heart a simulacrum of innocence, was immediately denied by the epic of conquest—clear evidence of historic necessity. Cortés and Pizarro corrupted the dream, subjecting it to the abstract demands of the imperial Spanish mandate—*Plus ultra*—and to the concrete demands of the hunger of individual will: that of the Renaissance *Homo faber*. Thus, Utopia was only an idea, an illusory bridge between Medieval geocentrism and Renaissance anthropocentrism.

It seems no coincidence that the first two parts of *One Hundred Years of Solitude* are equivalent to those opposing points of origin. The founding of Macondo is the founding of Utopia. José Arcadio Buendía and his family travel through the South American jungle, wandering in circles, until finding the precise place to establish the new Arcady, the promised land of origin: "The men on the expedition felt themselves overwhelmed by their most ancient memories in that paradise of dampness and silence, older than original sin." Like More's *Utopia*, Macondo is an island of the imagination: José Arcadio believes it to be surrounded by water. And from the island, José Arcadio invents the world, pointing out things with his finger, then learning to name them and, finally, to forget them. But in the moment in which founding father Buendía realizes "the infinite possibilities of forgetting things," he must, significantly, resort to writing for the first time. Having previously learned through divination, he now hangs signs on things, discovers reflective knowledge, and feels obliged to dominate his world with science: what he previously knew naturally, he will now know only with the aid of maps, magnets, and magnifying glasses. The utopian founders were seers; they knew how to recognize the hidden but pre-established language of the world; they had no need to create a second language, it was enough for them to open themselves to the language of things as they were.

In *The Order of Things*, Michel Foucault points out that modern knowledge abandons its ancient relationship with the Godhead: it has ceased to search for meaning through divination. Divinity supposes signs which precede it. In modern consciousness, the sign only has meaning in terms of its relationship with its own immediate, verifiable knowledge, and the turmoil of this rupture demands an eager search for the prolongations that might put us back in touch with the world that existed before us. Foucault cites, as examples, sensibility in Malebranche, and sensation in Berkeley. Later, and even today, these bridges would be, arguably, history and psychoanalysis.

But even as he abandons divination for science, and moves from sacred knowledge to hypothetical exercise, José Arcadio Buendía introduces the novel's second part: the epic, a historical course of time in which Macondo's utopian foundation is denied by the active demands of linear time. This part transpires, essentially and significantly, between Colonel Aureliano Buendía's thirty-two armed uprisings, the banana exploitation fever, and the final abandonment of Macondo, the utopia whose foundation was exploited, degraded and, in the end, assassinated by the modern epic of history, activity, commerce, and crime. The deluge—divine punishment—leaves in its wake a "Macondo forgotten even by the birds, where the dust and the heat had become so tenacious that it required effort just to breathe."

There remain the survivors, Aureliano and Amaranta Úrsula, "recluses in loneliness and love and by the solitude of love in a house where it was almost impossible to sleep thanks to the thunder of the red ants." Then the novel's third space begins to unfold, the mythic one, whose simultaneous and renewable character will not be made clear until the final meandering discourse, when we learn that this history has already been written by the gypsy Melquíades, the soothsayer who accompanied Macondo at its founding and who, in order to keep it alive must nevertheless resort to the same civilized ruse as José Arcadio Buendía: writing. Thus we come to understand the profound paradox revealed by a second reading of *One Hundred Years of Solitude*: all was known even before it came to pass through Melquíades's sacred, utopian, mythic, founding divination, but nothing will be known if Melquíades does not also compose a written record. Like Cervantes, García Márquez establishes the frontiers of reality within a book and the frontiers of a book within reality. The symbiosis is perfect. Once this realization is achieved, then begins the mythic reading of this sad, beautiful, joyous book about a town and people who proliferate, even parthenogenetically, with the richness of a South American Yoknapatawpha.

As with Faulkner, García Márquez's novel is self-creating: all creation is a spell, an androgynous fertilizing of the creator and, in consequence, a myth, a fundamental act, the representation of the founding act. At the mythic level, *One Hundred Years of Solitude* is, foremost, a permanent interrogation: What does Macondo know of itself? Meaning, what does Macondo know of its own creation? The novel constitutes a totalizing response: in order to know, Macondo must recount to itself all its "real" history as well as all its "fictive" history, all the notary proofs along with the rumors, legends, curses, pious lies, exaggerations, and fables that nobody has written, that the old men have told little children, that the housewives have whispered in the priest's ear, that the witch doctors have summoned up at midnight, that the quacks have touted in the center of the plaza. The saga of Macondo and the Buendía family includes the whole oral, legendary past for the purpose of declaring that we cannot content ourselves with official, documented history; history is all the Good and all the Evil which men dream, imagine, and desire that will both preserve and destroy themselves.

Like all mythic, ab-original memory, Macondo remembers creation and re-creation in a single instant. The novel's time is simultaneous, but we only realize this crucial fact upon second reading. Only then do first and last events acquire their totalizing significance: one day in the beginning José Arcadio Buendía decides that from then on it will always be Monday, and in the end Úrsula says: "It is as if time were spinning round and we had returned to the beginning." Memory repeats the models, the original matrices, in the same way that, time and time again, Colonel Buendía shapes little golden fish that he melts back down in order to forge them again in order to ... to be continuously reborn, an assurance of the permanence of the cosmos through rigorous, beloved, ritual acts. Such mythification is not gratuitous: men use their imaginations to defend themselves from the encircling universal chaos, from the jungles and rivers of the immense, devouring South American magma. Nature has dominions. Men have demons. They are bedeviled, like the Buendía family itself: founders, usurpers, creators, and destroyers; Faulkner's Sartoris and Snopes clans fused in a single bloodline.

An authentic rewriting of the Latin American utopia, epic, and myth, *One Hundred Years of Solitude* dominates and demonizes the dead time of historiography in order to metaphorically, mythically, and simultaneously enter the total time of the present. A Spanish galleon is stranded on a mountain, men tattoo themselves with penises, a wagon loaded with the bodies of peasants murdered by the banana company traverses the jungle and the cadavers are thrown into the sea; a grandfather lashes himself to a tree forever until he becomes an emblematic, shamanic trunk, carved by the rain, dust, and wind; the sky rains flowers, Remedios la Bella ascends into the same heaven. In each one of these fictional acts, the positivist time of the epic (the notion that this really happened) and the nostalgic time of utopia (this could have happened) both die, and the absolute present time of the myth is born: this is happening now.

But there is also something simpler and, at the same time, more clear and profound. Lévi-Strauss has indicated that a mythic system has the goal of establishing homologous relations between natural and social conditions. It is on this level that *One Hundred Years of Solitude* becomes a terrifying metaphor for man's frightening exile upon the face of the earth: the abandonment and fear of returning to an anonymous inhuman nature, the terror of begetting a child with a pig's tail and beginning the return to the absolute origin: to nothing. Edenic couple, the cousins José Arcadio and Úrsula are pilgrims who flee from the original world of their sin and fear to found a second paradise in Macondo. But the founding, of either a town or lineage, supposes the same repetition as the act of coupling, of taking advantage, of incest, with the earth or with the flesh. Lévi-Strauss adds that the matrimonial exchange is a mediator in the conflict between nature and culture. Marriage creates a second, controllable nature which man can influence. Thus arise the numerous myths about coupling of man and animal, of marriage between beauty and the beast, a double metaphor for natural dominion and forbidden incest, sin, violation, and rape which are, nevertheless, the condition of a synonym expressed by the Yoruba word for marriage, which also means food, possession, merit, increase, and acquisition. Through this understanding we approach the most profound meaning of *One Hundred Years of Solitude*: this novel is an extended metaphor, prolonged throughout an exhausting century of events, which only designates the instantaneous act of carnal love between the first man and the first woman, José Arcadio and Úrsula. They fornicate in fear, terrified that the fruit of their incest might be a child with a pig's tail, but they fornicate so that the world might be maintained, that it might eat, possess, acquire, deserve, dream, and be, with all the dangers that these enactments suppose.

Do we agree with Philip Rahv's insistence on the idea that myth denies history? Only if we mean the dead, oppressive, factual history which García Márquez leaves behind in order to situate, within a novel, the triple encounter of the Latin American age. First, an encounter with the primary, living, creative past, which is the tradition of risk and rupture: each generation of the Buendía family will know a son who dies in a revolution—an epic, heroic deed—which will never end. Second, an encounter with a desired future: ice makes its first, astonishing, supernatural arrival to Macondo's torrid jungle: magic and utility will be inseparable. Third, an encounter with the absolute present in which we remember and desire: a novel experienced as the long chronicle of a century of solitude in Colombia, but one that reads like the fable precariously inscribed on Melquíades's fluttering sheaf of papers. Macondo's secular document is the scattered pages of a mythomaniac witch doctor who inseparably mixes the relationships in the order of experience with those of the written order.

This split makes *One Hundred Years of Solitude* the *Don Quixote* of Latin American literature. Like the Knight of the Rueful Countenance, the men and women of Macondo can only appear in a novel— this novel—to prove that they exist. We see the creation of a novelistic language as a proof of being. The novel as an act of knowledge, as a negation of the false documents of the civil state which, until very recently, papered over our reality. Language-fiction-truth as opposed to lexicon-oratory-lie: *One Hundred Years of Solitude* versus the conquistadors' arrogant letters of relation versus the unobserved laws of the monarchical Indies, versus the liberators' violated constitutions, versus the oppressors' humiliating agreements. Against all those texts that disguise us, Márquez's novel is a fictional sign that indelibly identifies us, like Ash Wednesday crosses which will never be erased from the foreheads of Aureliano Buendía's thirty-seven illegitimate children: a cross of burned earth, a black mark of baptism as well as a target for the firing squads of the oligarchies and dictatorships that, thanks to that corporeal cross, will always recognize, and always murder, the rebellious children—the bastards—of the patriarch.

Against invisible crimes and anonymous criminals, García Márquez raises, in our name, a word and a place. Like the first Buendía, like Alejo Carpentier, Márquez baptizes all the things of an unnamed continent. And he creates a place. A mythic place: Macondo. As a fabulist, García Márquez understands that presence dissolves without a place (a place of resistances) which might be all places: a place which contains them all, which contains all of us: the seat of time, the consecration of times, a meeting place of memory and desire, a common present where all things can begin again: a temple, a book. *One Hundred Years of Solitude* reinitiates, reactualizes, and reorders—it contemporizes—all the present times of a zone of Latin American imagination which for a long time seemed to be lost to letters, subjected to the heavy tyranny of folklore, naturalist testimony, and ingenuous denunciation. This is not the least of García Márquez's virtues which, in his work, transform evil into beauty and humor. The dark side of Latin American history emerged in the novels of Gallegos, Rivera, and Icaza as multiple incarnations of an isolated, impenetrable, alarming evil which is, in the end, both defined and distant. García Márquez realizes that our history is not only fatal, not only lethal: we have also, obscurely, desired it. Additionally, he converts evil into humor because, since history is also desired, it is not solely an abstraction alien to our lives: it is the other, what we can see outside of ourselves but as part of ourselves, reduced to its ironic, proportional, fateful encounter with our quotidian debilities and imaginary representations.

2.

In *One Hundred Years of Solitude*, García Márquez leads us from a foundation utopia to a corrupting epic to the dawn of a myth which permitted us to recall our history in the present; to name it and write it. He achieved this realization thanks to an ironic and humanizing perspective about the total historic process of Ibero-America.

The Autumn of the Patriarch poetically radicalizes the literary technique of *One Hundred Years of Solitude*. To include all past experience in the present, García Márquez attempts a poetic conflation of times and characters. As in his previous novel, we encounter all that has ever been said presented as a *saying* and a *telling*: the official history but also the rumor, slander, gossip, dreams, and imagination woven into a single verbal plot line, a seamless web, a continuity without punctuation, divided only by commas: a long, solitary sentence in which the first person singular (I) is collapsed into a first person plural (We) before following the course though a third person singular (He or She) and ending up in another second person singular (You: the reader).

All things are brought together, separation is stamped out, the people occupy the palace, the balcony is abolished, the footlights are extinguished. The dividing line between the stage scenery and the auditorium rows disappears in the carnivalesque prose which Bakhtin attributes to Rabelais. García Márquez's prose is also a great critical, democratic, egalitarian prose, not a gratuitous exercise. If, historically, he leads us from the past, from a founding utopia (the original Macondo) to epic perversions (historic Macondo) to the memory of the myth (solitary Macondo), in both *One Hundred Years of Solitude* and *The Autumn of the Patriarch*, he situates us in a new territory of the present, where that experience reaches a degree of poetic intensity which permits us to see it with absolute clarity.

Thanks to the vision thus gained, we can, immediately, distance ourselves from the events, understanding them in historical perspective while assimilating them to our conflictive modernity. We made history and so maintaining it is our obligation. History, however, remains unfinished; continuing it is a collective obligation. The writer can only achieve a syntactical impact, affecting the order of a language he receives from the past, contextually besieged and determined by other voices and the convergent plurality of languages found in every social system.

With that, a writer like García Márquez fully achieves his literary and social function. Nevertheless, he leaves us on the threshold of historical continuity. His words and imagination have transformed that history. We can see it in a new and more creative way. I have spoken of utopia, epic, and myth. But reading *The Autumn of the Patriarch* permits me to change, enrich, and update these terms, and wonder, while reading Antonio Gramsci alongside García Márquez, if we have misread to the same degree both More and Machiavelli, and if we might not, as the Italian Marxist theorist and politician suggests, reinterpret utopia as a concept *in favor of* power, understanding Machiavelli as the author of a dynamic utopia, not merely as the political writer who describes what is, but rather, as the visionary of a duty to be realistic.

The Machiavellian theme of the Conquest of America is the theme of liberating the energies of new men who could not inherit, but instead had to earn, their kingdoms through a mixture of necessities and free will. But the vision of Machiavellianism as a utopia, and not only an epic of personal exaltation, is the theoretical novel Gramsci proposes. The author of *Note Sul Machiavelli Sulla Politica E Sullo Stato Moderno* (Notes on Machiavelli on Politics and on the Modern State) distinguishes the theme of newness in *The Prince*, but instead of rooting it in the terrain of what it is (Machiavelli as the author who describes the real ways of power) he argues that it is a work directed *toward* what must be; he describes a dynamic utopia concerned with the way that the prince must be and act if he wishes to direct his people to the founding of a new state.

In the Gramscian interpretation, the Machiavellian Prince works upon a people, crushed and isolated, to organize their collective will. He tries to persuade the people of the necessity of accepting a strong leader who knows what they want and how to obtain it, getting the people to enthusiastically accept this dynamic. This might have been, for example, the Spanish conquistadors' problem if, in the case of the theocratic empires of Mexico and Peru, they had gained power for themselves after usurping Moctezuma or Atahualpa. How does one convert the indigenous despot's vertical, autocratic power into the power of the Renaissance prince who is master of his will and liberated from fatality? Perhaps the only possible response is this Gramscian idea of Machiavellianism as a dynamic utopia: as an obligation to be a realist.

The Conquest—in itself and as a victory over indigenous power— is at the heart of the relationship of Ibero-American man and woman with power, that preoccupation which we have observed in diverse forms in the novels of Gallegos, Azuela, Rulfo, and García Márquez. Having conquered the Indians, could the conquistadors also conquer the Spanish crown? Could they, like the colonists in New England, be the fathers of their own local democracy? Bearers of an individualist ambition, they had to choose between individualism as democracy or individualism as a seigniorial right. They chose the latter, and thus delivered their response to the crown. Behaving as their ancestors had—like capricious and exploited gentlemen of leisure—imbued with feudal ambitions, they obliged the crown to respond, limiting them, subjecting them to abstract paternalistic laws—the legislation of the Indies—and to precarious practical decrees referred to in their titles and possessions.

Hernán Cortés had neither time nor occasion to seriously confront the Gramscian possibility of the dynamic utopia. Many of his letters, nevertheless, betray this ambition: to found and integrate a new community, governed by the new men of the Spanish middle class. Democratic individualism or feudal seigniorage? In every case, the Spanish crown, which had just defeated Castilian feudalism in the name of monarchical unity and absolutism, was not going to permit its resurgence in the New World, and nothing indicates that it would have respected a democratic orientation in the process of colonization. It had also just defeated the *comuneros*, the forces of the Castilian townships united in their revolt against the crown. Cortés defeated Moctezuma but the crown defeated and silenced Cortés. Monarchical authority displaced the conquistador, humiliating him at times, rewarding him at others, and always nullifying him as a political factor. Recall that the letters of relation from Cortés to Charles V were banned in 1527. Similarly, in 1553, the Crown prohibited chronicles of the Conquest from being exported to the New World itself. The popular, ascendent enterprise trumpeted by Bernal Díaz becomes an exclusive enterprise of monarchical power.

Gramsci makes a fundamental distinction between Machiavellian politics in Italy and Bodin politics in France. The first occurs in the *moment of force*, in the Medici city-state. The second, in the *moment of balance*, in the nation-state of Henry IV and Louis XIII, when the nation's political and economic life becomes centralized and placed into the hands of managers from the rising middle class: Mazarino and Colbert. Bodin can invoke the rights of the middle classes—the third estate—because the basic problems of foundation, unity, and equilibrium have been resolved in France. Machiavelli must invoke the rights of the revolution because all these things—territorial unity, national identity, a society freed from the bonds of feudalism— remained to be achieved in Italy.

In *The Autumn of the Patriarch*, García Márquez offers us the image of the last despot, anonymous, confused with his doubles and, in the end, dead and picked over by the vultures. The last patrimonial tyrant, archaic, before the time of revolutionary violence, but also before the time of democratic equilibrium. The governors of the past century had to confront or sidestep the same problem: How to move beyond anarchy and create viable nations? How to create national states in place of small balkanized *republiquetas*? How to fill the void left behind by the Spanish Imperial State now clogged with despots, priests, and military officers? For good or ill, these problems received responses: from Juárez and Díaz in Mexico, Portales in Chile, Rosas and Mitre in Argentina, and Justo Rufino Barrios in Guatemala. Some, like Rosas, perpetuated the seeds of anarchy and violence through unifying force. Others, like Juárez and Barrios, created basic, State institutions for the purpose of abandoning military partiality. Others, like Portales, tried to give a national face to an economically dynamic, increasingly democratic and diversified society. Others, like Mitre and Díaz, tried to create a facade of modern progress without transforming the royal nation.

More recently, leaders like Obregón and Calles in Mexico, Castro in Cuba, and the Sandinistas in Nicaragua, had to define the moment of violence as the moment of revolutionary foundation simply to obtain territorial unity, national identity, and institutional viability. Latin America's three twentieth century revolutions are, nevertheless, distinct. In Mexico, the society which emerged from the Revolution of 1910 ended up surpassing its predecessors: the Party and the State. Social transformations in Cuba, despite bringing improvements in health, education, and labor, have never achieved political equality.

In the end, a prolonged partiality cannot replace or contain Cuba's social dynamic. In Nicaragua, an agile political leadership tried to simultaneously create a national State (nonexistent before the revolution), to defend itself against a war of foreign aggression, and to break the circle of historical fatality as a puppet government of the United States. Modern tensions and conflicts gave birth to something Nicaragua did not have before: a modern civil society, despite backroom politics and obstacles to political partiality. The Revolution was later divided and power became vested in a single person, eliminating the other options available to *Sandinismo*, and returning to the partial and exclusive authoritarianism of the past.

A civil society already exists in Mexico, where the problem is to renovate the political dynamic and make it harmonize with the social dynamic. For a long time we had a strong State and a weak society. Then, an increasingly strong society gained ground from the corporate State. In Argentina, by contrast, a rather strong civil society has yet to create harmonious political institutions. Chile has a democratic civil society which, despite having fallen victim to military dictatorship, learned how to return to a democratic tradition. I choose just three examples to ask the question: Can Spanish America, through revolution or evolution, enduring or avoiding violence, invoking Machiavelli or Bodin, achieve something beyond brute force or precarious equilibrium: a dynamic of development containing justice and democracy?

From the autumn of the patriarch we move to the spring of the technocrat. But we have had to endure the winters of development without justice, and suffer the hells of debt, inflation, and stagnation at every level. The true democratic spring will survive these tests. It will not be able to be, again, a dream of prosperity for the few while setting aside and postponing the well-being of the majority. Many lessons have been learned. The new model for development, as a political democracy but also as social justice, will be challenging for all the actors of our political life: from right and left. It will impose obligations on everyone. It will require an effort unprecedented in our history. There will be no modernity that does not take into account the cultural totality of our countries. There will be no modernity by decree. No one believes any longer in an ideal country divorced from the real country. Thanks to novels like Márquez's *Autumn of the Patriarch*, we all know that there is another kind of writing, that of the imagination, which reveals both the power of desire and the will to change. Abstract, arbitrary law will never again return to preside in Latin America. Look what words can do! Words of power, but from now on, those of the writer and his community, too. Gabriel García Márquez's work has incarnated our imaginative possibilities as possibilities for our society. And for our contradictions. Look what words can do! Sometimes, in spite of themselves.

13. A Time Without Heroes: Vargas Llosa

The vision of justice is absolute; the vision of tragedy, ambiguous. This presence of both demands is one of the facts that give the modern Latin American novel its tone, originality, and power. Works like Vargas Llosa's *The Time of the Hero* and *The Green House* possess the force of confronting Latin American reality, no longer as a regional reality but instead the reality of all men, not one definable through Manichaean simplicity but a reality marked by movement of ambiguous conflicts.

Juan Rulfo in *Pedro Páramo*, Augusto Roa Bastos in *Hijo de hombre* (Son of Man), and Gabriel García Márquez in *No One Writes to the Colonel* are writers who convert traditional themes of the *hinterland* into mythic literature. Locality and characters appear to be the same as in traditional novels. Only in these works, the jungle and river are a legendary backdrop: nature has been assimilated and the stage comes to life with men and women not cast in any illustrious roles, instead they are truly totalities pierced by language, history, and imagination. Novels like *Explosion in a Cathedral* and *Hopscotch* indicate an even higher degree of complexity. In the dynamic of Carpentier's novel, Esteban's conflict is a knot of decisions in which the political, erotic, and moral options all affect or are affected by one another. Cortázar's comic characters also represent an anti-Manichaean ambiguity: La Maga and Oliveira, Talita and Manú are beings which simply exist: they are, they do, they let things be done, without discursive bondage to good or evil.

In Mario Vargas Llosa's *The Time of the Hero*, a Latin American city, Lima, is the scene of another drama of personal dilemmas involving a group of cadets and officers in a military academy and their external justifications and internal motives to denounce, punish, absolve or remain silent. Vargas Llosa's own case is particularly interesting. After having written a first novel of radical modernity as formal as it is *contenutista* (to use that monstrous vocable of Italian criticism which means emphasizing content over form and style, and without admitting that such a distinction, as it relates to Vargas Llosa himself, might be valid), he returns, in *The Green House*, to the most traditional of Latin American themes: man besieged by nature. I note, of course, that such a return is only part of a totalizing eagerness which would like to measure, bend, and resist that permanence of Latin America's inhuman background with the weapons of a language that pierces it in every sense. *The Green House* can serve as an example of a novel which would not exist outside of language and which, at the same time, and thanks to language, reintegrates the permanence of an inhuman world to our consciences and to our words.

"Lima the Horrible," as Sebastián Salazar Bondy would say. And Melville, a century earlier, in *Moby Dick*: "Nor is it altogether, the remembrance of her cathedral-toppling earthquakes; nor the stampedoes of her frantic seas; nor the tearlessness of arid skies that never rain ... it is not these things alone which make tearless Lima the strangest, saddest city thou can'st see. For Lima has taken the white veil; and there is a higher horror in this whiteness of her woe." I don't know if Mario Vargas Llosa recalled Melville's text as he was writing *The Time of the Hero* but from his novel rises that sadness and horror which scarcely symbolizes the cadets' lives at the Leoncio Prado Military Academy: Alberto, Jaguar, Boa, the highlander Cava, Rulos; the officers: Gamboa, Pitaluga, Huarina; the colonel-director of the training school; the girl Teresa; the thief Higueras; in the final analysis they live out the drama of all men, the drama of Justice.

Two symbols, like twin hearts, pulse throughout Vargas Llosa's oblique prose: the military academy, that microcosm which is school, barracks, prison, and the open city. This polarization affects and reveals, in an immediate way, a structure that echoes life and language. In the microcosmos, the whole precedes the parts; in the macrocosmos, the relationship is inverted. In the first case, language is subordinated to the previously synchronic structures; the second represents the chaotic liberty of the diachrony. But the barracks are only the society in miniature; society is the gigantic barracks, the social prison against which William Blake wrote. The novel's initial chapters immediately present this tension: escapes from school, sadistic games, stealing exams, contraband tobacco and alcohol; the whole language of the young men is an attempt to introduce into the school the free life they imagine exists outside in the city.

In the adolescent imagination, being free also means being an adult, and to be an adult means to expose oneself to danger and appear strong. At this level, Vargas Llosa demonstrates, like Robert Musil in his novel *The Confusions of Young Törless*, that fascism is a kind of fatal adolescence—temptation itself. The adult fascist prolongs his adolescence. Imprisoned in the school, the young men "only hear their own curses and their exalted blood that wants to burst out through the temples and breast towards the light."

But *The Time of the Hero* is not a *Bildungsroman* in the tradition of Samuel Butler and Thomas Mann (although it does possess the distinction of being a kind of collective *Bildungsroman*). While it is an extraordinary novel of adolescence, and if it truly contains the line of development of stories about juvenile crisis, *The Time of the Hero* does not dwell on the evidence of the pain of growing up. Its vision is more original and, again, closer to Blake: the adolescent is other, before itself and others, and this comes from that distance. How? For Witold Gombrowicz, who is really the greatest modern master of this theme, "when it is the adult (*l'Aîné*) who forms the young man (*le Cadet*), all goes very well from the social and cultural point of view. But if the adult is subjected to the adolescent, what darkness! What shame, what perversity! And how many traps along the way!" Gombrowicz's work revolves around this obsession: maturation means corruption; the adult wants the adolescent to mature in order to be corrupted, to participate in the putrefaction of the adult. In Vargas Llosa's work, adolescents, pretending to be autonomous rebels, actually sacrifice their menacing freedom from juvenescence by parodying the adult world. But Vargas Llosa sees further: young people are inventing the adult world. The adolescent is not ingenuous: he truly invents reality, he introduces it into the adult world and, as he himself turns into an adult, he only lives that pallid copy of his juvenile imagination. Adolescence cannot be preserved; maturity is not worth preserving. In reality, the academy's officers are forever stuck in the fascist temptation of the "exalted blood." In reality, some have formed others: "Created by form, man is created from outside: he is deformed, unauthentic. To be a man means never being oneself. Man is a constant producer of form: he secretes it" (Gombrowicz, preface to *Pornografia*). They make us. We make.

In *The Time of the Hero* we find a transposition of the theme in the passages characterized by a dog, Malpapeada (whose name can translate as "malnourished"). The brute animal, the silent compan-

ion, can take all the secret cruelty and tenderness, the great absolutes which the adolescent brings to the world. Cruelty: Jaguar gives
his dog the crab lice he caught in the pigsties of Huatita, until poor
Malpapeada is left looking "like a Peruvian flag, red and white, plas-
ter and blood" from rubbing herself so much against the wall of the
stable. Tenderness: "She'd climb on top of me at night and move all
around, without letting me sleep, until I scratched her a little behind her ears. Then she'd settle down ... ah, you little scamp, you
like that, don't you? Come here, I'll scratch your head and your belly.
And right there she settled down, quiet as a stone beneath my hand,
but I could feel her trembling with pleasure."

The world in *The Time of the Hero* is ritual, in the profound sense
which Lévi-Strauss attributes to this term: the rite as the great biological and social game between the living and the dead, between young
and old, between masters and servants, between the animate and inanimate worlds. But if on its first level Vargas Llosa's novel is a rite of
initiation, it soon becomes a rite of justice. Again, it is Malpapeada
who permits us to move from one theme to another:

> I thought it was only Malpapeada that didn't sleep, but later
> somebody told me that dogs are all the same, they stay awake all
> night. At first it made me nervous, it even scared me a little. The
> second I opened my eyes she was right there, looking at me, and
> sometimes I couldn't get to sleep because I'd be thinking about
> how she spent the night by my side without closing her eyes.
> It'd make anybody nervous to imagine they were being spied
> on, even if it was only by a dog that didn't understand anything.
> Though sometimes she did seem to understand.

The adolescent is seen and monitored, and beneath the watchful gaze
of others represents the ritual parody which invents reality: the tragic parodic reality and ritual of love, jealousy, denunciation, laws, and
compensation. Ricardo Arana, *"el Esclavo"* (Slave) is killed from a rifle
bullet in his back during the cadets' open country maneuvers. What
motivates Alberto to denounce Jaguar, the strong man of the fifth
year squad, as Slave's killer? The death of his friend who was hounded,
mocked, and despised by all? His own feeling of inferiority in the face
of the strong, commanding Jaguar? In any case, as he accuses Jaguar
without proof, Alberto sets in motion the ambiguity of a justice that

can only be expressed in absolutes in order to be considered any kind of justice at all.

The adolescent's imagination—his surrender to the primal, initiatory rite—clashes with the officers' reason. For them, the ritual is secondary, derivative, political: the school's good name demands that Slave's death be considered a simple accident. But there is a third factor: Lieutenant Gamboa, for whom justice demands an investigation. In order to prove that he is not lying, Alberto also denounces the illicit alcohol and tobacco, stealing of exams, and nighttime escapes from the school. The game of justice, compensation, and retribution knows no end: like the Hydra, each concerted stroke of justice's sword causes two more serpents to spring from its own head. Each affirmation gives rise to another denial and a contrary affirmation. Alberto is terrorized into silence: he is confronted with the pornography that he passes around the school. All the fifth year cadets are punished for their lack of discipline. All the young men believe that Jaguar denounced them: they attribute to the leader the arbitrary power of deciding what is just. Jaguar takes revenge for Alberto's accusation. The young men take revenge against Jaguar's denunciation of them. For his sin of seeking a truth that cannot coexist with the hydra-like demands of political justice, Lieutenant Gamboa is punished by being sent to a remote command post in the Amazon. The colonel-director's political reasons—to maintain the school's reputation—triumph over everything.

By absolving all, justice condemns all. But did Alberto really denounce Jaguar out of loyalty to Slave or because Jaguar stole Teresa's heart? Did Jaguar really murder Slave, as he finally confesses to Gamboa, in revenge for a previous accusation, or only to assume the terrible role that justice and chance offer him? Does Gamboa really believe in justice or does he, in turn, play an external role which compensates for his guilty internal conscience? Does the colonel really believe in the value of the Academy's reputation or is he only protecting his job and eventual promotion to the Ministry of Defense?

If the vision of justice is one of compensation, in *The Time of the Hero* all the external forms of compensation have been fulfilled and all that's left, silent and hidden, is the tragedy of ambiguity. What has been kept safe is the assumption of justice: the continuity between thought and action. All the characters know where they stand: caught in the chasm between knowledge and action. The rite of initiation is the bridge between both: the double illusion of permanence and continuity. But the role played by rite in Vargas Llosa's previous novel, *The Green House*, is assumed by the word. And here the word is the dark solar center of a stereometric novel of antiphonies, which can only be read on multiple and opposing levels of its immersion in the language.

The structure of *The Green House* is identical to everything that exists previous to the work. Those structural pre-existences represent diverse orders: a language anterior to the characters and narration, which imposes itself on them and which fatally reveals the immobile nature of an archaic and anachronistic system: Peruvian feudalism. System and language inform us on an anti-historical synchrony of Peruvian and Latin American life, about a permanence of the states of the system. On the opposite pole, that of change, in radical opposition to fixed structural poles, speech covers a revolutionary range. What is historically called spontaneous, against what must be anti-historically called hierarchy, not only defines a deep opposition of worlds but establishes an entire dynamic process: this is the very action of the novel, which integrates a polarizing diachrony.

Nevertheless, I have already indicated that in *The Green House* the poles neither cancel one another, nor remain isolated. From both historicism and structuralism, the novel obliges us to transcend an isolated mindset because, in order to exist, literature requires that the process connect with the system, demanding a connection between speech and language. These connections are, respectively, the event and the discourse. Through the event, the system, significantly anonymous, is personalized: *I, you, he, we,* and *they* appropriate the neutral and ahistorical system, coloring it, so to speak, with an individual and collective presence. In *The Green House* and the short story "The Cubs," Vargas Llosa constantly uses alternate pronouns with the purpose of converting system into event, and event into process and then, by means of a new verbal event, to return and affect the system with a double dose of change. This is no accident.

A novel of images, *The Green House* polarizes its meanings: its world stretches like a taut bow between jungle and city, between Santa María de Nieva and Piura, between convent and brothel. This polarization of images reverts, tacitly, to the opposition between structure and change: Santa María de Nieva is a petrified world, hier-archical and anti-historical, "a squalid little town, with naked savages, mosquitoes and rain that makes everything rot and fester, starting with the people"; Piura is a malleable world, wide open, historical: "The doors of Castilla and Mangachería are wide open to Indians who descend from the mountains and reach the town hungry and frightened, to witch doctors expelled from their villages by priests, to peddlers who try to sell their junk in Piura." Santa María's emblem is the convent; Piura's is the brothel. On the highway (and I emphasize *on the highway*: *The Green House* is not alien to the author's passion for novels of chivalry and their dynamic of travel, adventure, and secular pilgrimage), multiple adventures of time and space take place, simi-lar to the language's adventures which constitute the novel's action. This pilgrimage is identical to a contamination—of times, spaces, languages and, in a strict sense, of social and physical illnesses—which creates a second arc of tension: from the cloister to exile, from the maternal breast to desolate bastardry. Bonifacia, an illegitimate daughter, is taken in by the nuns of Santa María; she escapes from the convent to marry Sargent Lituma: she winds up in the Green House, the brothel in Piura, exploited by Sargent Fushia, a bastard, thief, and smuggler, who views the island of Huambisan, where he hides to plan his operations, as a maternal breast: "I think the island is the only home I've ever had." Traveling on the river he feels adventure, risk, and a premonition: "Are you always going to be on one side of the river or the other? . . . Haven't you thought that one day you might die in your boat?" But this premonition, which at bottom is a desire for freedom, is not fulfilled; just as Bonifacia, now called La Selváti-ca, ends up in the Green House,[5] in capital letters, Fushia also returns to the cloister, to the green house, in small letters: a hut in the jun-gle where, spent, exhausted, useless, without sex, devoured by leprosy and plague, toothless and wailing, Fushia, the Latin American ma-cho, discovers that he is only Fushia, the Latin American bastard.

A world of bastardy, of sons-of-bitches:

> Washer women returning from the riverside and servant girls
> from the Buenos Aires district heading to market are caught by
> groups of soldiers, thrown down on the sand, their skirts are
> pulled up over their heads, their legs are pried open, and one af-

5 In Spanish, *la Casa Verde*; besides meaning "green," verde can also signify "lustful."

ter another the soldiers rape them and then run away. The people in Piura say, well, that was just her luck, she got knocked down, run over, and caught in the crossfire, the whole operation was just a little target practice, and the resulting offspring just a son of a gun, born from seven kinds of spilled milk.

In Juan Rulfo's *Pedro Páramo*, Juan Preciado ceaselessly asks, *Who is my father?* In a different brothel, in José Donoso's *Hell Has No Limits*, the little Japanese girl cries out, *Who is my mother?* Both questions are met with anonymous peals of laughter, as are the bastards who live in the Green House: children of women knocked down and knocked up, sons-of-guns, little squirts of spilled milk, your mother's a whore, your father unknown. And nevertheless, the father had a name: Pedro Páramo, Don Anselmo the Harpist, Hernán Cortés, Francisco Pizarro. And it was the mother who was anonymous. But the bastards only ever really know their mother, never their father: they are a-patriated. In *The Green House*, as in *One Hundred Years of Solitude*, *Pedro Páramo*, *Hell Has No Limits*, and *The Lost Steps*, the Latin American novel offers itself as a new foundational impulse, as a return to the act of genesis as redemption for the original violation, of the founding bastardy: the Conquest was a gigantic knockdown, Latin America was trampled underfoot, target practice on a staggering scale which populated the continent with son-of-a-guns, little squirts of spilled milk, bastard sons of violated women: *hijos de la chingada.*

In order to start anew, Vargas Llosa corrupts, implacably; he salubriously contaminates all the levels of this degraded Latin American existence, significantly, between the Mass and the carnival spree. Against hierarchies he opposes a delirious verbal confusion in which the past is narrated in the present tense and the present in the past—in which the internally overlapping situations in the writing, although not in space and time, assimilate, match, and reveal a common, sinister, and bastardly condition. He de-hierarchizes the men who are polarized: the bandit Fushia and the honest, upright governor Don Julio, and the verbal forms indiscriminately assume all the caudal simultaneity of speaking and gestures, in order to enact that rupture of the oppositions between change and structure:

> They passed close by you on wild horses, who are those madmen, they're going to the river, now they're coming back, don't

be afraid sweetheart, and there her face turning, asking, her anxiety, her trembling mouth, her nails like sharp tacks, and her hand why, how, and her breathing right by yours. Now calm her down, you I'll explain it for you, Toñita, they've gone away now, they were going so fast I couldn't see their faces, and she tenacious, thirsty, searching in the blackness, who, why, how.

This totality of gesture and language which Vargas Llosa offers us does not, however, serve only to de-hierarchize Latin American verbal forms and level them into a common action. In the end we are delivered to the deepest and truest aspiration of personality; it is the sign of the inalienable individual (the "I-Am," as Faulkner would say) which fights to be known, to establish its right to dream, to tenderness, to the integral presence, in the world where man is bastardized, subjected to the fatalism of misery and the impersonality of nature. As the character *el Mono* (Monkey) claims: "A person always likes to discover secrets, what habits people bring with them from their own lands." To discover which secrets those might be is, doubtless, one of the keys to *The Green House* and one of its riskiest and most attractive aspects: the acceptance of melodrama as one of the axes of daily social life in Latin America. To put it provocatively: using *The Green House*, one could make a bad Mexican film with Rosa Carmina playing the role of la Selvática, Julio Aldama as Fushia, Fernando Soler as Don Anselmo the Harpist, and Arturo de Córdova as Father García. Vargas Llosa has not avoided the problem of melodramatic "content" of some lives that, in another way, would not know how to affirm their being. Abandonment, the feeling of non-existence which is expressed in action through bravado, machismo, sentimentality, and melodrama, encounters its popular linguistic outlets in such varied forms as circumlocution, the diminutive, scatological aggression and pornography, and the secret slang of the slums and outskirts known as *caliche* or *totacho*. Rubén Darío knew it well: only a Latin American could accumulate the gigantic and sublime verbal affectation found in his poem "Verlaine: Response" and, at the same time, reach the Quevedian, pince-nez perfection of "Fatality." Félix B. Caignet's *The Right to Be Born* remains Latin America's most faithful mirror of true, immediate, appreciable reality. When it lacks tragic conscience, historical reason, or personal affirmation, the melodrama supplies them: it is a substitute, an imitation, an illusion of being. Vargas Llosa does not overlook this evidence, he simply neglects tragedy, reason, history, and personality in order to confront them. There is a magnificent moment when Fushia, facing Aquilino, is aware of his tragedy: of the fact that now "I'm not even a man." There are the extraordinary encounters between Anselmo and Toñita, a mutual discovery of personality. And there is the permanent movement of language as it attempts to create a radical and historical context which, again, is conquered or overcome, by tragic awareness.

Thus, these debated and debatable lives, stretching in an arc between the convent of Santa María de Nieva and the brothel of Mangachería, ultimately discover that the jungle was not quietude, nor was the city movement. A suffocating immobility permeates the totality of the Peruvian world, and Vargas Llosa reiterates this image in both extremes of the polarity. In the jungle: "Thick, dark clouds, motionless over the lupuna trees, dumped down black water for two successive days, and the whole island became a muddy puddle, the inlet a roiled cloud, and a lot of birds fell down dead at the door of the cabin." At the Green House in Piura "a motionless, transparent smoke was floating between the ceiling and the dancers' heads, and there was the smell of beer, sweat, and black tobacco." Aquilino is *always going, from one side to the other along the rivers*; La Chunga is *always* in her chair, ruling over her father's brothel. And, as Kid says in the final, personal assimilation of apparent opposites: "I treat all women the same. Inmates or nuns, it's all the same to me."

Setting fire to the Green House is the revolution. But the Brothel-Phoenix will be reborn from its ashes and will continue devouring its pupils; the pupils from Mother Angélica's convent will continue feeding La Chunga's bordello; they will become pupils of the Green House. Vargas Llosa's novel never comes off as a political tract but rather a tragic literary creation which, in response to Reátegui's question—"Don't you want this earth to be livable?"—answers with the conflictive totality of what we are, a totality questioned by a language which already contains all the possibilities of what we can be.

Vargas Llosa responds to this "we can be" by questioning it in a series of great novels that culminates, recently, in *The Feast of the Goat* (2000) and *The Dream of the Celt* (2010). I'd like to highlight *Conversation in a Cathedral* (1969) and *The War of the End of the World* (1981) in order to focus my attention on *The Festival of the Goat*, while remembering the purpose of our long ago conversation in a London pub and conclude this literary meditation with the generic tyrant in the works of Gabriel García Márquez and Alejo Carpentier. In García Márquez's *The Autumn of the Patriarch* (1975), the models are fundamentally Franco and Salazar, although not without traces of Latin American dictators from the past, present, and future. In Carpentier's *Reasons of State* (1974) the model is the Venezuelan macho man Antonio Guzmán Blanco, a contradictory character who confiscated the property of the Church, created the system of primary education, and supported secondary education but who also governed with an iron hand, failed to end corruption, and suffered from a vanity as broad as the Orinoco River. Carpentier focuses on a semi-comic feature of Guzmán Blanco: his periodic retreats from power to enjoy life in France and nostalgically decorate his Parisian flat like a tropical jungle, complete with cockatoos. Power, however, mattered more to him than Paris: the moment a rebellion breaks out in Venezuela, Guzmán Blanco returns—slowly but surely, by ship—to retake power and sharpen his tyranny.

Roa Bastos, by contrast, chooses an individual tyrant—Doctor Francia—and Vargas Llosa another more contemporary, the Dominican satrap Rafael Leónidas Trujillo. But Roa Bastos can admit redemptive elements in the figure of Francia, and Vargas Llosa does not find them in Trujillo. If Francia is explicable in the light of nineteenth century post-independence instability, Trujillo is neither explicable nor admissible in the twentieth century: he is a bloody anachronism.

Initiated by Valle Inclán in *Tirano Banderas* (1926), the theme of the abuse of power, despotic authoritarianism, and the distance between law and practice continues with Gallegos's Ardavines family, Azuela's Don Mónico, Rulfo's Pedro Páramo, Guzmán's Caudillo, and, already cited, the various dictators of Roa Bastos, García Márquez, and Carpentier. The difference in Vargas Llosa is that he does not appeal to a literary pseudonym or a symbolic figure, but instead points us to a real dictator, who is personalized, with name, surname and certifiable dates of birth and death: Rafael Leónidas Trujillo Molina, Benefactor of the New Homeland, Restorer of Financial Independence and First Journalist of the Nation, although the Dominican people, to stay on the safe side, called him "Mr. Jones" or "Mr. Jackson."

This frank denomination—calling things by their real name—does not signify that Vargas Llosa limits himself to a journalistic exercise on the thirty years of the Trujillo dictatorship. The dates and biographies are present and lugubriously precise, but the novelistic frame reduces (or elevates) them to testimonies of an atrocious reality, to the extent that the same reality is enclosed (and revealed) by the narrative imagination, which is proposed, in turn, as *part* of a wider *reality*, which includes the reality of literary invention.

In this way, we learn in detail about the horror of Trujillo's oppression. Enemies of the regime? "We threw them to the sharks, alive, just as you ordered." The prisons are torture holes in which the dictator's excessive cruelty is amplified by each torturer's cruelty and rancor. Enemies of the regime are shot by twelve bandits who will, in turn, be shot so that no witnesses remain. Whole groups of naked men are humiliated, tortured, murdered. Trujillo can rely on a court of adulators, assassins, and subordinates. Johnny Abbes is the epicenter of all the evil: "For a government to endure thirty years, you need a Johnny Abbes who gets his hands dirty." A former grave robber and body snatcher, now a murderer of suspected enemies, a faggot, married to Lupita, a "horrible Mexican battle-ax . . . who went around with a pistol in her bag." "I'm your dog," Abbes says to Trujillo.

Henry Chirinos, called "the drunken constitutionalist" and "living garbage," wolfs down his food, possessed of an "insolent loyalty," a writer of poems, acrostics, and funeral orations. He is the man-who-never-sweats: he doesn't need a fan. His lips are the color of ashes; his words float on a cloud of stench.

We also see, at last, Agustín Cabral, an "expert in things unforgivable": traps, tricks, dodges, intricate betrayals. He attributes to Trujillo the saying that "We Dominicans discovered the wonders of punctuality." He is Urania's father. And, beyond good and evil, Joaquín Balaguer, who knows what is convenient and ignores the inconvenient. He knows how to keep his mouth shut. He is more Jesuit than the Jesuits themselves: he acts *as if he believed* . . .

Trujillo humiliates his collaborators. He specializes in humiliating those who serve him, learned, cultured, university graduates. He neutralizes his collaborators by provoking trouble among Trujillista factions. Has he read Machiavelli? Like Hernán Cortés in the conquest of Mexico, he doesn't need to. His instinct leads him to exercise a vengeful, bloody regime which, nevertheless, as *The Prince* said, bleeds in turn from various sides. Like all patrimonialist tyrants, Trujillo is the benefactor, not only of the Homeland, but also of his family. His mother "the Exalted Matriarch," "mother of the great hero who governs us," and Trujillo's wife, the First Lady, a "fat, stupid" old woman, a "two-bit" little lady "of dubious habits, dubbed *La Españolita* (the little Spanish lady)."

Ah! And we must not forget to mention the dictator's sons, Radhamés and Ramfis, so named in honor of Verdi's Aida. Radhamés is the "stupid, little ugly brute" and Ramfis is the spoiled boy, named colonel at seven years old, promoted to general at ten, sent to the Fort Leavenworth military academy. After not being treated like a "General Trujillo" deserves, he returns to his country to be feted like a hero: he is named Head of the Joint Chiefs of Staff of the Armed Forces. He grows up "surrounded by two or three friends who serve, celebrate, and adulate him, and prosper at his expense." He gives presents to the actresses he seduces—Kim Novak, Zsa Zsa Gabor—analogous to the United States's military assistance to the Dominican Republic. And his own benefactor, the Father of the New Nation, what does he do? What does he not do? He never sweats. He dissimulates. He controls his emotions. He whitens his mulatto skin. He has hundreds of uniforms, and many houses large and small. He likes to "make the little girls scream with pleasure." He trusts that his regime will be eternal—hasn't it been blessed by Francis Joseph, Cardinal Spellman, Archbishop of New York? Doesn't he count on U.S. support? After serving as an errand boy, he enters the National Guard during the U.S. occupation of the Dominican Republic and is promoted to colonel, protected by one Major Watson: "Trujillo thinks like a Marine!" In 1930, he becomes dictator through a coup d'état and never loosens his hold on power. In 1937, he murders, with impunity, seven thousand Haitian workers and, throughout his dictatorship, tens of thousands of Dominican citizens. Without him, the Dominican Republic would be "a mob, a tribe, a caricature of a country." How sad, for such a superior ruler, to leave such a legacy, one that is "the great mistake of my life," the incomparable calamity, "they only live for drinking, money, and fucking"! And it is in spite of, not thanks to them—the mob, the tribe—that the regime knows itself to be eter-

nal. "Who would ever think that some day the Earth could stop revolving around the Sun?" This "faith" permits the dictator to bear his
own personal miseries. An infected prostate. Incontinence. Pissing
his pants. A loose sphincter. Unable to "make a little girl scream with
pleasure." And unable to avoid death as well.

The tyrant's death is anticipated by men who are brave and im-
patient, ill-prepared opponents who fashion the final trap to assassinate Trujillo. And these brave men, themselves disposed to die in the
attempt, manage to carry it out in a haphazard manner. From the
country of "squabbling windbags, vampires, and ham-fisted idiots"
despised by the dictator, emerge the ones who are mad for justice,
who kill him and put him on ice, as if the cold might resuscitate him.
Trujillo persecuted the clergy, he lost the backing of Washington, and
left behind a vacuum filled by the little man Balaguer, and by Ramfis
in his transitory position as head of the army. Everything is hurried,
everything is passing. "The terrible, vengeful" and very astute first lady
always understood how to manipulate things, accumulating millions
of dollars in secret accounts in Swiss banks, the ultimate beneficiaries
of Trujillo's rapacity. She never disclosed or recovered her hidden millions. She died in poverty, in Panama, and was taken to be buried in
the cemetery by taxi.

Vargas Llosa's novel is not journalism; it reveals nothing that has
not already been published about Trujillo's tyranny. Nor is it history: too many Dominicans suffered or benefitted from the three decades of Trujillo's power to pretend that their experience could
be encapsulated in a book and consigned to the past. It is a novel, a novelty, and also, à la Unamuno, *nivela, nube y niebla*;[6] that
is, a cloudy, misty, multi-leveled novel. This is thanks to a presence
which communicates the events and humanizes them, makes them
new and novel-worthy again. That presence is Urania. She is the
daughter of Senator Agustín Cabral, a man who was the "brains"
of the regime and is now a human vegetable, stripped of willpower, and abandoned by his daughter. She is protected by nuns,
to save her from the fate of Rosalía Perdomo, and so many other girls raped by Trujillo, by the Trujillos, by the gangs of the Ardavines family, by the Pedro Páramos, the sons of the patriarchs,
and the descendants of the tyrant Banderas: the legions of lawless
power in Latin America.

6 *nivel*: level; *nube*: cloud; *niebla*: fog, mist

Urania Cabral saves herself. She goes to New York to live her own life as an independent professional, far from the fatality of brute force. She returns to acknowledge her invalid father. She returns to relate this novel to her aunt Adelina, to her cousins Lucinda and Manolita, that is, to all of us, the readers of Mario Vargas Llosa's novel. She not only tells what we already knew but what we did not know: the effect of this history on the soul of a woman, Urania, who escapes from history to tell history, from the frame of a personality shaped by history but taken out of history in order to recount it—Urania Cabral—giving it a personal frame, a protagonist, who renews history and makes it intelligible.

14. José Donoso:
From Boom to Boomerang

1.

Mario Vargas Llosa called José Donoso the most literary writer of the Latin American Boom. Looking back over the years, what did that vaunted generation, whose initial works were published from the mid-1950s to mid-1960s, really stand for? The novels of the Boom departed from the idiotic alternatives established by two wings of an equally dogmatic set of precepts: nationalism or cosmopolitanism; realism or fantasy; compromise or formalism. They refused to be pigeonholed by narrow genres: urban novel or indigenous rural novel, proletariat novel, historical novel, etc.

The novel of the Boom restored the breadth of literary tradition. It acknowledged and embraced the fathers of the new novel — Borges, Carpentier, Onetti, and Rulfo. It reclaimed for itself the great uninterrupted poetic continuity of Latin America, from the Nahuatl lyric to the colonial Baroque poets to the great contemporary poets: Neruda, Vallejo, Huidobro, and Lezama Lima. This gave the novel a range that reflected reality and also made it a creator of a greater reality. It tremendously broadened the technical resources of Latin American fiction, grounding its social effects in the domains of language and the imagination, and encouraging an extraordinary individuation of writing beyond the narrowness of genres. As if that were not enough, the Boom spectacularly enlarged the Latin American market for reading and internationalized the literature from Mexico and the Caribbean to Chile and Argentina.

The generation of the so-called "Boom writers" transcended many limitations. Not only did it expand the genre and internationalize the Latin American novel but, I would add, it assumed the burden of our tradition. (When asked to identify the apparent influences in the fiction of Juan Rulfo and Juan José Arreola, Alfonso Reyes simply replied: *two thousand years of literature*.) The novel does not reflect reality: it creates reality. The novel's social effect is first given in terms of language and imagination. Everything matters: genres submit to the writer's personalization.

No one overcame those oppositions or affirmed these positions more naturally than José Donoso. No one made more patent the rigid social hierarchies in Latin America—the cruelty of the Chilean class system, background for a theme that receives such lustrous treatment in Isabel Allende's *The House of the Spirits*.

In Donoso's work, nothing is what it seems to be. Everything is on the verge of being *something else*. Disguise, homonymy, even organ transplant; makeup, as Juan Villoro has noted: it all serves Donoso to dramatize a written revolt under the twin signs of destruction and recreation, both unstable, passengers in the great Baroque poetry of our language: "I am a *was* and a *will be* and a tired *is*."

I have cited Claudio Magris when he states that one must learn to read Latin America anew; to do our homework in seriously penetrating the hard, melancholy, difficult prose of the South American continent.

Regarding world literatures, Magris adds that European literature is menaced by incapacity, North American literature by negativity, and Latin American literature by totality. And although Magris celebrates the Latin American dilation of imaginative space, he also points out the European guilty conscience, ashamed of reveling in the Latin American celebration. For that reason, the critic from Trieste asks us (Europeans, Latin Americans) that we make an effort to read Latin America anew, resisting the tempting perspective of literature as exotic adventure.

One cannot begin this apprenticeship better than with José Donoso. There is something in him which occasionally recalls what T. S. Eliot said to James Joyce: "You have enormously increased the difficulties of being a novelist." But Donoso's difficulty is also an invitation, that of letting us fall into a forgotten world, the world of origin, the magic world, with our eyes open. Donoso's fall into origin does not signify a return to an ideal primitive world, into a Golden Age giving way to an Iron Age. Donoso's first age is not a paradise lost. The present horror of his novels is a twin of the original horror. His fetuses and dogs, his gigantic grotesque heads, his spells and witchcraft, his duplicated babies, are the mirror of divine creation. The monsters were already there at the dawn of Eden.

The only thing separating us from them is a pile of dirty rags. Unlike Cortázar, where the houses are taken over, in Donoso the houses have always been occupied: we move through them following corridors without destination, useless patios, blind, dead-end dwellings.

It's no coincidence that Humberto Peñaloza, El Mudito (the little mute) of Donoso's masterpiece, *The Obscene Bird of Night*, has simultaneously lost the power of speech (or feigns having lost it) (or has converted silence into the very eloquence of the origin of the speaking being). In Donoso's novels, everything occurs as if we all required a new, but also very ancient, discourse in order to walk between a world that is the "forest of symbols" of which Baudelaire spoke and which, in Donoso, surrounds our "country house" and also our little urban rooming house.

As a reader of English literature, Donoso invites us to fulfill the imaginary requirements proposed by Coleridge. The writer must, above all, mediate between sensation and perception, only in order to immediately dissipate any reasonable relation between things. The goal is re-creation with an imagination stripped of the rationalism that reduces everything to a single meaning and sacrifices the very essence of the poetic act which consists of multiplying the meaning of things. As if in response to Wittgenstein's request, *The Obscene Bird of Night* shows that there is nothing more to say, save what cannot be said: poetry and myth.

For all these reasons, Donoso allowed himself the luxury of changing genres and narrative styles again and again, telling us that the reader must obviously be asked to read the novel as it was written but that one must also learn to read it as it will be read. You must learn to write it, at last, as it will be written by the reader. This is the twist which places Donoso within the tradition of Cervantes; the tradition of La Mancha.

Luis Buñuel was right when he said that Donoso was the master of a natural and inexplicable irrationality, very close to surrealism. Donoso's literary merits, his constant mediation between sensation and perception — the novelist's diapason — affords him equal license to borrow a delicate, melancholy string quartet or to stage a somber, dolorous opera. We listen to Donoso: he is Brahms played at the rhythm of the Chilean *cueca*; he is Wagner injected with Frankenstein.

José Donoso plays an active role in all the phases attributed to the Boom: the *pre-Boom*, the heart of the movement, the *proto-Boom*, the *mini-Boom* and the *sub-Boom*. And I add, now, the *Boom-erang*. Because Donoso exercises his mastery in a double sense, a mastery proceeding from the work itself and a magisterial capacity for teaching and shared enthusiasm. That is why I place his work as a prologue to the new Latin American writers. The amplitude of Donoso's work has opened the way for a great generation of Chilean novelists, in the very country which supposed itself to be the exclusive province of the greatest modern poets of America. Today, the Chilean novel's family tree boasts magnificent fruit: Diamela Eltit, Marcela Serrano, Arturo Fontaine, Carlos Franz, Alberto Fuguet, and Sergio Missana, many of them formed in Pepe Donoso's literary workshops, a generation of novelists expressing itself in a variety of free, personal voices.

(A personal note. Donoso and I became friends when we were both students at The Grange School in Santiago de Chile. Later, he lived for a time in a small house on my property in Cerrada de Galeana in Mexico City, while he was writing *Hell Has No Limits* and I was writing *A Change of Skin*. He suffered from maladies that many in our circle judged to be imaginary, illnesses from which his wife María Pilar also seemed to suffer, until one day his hypochondria turned out to be all too real, to the degree that it has been suggested that, as a *memento mori*, his gravestone bear the inscription: *¿No que no, cabrones?* ("Do you believe me now, you pricks?"). But the near-simultaneous deaths of Pepe and María Pilar, as simultaneous as their illnesses, take us again into the literary terrain where Sacha Guitry defines love as the perfect egoism between two, and Quevedo invokes a love constant beyond death: "they will be ash, but ash with sense and feeling; they will be dust, but dust in love.")

2. The Boom

What has this storied generation left behind? In summary, I think that it made five principal contributions. First, a handful of good novels. Next, the Boom internationalized the Latin American novel. It also broke the rigid strictures which the genres had until then imposed on fiction (rural, urban, indigenous, etc.) For that reason, it personalized fiction's task to an extraordinary degree. Finally, it created an internal and international market for our literature.

Thanks to the Boom, there is today a new Latin American novel which we could call, not without irony, the Boomerang. It has benefitted from both the formal liberties and the individuation of the

Boom. One need not speak of genres or apply labels to describe a novel by Luisa Valenzuela in Argentina, or one by Ángeles Mastretta in Mexico. On the other hand, and dramatically, the current novelists lack the distribution, information, and influence of past years. Thus, not surprisingly, I have to travel twenty hours to reach Buenos Aires in order to discover the true, contemporary richness of Argentine fiction. But if I don't go to Buenos Aires, I'm not likely to discover writers like César Aira, Matilde Sánchez or Martín Caparrós. And if I don't travel to Chile, I won't discover the most interesting new fiction on the continent: Arturo Fontaine, Carlos Franco. But they, in their turn, would have to make the long trip to Mexico to find out about the excellent work of Laura Esquivel or Gonzalo Celorio. From the Boom to the Boomerang: save for exceptional cases, like those of Laura Esquivel, Isabel Allende or Luis Sepúlveda, the Latin American novel today tends to stay in its national ghetto.

What has happened? Starting in the 1930s, Argentina managed to create a powerful distribution network for books. For three decades, thanks to distributors around Buenos Aires, an enormous variety of titles reached an immense number of bookshops and readers all throughout Latin America. The basis for this success was a reward for exportation, up to thirty percent, for each book shipped abroad, provided by the Argentine government and a commercial infrastructure which permitted an editor, however small, to dedicate himself to publishing books without the need to get involved in a distribution network. Thus, the massive distribution permitted Latin American booksellers, however small they happened to be, to acquire many titles at a low price and in small quantities. The beneficiary was the Latin American reader, from Chihuahua to Patagonia. We writers also benefitted; we got to know each other, and we stayed current on what was new.

Military dictatorships in the Southern Cone and the economic crisis put an end to this situation. Pinochet, Videla, and their emulators targeted the intellectual class, accusing it of fomenting and idealizing violence. Among those pursued and disappeared, were not only writers but also readers. Fascist ideology modified and narrowed curricula. Many intellectuals went into exile. The international market shrank, bookshops closed, the distribution system collapsed.

Mexico, the other great publishing pole of Spanish America,

could not make up for the Argentine deficiencies. Lacking a distribution system, Mexican books had to be acquired by Latin American
booksellers in an itinerant manner, going from publisher to publisher, and not through a global distributor. The void filled by Spanish
publishers now experiences other limitations: the fear of selling mas-
sively in America but never getting paid by the distributors for the
book sales, and ending up with piles of debt. Finally, the brutal de-
cline of buying power among the middle classes and the pauperization of pauperization itself, offer a desolate panorama which turns
the book into a luxury item.

3. The Post-Boom

That is why being a novelist today in Latin America is more difficult
but also more important. The practical problems — the market, distribution — have been overcome by excellence and number. At the
2008 Paris Book Fair, dedicated to Mexico, more than forty Mexican novelists were present. Others who could not attend were represented as well, totaling more than fifty authors for a country that in
1930 counted barely half a dozen published or publishable novelists.

Problematic though it is, the growth is nevertheless noteworthy,
and I dare to attribute it, in large part, to what Vargas Llosa attributed to Donoso: being literary, believing in the novel as a fiction which
is reality, believing in literature as a creator of reality. If not, how do
we confirm and accept the reality of *Don Quixote* in *our* reality? Before Cervantes, *Don Quixote* did not exist. After Cervantes, we cannot conceive of reality *without Don Quixote*. This is what José Donoso
understood supremely well, and from that understanding is born the
great arc that stretches from the Boom to the Boomerang and from
there to the new literature, inconclusive but bloodless, which I will
consider next.

What had not been said still needed to be said. Twentieth century novelists — Borges, Carpentier, Lezama Lima, Onetti — and those
of the Boom filled that historical void, while the Baroque, widely understood thanks to being an art of European, indigenous, and African miscegenation, was the style capable of embracing and unifying
different eras. Perhaps the desired synthesis was achieved. Perhaps the
unsaid was not only said but fortuitous, as well.

Perhaps all this twentieth century writing liberated the fortunate thematic freedom I next describe from the burden of saying the unsaid. Nevertheless, recent writers—from the Guatemalan Rodrigo Rey Rosa to the Mexican Mario Bellatin—inherit a tradition and enrich it with new creation. Such is the synergy—the concerted action of the past in order to make way for the future, and the action of the future to vigorously assimilate the past as well.

What was previously *unsaid* is, in this way, associated with what needed to be said *today*. My intention in this second part of the book is to survey the variety of our current writing. If I privilege Mexican writers, it is not out of Nahuatl-Hispano chauvinism but proximity of knowledge. In every case, from Sergio Ramírez to Luiz Rafael Sánchez, and from Sylvia Iparraguirre to Juan Gabriel Vázquez, it is stylistic and thematic variety that truly identifies the contemporary literature which includes Margo Glantz and Juan Villoro as parts of a whole rather than national exceptions.

15. The Boomerang

1. Augusto Roa Bastos and the Power of the Imagination

In the Autumn of 1967, I happened to run into Mario Vargas Llosa in London. We had both recently read and admired *Patriotic Gore*, Edmund Wilson's collection of portraits from the American Civil War. Seated in a Hampstead pub it occurred to us that a similar book about Latin America wouldn't be a bad idea: an imaginary gallery of portraits. Suddenly, various ghosts floated into that London pub, claiming the right to be incarnated. They were Latin American dictators.

Individuals like the Mexican Antonio López de Santa Anna, the limping aficionado of cockfighting who gambled and lost half the national territory in the war incited by President James K. Polk and his expansionist slogan of Manifest Destiny. Santa Anna was president of Mexico for eleven terms. He lost a leg in the so-called "Pastry War" with France. He buried it with pomp and circumstance in the National Cathedral. When the tyrant fell from power, the people disinterred the leg and dragged it through the streets. But each time he returned to power, Santa Anna ceremoniously reburied the leg, only to see it disinterred and dragged through the streets again. Juan Vicente Gómez, president of Venezuela for thirty years, announced his own death in order to punish those who would dare to celebrate it. The tyrant Maximiliano Hernández Martínez protected San Salvador from scarlet fever by wrapping the streetlights in red paper. The Bolivian Enrique Peñaranda, of whom his mother famously said: "If I had known that my son would grow up to become president, I would have taught him how to read and write." They all constitute a challenge for the Latin American novelist: how can we compete with history? How does a writer invent characters who are crazier, more powerful, or more unbelievable than those who have appeared in our history?

Vargas Llosa and I invited a dozen Latin American authors to respond to this question. Each one was asked to compose a novella about their favorite national tyrant, with a limit of fifty pages per dictator. The collected volume would be called "The Fathers of the Fatherlands." Claude Gallimard, our editor in France, became the project's godfather. Unfortunately, in the end, it proved impossible to coordinate all the writers' different schedules and wishes. If my memory is as sharp as that of Augusto Roa Bastos's dictator in *I, the Supreme*, besides Vargas Llosa and myself, the group included the Argentine Julio Cortázar, the Venezuelan Miguel Otero Silva, the Colombian Gabriel García Márquez, the Cuban Alejo Carpentier, the Dominican Juan Bosch, and the Chileans José Donoso and Jorge Edwards (Donoso promised to focus on a Bolivian dictator; his wife, María Pilar, had been born in that penthouse of the Americas). When the project fell apart, three of the writers mentioned decided to move ahead and finish their own novels: Carpentier (*Reasons of State*), García Márquez (*The Autumn of the Patriarch*) and Roa Bastos (*I, the Supreme*).

Carpentier invented a composite character, made up of the Venezuelan dictator Guzmán Blanco and Guatemalan president Manuel Estrada Cabrera, recreating the figure of the enlightened despot who preferred to spend the greater part of his time listening to opera in Paris, but who would return to his native land in a flash to crush military uprisings without missing a beat of *Rigoletto*. Carpentier's head of state ends his days in a Right Bank apartment which he has decorated with orchids, hammocks, palm trees, and monkeys. García Márquez's patriarch comprises characteristics of the Venezuelan Gómez, the Bolivian Peñaranda, the Dominican Rafael L. Trujillo and, especially, the contemporary Iberian dictators, Francisco Franco and António Oliveira Salazar. Both men took so long to die that their deaths seemed to last longer than their lives: were they, after all, immortal?

Augusto Roa Bastos had his hands full with just one life, that of the Paraguayan despot José Gaspar Rodríguez de Francia who governed his country as "Perpetual Dictator" between 1816 and 1840, the year of his death at the age of seventy-four. The result is a brilliant, richly textured book, an impressive portrait not only of El Supremo but of a whole colonial society in the process of learning to swim, although it might be in the Paraná River, since Paraguay has no coastline. Learning to swim, upriver or out to sea: the Paraguayan experience, the transition from colonial dependence to national "independence" has been in our own time the same experience as many countries in Asia and Africa. Starting at the end of the eighteenth century, Latin America began the process of decolonization. It was an initial revolt, not only of what would later be called "the Third World," but of the sons and daughters of the West against the West itself, although with Western ideas. Latin America, Alain Rouquié has written, is "the Far West."

In this way, the government of Doctor Francia first coincided with the epic of independence, then with the drama (and melodramas) of organizing a post-colonial republic. The Paraguayan situation was difficult. Isolated in the heart of South America, where the Jesuits had maintained their colonial reservation, surrounded by gigantic, ambitious neighbors—Argentina and Brazil—which Paraguay would have to fight right down to the last able-bodied man old enough to bear arms, and besieged by an endless territorial conflict with Brazil for the possession of the Chaco region. At the beginning of its national life Paraguay saw itself faced with a dilemma: had it gained independence from Spain only to become a province of Argentina or a Brazilian satrapy?

The possibility of a community of Hispanic nations was frustrated when no one listened to Charles III's minister, the Count of Aranda, who, upon proposing unity at the time of Latin American independence, was trying not only to promote Spanish American independence, but also to create a viable alliance in opposition to the growing power of Anglo-America. Napoleon's occupation of Spain in 1808 unleashed the wars of independence in Spanish America. These wars foiled the ambitions of numerous provincial satrapies. In many cases, the Spanish Empire in the Americas degenerated into mere *republiquetas* or guerilla factions seeking independence. Among them, a series of petty tyrants and local bosses affirmed their actual local dominion as opposed to the governmental authority of the national republic. The *republiquetas* stretched from the hacienda of Padre Ildefonso de las Muñecas on the shores of Lake Titicaca to the violent fiefdom of Juan Facundo Quiroga in La Rioja, described by Domingo Sarmiento in his classic book, *Facundo: Civilization and Barbarism.*

Civilization or barbarism? Legality or violence? National or local government? Unable to restore the Iberian community upon democratic bases, Spanish America instead chose nationalism, seeing it as the lesser evil of all the philosophical blessings Enlightenment doctrines had to offer. As the young Francia informs an enraged priest in Roa Bastos's novel, "We, by contrast, plan to construct everything anew through builders like Rousseau, Montesquieu, Diderot, Voltaire, and others just as good as them." In Paraguay, Francia decided to convert necessity into virtue, transforming his parochial power into national power. He converted the fact of Paraguayan isolation into a pretext to save his country from absorption by Argentina or Brazil. Naming himself "El Supremo," Francia prohibited commerce, travel, and even the postal service between Paraguay and the outside world. Like some lost Evelyn Waugh character, the foreigner who ventured into Paraguay would remain there forever: El Supremo hung an enormous warning on the gates of his fiefdom: NO EXIT. He also wrapped his iron chauvinism in a populist mantle. His introverted republic had to be, by necessity, autocratic. Doctor Francia created a subsistence economy; he favored mob politics, and he attacked and weakened the church, but in the end, he protected and strengthened traditional oligarchical interests. His prolonged rule demonstrates a fact of our history that is generally ignored: Latin American nationalism has its origins on the right, more than on the left which is intellectually oriented towards internationalism. It also illuminates a rather well-known fact: despotic populism disguises the paralysis imposed by the tyrant of society. There is the impression of a movement but nothing changes.

Born in 1917, Roa Bastos left Paraguay in 1947 and from then on lived in exile through the reign of General Alfredo Stroessner which lasted longer than that of El Supremo. As his country's most eminent writer, Roa Bastos's legend will clearly outlive both tyrants put together. His novels are few in number, restrained (as befits a Paraguayan work), and brilliant. Nevertheless, his masterpiece, *I, the Supreme*, appeared in Spanish in 1974, and was not published in English until 1989, in a masterful translation by Helen Lane. *I, the Supreme* is a *summa* which absorbs all the author's previous work. It takes the form of Roa Bastos's dialogue with himself through history and thanks to the mediation of a monstrous historical figure which the novelist must imagine and comprehend in order to finally understand himself and his country. The novel absorbs the historical material in order to imagine history and create another nation, one living through the gestation of its cultural events. This second nation of the imagination and culture is the real force of a people, not the fragile nation of the official discourse and the historical archives.

Roa Bastos's literary technique primarily proposes a relationship between the self and others, between individual destiny and shared, truly historical, destiny. The technique is the writing itself: the writing of history and the writing of the novel united in the writing of a life that can only be ours if we take charge of the life of the other. *I, the Supreme* is a voice directed at you, the reader, but also at the historical figure of Doctor Francia, at the fictive character called "El Supremo" and to Augusto Roa Bastos the Paraguayan writer. It begins, biblically and literally, with the writing on the wall. A pamphleteer has nailed a declaration on the door of the cathedral (intimations of a Lutheran rebellion!) bearing the forged signature of El Supremo. In this apocryphal decree, the Perpetual Dictator commands that "upon my death my cadaver be decapitated and my head placed on a pike for three days." When summoned by the church bells, the people must also gather to pay homage to the head of El Supremo while his entire civil and military cabinet must be immediately hanged.

This strange, oracular foretoken of the Eternal Tyrant's demise, supposedly written by the dictator himself, unleashes the novel's protean writing. The dictator demands that his incompetent secretary locate the author of the libel (he is never found). The secretary records El Supremo's dictation. El Supremo corrects it, he speaks to his dog Sultán, he writes his own secrets in a private notebook which is, actually, in a playful Dickensian echo, "an oversized ledger, of the kind which El Supremo used since the beginning of his government, to keep track, in his own handwriting, of the treasury accounts down to the last real." In these folios, El Supremo now writes, "disjointedly, incoherently, events, ideas, reflections, minutely detailed and well-nigh maniacal observations on a sweeping range of very different subjects and themes: those which, by his estimate, were positive in the Credits column and negative in the Debts column," says the compiler who notes his observations throughout the novel, thus creating a second spectral text, parallel to, at times opposed to, at other times in support of, the divagations of El Supremo himself. Add to these official documents, a log book, traces of the memories of people who knew El Supremo, selections of biographies dedicated to him (including one written by Thomas Carlyle), illuminating footnotes provided by translator Helen Lane (they should become part of the Spanish edition) and the shudderingly ingenuous response of the Piarist fathers' pupils to the government's question: How do you see the Sac-

rosanct Image of our Supreme National Government? "The Supreme
Dictator is one thousand years old like God and wears shoes with
golden buckles trimmed and laced with leather," answers ten-year-
old student Liberta Patricia Núñez. "The Supreme Dictator is what
the Revolution gave us. Now he rules because he wishes it to be so
and forever," writes another student, nine-year-old Amancio Recal-
de. Roa Bastos possesses a special talent for revealing to us, in a flash,
Latin America's cultural abyss. The elite venerate modernity, progress,
and law. The people venerate the gods of the jungle. The tradition of
Roman law is one of the strongest components of Latin American
culture; from Cortés to Zapata, we only believe in what is written
and codified. But alongside this sort of worship there is another, one
that accepts the power of a despot capable of making himself invisible by sneezing three times.

Suspended between Voltaire and Moctezuma, the Eternal Dictator fills the desperate void between reason and magic, between law
and practice, a feat he accomplishes through caprice and repression.
"The problems of political meteorology were resolved once and for all
in a week of mass executions" but also through reform (the dictator
deprives the clergy of riches and power accumulated during the colonial era). He holds the strong conviction that he must do what he
does, and do it as it seems best to him, because if he does not do it,
no one will. El Supremo unwittingly reveals that he is occupying the
space of a weak or nonexistent civil society. But instead of nourishing
it, he simply appropriates society's own tragic conclusion for himself:
I am indispensable, therefore I am history. "I do not write history. I
make it. I can remake it as it pleases me, adjusting it, emphasizing it,
enriching its reality and meaning."

Writing and rewriting history: therein lies the grandeur and servi-
tude of El Supremo. To his people he offers a sick Utopia, where order
is an end unto itself. Paraguay under Doctor Francia was undoubtedly a tranquil place. So are cemeteries. The character's grandeur is
that, in the end, he has no way of approaching history without writing it; only in this way can he remake, adjust, emphasize or enrich it.
He says that he can distribute a "perpetual circular," a kind of metaphysical *ukase*, for all times. But he is sorrowfully conscious of what
awaits him: he is master, almost, of a tragic conscience. He knows
that he himself is an illusion: "A chimera has usurped the place of my

person." He is not capable of controlling everything, and he knows it: "The fact is that nobody manages to comprehend how our actions outlive us." Unlike Conrad's character Kurtz in *Heart of Darkness*, he cannot whisper: "The horror, the horror." Kurtz has exerted power over nothing; this is his horror and his awareness of his horror. The twisted human interest shown by Roa Bastos's creature consists in having delivered us into the hands of a man at war with himself, one far different from the stereotypical Latin American dictator: a monster blessed with a kind of Baroque freedom. He can feel irreplaceable and, simultaneously, conceive of his own body as a few scraps inside an old noodle box, which is where, in effect, he ends up.

El Supremo has no fondness for writers. He would rather shrink them down and trap them in a bottle. Nevertheless, while he battles the words which will prolong his life beyond the actions and events of his life, El Supremo increasingly depends on that other Paraguayan, the novelist Roa Bastos. It is this man who maintains the despot's perverse humanity through words, stories, papers, and especially, images and metaphors. In one part of the book, the dictator, as a child, is rowed upriver in a canoe by a man who says he is his father, and who takes him to the university in Córdoba. This image of El Supremo's humanity contrasts with the description of his power played out on the same river when a political prisoner is condemned to row forever. He can stop in predetermined spots to pick up his rations but must immediately keep rowing, upriver or downstream, incessantly. "He is just one single knotted mat of hairs more than three meters long which drags along in the current as he rows." Meanwhile, three acolytes carry lit candles that neither the rain nor the wind can extinguish. An old despot avoids the moonlit nights which make him break out in white mange, and walks with lit candles burning atop his hat. The Paraguayan riders charge, dismount, saddle the horses and unsaddle them again, return to the charge and snatch up lances out of the ground. A head is exhibited inside of an iron cage and the clothing of El Supremo turns red in the light of a sun that suddenly appears in the sky, magically stopping the wind and the rain. "I crossed the Plaza of Arms, followed by a growing crowd of people acclaiming my name."

El Supremo enters Asunción, "this red South American Jerusalem," one last time, never more to leave. The novel's papers solemnly affirm his final arrival. The papers survived, despite the rats and the fire that almost consumed them a few days before El Supremo's death. Augusto Roa Bastos has outlived all the tyrants of Paraguay, from Doctor Francia to General Stroessner, in order to reach the age of Cervantes, the man for all ages. The themes of this great Latin American writer are the self and the other, individual destiny and historic destiny seen as a shared destiny. Roa Bastos knows that he can only deal with them by writing them. In writing the novel he writes the true history. As he writes the novel and history he writes a life that only can be ours if we assume responsibility for understanding the life of the other. This effort makes Roa Bastos a great writer of the imagination of power in its constant battle against the power of the imagination.

Nothing more alien, more distant, more *other*, if otherness is indeed the novel's primary interest, than this monstrous dictator, locked in the prison the size of a country he has ordered built but in which he himself is also a prisoner. The mission Roa Bastos proposes to carry out is to understand the monster that exercises power in the name of the citizens who are the true origin of power; thus, the writer creates a society through language. He recovers the language of civil society, stealing it away, step by step, from the abstract power of such dictators as I, the Supreme, from all the supreme tyrants, to deliver them to a vast *Nos-otros* (Us-others).

2. SERGIO RAMÍREZ: THE RIGHT TO FICTION

When my parents decided that I should study law, because following my calling to be a writer would surely mean starving to death, they sent me to visit the great Mexican polygraph Alfonso Reyes who, in addition to being a writer, was licensed to practice law. Don Alfonso reminded me that Mexico is a very formal country, and that a professional title gives others the permission to offer us a helping hand. With a smile, Reyes asked me: "Why do you think that Stendhal said the French Civil Code was the best model for writing a novel?"

I've recalled this conversation while reading *Castigo divino* (Divine Punishment), Sergio Ramírez's Central American novel. His most immediate language is that of penal codes and trials, accusations, and the accumulated tests of our Roman, Latin American, and French legal tradition. Historically, among ourselves, faith in the written law of

Roman origin is constantly corrupted by the practice of conspiracy and shady deals ("the law is obeyed, but disregarded"). French rationalism incarnated in the juridical and syntactical architecture of the Napoleonic Code establishes a compromise between written law and political practice.

In his novel, Sergio Ramírez includes the three aspects of Latin American legalism; each one implies a displacement with respect to the other two. First, though Roman law converts the written word into the foundation of reality, Latin American legal customs merely pay lip service to this concept while, in fact, consigning us to a world evoked by the gypsy curse: *Entre abogados te veas* ("May you find yourself surrounded by lawyers"). Second, we always have been surrounded by lawyers: in 1521, even before the fall of the Aztec capital, Tenochtitlan, the Hapsburg bureaucracy had already filled all the administrative posts of the future colony. Of course, these were not granted to the conquistadors, but to the pen pushers, hack writers, and grubbing lawyers that since then have swirled above the fields and cities of Latin America like a murder of crows.

But the third aspect, which we could call the Stendhalian aspect, sifts the original letter of the law as well as its passionate violations through a sieve of order, irony, and rigor. This is Sergio Ramírez in action. Thanks to him, the writer can observe a criminal trial with irony and distance, as well as with extraordinary intimacy and humor: specifically, the trial of Oliverio "Oli" Castañeda, a young, dapper Guatemalan diplomat and lawyer accused in 1933, in the Nicaraguan city of León, of having poisoned three people: his own wife, the distinguished León printer Don Carmen Contreras whom he lodged in his house, and this man's daughter, Matilde.

Like Stendhal in *The Red and the Black*, and Flaubert in *Madame Bovary*, Sergio Ramírez bases his writing on real events. But the French novelists converted the *fait divers* into literature through displacement. The information which Stendhal gleaned from *The Tribunal Gazette* about the crime of seminarian Antoine Berthot becomes the information which the novelist provides on the passion of Julien Sorel. The interesting thing in Stendhal's case is that the novel must necessarily conclude in the same way as the newspaper article. Berthot / Sorel shoots down his lovers while they are praying in church. To the facts gleaned from the paper, which is the tale's opening and closing, Stendhal introduces another order of information, that of the imagination, which is the literary path of knowing.

By contrast, Sergio Ramírez employs the Stendhalian sieve to distance and objectify the narrative of events, but the denouement confers on them a tremendous ambiguity. Oliveira Castañeda's judicial melodrama terminates not in a single way (unlike Berthot/Sorel), but in many ways. The fact that this ambiguity is linked to political uncertainty, to the probable abuse of authority, to the cynical fatality of the law-followed-but-disregarded, in no way diminishes the tragic force in the denouement of divine punishment; it enlarges, diversifies, and sows it into each one of the probabilities which remain open in our spirit as we witness the fate of the suspected poisoner, Oli Castañeda.

I will not reveal the ending; I simply call attention to the turn that Ramírez gives to the literature derived from chronicle. Flaubert, of course, converts novelistic displacement into art that is self-aware; Emma Bovary is not the typical provincial adulteress who commits suicide and makes the pages of scandal sheets, because Madame Bovary is the supreme example of a character who, within the novel, displaces herself in order to see herself as the other, but without anticipating the abyss which thus opens between her social condition and her psychotic illusion. Henry James writes correctly that she is the first character in a novel whose interior current we can follow from one extreme to the other. The drama is that the internal current flows out into the external nothing because Emma Bovary's capacity for seeing herself as other leaves her incapable of seeing herself as she really is: her displacement is immobility; it is suicide.

Ramírez extends Flaubert's technique to an entire society, true microcosms of Central America, because although situated in León, the action reverberates through Costa Rica and Guatemala. Nevertheless, more than in any other novel I have read, we find ourselves in Central America, and we are there within an embrace as humid and suffocating as the climate itself and its accompanying provincial attributes: the cloying tackiness and stupidity, the worst hypocritical prudery, sanctimony, and unpunished violence. A society of invisible boundaries where urban businessmen still own dairy farms and come to the office with their boots caked in cow dung, and where the hasty, almost anguished, importation of modern objects fails to disguise an empire of the most archaic caprice and violence.

Civilization and barbarism: Sergio Ramírez transposes our nineteenth century theme to a great novelistic comedy about the ways we Latin Americans disguise, deceive, and even sometimes enjoy ourselves, casting veils over the Conradesque "heart of darkness." In opposition to the jungle that, on another day, swallowed up Arturo Cova, a physical, moral, and political malaise, we raise the constructions—sometimes mere Potemkin villages—which Sergio Ramírez critically describes and employs, observing how they serve us to distance ourselves from the unpunished violence noted by Rómulo Gallegos.

Nobody before has been so conscious of what he is doing in this respect. *Castigo divino* is a novel written with the diversity of languages which identifies the essence of novelistic style, after Cervantes, but especially with the style of the comic novel, including language of the cinema, the supreme modern spectacle. The arrival of cinema to villages and small towns is one of the principal cultural events of twentieth century Latin America, and Ramírez utilizes it from the start: *Castigo divino* is the title in Spanish of *Payment Deferred*, a criminal melodrama starring Charles Laughton, based on the eponymous novel by C. S. Forester. The movie plays in León and also tells the story of a poisoner.

Besides the cinema, the modernizing disguise—the "heart of darkness" fugue—is present in the finely detailed litany of consumer products that make their first appearance in Central America: the bottle of Vichy-Célestins mineral water, the Marshall & Wendell grand piano, the Victor gramophone, Pan Air flights, Philco radios, Underwood typewriters, Barry's Tricopherous, Parke-Davis sleeping pills, and Scott's Emulsion Cod Liver Oil.

This nominative diversity of consumer products runs parallel to the diversity of languages which animates the writing of *Castigo divino*. The products are gathered in specific places: Don Carmen Contreras's shop, La Fama, and Doctor David Argüello's pharmacy. As in *Madame Bovary*, the pharmacy is a privileged space of urban-rural life, which sells poisons akin to the dark fluid of the plot: who sells them, who buys them, who swallows them. Émile Zola, Federico Gamboa, and the perverse touch of some drawing by Julio Ruelas: naturalism bears its putrid breast only so that immediately afterward it may be covered by two languages, two different but complimentary styles. Naturalism is the first cousin of Latin American positivism: a novel of the learned class, *Castigo divino* presents a highly amusing group of provincial doctors determined to demonstrate that they are scientists not bush doctors or quacks.

Doctor Darbishire and Doctor Salmerón, apostles of the most civilized civilization—the modern scientific one—nevertheless cannot evade that other mask which veils and protects us from the anopheles mosquitoes of barbarism; this is the sublime mask of tackiness and affectation, the language of frustrated poets converted into pompous journalists. Rosalío Usulutlán's splendid articles in the local newspaper are a true high point of this style in which the señoritas are always "the spring of goodness and charm" and their mothers, "crucibles of virtue," when they are not "inconsolable widows."

The novel's symbolism takes shape in the bolero; Luis G. Urbina is not very far removed from Agustín Lara, and at times one of the delights of *Castigo divino* is to imagine this novel sung by the voices heard on its pages, the voices of María Grever and Doctor (yet another!) Ortiz Tirado. At this level, *Castigo divino* is a great camp monument of Latin American culture, filled with an abundance of signs, symbols, and artifacts, so bad they turn out to be good. The tackiness (*cursilería*) is the failure of another attempt to civilize a barbarous environment. According to El Inca Garcilaso, the word *cursilería* is a corruption of an old Lombard virtue, which is courtesy; it is the caricature of an English gesture, the curtsy or courtly bow before those who deserve our respect or our desire.

A combat of languages, hybrid languages which illuminate one another but in the end acquire their sense through the sieve of judicial language. The language of law guides the writing in *Castigo divino*, an urgent autocratic mode of expression but one that is also scientific and modernizing—its replaces the village witch doctor with the eminent Lombroso, and the purification of souls with the study of phrenology. A titanic, astonishing effort, accomplished by submitting the heteroglossia of gossip, prissy affectation, sentimentalism, science, journalism, and politics to a rational rigor worthy of Napoleon and Stendhal. The language of law which dominates this novel's structure fulfills its purpose but it does so comically, revealing even more the stratification of languages and the distances between those who practice them. It also fulfills it tragically: in the end, the mask of law cannot hide the face of injustice. The heart of darkness has not been domesticated.

Melodrama is comedy without humor. Sergio Ramírez gives the smile back to the soap opera, but in the end that smile freezes on our lips; we are back in the heart of darkness. Between the abundant comedy and imminent tragedy, Sergio Ramírez has written the great Central American novel, the novel necessary to touch its peoples intimately, to travel to the very frontier between their persistent traditions and their possibilities for renewal.

The denouement of *Castigo divino* justly occurs among the repeated fatal elements, of a volcano spewing ashes, a boy with the image of Jesus the Redeemer "imprisoned behind wooden bars," a burro driven by a different boy, and the reporter Rosalío Usulutlán wrapped in oilcloth, using a lantern to flee from the ash-smothered town, López Velarde's "Eden subverted by shrapnel."

These fateful images, nevertheless, appear to be wrapped in ambiguities, the result of our imagination freely and creatively interacting with the writer's art. This reminds me of another way in which real events read in a newspaper are employed in the novel. It is Dostoyevsky's method. From 1860–1870 the Russian novelist routinely devoured newspapers and magazines as part of his interest in the relations between life and the novel, but in the newspaper he found nothing that could surpass his own imagination. Consequently, he wrote *Crime and Punishment.* But shortly before the novel was published, a handsome, lonely, intelligent student named Danilov murdered and robbed a pawnbroker and her maid. In this way, Dostoyevsky had the surprise of seeming to read his own forthcoming novel in the yellow press. "My idealism," he wrote upon finding out, "is far more real than the realism of the realist writers . . . Thanks to my realism, I have prophesied what has just happened." The same can be said of Sergio Ramírez and *Castigo divino*, if not anecdotally, then in its historical and personal intimacy: a chronicle of Central America, this novel is also an irreplaceable prophecy of what we are. The punishment (*el castigo*) is divine, but the crime is human and, consequently, not eternal. Its name is injustice.

"Comedy has no history because no one takes it seriously." This phrase comes from Aristotle's *Poetics*, and the idea it expresses evolved through the medieval Christian "comedy" in the archetypal image of a soul's turbulent pilgrimage towards salvation by the side of a God whose Eternity liberates us as it welcomes us forth from the vicissitudes of the human "comedy." Dante, incidentally, merely called his poetic pilgrimage *commedia* when it was published in 1314. The term "Divine" is an addition made by Lodovico Dolce in 1555. Thus the ground of Renaissance terrain was fertilized so that Cervantes and Shakespeare might give the word "comedy" its humanist connotation: the actuality of the absurd, fleeting, and requisite fact of a changing and diversified language.

I begin with this requisite prologue only to more closely approach the question of what is "comic" as one of the most notorious absences in Ibero-American literature. In spite of the colonial satire of Rosas de Oquendo in Peru or the pro-independence picaresque novel of Fernández Lizardi in Mexico, our literature has tended to be serious when not solemn. Romantic, naturalistic, or realistic, it sometimes avoids humor in favor of melodrama, other times in favor of the epic of our rediscoveries. The exception in this and in all, is Machado de Assis, but, in order for comedy as a narrative axis to appear in Latin America, one will have to wait (again the River Plate is the exception) for Macedonio Fernández, Roberto Arlt, and his descendants: Borges, Cortázar, and the fusion of Bioy Casares and Borges: Biorges. The Boom brought a humor that was implicit, masked, ironic, and cut against the grain — *One Hundred Years of Solitude*; *Aunt Julia* — but only the Boomerang burst out laughing openly through the authority of the comedy: Bryce Echenique, Luis Rafael Sánchez. Now, with its immigration papers and official literary citizenship in hand, Latin American comedy has become a story that takes itself seriously because only comedy provides enough room for the incidents of our confused, perpetually unfinished modernity, always ready to fall flat on its face and break its nose.

Sergio Ramírez is a recognized master of the comic absurd derived from variable incident, the small red note in *Castigo divino* (inspired by *Madame Bovary*, *Red and Black*, and *Demons*), or from historical farce (the conjunction of Rubén Darío and the Somoza family in *Margarita, How Beautiful the Sea*). Recently, in "Catalina y Catalina," Ramírez displays his comic talent through the story's tightly controlled brevity. We have round trip tickets from one marvelous thing to another and from smile to cackling laughter: Ramírez opens up a wide range of situations and characters which lends a smile, at times a cackle, to our gloomy, disenchanted Latin American life: the effect is comparable to René Clair's *An Italian Straw Hat*; one comic situation leads rapidly to the next, and everything revolves around a mystery: Who peed in Widow Carlota's chamber pot? It was "the loveliest chamber pot, decorated with roses in relief and painted cherubim floating in the clouds ... Now a woman cannot even pee peacefully without people in the street gossiping about her urine" exclaims the exasperated seductress Doña Carlota, and although she complains, "I grew tired of hearing them talk all morning about peeing as if I were some kind of lazy, vulgar, woman of leisure," the comic situation staged by Ramírez ends up creating an irresistible feminine figure, infinitely secret and desirable.

In the story "Vallejo," we discover an old advertisement with the face of a girl "fading out forever, like a ghost from the past hiding inside itself, erasing itself and dissolving into nothing." In the end, the comedy yields to the powers that gradually fade out: love, memory, presences. Behind the political power there is a Nicaragua, as there is a Mexico, a Colombia, an Argentina, which only literature reveals to us.

3. Héctor Aguilar Camín: The Truth of the Lie

I had the good fortune of reading Héctor Aguilar Camín's novel *La guerra de Galio* (Galio's War), at the same time that I was reviewing Franco Ferrucci's book *The Poetics of Disguise*. Aguilar Camín's novel topped the Mexican bestseller lists for several months. Many readers and commentators attributed this great success to the fact that numerous figures from Mexican public life appear in its pages as central and secondary characters.

The characters are easily identifiable. So is the situation: guerillas from the seventies; recent struggles between the press and the powers that be. Vicente Leñero, one of our most versatile and outstanding writers, had already written about the latter theme, in a kind of journalism verité. Thus, some critics wonder whether this novel by Aguilar Camín was truly necessary. Does it hold any other interest apart from the morbid desire to identify the characters? My response, in both cases, is affirmative. The novel contains its own coded risks and Aguilar Camín has taken them, although the author's epigraph warns that "All the characters of this novel, including the real ones, are imaginary." The same could be said of Aldous Huxley, who put the post-World War I English literary establishment on display in *Point Counter Point*; or Simone Beauvoir, who did much the same for the Parisian coteries of another postwar generation in *The Mandarins*. But unlike Roger Peyrefitte in his novels, Aguilar Camín has not made a career out of mystery.

Instead consider an illustrious model, that of La Bruyère, whose late seventeenth century novel *Les caractères* caused a sensation, more for the series of keys identifying the figures of the time than for the extraordinary quality of the writing and ideas. The correspondences between the literary characters and their real life models were found in marginal annotations designed to make the book sell more copies. In the end, a key was published for reading *Les caractères* so the reader could follow La Bruyère with a small accompanying book explaining who was who. Perhaps Héctor Aguilar Camín will end up doing the same, although his playful spirit could lead him to attribute identities to his characters different from those conferred on them by the *vox populi*.

But if people are still reading *La guerra de Galio* fifty or one hundred years from now (again, I bet they will be) it will no longer be from curiosity about whether Mr. or Mrs. So-and-So makes an appearance, but rather for the values that make this an indispensable novel. Because if, by all rights, the author disguises his models to make them "imaginary," the work's true disguise lies in itself, in its interior, in its *raison d'être*, and in its most intimate truth. Here is where my reading of Ferrucci turns out to be timely and fortuitous. The distinguished professor alleges that every literary work has its own autobiography, insisting that it is distinct from the author's autobiography and, of course, from the characters' biography.

For example, a novel creates its own biography in the moment that it diverges from its model, in reality or in literature, and thus creates its own reality and its own literature (in the end the same thing). Cervantes, let's say, destroys the model of the novels of chivalry. Dostoyevsky destroys the model of serial novels. But at the same time, the author disguises the model which serves him to create a new work with symbolic strategies. It is always easier to judge what a novelist leaves behind, than to guess the horizon that it opens. And rare is the novelist who, like Laurence Sterne, makes evident, in Shklovsky's words, the structure and technique of his work.

Closer to Dostoyevsky than to Sterne, Aguilar Camín, nevertheless, participates in the gestural, gestating, expectant universe of our father Homer. In *The Odyssey*, says Ferrucci, we can observe how the work is made, how it develops, how the poem's autobiography is formed. But that truth is based on an act of deception. *The Odyssey* is the story of a man who must disguise himself to obtain what he wants: his return home to Ithaca. In order to escape the giant Polyphemus incognito, the hero declares that his name is Nobody. But only Nobody can then become Somebody. Odysseus travels in disguise even as he is captive to a collective, archetypal past which identifies him. This is the past which he shared with Hector and Achilles. Only they did not return from Troy. Odysseus's return is a violation of the past because it violates tragedy. This time, the return to the city has a happy ending. Odysseus is not Agamemnon. And Odysseus returns only because he comes in disguise. Nobody becomes Somebody. By means of this strategy, Homer permits us to observe the poem in the process of development. Through the disguise, through the lie, the poet offers us access to the autobiography of the poem.

I cite the autobiography of *The Odyssey* analyzed by Franco Ferrucci as a recommendation for reading *La guerra de Galio*. I consider Héctor Aguilar Camín to be one of the most intelligent Mexican writers of the generation—twenty years younger—which succeeds my own, with more than enough talent to present an apparent biography of his novel, which sweetens and distracts many critics and readers, permitting the work to construct itself in disguise. But truth lies behind the disguise of the *roman à clef,* and the truth of this novel is that it is a song about waste, a poem from the basements of the existence of what Adorno called damaged humanity. Like Adorno, Aguilar faces human damage head-on, but he denies himself, and denies us, any romantic impulse to return to the pristine past, to the restoration of a lost unity. Adorno and Aguilar tell us that we could not endure a just world. But we can go forward with the critical conscience that, if we have to create values, we will find them in the absence of unity, in diversity, in what Bakhtin celebrates as the centrifugal force and its novelistic manifestations: the diversity and conflict of languages, the novel as an arena where not only characters but times, civilizations, and ideas clash with and encounter one another. The time and place of that encounter in *La guerra de Galio* is the history of Mexico. Between the picaresque and melodrama, between Lizardi and Revueltas, between Payno and Azuela, between Guzmán and del Paso, Mexican literature has offered works which transcend and even crown the models of unity which have constituted the disguises of legitimization in our country. The virtue of *La guerra de Galio* is that it defines the boundaries of, and clearly distinguishes, although in a turbid atmosphere, the real passions and positions of political disguise. In one corner, Medieval Thomism. In the opposite corner, Eighteenth Century Enlightenment. The referee is Modernity. But the ringside seats are lined with uneasy savages, barbarians, and cannibals, anxious and grumbling.

A Thomist country in a certain sense, Mexico has always given its central authority the power necessary to secure the common welfare, which is the supreme objective of scholastic politics. *La guerra de Galio* not only demonstrates this but rather dramatically incarnates it in the combat between two elites: the government and the press, The Republic and the newspaper *La República*, the President's Estate and the Fourth Estate. Between both sides is established "an internal correspondence among the country's elite," in which words are reality. A journalism of declarations, more than facts, also corresponsive with a politics of declarations and with facts that do not coincide with words. It is no surprise that characters, above all Galio, poison themselves by talking; words are his vice, his compulsion, his only proof of, and similitude with, power.

But if the words of the intellectual elite are exhausted by themselves, words of power can turn into acts, in spite of the fact that, or precisely because, they contradict words. The whole debate revolves around that question: What kind of political acts will give an account of our words? Will we Mexicans, as the English historian David Brading saw clearly, continue to impose a liberal, enlightened, compromised project (in the sense of a compromise between many parts) on "a country constructed in the inverse tradition," which is sacralizing, conservative, intolerant and, in the end, a child of Phillip II and Moctezuma? Or will we abandon the liberal compromise, made up of equal parts of concessions, self-deceptions, and *Aufklärung* (clarification, enlightenment), in order to descend to "That horror you do not suspect": an underground criminal chaos, newly artificial, comparable almost to the first cry and the first stabbing? Time seems to justify the "horror": narco-trafficking, kidnappings, murders . . .

La guerra de Galio is a story of the duel between Mexico's elites: the official elite and the critical establishment. Of course, the country doesn't end there. The "liberal mystery" to which Brading alludes has never wanted to give the possible, alternative society a chance. It fears the "wild, untamed Mexico," the "unleashed tiger" which burst from its cage at the beginning of the twenty-first century.

The alternative society showed itself in two factions during the Mexican Revolution: those of Pancho Villa and Emiliano Zapata. Zapata's aura is that of having managed, for a brief time, to realize a local, alternative society based on the culture of self-government.

In *La guerra de Galio*, the young, middle-class guerilla fighters abandon their homes, studies, and cities to give the lost revolution another opportunity. The critical question is the following: What will prevent the guerillas, in the event they come to power, of imposing their own ideology as a new elite motivated by historical reason and the common good?

All of these dangers have been made palpable in South America. The deranged Pol Pot-style methods of the Shining Path in Peru represent another barbaric face of the torturing dictatorships of Videla and Pinochet. Between scholasticism on the right and the left, modern power in Mexico has presented itself as an imperfect liberal option, perfectible and, in every case, viable, whose enlightenment depends on two things: admitting criticism but not loosening its hold on power. Frederick of Prussia and Catherine the Great would have felt right at home in Mexico after 1920; Voltaire and Diderot as well. Thomas Paine, never.

To what degree has power in Mexico managed to not only steal or take possession of but identify itself with the profound keys to the country's peasant classes? Wilhelm Reich claims that National Socialism successfully understood and kidnapped German culture, while the communists and socialists discussed economic infrastructures and abandoned the cultural "superstructure" to Hitler.

Aguilar Camín's novel is debated, shaken, and suffers at the level of that *superstructure* which, as current history reveals every day, is society's true infrastructure. If Marx turned Hegel upside down, Nietzsche has now done the same to Marx. But Aguilar Camín's characters, a product of the dominant interpretation after Hegel, don't even know it. They would like the power to change the economic "infrastructure." They do not know how to employ cultural power, nor do they realize that because they act, or can act, in the cultural superstructure, they already possess power. From there comes the confusion, bitterness, and defeat of the Galio, Sala, and Santoyo families, above all, the protagonist, that "waste called Vigil," the historian turned journalist. The truth is that all Mexicans have lived through at least some part of Galio's war. We all know the brilliant men who wasted their talent chatting in cafes, in drunkenness, in politics forged between the brothel and the cantina, between gala dinners and the señor minister's antechamber. We all know the women who lost their love because love was the greatest waste of these thriftless generations. We all smile and shrug our shoulders as we recognize ourselves in this culture of the Cuba Libre and the bolero. Aguilar Camín has lived and written this all for us and thus earned the admiration and the gratitude of many readers. These lacerated biographies are, or could be, our own; they are born from wastefulness, from disgust. More than Sartre's novel, it is Aguilar's which merits the title *Nausea*.

It is no secret, then, that this book leaves the reader feeling torn and uneasy. But to criticize the author for an absence of love is to deny the book's very *raison d'être*: there can be no love here, because love is the first victim in Galio's world. But if there can be no love, can there be democracy? Nobody, in Mexico, or in any place in the world, wants to lose that double hope, democracy and love, political happiness and amorous felicity. We try to find love, but we fail. We attempt democracy, but again and again the authoritarian scheme — sometimes enlightened, sometime repressive — takes over. Nevertheless, with no bias against anyone's good faith, it can be said that there is almost no single Mexican intellectual (myself included) who in one moment of their life has not approached power, confident that they could collaborate to change things, to stave off the worst, and save what is salvageable.

Galio is the most atrocious example of the cynicism possible in this effort. Virgil himself is the best example of a hopeful surrender to public life. Both fail. They ignore the fact that in Mexico (this is the logic of power) everything occurs only once and for all time, although it repeats itself (almost ritually) on a thousand occasions. Although it failed, one agrarian reform was enough, so there need not be another. One massacre in Tlatelolco was enough so that the error need not be repeated. In other words, one Mexican revolution was enough so there should never again be another one. This is the power elite's cynical defiance of the populous. Will a civil society in gestation, alternately energized and exhausted, choose to confront it? In the end will a wider, more representative Mexican democracy triumph? Will the triumph belong to liberal compromise? Or will *pistoleros*, impunity, and the dungeon triumph?

Staring into the abyss of horror, of what Rómulo Gallegos called "unpunished violence," Héctor Aguilar Camín finds encouragement in his own critique. The novel's autobiography becomes the autobiography of the novel's theme—Mexico, its politics, its society—when the author speaks to us about "the tragic generosity of Mexican life, its enormous capacity for human waste and resistance . . . I don't know what stoic fatality, mistress of the hard, unjust life, severe, capricious, and impassible as time itself, matron of adversity and the incessant, very costly struggle for life's plenitude."

Like Odysseus, Aguilar Camín has traveled captive to a collective, archetypal past. But upon writing it, he has violated its codes, betrayed its world, opened it up to its own truth, and revealed its secrets: we can only be something after we are the nothing that is described here; we can only know something better after knowing this horror which I show here; the measure of our salvation lies in the energy of our degradation. I do not know if this is, in the end, the response of a Christian culture; not of a blessed Christianity but rather that tragic Christianity of hard choices prefigured, among us, by José Lezama Lima. Is *La guerra de Galio*, secretly, a great religious oratory, a degraded Mass officiated by Saint Thomas Aquinas, Voltaire, and Al Capone?

The contemporary world demands that we see directly, without deception, what we have been. But in order to know the truth, there is no path more certain than the lie called the novel. Perhaps the secret of Héctor Aguilar Camín's novel is that of a tragic culture as an indispensable part of modernity. I do not dare judge it. Being a novelist, he has been careful to not reveal to us the autobiographical nature of his work. The key to the novel is not found in the key to the characters' identities, but in that artificial part, the part that is a lie, which is always the truth of a novel.

4. Reyes Heroles: Politics, Sensuality, and Memory

Noche tibia (Warm Night) by Federico Reyes Heroles is a beautiful, complex novel. Beauty and complexity, in this case, neither exclude nor frighten one another. In *Noche tibia*, one of them would be uncomfortable without the other. A reluctant, and therefore more acerbic and equanimous political scientist, a man of ideas who delivers them first in the public square, Reyes Heroles the novelist comes to his narrative task free of dogma and even opinion, but full of thought and sensibility. What I mean by the previous comment is that if *Noche tibia* is a political novel, it is also a love story, a novel of intimacy, memory, and nature. In Reyes Heroles's writing these terms acquire a decidedly unusual structure, at times provocative, at others striking, and in the end as convincing as the internal framework of a tall building of which we can only see the exterior, well-aware that it would be nothing without the naked architecture of the framework.

Reyes Heroles's novel rests upon three columns: memory, politics and intimacy. These, in turn, rest upon an extensive terrain which goes from country to city and back again. In this way, the vertical novel (memory, politics, intimacy) rests upon the horizontal one and this, in turn, encompasses its two dimensions (country-city) in the common embrace of nature. So intense is the presence and differentiation of these two natures in Reyes Heroles's work that one could rightly speak of both a *natura naturans* and a *natura naturata* in this novel. The first was explained by Averroes as "what is in itself and by itself conceived." *Natura naturans* is, therefore, another name for God. Spinoza, by contrast, spoke of the *natura naturata*, derived from God, as something which, being in God, can neither be nor be conceived without God.

To that nature which is sufficient unto itself, Reyes Heroles dedicates pages of a rare sensuality, demonstrating the writer's knowledge of trees, plants, flowers, fruit. In this, he is comparable to D. H. Lawrence, the twentieth-century English writer with the greatest intimacy with nature. Reyes Heroles improves upon this in one aspect: the Mexican tropics have not yet been overwhelmed by industrial chemicals. In Mexico there still exists A.P. (Ante-Plasticus) time and Reyes Heroles delivers it to us with a magnificence that is not in the least gratuitous, all the while offering a sensual portrait of the divine nature which infects or, rather, reproduces itself in the physical sensuality of characters like the "wood-colored" Elía.

The move from natural to physical sensuality permits the author to offer us a correspondence between nature and sex which forms the base of one of the book's columns: the constant intimacy which animates it. I will say more about Reyes Heroles's intimacy, because it reaches degrees of intensity rarely seen in our literature. For now, I only indicate that the column of intimacy is raised upon the ground of natural and physical sensuality, and the political column is also built upon this foundation. But if these corresponding elements complement one another, they also fatally wound and reject each other. Political (or economic) necessity devastates nature, clearcuts the forests, erodes and washes away the land, and leaves us, in the end, a country without a future, devoured by neglect. Corrosively loyal to himself and his project, Reyes Heroles extends his metaphor of destruction: the earth is devoured, then so is the novel. Both—the earth, the novel—without the goal of extracting food or sustenance, or (à la Gide's *nourritures terrestres*), the fruits of the earth.

In the city, the war has ended. Garbage and waste serve as "nature" in Mexico City. The protagonist reflects upon the only possible growth, in the disorder, "with depredation and filth, as if this earth did not belong to us, as if it were there so that we would devour it." In order to stave off the detritus, Reyes Heroles seeks new support through intimacy with nature, and there he finds the triumph of his novel. In two senses. They are the best passages in the book, the most beautiful, the most audacious. Few of our writers have gone so far in the novelization of solitary sensuality, the strength of desire, the underlying pulse of sex: everyone desires but no one dares. However, when sensuality finds its object (or its objects: Manuel-Elía-Mariana or Gustavo-Liliana), it enjoys it with a moroseness that is prodigious in its very slowness: taste and aftertaste. We all know that sex requires time but we do not always give it that time. It also requires humor, which Reyes Heroles renders with a fine playful sensibility, especially in the scene in which Elía knows that she is having her naked portrait painted by Manuel but only later discovers that there was a witness, Sebastián. The excitation and humor are paired up, and we end up "playing" with ourselves again.

Instead of confirming any suspicion that the intense intimacy will also be conquered by politics, *Noche tibia* shows a contrast between both. Politics devastates nature: it is a disguise for the deaf struggle here present between bureaucracy and love, two singular and almost obscene contenders. The fact is that the political comedy in Reyes Heroles is so very sharp because it is so varied: it goes from the tragicomic description of a bureaucrat governed by his portfolios to a cruel Hegelian dramatization of the master-slave relationship in its boss-employee frame. The political scenes add up to a corrosive portrait of a country built by inefficiency. Thanks to it? In spite of it? Nevertheless, we grow. Is it worth doing so to build "the same nation with nothing in common" stigmatized by the insuperable distance between political actors and citizenry? Reyes Heroles answers this dilemma brilliantly, not with a thesis but with a scene, a set piece but one made dynamic by something we might call the exposition of the intimate being in the public plaza. The novel here reaches a great symbolic-narrative height.

And at this height it would, ironically, remain, if not for the following chapter, which is that of memory. It colors, invades, and impedes the repose, settlement, triumph and even failure, of the private-voice-made-public and its paradoxical marriage of "intimacy" and "politics." The memory is the flow, the river that bathes, overflows, cleanses, empowers, sweeps away and sometimes drowns. The moments of memory are the day and night of all previous relations, country and city, politics and intimacy. Elía and her father live an emblematic life on the banks of the river, which is, in a way, the hope of this book which often despairs of our inability to love, govern, and respect those near us, to give and receive, to maintain the beauty which does not belong to us but which the immensely beautiful country gives to us in spite of our history of masochisms and terrifying, murderous attacks against our very being.

For all this, *Noche tibia* is a novel and, in the end, one that contains a hope inseparable from obligation. The hope consists of understanding that we are still here, a country of survivors who have hardly said their last words. The obligation is the same one, neither more nor less, that Milan Kundera attributes to the novel as both genre and function: to propose human beings, again and again, as conflictive beings who, for that very reason, assure the continuity of life.

Noche tibia is a narrative edifice supported by the columns of politics, intimacy, and memory, raised upon the ground of the natural environment and urban nature. It saves its own life and, despite its nocturnal suggestion, confirms the inherent warmth of its title. It opens the windows of questioning and the doors of future language; through them circulate the necessity of telling this history in order to remember those histories that have already happened, and to guess about those that still remain to be told.

5. Return to Ramírez: the Art of the Autobiography

Many of the writers mentioned here have written about themselves, from Bernal Díaz del Castillo, who as he writes the chronicle of the Conquest of Mexico also writes the autobiography of the soldier Bernal. Almost all have written, contemporaneously, about their lives, novelists like García Márquez and Vargas Llosa, authors like Jorge Luis Borges with his ironical self-reflection "Borges and I," and poets like Pablo Neruda. I've chosen to discuss Sergio Ramírez's autobiography, *Adiós, muchachos*, because it both closes and opens: it encloses itself in Nicaragua and it presents politics. It opens itself to the world through imagination and language.

Frank and reserved. Candid and wise. Direct and calculating. Absolutely free and disciplined. Devoted to his wife, his children, his friends. Intransigent with his enemies. Eloquent in public speaking. Discreet in his private life. Firm in his ethical beliefs. Flexible in his political action. Religious in his literary dedication. All the different dimensions of Sergio Ramírez appear in his autobiography in order to introduce us to a man of extreme complexity, disguised by tranquil external bonhomie and revealed through the creative spirit in constant ebullition. Strictly speaking, Ramírez's life possesses two great sides: the political and the literary. The first cannot be understood without the second, although the latter, the literary vocation, ends up imposing itself on the former, the public performance. The course of a life and the tension among its components give this book not only its vigorous quality but also its serenity. Not only its action but also its imagination.

When I visited Managua for the first time in 1984, amid the fervor of revolutionary celebrations, I was most immediately struck by the city's unfinished aspect. The destruction from the great earthquake in 1972 had not been repaired—neither before by the Somoza dictatorship nor afterwards by the Sandinista revolution. The Cathedral was a ruin. The streets had no names. The city had turned its back on the lake, using it as a dump for raw sewage.

I asked various bureaucrats of the Sandinista government the reason for such neglect. The response was in their gazes before their words. Nicaragua was at war. The small Central American nation, so many times invaded and humiliated by the governments of the United States of America, was once again defending itself against the Colossus of the North. Washington's constant backing of the dictator Somoza and his appointed successors had turned into ferocious opposition, blind and arrogant, against the Sandinista regime's unassuming declaration of independence. Along with Sergio Ramírez, I visited the admirable Dora María Téllez, the hospitals full of mutilated children and wounded civilians, victims of the Contra assault armed and directed by Washington.

How could one not be on the side of this heroic group of men and women who forever changed Nicaragua's historical road—dictatorship, humiliation—with a promise of dignity, at least for dignity's sake? This was reason enough to not look too deeply into sins or minor offenses so much less important than two things: the internal politics of the Revolution, especially the literacy campaign, and its foreign policies: the affirmation of sovereignty in opposition to the United States. Sergio Ramírez says it with beauty, nostalgia, and longing: "Inspired by a swarm of dreams, mysticism, struggle, devotion and sacrifice, we wanted to create a more just society." That was the goal. Today Ramírez questions the means: "we tried to create an apparatus of power which would be relevant to everything, dominating and influencing everything."

The Sandinistas felt like they "had the power to erase the past, to reestablish the rule of justice, redistribute the land, teach everyone to read, abolish the old privileges . . . to reestablish the independence of Nicaragua and give dignity back to the poor." It was the first day of creation. But on the second day, the North American dragon began to belch fire from its nostrils. How could the ever-subjugated province, right in its own back yard possibly be independent? Ronald Reagan's policies towards Nicaragua deemed the Sandinistas capable of fantastic and unlikely feats against North America: on television, Reagan claimed the Sandinista National Liberation Army could reach Harlingen, Texas in forty-eight hours, rapidly crossing Central America, all of Mexico, and the border along the Rio Grande. The wounded nation had turned itself into the "potential" aggressor. No: the real aggression was in the Contra guerilla fighters, in the Nicaraguan ports mined with explosives, in Washington's complete disdain and disregard for international juridical norms. Nicaragua felt obliged to defend itself. But once again the question was framed in radical terms. Is the revolution better defended with methods that limit freedom or through measures that extend it? The Sandinista Revolution tried to do both things. It made a mistake in silencing newspapers and imposing dogmas, especially economic ones, that, with or without U.S. aggression, failed to lift Nicaragua out of poverty and only increased the general misery. The agrarian reform failed because those who had a stake in it, the farmers themselves, were not given a voice. Insufficient trust was placed in those whom the Revolution wanted to help, and trust was, unnecessarily, taken away from those who were not opposed to the revolution but who diversified it: the incipient civil society.

By contrast, the revolution imposed unity upon itself at all costs. "To divide ourselves was defeat. The problems of democracy, the early stages, of tolerance, were going to come when we put the war behind us." Before any celebratory *piñata* came *la piña*, "the pineapple," meaning, in this case, a unified blow: all the Sandinistas banding together against enemies real and imaginary, present or potential. But "it was a mistake to think that political friendships have a personal, intimate dimension." Presenting a unified face to the world masked differences of character, agenda, sensibility, and ambition within any particular governing group: revolutionary or reactionary, stable or unstable. In the end, the leaders not only stopped listening to each other but "We stopped listening to the people." The Sandinistas, Ramírez tells us, understood the poor from within the context of the social struggle, but once they achieved power their new position created distance and a loss of perspective. The thread between government and society was broken.

The chosen model did not help. As Ramírez reflects: "With or without the war, the Sandinista movement would probably have failed at any rate in its economic project of generating wealth because the model we proposed for ourselves was wrong." Might there have been another? Surely. Did it lack foresight, imagination, and information? Without a doubt. But today when the world is incapable of proposing a new paradigm of development which avoids the extremes of the Marxist zoo and the capitalist jungle, can we criticize Nicaragua for not having prophetically intuited the real possibility of an authoritarian capitalism, such as what is being practiced today in China? Better to have been mistaken before and not now.

The revolution brought democracy and, in the end, corruption. The code of ethics that was the password of the young Sandinistas was destroyed by the Sandinistas themselves. "Fortunes changed hands and, sadly, many of those who spread the dream of the revolution were those who finally grabbed what they could from the piñata." Sergio Ramírez did not lower himself to scrabbling for the peanuts of power. He did not kneel before money. He had the strength of a personal project he could not renounce: literature.

Because Sergio Ramírez was a writer before, during, and after the revolution, he knew that governmental leaders come and go but writers remain. A president can retire. A novelist, never. Sergio Ramírez will die with pen in hand. May he enjoy a long life from now until his last page. Meanwhile, we have the abundant accumulated works of a writer who achieves increasingly wider levels of projection. He is Nicaraguan but the nature of his work broadens and strengthens the idea of a Central American literature which, in the end, is only one part of world literature, the *weltliteratur* proposed by Goethe.

I have written about *Castigo divino*; *Margarita, How Beautiful the Sea*; and "Catalina y Catalina." In these works of fiction I have seen notable qualities I will now summarize. Irony and distance. Intimacy and humor. The capacity to take the copper of the journalistic chronicle and transform it into the gold of verbal imagination. The assault on literary solemnity through comical resources which concede to the novel the revolutionary power of diversified speech, far removed from monotonous, monolingual, centripetal discourse. Ramírez's comic fictions are, on the contrary, multilingual, polysyllabic, and centrifugal. He includes fashion, the yellow press, law, cinema, and medicine. The splattered brains of Rubén Darío and the publicized pisses of the widow Carlota.

In the territory of La Mancha, the vast realm of the Spanish language, Ramírez recovers the eternal theme of Sarmiento and Gallegos: civilization and barbarism. His conclusions are tragic. We have not tamed barbarism. We carry on as captives of unpunished violence. Then we must offer a human smile, skeptical and ironic, to injustice and barbarism. The two supreme artists of Nicaragua in these moments are Sergio Ramírez and the painter Armando Morales. Implicit in the former, explicit in the latter, the jungle surrounds, the violence bursts forth, the smile humanizes.

Sergio Remírez speaks for all writers in the world when he affirms that "one never retires from the writing trade. Writing is a passion, a necessity, a happiness." There are no writers drawing a pension. Governments come and go. Literature remains. Who, to begin with, remembers the names of the United States' Secretaries of the Interior, of the French Ministers of Agriculture, of nineteenth century Latin American municipal leaders? Who, on the other hand, can forget the office clerk Nathaniel Hawthorne, the librarian Ricardo Palma, the hermit Gustave Flaubert?

Sergio Ramírez exemplifies the old Latin American tension between nationalism and cosmopolitanism, between *artepurismo* and *compromiso*—pure art and compromise. He exemplifies them and dissolves them. Alfonso Reyes clarified the first dispute some time ago: let us be generously universal in order to be profitably national. After Borges and Neruda, opposite in every way save their profound literary vocation, following the Boom generation, and now, after the Boomerang and the Crack, Latin American literature has only served to confirm Reyes's directive. From Cortázar and García Márquez to Volpi and Padilla, our writings form part of the national, continental, and universal patrimony. The old separation has disappeared. In the very center of that transition, stands Sergio Ramírez as a prophet of the past and a memorialist of the future.

Add to this essential location the dissolution of the quarrel—compromise / pure art—following from the conviction, as exercised by Ramírez, that political militancy is not obligatory but rather results from the reasoned choice of the writer whose collective obligation is fulfilled, with interest, by exercising imagination and language. A society without the one or the other soon falls as a prisoner of tyrannies that, not without reason, see their worst enemies in words and dreams. Thomas Mann in the Nazi bonfires, Osip Mandelstam in the Soviet cooler, are proof of that. Although, as Philip Roth says, the difference is that tyrannies send writers to concentration camps while democracies send them to television studios. Judge for yourself which poison is more harmful.

Without ever straying from his primary vocation as a writer, Sergio Ramírez actively attended to his second muse, politics. Such is the essence of this engaging book, in which the revolution appears neither as an absolute disaster nor an indisputable triumph, but rather as what María Zambrano hoped for: Revolution as Annunciation. Like liberty itself, the deep heart of the revolution is never fulfilled: both of them are a struggle, bit by bit, for the amount of possible happiness that, as Machiavelli said, God has granted to all human beings.

16. The Post-Boom (1)

1. A New South American Narrative: The City

The great poetic liberation of language gives wings to a prose that is imaginative, innovative, and ultimately poetic in the sense of founding reality through the word. Half a dozen authors — Rulfo, Borges, Carpentier, Asturias, Onetti, and Lezama Lima — all incarnate what we might call the Latin American *pre-boom*. The Boom would continue with some dozen more, as many as twenty writers. Next, the shock wave spread out to the post-boom, the mini-boom, and even the anti-boom, until it numbered some hundred excellent novelists writing in the Spanish language, from Mexico to the River Plate.

A notable fact is the flowering of women writers. Another is the movement from the countryside to the modern city. Another still, the variety of styles, tendencies, arguments, references and options. Today one cannot speak about one single literary school, social realism, or magic realism, psychological novel or political novel, *artepurismo* or *compromiso* — an art of purity or one of compromise. The categories of the previous debate have been surpassed by two elements that truly define literature: imagination and language. The sign of the Latin American novel is variety — a variety as numerous as the size of our cities. My city, Mexico City, exploded in my lifetime from one million inhabitants to twenty million, and Santiago de Chile, Lima, Caracas, and Sao Paulo: creeping up the hills, invading the flats, hiding in the culverts and sewers, Latin American urbanity is the virtual or evident scene of the contemporary novel — leaving behind the agrarian or rural novel that goes from Gallegos to Rulfo.

I choose, nevertheless, Buenos Aires as the *emblematic* city. It is not as old as Mexico City (founded by Nahuatl immigrants in 1325) nor as important as Lima or Quito were during the colonial era. It is, however (or was until very recently), the modern city which was born thanks to European immigration and transatlantic commerce as well as commerce from the interior, rapid urbanization carried out with an aesthetic criteria — plazas, boulevards, public buildings — and a spirited cultural life with theaters, cinemas (Lavalle Street), bookshops, atheneums, universities.

City / city, Buenos Aires permits us to observe with intensity the theme of the large Latin American city, which I have previously discussed in relation to Borges and Cortázar. It is both natural and paradoxical that the country where the urban Latin American novel reaches its highest narrative degree is Argentina. Obvious, natural, and paradoxical. After all, Buenos Aires is the city that almost wasn't: virtually aborted at first, followed by an astonishing rebirth. The city's original founding by Pedro de Mendoza in 1536 was, as is commonly known, a disaster that ended in hunger, death, and, some say, cannibalism. Mendoza's corpse was thrown into the River Plate. However, the second founding, in 1580, gave the city a function as rational as the first was senseless. Now designed on a checkerboard pattern, Buenos Aires became a well-ordered center of bureaucracy and commerce, an axis of mercantile trade between Europe and the South American interior.

Buenos Aires is the city of meetings. The immigrant from the interior arrives seeking work and fortune, the same as the immigrant from the factories and fields of nineteenth century Europe. In 1869, Argentina had barely two million inhabitants. Between 1880 and 1905, almost three million immigrants entered the country. In 1900, one third of the population of Buenos Aires had been born abroad.

But a city founded twice must have a double destiny. Buenos Aires has been a city of prosperity and also of necessity, an authentic city and a city in disguise, which at times can only be authentic by turning itself into what it imitates: Europe. "We Argentines are exiled Europeans." Borges said this—or something comparable—and Cortázar confirmed it.

Above all, Buenos Aires is, simultaneously, a city of poetry and silence. Two immense silences meet in Buenos Aires. One is the silence of the limitless pampas, the vision of the world in a perpetual 360° circle. The other silence is that of the vast reaches of the Atlantic Ocean. Their meeting place is the city by the River Plate, exclaiming, amid both silences: *Please, verbalize me.*

Built upon silence, Buenos Aires becomes a city that is also raised upon absence, responding to silence but founded in absence. Paradoxically, Buenos Aires has been at the same time (or has seemed to be) Latin America's most complete, polished city, the one most conscious of its urbanity, the most urbane city of them all. Apparently, I say, when compared with the permanent chaos of Caracas, the gangrene of Lima, or *la mancha*—the spreading stain—of Mexico City. *Mancha*: La Mancha, men and women of La Mancha, the kingdom of Cervantes, writers in Spanish, citizens of La Mancha. Nevertheless, as evidence of a city built on dreams and classically urban themes, works like Leopoldo Marechal's novel *Adam Buenosayres*, the novels of Eduardo Mallea, or the colorful, highly evocative psychodramas of Ernesto Sábato, offer less contrast for understanding the relationship between city, history, and fiction than other Argentine works marked by what I would call a radical absence. These are visions of an absent civilization, capable of evoking a devastating feeling of emptiness, a kind of parallel ghost which only speaks in name of the city through its specter, its impossibility, its contrariness. Buenos Aires, wrote Ezequiel Martínez Estrada, is David's body with Goliath's head, which is Argentina. A lot of city, a little history, but how much reality?

Is the degree of absence the measure of Argentine fiction? This is the absence which Borges fills with his fabulous constructions— Tlön, Uqbar, Orbis Tertius—which exist only in the memory of other cities. More recent writers, by contrast, are incapable of filling the void. Their project, perhaps, consists of letting the absence continue to be absent. The only presence is that of words. For these authors, in a society devastated by the total, omnivoracious use of violence, literature serves as a way to put its own material, language, and imagination, to the test. Argentines disappeared. Did the nation disappear? The writer can only respond by exploring the depth of these absences through his question: did words disappear?

Words, it is true, often fail in their intent to conquer the absence found at the root of many Argentine histories. Discovery, for example; colonization; the fate of the indigenous population. Borges creates another reality in the name of imagination. At times, inclusive, he desperately forgets it in order to supply perceived absences. If there is no Yucatan and Oaxaca, then there will be Tlön, Uqbar and Orbis Tertius. But Héctor Libertella or Juan José Saer can only give us the gaze of Pigafetta, the navigator on Magellan's expedition, like a bottle cast into the sea, and radicalize the absence of the Indians or, rather, the absence of the isolated, hermetic, tribal universe, which constitutes the other American civilization, while Abel Posse discovers, in his novels, that the discovery of America is, in reality, the covering up of America. The writer imposes the obligation of truly discovering through the literary imagination.

Can nothing be replaced by nothing more, and nothing less, than the word? This is the most radical example of Argentine fiction, and nobody takes on the theme better than César Aira:

"The Indians, seen clearly, were pure absence, but made of an exclusive quality of presence. Thus, the fear they provoked." And if Posse, Aira, Saer, and Libertella disturb us because their return to the explicit absence of uninhabited nature is disquieting, their immediate ancestors, Adolfo Bioy Casares and José Bianco, do not make us uneasy: their landscapes are more immediately recognizable or, only apparently, less solitary. In Bioy's *The Invention of Morel*, absence is presented through a mental or scientific artifact, an implacable apparatus, a kind of impossible machine, as in Rube Goldberg's cartoons, whose metaphysical dimension, nevertheless, is to function like a memory of devastating primitive recognitions, while the scientific function is, perhaps, that of predicting (in 1914) laser holography. In the end, it is about recognition of the other, the companion, the lover, the enemy, or I myself, in the mirror. In Bianco's *Shadow Play*, absence is a spectral, parallel, and profoundly troubling reality, because it lacks the finitude of death. Bianco masterfully introduces us to a suspicion: death is not the end of anything.

Not death, but rather a much more insidious absence, that of disappearance, finds its contemporary resonance in the novels of David Viñas, Elvira Orphée, Luisa Valenzuela, Daniel Moyano, Osvaldo Soriano, Martín Caparrós, Sylvia Iparraguirre, Tomás Eloy Martínez and, finally, Matilde Sánchez. In them, we witness the disappearance, not of the Indian or nature, but of the city and its inhabitants. The head of Goliath disappears but drags along with it all the small enthusiastic rock slingers, the little Davids who have no right to modern security and comfort, or to life and liberty. The metropolis acquires the solitude of the endless plains. The city and its inhabitants are absent because they disappear, and they disappear because they are kidnapped, murdered, and repressed by the all-too-present military and police apparatus. The absence thus becomes a simultaneously physical and political fact, transcending any aesthetic of aggression. Violence is a fact.

Julio Cortázar foresaw the tragedy of the disappeared in his novel *A Manual for Manuel*, in which the parents of an unborn child prepare for him a collection of newspaper clippings with all the news of violence with which he will have to live and remember upon being born. It is Cortázar who most generously fills Argentina's absence in his great urban novel, *Hopscotch*, in which he constructs an anti-city, equal parts Paris and Buenos Aires, each one completing the other's absence. From this anti-metropolis flow the anti-myths that cast a shadow over our capacity to communicate, write, or speak with one another in the accustomed manner. Language falls, fragmented. In it, Cortázar observes the corruption of solitude turning into violence.

Cortázar offers a gift to our conflictive urban modernity. More than a language, he invents a counter-language as a response to the anti-city, in the same way that in order to combat a malignant virus one is inoculated with a portion of the same, a mortally attractive double. Like the inoculated body, Cortázar's invented counter-language requires complicity between writer and author, a kind of shared creativity. A language capable not only of writing, but rather of re-writing and even, radically, of un-writing or de-scribing the modern history of Latin America.

Cortázar's demanding critical concept about what is modern is founded on language because the New World is, after all, built on a foundation of language. Except that this is the language of another absence, of the link between humanist ideals and the religious, political, and economic realities of the Renaissance. With the language of Utopia, Europe transfers its dream of a perfect Christian community to America, a terrible operation of historical and psychological transference. Europe liberates itself from the need to fulfill its promise of happiness, but it dumps it on the American continent, fully aware of its impossibility. Because history and happiness rarely coincide, our historical failure becomes inevitable. When will we stop being a chapter in the history of human happiness, not in order to turn ourselves, fatally, into a chapter about unhappiness but rather into an open book about the conflict of values that do not destroy but instead resolve one another?

The great Ibero-American writers propose a contribution from literature itself. Language is the root of hope. Betraying language is the longest shadow of our existence. The American utopia went down to live in the mine and work on the hacienda. From there it moved to the miserable village, the shantytown, and the lost city. With that movement, from jungle to urban jungle, from the mine to the slums, have flowed a multitude of languages, European, indigenous, black, mulatto, mestizo.

Cortázar asks us to expand these languages, all of them, liberating them from custom, oblivion or silence, transforming them into inclusive, dynamic metaphors, which admit all of our verbal forms: impure, Baroque, conflictive, syncretic, polycultural. This has become a part of the Latin American literary tradition, from Pablo Neruda's *Residence on Earth*, when the poet stops in front of the shoe store windows, enters the barbershops, and names the lowliest artichoke, to Luis Rafael Sánchez, stuck in a San Juan traffic jam on his way to a tryst, with nothing to do but turn on his car's FM radio, broadcasting its endless Heraclitean flow of soap operas and tropical songs: *Macho Camacho's Beat*. The relationship between civilization and its fiction can proceed from the direct, material presence of such writers as Pablo Neruda and Luis Rafael Sánchez, or from the different kinds of absences of a variety of writers: the physical absences of Tomás Eloy Martínez and Sylvia Iparraguirre, the metaphysical absences of Bioy Casares, the phantasmal absences of José Bianco, the deadly absences of Luisa Valenzuela, the ironical absences of Martín Caparrós, or the expectantly critical and creative absences of Julio Cortázar, Tomás Eloy Martínez, and Sylvia Iparraguirre.

2.

Iparraguirre's extraordinary novel *Tierra del Fuego* narrates the story of Jeremy Button, a Patagonian Indian taken to England in order to "be civilized": language, clothing, manners. When he returns to his native land in order to educate it, Button quickly strips off his British habits and returns to be what he *is* and *wants to be*: an Argentine Patagonian. In *El Muchacho de los senos de goma* (The Boy with the Silicone Breasts), Iparraguirre tells three stories simultaneously separate and intertwined. One is about Mentasti, a perpetually contradicted philosophy professor. Another is about Mrs. Vidot, caught between nostalgia for death and the question: Who is going to take care of my cats when I die? The third is about the young protagonist Cris, unsettled by his fascination for "Renato" (the philosopher Descartes as revealed to him by Mentasti), the sexual confusions of the widow Vidot, and the need to earn his living selling useless objects: the titular silicone breasts. Iparraguirre describes Buenos Aires as the all-embracing protagonist, mother, godmother and stepmother: "Neighborhoods of millionaires and tenements filled with anarchists, architectonic grandeur built on cows ... Embracing and voracious, corrupt and innocent ... Too young to be definitively evil ... Only in the contradiction does it find its form." She also describes Lima, Caracas, and Mexico City in their most radical aspects.

Luisa Valenzuela is a writer disguised as herself. By this I mean that she is always present in her novels. If her writing hides the writer, she takes charge of re-introducing herself through brief philosophical or essayist exercises—intrusions—which appear to be just slightly removed from the stories being told. But this is a trick: Valenzuela likes to make herself present in her books so that, at that moment, the fiction itself becomes absent and obliges us to forget it for a while and then return to it, not without a certain sense of the sin itself.

Why this complicated authorial game? Because Valenzuela's great theme is the secret. In her *Black Novel with Argentines* from 1990, Valenzuela describes disguised characters. They are all what they are because they are not what they seem to be. It turns out that Valenzuela plays a game of games. As an author, she makes herself present only in order to distance herself from the book and its characters, but behind their disguises, they are, in turn, bearers of a secret. What's more, they need the authorial intrusion and their own disguise (in the end disguised as the author herself) in order to reveal to us the truth of their lives, which depends neither on Valenzuela's authorship nor her personal disguises. The truth is a secret. Language is a power between language and truth. Valenzuela locates the secret as the real reality of power. The thinking *I* is not equal to the existent *I*. Between the two, for example, the dream is inserted, which is "the bloodhound of the secret." On the other side is the reader, for whom the novel is also a secret, to the degree to which every reader is, simultaneously, present in the reading as well as the fiction.

The extraordinary thing about Valenzuela's novels is that her stories originate in Argentina's most immediate and palpable reality, during the decade from 1979 to 1989. Writing was banished from a nation dominated and degraded (torture, murder, concentration camps, disappearances) by a military junta indiscriminately shielded by Cold War anti-communist politics, as well as by the persecution of every person not addicted, whether they openly admitted it or not, to the military dictatorship. Valenzuela returns to Argentina in 1989 and does not recognize her country. The military tyranny, the farcical regime of Isabel Perón and the witch doctor López Rega, have deformed the country that Valenzuela left a decade earlier. She does not recognize her country because it has ceased to know itself. Valenzuela joins a long search, not only for the lost nation, but also to find the new nation. The reality created by the repression is a trick which disguises the country. Valenzuela responds with another trick to entrap the tricksters. A language of multiple meanings, against the dictatorship's language of single significance. A textorial text, says Valenzuela, a textile-text, visible, but covering the secrets that we hide the best: the common everyday secrets of the body, its illnesses, its manias, its necessities. A grim way to rebuke tyranny: you have violated my body, you have tortured what is common to all of us. The miserable human body. I would add that Valenzuela clearly locates the secret among Argentina's ruling class and obliges it to recognize a question (although it does not know how to respond). Have you substituted the secret for God? Is the secret the God of power? Can a novel offer us a language without power, but with new meanings: a *butterfly* language, elusive, volatile, and colorful, which cannot be pinned down?

3.

Víctor —"I will not give his last name"— he's got the eyes of a doped ogre. He gives off a primitive stench. He is obsessive, indolent. His laugh is a wheezing echo of gangling catarrh. He speaks with the falsetto of deception. He is a narcissist and a megalomaniac. He is a thief and enjoys a ferocious impunity. He brags about his experiences but only repeats the same incidents continuously. He would like to be a scoffer but he is only the king of masks. He really has no experience: everything happened to him before. He attracts gratitude and morbidity, at the expense of human life. He is only interested in every kind of woman. He is possessed of a violent vulgarity. He is a flatulist —a fart artist. He shows no sign of tenderness. His vanity is infinite. He is only moved by compulsion, impunity, intolerance. He is the appendix of his own sex. The street is the theatre of his ego.

He is a peripatetic genius. He is full of attributes which leave the world indifferent. He is obsessive and indolent. His manias lack effort. He is a cheat. He boasts about his acting talent but he only ever lands tiny roles as a movie extra. His exhibitionist pleasure carries him through every disaster. It's enough for him to contemplate his impact on women.

He is no simple Don Juan: "He is a castaway in brothels without time zones, a vagabond of two hemispheres." It's not that he leads a second life ... He is the exponential multiple with a dozen fictitious names and an alternating series of addresses. He creates an address and an identity, goes fishing for a few female passengers—that's the word used to describe them—he visits them during his stay and then he vanishes ... the address, the name, the person disappear, "it's like he moved to the moon." But they are all of them "the lady of his life." He wants to be the *caudillo*, the patriarch of a whole "hothouse of lovers." One of them is the narrator of this novel, *Los daños materiales* (Material Damage by Matilde Sánchez). Víctor describes her as corrupt, an extortionist, a hopeless compulsive gambler, a drug addict, infected with AIDS, "he'll say something about my rotten mouth ... say I'm a greedy, a coprophagous thief, a usurer, a defaulted debtor, and, as the author of this book, a libeler."

Does the narrator envisage these insults from Víctor when he reads *Los daños materiales*? Has she endured them already and is she only repeating them here? Or did Víctor never say all this, and these are only injuries which she blames on him, wishing that he had said them to her? These questions figure into this novel's literary mystery. Does she invent Víctor or is what she says here true? She does not believe Víctor for a single moment. Should we then believe her? Does she imagine Víctor or does she really experience "roaring intercourse" with him, hanging from a chandelier, from a revolving fan, "penetrated with legs flying"? Or is the narrator the victim of her own atavistic passion, a "cerebral fossil," hunted like a beast and chained asleep in bed by and for submission? Does she want to have, perhaps, a monopoly on grievance? Why then does she apologize when she suffers Victor's gaze of exalted hatred, "ready to set me on fire"?

She makes a long apology for "the enslavement of the African peoples and the extermination of the Cherokee nation," for the Tonton Macoute along with Videla, Pinochet, and Somoza: she apologizes

and then cracks up laughing, in a "homage to laughter": more than
a laugh it is a "roar of vitality." Perhaps this roar of laughter contains
the most profound key in *Los daños materiales*. True or false, lived
or remembered, what Matilde Sánchez tells is atrocious: the emptiness of macho grandeur, the absurdity of *el Buco Cabrón*— "the Buck
Goat." The author does not want to take over the "monopoly on
grievance," she wants to touch "the bottom of the bottom" before expelling it all for good. She wonders if she can forgive those who do
not deserve it and whether or not that question contains a certain
amount of self-irony. She sends Víctor to the purgatory of hospitals,
morgues, and funeral parlors. She understands that Víctor does not
like all women; he likes any kind of woman.

Is she just "any kind of woman"? Or does she possess the power
which Víctor lacks: the power of literature? As a matter of fact, Víctor,
with all his cruelty, cannot say why he lives such a crazy life, periodically
injured, trapped in his public figure, cornered, *in extremis*, to destroy
himself by trying to destroy whatever he touches, like the narrator's
mother's fine crystal? The narrator, on the other hand, can abandon
Víctor to a wheelchair, a punishment fitting the character's ubiquity
and ambulatory mania: "Víctor isn't going to fuck anybody again."

While she sleeps, the narrator experiences epiphanies. Upon waking, she writes them down (well aware that Víctor will never sit down
to do it). But like a good Argentine narrator, who has written the
book that we are here reading, she tells it all to a Buenos Aires psychiatrist, and the doubt returns to assault: does the psychiatrist lie to
her? Has she lied to us readers?

Matilde Sánchez has written various noteworthy novels: *La ingrat-
itud* (Ingratitude) (1990), her first work; *El dock* (The Dock) (1993),
about a man who moves away from political violence to a lost town
on the Uruguayan coast with his wife and an orphan boy; and *El des-
perdicio* (Waste) (2007), which is the story of Elena who moves with
her sister and cousins from the provinces to Buenos Aires. There, her
promising intellectual life is derailed by the very ordinary problem of
an unwanted pregnancy. In the end she finds herself alone again in
the same country landscape of beggars and hunters which she wanted to escape. Will talent and friendship see us through the reality of
our suffering?

4.

Blanco nocturno (White Nocturne) by Ricardo Piglia appears to be a
detective novel, and this time appearances do not deceive, except that
Blanco nocturno, besides being a detective story, is also a family drama, a new X-ray of the pampas, a novel which knows itself to be both
a fiction and a narrative rooted in its characters.

An X-ray of the pampas: in the center of a world which is pure
horizon, muleteers, herders, horse breakers, farmers, tenant farmers,
migrant workers who follow the route of the harvest, gauchos capable of killing a puma without a gun, with only a poncho and a knife,
people without any other particular status than egoism and imaginary illnesses, move or stay, are visible or invisible, are the human
"material" of a vast endless land.

Family drama. Upon this natural immensity, an artificial nature
is raised: industry, more precisely the factory of the Belladona family, the patriarch Cayetano, his sons Luca and Lucio, sisters Ada and
Sofía. The patriarch enclosed in his dominions. The rival sons, the
promiscuous, liberated young women, given to pleasure, especially
if paid for by the foreigner, Tony Durán, a Puerto Rican man from
New York, who comes to the town on the pampa, lover of the sisters,
elegant, jaunty, disruptive, and murdered. And the fugitive mother,
an Irish woman, who flees when her sons turn three years old.

A narration of characters. To the proprietary family are added,
decisively, the lawyer Cueto and the chief of police, Croce. Croce
knows everything, scratches around in every corner, knows that the
other characters know that he knows: knowing is his destiny and his
downfall. When he learns what no one else knows, he commits himself to an asylum and observes the "Human Comedy" which involves
the lawyer Cueto and Tony's suspected killer, the Japanese servant Yoshio.

Detective novel. Who murdered Tony Durán? The suspects blame
the Japanese man Yoshio, who is arrested and jailed. Except that Yoshio is outside the family drama, which is central to the plot or, as
Graham Greene would call it, "the heart of the matter." It is not by
chance that I cite Greene, whose "entertainments" (*A Gun for Sale*, *The
Ministry of Fear*) are intense novels of morality disguised as crime stories. Is not *Hamlet* a detective story in which the Prince of Denmark,

informed and sworn to revenge by his father's ghost, investigates and captures the criminal Claudius? Is not *Les Misérables* a detective novel, in which Inspector Javert pursues with rabid jealousy the criminal Jean Valjean? I offer no further examples. I only wish to situate Piglia generically and far beyond any reductivism.

A novel that knows itself to be fiction. Part of the structure (and of the prose) of *Blanco nocturno* are the numbered footnotes Piglia uses to refer to events related to the novel, and introduce political, economic, financial comments which enrich the plot without encumbering the narrative. This style peculiar to the author guides us with subtlety through an Argentine Republic whose past not only illustrates its present, but rather, with another turn of the screw, reveals to us the newness of the past.

Renzi. I don't run the risk of revealing the mysteries which Piglia so skillfully weaves if I discuss the quasi-narrator character, the journalist Emilio Renzi, whom we already know as the young writer of Piglia's earlier novel, *Artificial Respiration*. A fledgling author, then, Renzi writes the story of the betrayals (and traditions—at times the same thing) in his family history before finding himself with the main protagonist of those double dealings, his uncle, Marco Maggi. This points the reader to the dictatorship of Juan Manuel de Rosas and, in the end, to the drama of the Argentine nation: why, with such rich, abundant potential, it ends up having nothing. Another "detective," Arozena, seeks the answer to the enigmas. Failing to find them himself, he sends us to *Blanco nocturno* with Renzi, grown old and cynical, a useless hack, lost to literature, saved by the imagination of Ricardo Piglia.

5.

Concerning women, in 1943 the actress Eva Duarte performed in a series of radio plays focusing on such famous women from history as Marie Antoinette, the Empress Carlota, Madame du Barry, and others. Although these programs were broadcast on *Sintonía*, the bible of Argentine radio, they were downright awful and Duarte was a wretched voice actress. In his novel, *Santa Evita*, Tomás Eloy Martínez transcribes the ham-fisted melodrama of her radio voices perfectly: "Masmillion ees soofring, soofring, and I veal go maaad!" Eva

Duarte's films were equally pathetic; I once endured an adaptation of Alarcón's *La Pródiga* (The Prodigy) which Martínez declares so primitive as to appear pre-cinematic. Eva Duarte also occasionally appeared on the cover of *Antena* magazine, wearing sailor outfits or tacky, unflattering swim suits.

So, my own acquaintance with the hallowed Eva Perón was an aural one, an intimate familiarity with the sound of her voice which occurred even before Colonel Juan Domingo Perón himself met the ambitious provincial socialite. Serving then as Minister of Labor in the military cabinet of General Edelmiro Farrell, Perón was already rumored to be the real person in charge behind the scenes. Imagine my surprise, upon returning to Mexico in 1945, to learn that Perón and Eva Duarte had become an item in 1944, and were now acting out their own radio soap opera before the collective gaze of Latin America and the world beyond: he was Caesar, and she was Cleopatra. The first time that I saw them together, on the EMA news broadcast, standing on their balcony overlooking the Plaza de Mayo in Buenos Aires, I sensed that their once and future roles would be two grand characters named "Eva Duarte" and "Juan Perón." As Tomás Eloy Martínez writes, they began to act very much like novelists. They decided that reality would be what they wanted it to be. They abandoned any need to distinguish between truth and lies. "Doubt simply vanished from their lives."

Reality and Fiction: one recent cliché claims that Latin American fiction generally cannot compete with the Latin American realities that inspire it. The powerful novels of Alejo Carpentier, Gabriel García Márquez, and Roa Bastos provide supreme, peerless examples of this hyperbolic truth. It was not—it is not—possible, in this sense, to surpass *The Autumn of the Patriarch* and *I, the Supreme* which are, as we know, directly inspired by the grotesque realities of Latin American demagoguery. Once, when discussing an incredible sequence of events in Latin America, García Márquez told me: Books should just be tossed into the sea, reality has made them obsolete.

Tomás Eloy Martínez turns to the very sources of this Latin American paradox to remind us, first, that it contains the origin of the novel; next, to submit the paradox to the proof of biography (the life and death of a historical character, Eva Perón); and finally, to return a documented and documentary history to its true truth, which is fiction itself.

Martínez quotes one of Oscar Wilde's pithy, pointed quips: "The one duty we owe history is to rewrite it." And the Argentine author himself elaborates: "Every tale is, by definition, unfaithful. Reality can neither be told nor repeated. The only thing that can be done with reality is to invent it anew." And if history is simply one more literary genre among so many, he asks, "Why deprive it of imagination, folly, exaggeration, and defeat, which are the *materia prima* of literature?"

Walter Benjamin wrote that when a historical being has been redeemed you can cite his entire past, both the apotheosis and the dark secrets. Imagine, for a moment, what the unredeemed life of Eva Duarte might have been like. Born an illegitimate child in the "little town" of Los Toldos on May 9, 1919, Eva was a practically illiterate girl who never learned to spell, who said "I'm going to the *endtist*" when she was going to the *dentist*, and who was forced to learn basic social manners, an Eliza Doolittle from the Argentine heartland, waiting for the Professor Higgins who would show her how to roll her R's. Instead she met the director of an orchestra that played comic tangos, a man named Cariño with a bent for dressing up as Charlie Chaplin. He spirited her away to Buenos Aires when she was fifteen.

As Eva Perón began her social ascent, it was the Argentine elites and oligarchy who showed her the most ferocious disrespect. To her social enemies she was, variously, viciously: "That tramp, that slutty waitress, that piece of shit." Eva Duarte was "a dark resurrection of barbarism." In a country convinced—wrongly—of being "so ethereal and spiritual that it had achieved sublimation" the defeat—mediate and immediate—of the Argentine oligarchy and its pretensions by "that cheap floozy" offers one of the best real life stories of political vengeance in recent times.

Evita's vendetta operated on a single, unyielding principle: to never forgive or pardon anyone who had humiliated, insulted, or battered her. But her own personal mythos became a much more powerful instrument: Eva Duarte believed in the miraculous stories told by those wretched soap operas where her career had started. "She thought that if there had been one Cinderella, there could be two." Of this she was certain, and this is precisely what her enemies ignored. Argentina was not the European Olympus of Latin America. Evita was a Cinderella with lethal weapons.

Cinderella in Power: As sordid and true-to-life as the story of Eva Duarte's youth and social ascent might be, it is also accompanied from the beginning by another story, one that is mythic, magical, and hyperbolic. While Evita's enemies saw nothing more than a naturalist novel, in the style of Zola: Evita Nana, she herself proposed to turn romantic plots into her personal political reality, in the style of Dumas: Cinderella Montecristo. But neither she nor her enemies saw beyond the cultivated, Parisian, Cartesian Argentina which the elite of Buenos Aires, headed by Victoria Ocampo and *Sur* magazine, offered to the world.

In a country like Argentina, where the soldiers of an army camp in the lost Patagonian outback might chain up six or seven dogs against a wall, and in a farcical, demented military execution, wildly gun them down amid howls and blood, can it not be said that fiction and imagination conquer history and reality? "The only thing that keeps us entertained here are the executions." Tomás Eloy Martínez remembers and describes the Argentine officers' fascination with sects, cryptograms, and occult sciences, culminating with the reign of the "witch doctor" López Rega, the *éminence grise* of the next Mrs. Perón, Isabelita. Only such a fantasy realm could foster an Argentine colonel's plan to murder Perón by cutting out his tongue while he slept. When Eva met Juan Perón in 1944, she was already beginning to practice her philanthropic vocation by supporting a tribe of mute albinos that had escaped from an asylum. When she took Perón to witness her charity he found the miserable souls naked, frolicking in a manure pond on a farm. Horrified, Perón sent them away in a Jeep but the albinos slipped away once more, vanishing into the Argentine countryside. Fiction or Reality? Reality is Fiction.

Tomás Eloy admits as much: his novelistic sources are, perhaps, dubious but only in the sense that reality and language are also, always, open to question. Memory slips are no more, no less than filtered, impure truths. "Maybe nothing was happening which seemed to be happening. Maybe history is not built of realities but dreams. Men dreamt events, and then the writing invented the past. There was no life, only tales."

Cinderella in power, Eva Perón exercised hers like a strange fairy godmother. Like a Robin Hood in skirts, she gave away everything, attended to the immense queues of people who might need furniture, a wedding dress, a hospital. Argentina became her *Ínsula Barataria*, her private fantasy island, except that she was Don Quixote, and her plain, pragmatic husband Juan Perón was her Sancho Panza, a man of common character who plodded through his time in office like a day laborer, who lacked the charisma that she lent him, who was in no way the mythic persona that she invented for him, a scripted part which he duly accepted and acted out. Mythic as she herself was, Eva Perón could nevertheless be as steely as any politician or general. But this was secondary to the central fact: Cinderella didn't have to make bad movies and act in sappy radio plays anymore. Cinderella could shape history, and what's more, see herself in history. Tomás Eloy narrates a marvelous episode in which the real-time Eva sitting in the cinema watches the filmic Eva on the screen having an audience with Pope Pius XII. The once frustrated actress sits in the orchestra seats, repeating in a low voice the mute conversation between the First Lady and the Holy Father. A far cry from the pathetic sets of Argentina Sono Film studios. Now the stage is nothing less than the Vatican, the World ... and heaven. After all, only God can write the perfect story. But imitating God's imagination is to accede, on Earth, to his virtual kingdom, and Santa Evita did precisely that in her life on Earth. In 1951, a sixteen-year-old Argentine girl named Evelina mailed some two thousand letters to Evita, about five or six per day, all with the same text, written like a fervent petition to a saint. Indeed, Evita, had already become one in life, the Argentine incarnation of *la Virgen de Guadalumpen*, as Ricardo Garibay has dubbed Mexico's patron saint.

How was that body, that image, going to confront sickness and death? "I prefer to be killed by pain rather than sadness," says Eva Perón when her cancer becomes terminal. At the age of thirty-three, the powerful woman, beautiful, adored, capricious, philanthropic, wife of Perón but also *La amante de los descamisados* ("the lover of the shirtless ones"), *la madre de los grasitas* ("the mother of the greasy ones"), sinks into an intolerable early death, carried away by fate. The fiction surrounding her life becomes increasingly accentuated with agony. Her majordomo, Renzi, removes the mirrors from the dying woman's bedroom, freezes the scales at 101 pounds for eternity, and dismantles the radios so that she cannot hear the crowds' lament: Evita dies. But once dead, Eva Perón goes on to begin her real life. This is the essence of *Santa Evita*, Tomás Eloy Martínez's phantasmagorical novel.

Cadaver-errant: Dr. Ara, a sort of *criollo* Frankenstein, takes charge of trying to revive the embalmed cadaver of Eva Perón. "Evita had become tense and young, like a twenty year old. Her whole body gave off a soft scent of almonds and lavender . . . a beauty that made one forget the other happy things of the universe." Dr. Ara's final, theatrical touch is to have the dead woman floating in mid-air, hanging from invisible strands: "The visitors fell to their knees and stood back up feeling faint and dizzy."

When Perón fell from power in 1955, the new military dictators decided to make Evita's body disappear. As easy as it would have been to burn her chemical-sodden clothes they eschewed cremation: Evita would have exploded at the touch of a lit match. The president, however, ordered that she be given a Christian tomb. Hers was a body "bigger than the country itself," into which the Argentines emptied all "their shit, their hatred, and their desire to kill it again." And their tears. Perhaps, by giving her a Christian tomb, Evita would sink into oblivion.

But Eva Perón, mistress of her own destiny to the last, refused to disappear. Tomás Eloy Martínez masterfully unveils for us the way in which Evita, by continuing to live, guaranteed her immortality. Her body became an object of pleasure even for those who hated her, including her guardians. Fetishism, says Freud, is an alteration of the sexual object which provokes both an ersatz satisfaction as well as frustration. The guardians of Evita's body not only replaced their impossible sexual love with Argentina's national goddess—its hetaira, they also ensured the cadaver's survival, assisted by Dr. Ara who clung to the idea that his masterpiece should endure. They managed an unholy trinity of bodies: one real cadaver and two copies, the real one identified by hidden marks on the ear and the sex. They moved her body—her bodies—to throw people off the trail, to dishonor Eva Perón even while continuing to honor her, to monopolize the possession of Evita in her funereal errancy. They moved her from storeroom to projection room to jails in Patagonia to army trucks to transatlantic ships, by way of safe houses and family attics. They called her The Deceased. They called her E.M.: *Esa Mujer* (That Woman). They called her *Persona*: "Person."

Person: the French language lacks a word like our rounded Spanish *nadie* (no one), or the Italian *nessuno*, or the English *nobody*. Instead, the French *personne* stands for both presence and absence, an unknown body, a no-body. *Person* is a negative response, an ellipsis of nonexistence, an abstract noun. And it is that Person who is Nobody, with whom the body's successive jailers fall in love. Entrusted with the body's secret (she is a nomad Evita who comes and goes through the city because there is no safe place for her), Colonel Moori Koenig nearly shakes the corpse to pieces. In the end, however, the only safe place for her lies within the Colonel's own obsession. He hates her. He needs her. He yearns for her. He orders his officers to urinate on the body but he cannot bear Evita's absence when another officer, "El Loco" Major Arancibia, hides her body in the attic of his house and unwittingly unleashes a family tragedy: when Arancibia's wife collapses and dies after stumbling into the dead woman's sacred space, Arancibia loses his mind. But Evita survives every calamity. Her death is her fiction and her reality. Wherever she is taken, the body is mysteriously surrounded by candles and flowers. The caretakers' job becomes impossible. They must fight against a death in whose life millions believe. Evita's reappearances are multiple and identical: her only message is that the times to come will be gloomy and, as they always are, Santa Evita's prediction proves infallible. The embalmer understood this perfectly, always: "Dead, she can be infinite."

With Evita dead, Dr. Ara takes charge of answering the letters her faithful followers continue sending, begging for wedding dresses, furniture, jobs. And so the dead woman answers: "I send you kisses from Heaven. Every day I speak with God." The cadaver's jailers are, themselves, prisoners of the ghost of Person—The Person, The Deceased, That Woman. "She stopped being her own words and deeds to become the words and actions floating on the gossip of others."

Eva Perón's body dies but does not abandon its destiny. The embalmer's art is similar to the biographer's. It consists of paralyzing a life or a body, says Tomás Eloy Martínez, "in the pose in which eternity must remember them." But Evita's is an incomplete destiny. She needs an ultimate destiny "but in order to reach it she will have to pass through any number of others." Lovesick for Eva, Colonel Moori Koenig thinks he witnesses Persona's destiny when he sees the American astronauts land on the moon. When Neil Armstrong begins gathering lunar rocks, the colonel exclaims: "They're burying her on the moon!"

I conclude, then, with this other climax: artillery captain Milton Galarza accompanies Persona's body to Geneva on the ship *Contessino Biancamano*. The embalmed body travels, bumping around inside an immense coffin packed with newspapers and bricks. During the crossing Galarza's only amusement is to descend to the storeroom each night and converse with Persona. Eva Perón, her cadaver, "is a liquid sun."

The Last One in Love. Russian formalist Viktor Shklovsky admired the temerity of those writers capable of revealing the structure of their novels, shamelessly putting their methods on display. *Don Quixote* and *Tristram Shandy* are two of the most celebrated examples of "undressing the method"; *Hopscotch* is a great contemporary example. *Santa Evita* also belongs to that club. The construction of Tomás Eloy Martínez's novel bears comparison to Orson Welles's *Citizen Kane*, with testimonials from a varied cast of people who knew Evita and her cadaver: the embalmer, the majordomo, the mother Juana Ibarguren, the projectionist in the cinema where the coffin was hidden — the second feature — behind the screen, Evita's hairdresser, the military officers who took charge of her body.

Two authors transcend that gaggle of witnesses. One of them is, openly, Tomás Eloy Martínez who is fully conscious of his literary method. "Myth and history take separate paths and between them lies the defiant realm of fiction." He wants to give his heroine a story because, in a certain way, he wants to save her from history. "If we could see ourselves within history," says Martínez, "we would be terrified. There would be no history, because nobody would want to make a move." To overcome that terror, the novelist offers us only stories instead of life itself. "Perhaps history was not built with realities but with dreams. Men dreamed of events, and then writing invented the past." The novelist knows that "reality does not resuscitate, it is born in another way, it transforms, it reinvents itself in novels." In serving this credo, the novelist is condemned to live with the ghost of his creation, with the dream that invents the past, with the fiction that is inserted between myth and history. And so Martínez writes: "Thus I go on advancing, day after day, along the fine line between myth and truth, sliding between the lights of what was not and the darkness of what could have been. I lose myself in those folds, and she always finds me. She does not cease to exist, to make me exist: she makes, of her existence, an exaggeration."

Tomás Eloy Martínez is the ultimate guardian of the deceased, *la Difunta*, the last man in love with Person, the last historian of That Woman. *Santa Evita* is the story of a self-deceived Latin American country, which imagines itself European, rational, and civilized, only to awaken one day stripped of its illusions, to see itself as a nation as fully Latin American as Venezuela or El Salvador, one far crazier, perhaps, because it never believed itself to be so vulnerable; wounded by its amnesia because it had to remember that it was also the country of Sarmiento's *Facundo*, of Rosas, and of Arlt; and just as brutally savage overall as the men who were its military torturers, murderers, and destroyers of whole Argentine families, generations, and professions.

Just as Latin America invades the Argentine Republic, just as the *cabecitas negras*[7] in Argentina move in and settle around the Parisian capital city, in the same way Eva Duarte invaded the heart, the head, the guts, the dreams, the nightmares of Argentina. What is *Santa Evita*? A beguiling, gothic novel, a perverse love story, an impressive tale of terror; a stunning, twisted, hallucinatory, national history *à rebours*. All that and more. It is the proof of Walter Benjamin's assertion: When a historical being has been redeemed, one can cite his entire past, the apotheosis as well as the secrets.

The Disappeared of Tomás Eloy. As the constant bearer of doubt in the face of ideological faith, religious certainty, or political convenience, the novel's language cannot abandon ideology, religion, or politics. Nor can the novel be dominated by any of them. What it can do is convert ideology, religion, or politics into a problem, opening the door of investigation on them, raising the roof of the imagination, descending to the basement of memory, entering the bedchamber of love and, above all, leaving open the window to Pascal's words: *J'ai un doute à vous proposer.*

In that way I return to a novelist who is my contemporary, Tomás Eloy Martínez, and his ultimate work—his final work—*Purgatory*, in which the author proposes to write a novel on an inescapable theme: disappeared persons. Namely, the Argentine military dictatorship's grim, brutal practice from 1976 to 1981, officially called the "Process of National Reorganization." Its methods were to make dissidents vanish, to torture them in front of their wives and children, to assassinate anyone suspected of reading, thinking, or criticizing

---

7 In Argentina, a pejorative term for people with dark hair and complexions.

in any way not approved by the dictatorship, even kidnapping their children, changing their names and their family.

All this odious violation of the human person can be denounced in a newspaper, a speech, a demonstration. But how does one incorporate it into fiction, when the reality is worse than any fiction? In *Purgatory*, Tomás Eloy Martínez tells the story of a woman, Emilia Dupuy, daughter of a powerful Argentine man who supports the dictatorship and celebrates its distractions, to the point of inviting Orson Welles to film the world championship soccer match; a cinematic act comparable to Leni Riefenstahl filming the 1936 Berlin Olympics. Emilia is married to a cartographer, Simón Cardoso, whose job requires him to travel and survey the country. The police confuse Simón with a terrorist. He disappears.

Where do the disappeared end up? Desperate, Emilia Dupuy follows her missing husband's possible routes, from Brazil to Venezuela to Mexico and, in the end, to the United States. Finally, as a sixty-year-old woman, living in a small college town in New Jersey, she recovers her lost husband. Except that Simón is still a thirty-year-old man. Now Emilia must give up her old habit of longing for the person she loved most in life. He has returned, with a "smile from some place very far away."

I'll say no more, except that Orson Welles's condition for appearing in the film as well is that the military makes the disappeared reappear. In the novel, as in the cinema, one can believe any and every reality, imagine what does not even exist, and make time stop. In the novel, then, we must seek the reality of what history forgot. And because history has been what it is, literature offers us what history has not been. Tomás Eloy Martínez was—is—a master of this art.

17. The Crack

1.

Mexico City was a novelty. As was the Revolution itself. After 1910, Mexico, a country traditionally out of touch with Mexico City, began to discover itself. Great processions of armies, from Sonora in the North to Morelos in the South. Revolution by railroad: soldiers, men, and women alike. Zapatistas eating breakfast in the old Jockey club on Plateros Street, seeing themselves in a mirror for the very first time (*The Old Gringo*).

Poetry of the revolution: *El corrido,* the popular ballad. "In nineteen-fifteen / Holy Thursday morning / Villa de Torreón rode out / to fight in Celaya." Poetry of the counter Revolution: Ramón López Velarde and his "sad intimate reactionary." Painting of the Revolution: The "three big ones," Diego Rivera, José Clemente Orozco, David Alfaro Siqueiros. Cinema of the Revolution: Eisenstein, Soviet. Fernando de Fuentes, Gabriel Figueroa.

So then, Nativism? No, there is no Rivera without Paolo Uccello and Paul Gauguin. Nor Orozco without German Expressionism, Otto Dix and George Grosz. Nor Siqueiros without Italian Futurism: Boccioni, Carrá. Vasconcelos, minister to President Álvaro Obregón and the Revolution's first educator understood it thus. Rural teachers to carry the alphabet to the countryside, although the land owners would cut off their ears or hang them from the trees: ninety per cent of the country was illiterate and the feudal landholders did not want peasants who knew how to read and write. At the same time, Vasconcelos gave us editions of the Greek and Latin classics produced with the greatest care, from Dante to Goethe, because what were the illiterate going to read when they stopped being illiterate? *Don Quixote* or comic strips? And he handed over the public spaces to Rivera and Orozco, establishing an amusing paradox: revolutionary artists criticizing revolutionary governments. While unthinkable in Stalin's Soviet Union, the Mexican Revolution demanded this aesthetic liberty in exchange for, certainly, the many political liberties it denied to the citizenry. The reason being that the Mexican Revolution preceded the revolution in Russia, in China, in Cuba . . .

There was a great creative explosion. But once the revolution dismounted from its horse, a negative chauvinism surfaced. When it comes to this, no country outdoes Mexico. He who reads Proust *proustitutes* himself. One who is not exclusively concerned with Mexico is a traitor. Or as one of novelist Ignacio Solares's characters says, "I'm pure Mexican, without any Indian or Spanish in me."

Alfonso Reyes, who was, according to Jorge Luis Borges, the best prose writer in Spanish of his time, became a target of the extreme nationalists. He lived in a foreign territory occupied by Goethe and Mallarmé, Homer and Virgil. He turned his back on Mexico. Reyes answered these attacks with a text: *A vuelta de correo* (By Return Mail), which not only defended Reyes but also all those who were so arrogant as to see beyond what José Luis Cuevas would call "The Nopal Curtain." In *A vuelta de correo*, Reyes responded:

"The only way of being beneficially national consists of being generously universal. Because the part is never understood without the whole. No, nobody has ever forbidden my compatriots, and I will not agree to let anyone forbid me, to be interested in all the things that interest humanity."

I evoke this "immediate past" as a liberating antecedent for the Latin American Novel, which reaches a high point with the works of Yáñez and Rulfo, the crown of sun and blood for rural, revolutionary Mexico, and which opens up to modern urban life through the works of two of my excellent contemporaries: Sergio Pitol: *El desfile de amor* (The Parade of Love); *La vida conyugal* (Married Life); *El tañido de una flauta* (The Whistling of a Flute), and *Domar a la divina garza* (Tame the Divine Heron); and Fernando del Paso (*News from the Empire*; *José Trigo*). In Gustavo Sainz's *Gazapo*, and José Agustín's *De perfil* (Profile View) and *La Tumba* (The Tomb), the novel is used to liberate the language. It also restores the *sorjuanista* voice of a distinguished group of women (Margo Glantz, Elena Poniatowska, Ángeles Mastretta, María Luisa Puga), and offers paths of newness and loss: Héctor Manjarrez's *Rainey el asesino* (Rainey the Killer), *Pasaban en silencio nuestros dioses* (Our Gods Went Silently By), and *El camino de los sentimientos* (The Way of Feeling). And to reach a contemporary culmination, let us not forget José María Espinasa and Tomás Mojarro in the self-styled "Crack" generation.

Mexican literature after the Crack generation, sometimes before it (Rosario Castellanos), and, in every case, parallel to it (Salvador Elizondo), is perhaps a response to Vladimir Propp's thesis in his *Mor-*

phology of the Folktale which posits a matrix of fiction that gives rise to a dozen variants. Functions are repeated, presenting innovators with a dilemma: to find the originality in very limited functions and variants. This poses an interesting problem for the younger authors who succeed the ones I have already discussed here. The great forms of gestation—myth, epic, utopia—culminate but are adapted to the writing that I am describing. Creation requires a tradition, and tradition requires creation. The one without the other perishes or stagnates. *Pedro Páramo* and *One Hundred Years of Solitude*, *Paradiso*, and *Hopscotch* are, thematically and stylistically, culminating works, in themselves singular and unique. Juan Gabriel Vásquez cannot write *like* García Márquez nor *without* García Márquez. Or Matilde Sánchez *like* or *without* Borges. Or, to go further, Vargas Llosa *like* or *without* Gallegos. And if *Paradiso* or *Pedro Páramo* cannot be duplicated, they only reach an apogee in order to move ahead.

I say this in order to point out something in Mexican literature that could be called "the Elizondo effect." Salvador Elizondo was a brazen critic for whom Joyce's *Ulysses* was the ultimate novel. To prove his point he wrote his own enigmatic novel, *El hipogeo secreto* (The Secret Hypogeum, 1968). He also left us an unlikely book, *Elsinore* (1988), a memoir, full of humor, disguise, and even metamorphosis, about his time in a United States military academy where "Elizondo" was turned into "Elsinore," the castle of tragedy as well as the stage for the play within a play and the comedy that does not know itself as such.

The book by Elizondo which most holds my attention, in itself, of course, but also for the purposes of this present volume, is *Farabeuf* (1965). Presented as "The chronicle of an instant," *Farabeuf* is also a stylistic bridge without which I see, retroactively, it would be difficult to conceive of the novels later written by Ignacio Padilla or Jorge Volpi. If these writers and their contemporaries represented a rupture with the past generation of Azuela-Guzmán-Yáñez-Rulfo, Elizondo's *Farabeuf* is the bridge between the former group and the latter—or, if you prefer, the rupture. The novel tells the story of Farabeuf, a doctor who "specializes" in transformations, and who would like to enclose all metamorphoses within a single instantaneous one which would abolish all times in favor of one single time which would, in turn, contain all spaces. The means for such an operation is evil, pain, torture, and the negation of all things in order to affirm them all.

A daring—and risky—literary operation, which Elizondo undertakes with a slight smirk. Between the two, he finally opts for a literary freedom which will be that of his successors. Far from closing the chapter on narration, Elizondo opens it, in a cruel, extreme, and fascinating way, with the novel that goes beyond the pale: *Farabeuf, or The Chronicle of an Instant.*

In English, the word *Crack* is polyvalent. It signifies rupture, separation, and superiority. It stands for a strike or a blow, a fissure, novelty, and virtuoso skill. It signifies madness, conversation, and above all, the announcement of something new, by means of an explosive noise. Following the Boom, the Crack generation is the first one to deliberately adopt a name. It did well to establish a space and a difference, not for the purpose of denying tradition, but rather to give evidence of a new creation—and no creation matters without tradition to support it.

In a way, the Crack is the culmination of the demand for the right to diversity. Critics of the useless or excessive, who thus stake their claim to maintain a "tradition of rupture," uncompromising cognoscenti of art and writing that, half a century ago, would have been burned in the Zócalo, their experience, perhaps, also includes disillusionment at the contemporary acceptance of such work. "Turncoats" yesterday, radicalized radicals today, their works are the barometer of a critical diversity which reflects and even anticipates such values in a political society not completely resigned to abandon deep-rooted uses and customs of the past.

The name, with its inexhaustible multiple references, requires a double dose of respect: Mexican novelists and only six of them, the Crack group are: Jorge Volpi, Ignacio Padilla, Pedro Ángel Palou, Eloy Urroz, Cristina Rivera Garza, and occasional member Xavier Velasco. If any of them had published their novels in, say, 1932, they would have been taken to the summit of the pyramid at Teotihuacan to have their hearts cut out and thrown to the nationalist hordes, accused of being traitorous, cosmopolitan, Frenchified turncoats against reality and enemies of the Revolution. The normality of their presence today, the applause they receive, the international recognition they garner, all speak very clearly of overcoming a dogmatic and reductivist era of our literature.

The Crack writers do not need to be justified, neither before the Virgin of Guadalupe nor before La Malinche, the good and bad Mothers of Mexico, the miraculous one and the one who believes in miracles, the one who throws us the life preserver of faith when we no longer believe in anything—a recurring rule—and the one who, with sad irony, advises us that we must not trust anything—especially, and ever more frequently, politics.

2.

In his dedication to my father in *A vuelto de correo*, Don Alfonso Reyes writes: "*Un agarroncito a la mexicana, para no perder la costumbre.*" ("A little Mexican dust-up, just to stay in shape.") In its own way, the Crack was another, inevitable, "little dust-up," as are all movements of renewal. Nevertheless, we should not accept them today simply as proof of a creative norm, but as vindicatory virtues of both newness and the tradition of newness. Let me explain: Ignacio Padilla's work leads us to the very uncertainty of the novel, to the generic rupture, to Cervantean tradition. In *Amphitryon*, Padilla gives the word "hypostasis" all its levels of paradoxical meaning. authentic existence, but also movement from one meaning to another and, finally, a relation between the three persons of the Trinity, in order to turn the tables, and the chessboard, on Europe, to load the old continent with our own search for identities and establish, through a deadly game, an Austro-Hungarian switchman switching rail signals during the First World War, a project to create doubles of the Nazi leaders during the Second World War, and the true identity of Adolf Eichmann, another master of a deadly chess game. Adolf Eichmann, the executioner of "the Final Solution": to eliminate eleven million Jews.

And further: in *La gruta del Toscano* (The Tuscan Grotto), Padilla leads us to a cave in the Himalayas where in the deepest, most mysterious and impenetrable spot one might — might — find Dante's inferno, which is to say, discover the material space of a literary reality. Visionaries, men of faith, military troops: one expedition to the grotto follows another, all ending in disaster. But all of them give an official version of the cavern. They all lie. But not all of them tell the truth, because the cavern is a fiction, it is a legend which is only understood by *reading*, not seeing or measuring. Reality is a convention. Literary reality is a lie, but that lie, as Dostoyevsky says about *Don Quixote*, saves reality.

Paradoxically, Padilla's novels obey an incredulous creed. Their desire to create is not, in the end, the desire to deny. I mean that Padilla does not deny tradition because he knows that without it no creation can prosper. What Padilla does—second paradox—is to feel fatigue. A tiredness where the past is tiring: the flip side of the coin. With the fable declared, for example, before magic realism, not before Carpentier and García Márquez, but rather towards the tired followers that in the unnecessary hereafter of *The Kingdom of this World* or *One Hundred Years of Solitude* were closing doors and exiling suns below a thick foliage of plastic and cardboard and jungles. Writing badly in order to be read, not better, but more. This is the fatigue that enervates Padilla or moves him, exhausted from imperious legislation, to venture into new terrain: *Amphitryon* and *La gruta del Toscano*, which occur in what Padilla calls "The empire of chaos": the construction of a literary cosmos which reserves the right to self-destruct.

For that reason, Padilla proposes to renew language from within, from the ashes of language, which is often fires only forgotten but not extinguished. To read Padilla, one would have to read the troubadours anew, or for the first time, but learn—how much more difficult—to hear rhapsodes, folklorists, archaic voices, and atavisms of the language. To listen to what is not written. To remember what is forgotten and how the unwritten and the forgotten sometimes leave no trace, to invent the language of the forgotten and the unwritten. The "legality" of Padilla's method is absolute, not because it is verifiable, but rather because *it is not*. What does Padilla wager, thus? That the unspoken and the forgotten have shown the greatest resistance to the passage of time—precisely because we cannot prove their authority but, for the better, guess at it.

Padilla's broad, comprehensive faith consists of believing that writing novels is necessary. This is true because the means of communication and information that have tried to displace it—the press, radio, television, cinema, internet, Twitter, iPad—have only proven that the novel says what cannot be said in any other way: the reasons of the heart and head which the head and heart ignore. This is Pascal's permanent lesson and nobody has understood it better than Ignacio Padilla.

3.

Hero or traitor? Faithful or unfaithful to science? Loyal or disloyal to his country? Did he advance as rapidly as possible in the construction of the atomic bomb in order to give victory to Hitler? Or did he purposely delay his work to deny it to the Führer? This is the vital dilemma of Werner Heisenberg (1901–1976), the German physicist who won the Nobel Prize in 1932 and is most famous for his "Uncertainty Principle," according to which no mechanical system can simultaneously possess identical velocity and position. This theory was a corollary of Heisenberg's great contributions to quantum theory, in accordance with the idea that measuring a time-space variable with precision means measuring the relative variable imprecisely.

Heisenberg was a disciple of Niels Bohr, the great Danish physicist (Nobel Prize, 1922) and author, in turn, of the no less famous "Complementarity Principle": the evidence of physics experiments are always "complementary," given that "only the totality of the phenomena exhausts the possible information about the objects."

In 1941, Bohr and his disciple Heisenberg met in Nazi-occupied Denmark. Affection brought them together, politics separated them. What did the two of them have to say to each other in that mysterious encounter? No one knows. Heisenberg returned to Germany to continue working on the Nazi atomic project. Bohr fled to Sweden and from there to the United States, where he participated in—or at least witnessed—the success of the North American atomic project which culminated with the destruction of Hiroshima and Nagasaki and the end of the Second World War. Could the war have ended with the destruction of London and New York and the victory of the Hitlerian "New Order"? Werner Heisenberg is found at the center of these questions. As in Borges's fable, in some versions of history he is a hero, in others a traitor.

A debate about these matters took place in the prestigious pages of *The Times Literary Supplement*. Apart from the horrendous *Les Misérables* and *Miss Saigon*, the hottest ticket in the world's theatre capital, which is London, was *Copenhagen*, Michael Frayn's play about the Bohr-Heisenberg meeting. And on the beaches of Spain in the summer of 1999, again, apart from the startlingly bad offerings from

Ken Follet and company, the most widely read book was Mexican writer Jorge Volpi's novel *In Search of Klingsor*, which won the Biblioteca Breve Prize. In this story, Heisenberg occupies a mysterious protagonistic role.

The interest is comprehensible. Stable Newtonian science, which had explained the world since 1687, was shivered to pieces when Albert Einstein demonstrated that, unlike Newton's postulation, time and space are not absolute but purely relative. Heisenberg's Uncertainty Principle, in a certain way, is the culmination of Einstein's theory of relativity. Each observer of a phenomenon will observe it in a different manner. Between both reflections, the twentieth century's revolutionary transformation of culture takes place: Joyce's rupture of linear expository logic in the novel and Mallarme's in poetry. Eisenstein in cinema, or Picasso in painting, sometimes anticipate, at other times continue, the new visions of science and, regarding war and violence, of politics. As Picasso said, "We Cubists invented camouflage."

One of the great virtues of Jorge Volpi's novel is that he resists the temptation of giving it the avant-garde format authorized by the scientific revolution of the perception of things (Husserl said that perception is not solipsistic: it is the relation between perceiver and perceived). Instead, without renouncing the game of temporal planes and spaces, the Mexican novelist gives his narration an underlying unity that is not simply linear but logical, exactly like the arguments scientists fenced over, and which Volpi explains with astonishing clarity and knowledge. But *In Search of Klingsor* is not a treatise on quantum physics. It is, if you like, a superior thriller, as good in this sense as the films of Fritz Lang about the mysterious Doctor Mabuse who directs his criminal operations from his jail cell, or like Eric Ambler's novel *A Coffin for Dimitrios* which shuffles times and spaces in search of the eponymous antihero.

However, as entertaining as its continuous game of suspense is, *In Search of Klingsor* is primarily a moral fable for our time. The solidly scientific expository base, as well as the novel's passionate narrative intrigue, propose an essential question: has science lost its innocence? Does genius scientific innovation exonerate us from all guilt? Volpi tells us that all absolutes produce traitors, and love is the greatest of them all. The physical love of the American serviceman Francis Bacon and his women, but especially the intellectual love between great men of science, produce not only betrayals but passionate rivalries that stain the abstract purity of scientific work.

The search for Klingsor—the mythic Germanic hero locked away in his castle, staring at himself in the mirror, jealous of his own image—possesses a powerful cultural substrate, and places us amid the true combat of civilizations, not the very simpleminded notion conceived by Huntington, but rather another, more profound, in which religious faith—the truth of what is unbelievable, as Tertulian defined it—is replaced by scientific faith, only to discover that it merits less confidence than religion. As one of Volpi's characters says, all great physicists have a criminal profile. Yes, because science has ceased to be "innocent"; it cannot only alter the nature of the universe, but also destroy the universe itself. Nevertheless, a demand for tolerance and human warmth hangs over the conviction that, if everything is relative, so must be relativity itself, and that the universe which contains us all can be both terribly infinite and mercifully, humanly finite. It is up to us to keep it alive as a place of love.

The work of a young narrator, *In Search of Klingsor* is not free of defects, especially when the powerful, fascinating narrative flow is interrupted by conversations between scientists (the visit with Erwin Schrödinger) who already know what they are going to say, and tell one another what they already know, but which the reader does not. By contrast, the same figure of Schrödinger is the object of a quasi-Mozartian narrative brio when Volpi narrates the adventures of the insatiable lover who was the Austrian physicist (Nobel Prize, 1933).

4.

Pedro Ángel Palou promises to be—already is—a polygraph, like Alfonso Reyes between 1930 and 1950, Octavio Paz from the 1960s to the 1980s, and José Emilio Pacheco from then until the present time: all of them, to a greater or lesser degree, poets, essayists, narrators, conquerors of limits, authors involved in a dialogue between genres.

With extreme versatility, Palou moves from the Germanic theme—so attractive for his generation—in *Malheridos* (Badly Wounded), where he situates a pair of lovers and two destructive beasts captured in the enigmas of evil, violence, and war on a British isle, to *Con la muerte en los puños* (With Death in His Fists), a history of the boxer Baby Cifuentes, a stuttering monologue caught between sex, drugs, alcohol and, in the end, life and language forever boxing with their shadows.

Palou is also the author of a biographical novel about Emiliano Zapata. Yet another book on Zapata? Could anyone ever surpass John Womack's biography of the great leader? Yes, Palou tells us: *Zapata* is not only a history, it is a psychological study, a number of different dreams, and the story of a life lived to the fullest, worthy of being celebrated in song. Palou recounts the great events of the Zapatista legend but reserves for himself the enormous liberty of telling us, as well, the marginal events, the details that only the novelist observes, the character's oneiric world, his secret sensuality, his relationships with women and, in a manner that is simultaneously rebellious and servile, with a man, the boss whom Zapata obeys but also, with his rebellious carnality, humiliates.

All that would be enough to make Palaou's *Zapata* a subversive work, in this sense: the official version of the hero Zapata offers an endless number of subversions or alternate narrative inquiries which documented history does not record and the Revolution's register of saints ignores. The interesting thing about Palou's book is that his portrait of Zapata, the sensual, dreaming, choleric, inadequate man, fugitive from emotion, *enlarges* the epic lived by the man of the Revolution and his people.

One must know about Zapata's love affairs with Josefa, Gregoria, with the female colonels Carmen and Amelia, with Petra Torres, to understand how much a man in the middle of "sickly hunger and bastardly war" gives and receives. One must walk among nightmares with feet covered in blood, among burnt houses, mad dogs, and women who flee with their children in arms, to have—to be able to have—the dream of an agrarian revolution which "in three months satisfies the demand of centuries." One must know how to escape "again and again from all omens" only to fall, in the end, betrayed in Chinameca. Zapata slips out at night and enters silently like "a solitary nahuatl" so that "a woman scratches his back, smiles at him deeply, as if she were dying and had seen an angel." Are these epiphanies sufficient to handle such an ambush, such betrayal, such sadness?

Zapata is filled with columns of silent men, "tired warriors, in sandals, numerical and exhausted amid the thunder." How then to

not hate the "birds that announce their desperate existence, mysteriously awake before sunrise"? Here lies an unbearable tension between a land which tells the Zapatistas "that it is awaiting them" and
the ultimate final loss of that same land, barely recovered in cemeteries which no longer have room for more dead. The novel exhib-
its a rebel exaltation of spectral men and women who invade their
own lands and find a fleeting paradise—control, justice, self-government—and then lose it through Mexico's mistaken fusion of central and authoritarian power, the mistrust among revolutionaries, the
misunderstandings between comrades, and the war between tribes.
Perhaps all of this is true because, like Zapata, reality is "a ghost
made of symbols." What remains is the perpetual Mexican (and Latin
American) question: the promise on paper and the reality that denies,
postpones, or affirms words. When "death is no longer more than a
promise," then what remains is the Plan of Ayala which "inscribed
with words on paper what the gunpowder wrote."

"What a wish to have no wishes!" thinks Zapata as he becomes
a "ghost of himself" and enters "a mirror made of symbols" where
he waits to be spirited away one day by the history which remains
to him. For the moment, Pedro Ángel Palou's great cantata appears,
with honor, in a single Mexican *corrido* which, like the Spanish ballads, permits the novelist to not tell "the truth of the lies" but rather
to create "another truth."

5.

There are books which, perhaps to their own credit, are slow to receive
the recognition they deserve. One such case, it seems to me, is Mexican writer Cristina Rivera Garza's extraordinary novel, *No One Will
See Me Cry*, which appeared in 1999. I overlook—I take it for granted—the beauty and exactitude of Rivera Garza's prose. One does not
write a description of a character like this one with impunity: "Pru-
dencia Lomas from Burgos. When he forgot her face, her name was
enough to soften the difficulties of his old age." I cite this sentence,
not only for its evocative beauty, but rather because it situates us in
the center of the novel, which is the sense of sight. The connecting
thread is the gaze. What guides the narration is an early twentieth
century Mexican photographer, Joaquín Buitrago, determined to

travel around the sorrowful city—*la città dolente* of Dante—with the eyes of a camera capable of capturing that sorrow in the very instant it is transformed into its own absence. Into nothing. The light is found within sex; born from the mouth it dies in the eyes. Or rather, it is fleeting, it is perishable. But at times, by the simple fact of revealing an appearance, it saves.

The photographer has two favorite spaces because in them "the blue dog of memory" bites his ankles and Buitrago knows that in those places—the brothel and the insane asylum—hope is crucified, without remedy. The hopeful traveler is Matilda Burgos, an errant woman, a woman lost between the two poles of her existence: the bordello and the madhouse. There among the madmen, charged with photographing them, Buitrago recognizes, in 1920, a young woman whom he had met years before in a brothel. It is Matilda Burgos, heroine of this extraordinary novel which, like Juan Rulfo in *Pedro Páramo* assumes the conventions of the genre—the novel of the Mexican Revolution in Rulfo; the melodrama of the fallen woman in Rivera Garza—in order to transform them into something new and unusual that only exists thanks to the power of tradition transformed by imagination. The name of that process is artistic creation.

As in *Santa*, Federico Gamboa's classic work of Mexican naturalism, Matilda comes from the open country where her father "cared for the vanilla as one must care for a woman." Alcohol is the worm in the apple, and Matilda must leave the countryside and take refuge with a doctor uncle in old Mexico City. There, the city's highly dignified chronicler, Don Artemio del Valle Arzipe, celebrates the arrival of public lighting to the Mexican capital in 1900 because electric light "frightens the thief, moderates the intemperate, stops the vicious and influences . . . the development of good habits." What "electric light" does not impede (the theme of a delicious celebratory *corrido* which the painter Rufino Tamayo used to sing incomparably well) is the bad habit of rebelling against political despotism.

From the ranch to the capital: Matilda's personal movement leads her to the revolutionary circle of Diamantina Vicario and the sleepless rebel Cástulo; pursued by the dictatorship, he is a live wire of a man, crackling with that same celebrated electricity, for whom sleeping is no pleasure, merely an interruption in political activity. Diamantina conspires. Cástula acts. And coming between the both of them is

Brecht's Mackie (Mack the Knife), asking the revolutionary: "Which is worse, to found a bank or rob a bank?"

In this novel of long black skirts, Cristina Rivera Garza imagines, like no one in Mexico has done since José Revueltas, the tragic options and psychic upheavals between revolutionary theory and action. She does it with such an intensity and grandeur that together with the protagonist Matilda, we must, as readers, kneel down when Diamantina dies, Cástulo is lost, and Matilda prays for them; from there on she only remembers their names in secret, as if her soul was the pantheon of all disastrous heroism.

Thus, unlike Gamboa's *Santa*, Matilda does not end up in the brothel by deceit or by accident, but rather because she is in mourning: for Cástulo, for Diamantina, for Mexico, for the Revolution which devours its own children. As Roland Barthes remarks about the novels of the Marquis de Sade, the dissolute moves from one place only to become enclosed in another. The isolated enclosure is indispensable for the sadist to practice his vice in secret. For Matilda this is the vice of pain in a disguise that fascinates the photographer, the joy, the shamelessness, the carnival, exhibitionism. But Cristina Rivera, with cruel astuteness, reminds us that Zola's naturalism went hand in hand with Lombroso's deterministic criminology.

For Lombroso, man was criminal due to atavism, by regression to a primitive state of evolution. Writing in the *Nuova Antologia* (New Anthology) in 1886, Lombroso states that whores—like monkeys—possess a prehensile foot which serves for encircling, grasping, and fucking. Matilda, who has read neither Lombroso nor Zola, breaks this determinism and enclosure by rebelling. A rebellion of prostitutes. Or rather, proof of Matilda's madness in rebellion against her predetermined destiny.

Which is, moreover, the destiny of women in a macho society. "The first women ... were not made to be kept. Pity the man that stays with them." A woman is used, enjoyed, then thrown in the trash. And is there a more infamous trashcan than an insane asylum, "the place where the future ends"? Cristina Rivera Garza has scrutinized the files of the inmates of La Casteñada, the old general asylum in Mexico City: *Obsessed with praying. Imitates animals. Licks food up from the floor. Absolute memory forward and backward, so absolute as to be useless.*

And the endless physical abuse. Many asylums nowadays have still not improved their conditions. Yolanda Monge reports in *El País* on psychiatric hospitals in Bulgaria: Electroshock therapy without anesthetic. Women tied with belts to metal beds bolted to concrete floors. Children driven into idiocy by physical and mental isolation. Madmen obliged to devour their own feces. I refer to a recent report by Amnesty International. What about conditions in insane asylums in the 1920s? Cristina Rivera Garza transcribes reliable documents and presents them without commentary. As a novelist she is preparing her subsequent narrative, which deals with the mass escape of the inmates (women in the asylum of Divino Salvador, men in San Hipólito) transferred to the new general asylum in 1910.

The inmates' encounter with the city comes as a shock. The thousand demented individuals who arrive in Mixcoac, in those days within the Mexico City limits, feel desolated by the life which they find outside the asylum walls. "The people hurrying about caused the air in the streets to change direction." Leaving the refuge of madness is to approach an "urban animal" even more fearful than the inner beast of madness itself. The fugitives realize that their true confinement was the exterior, not the interior. And little by little, desolated by the life that they find outside the madhouse, "they willingly returned to the asylum."

Matilda will never again leave the asylum. It will be her "play city" for the rest of her life. She wants to forget. But one can go mad from not remembering. Nevertheless, there is someone who discovers her because he remembers her. It is the photographer Joaquín Buitrago, the witness. A man who at forty-nine years of age "is still capable of falling in love as if he had all the time in the world and nothing else to do." Time for everything except love. Love a crazy woman? Remember with passion Matilda's body, "the pear of her naked hips"? Is her soul's furniture covered with white sheets, like cadavers? Must Joaquín accept that his life is also a failure, that his money is gone, that there is nothing left to do but bathe with buckets of cold water and put on his one and only black suit in order to face the world? Or is there room to admit that, in the end, in the asylum, Matilda Burgos is disposed to spend "the happiest years of her life" in confinement, the peaceful years in which she does not have to give answers? Like that crazy woman of whom they ask the following question in order to certify her madness:

"Who is the president of Mexico?"

"I don't know."

Perhaps Matilda's madness is wisdom of a different order, in which Buitrago can understand that between a man and a woman certain distances provoke happiness, and that failure can be welcomed as repose, peace, and silence. Because outside the walls, in the Dantesque city, the war never ends, the state of siege is permanent, and every day in Mexico hope is crucified.

Some residue of the original but recoverable nobility does exist. The tropics embrace it. It is the pyramid of El Tajín in Veracruz. There, the architecture is perfect, the beauty is unspeakable, and the age is immemorial. From that place come Matilda Burgos and her novel.

6.

Roberto Soto (el "Panzón" Soto) was a stage comedian in Mexican revues in the 1920s and 1930s. Like Leopoldo (el "Chato") Ortín and Carlos López (el "Chaflán"), Soto was displaced by the implacable personality of Mario Moreno ("Cantinflas") who did not even tolerate his first comedy partner (Manuel Medel) and only later had a rival, Germán Valdés ("Tin Tán") and secondary competition ("Clavillazo," "Resortes"). My motive in recalling these anecdotes about Mexican stage and screen comedians is to make a wicked allusion to a different Roberto Soto, the character in Eloy Urroz's novel *Friction*, whose name recalls el Panzón, except that Urroz's character is named Roberto Soto Gariglietti. He claims that he is not, like his Mexican homonym, a traveling tent show comedian, but rather a pre-Socratic philosopher, Empedocles, the fifth century B.C. disciple of Parmenides.

Does Urroz get to have his cake and eat it too? Of course he does. His reference to a popular Mexican comic as well as a Sicilian of Antiquity, is not gratuitous, if we take into account that Empedocles professed a philosophy of reincarnation, namely: "No mortal thing has been born, nothing has ended with funereal death. There is only a mixture of iridescence of fragmented things. This is what men call birth."

To be a born survivor means that nothing dies completely, and that Roberto Soto Gariglietti is a mirror image of both the Mexican comic and the Sicilian philosopher, to the extent that both are part of the human tragic-comedy. After all, it is funny that Empedocles ends

his life by leaping into the crater of the volcano Etna, which gave
birth to the celebrated couplet:

Poor Empedocles, that restless soul,

Jumped into Etna, and was roasted whole.

Other versions say that Empedocles was hurled up by the volcano to
a heavenly Elysium; others that he fooled the whole world and only
left a sandal atop the volcano to make them believe in the myth of
his death.

However it happened, Empedocles's comedy contrasts with the
tragedy of Soto, whose comic pre-eminence was stolen by Cantinflas,
who reduced el Panzón to movie flops like *La corte del Faraón* (The
Pharaoh's Court), although his son, "Mantequilla" ("Butter") Soto,
did in fact establish himself as a supporting comic figure in the films
of Luís Buñuel (*Mexican Bus Ride* and *Illusion Travels by Streetcar*)
and Pedro Infante (*We the Poor*).

I say all this by way of entrance, on uncertain footing, to the parodic, ever-changing world of Eloy Urroz. His novels offer encounters between Sergio Pitol and J. M. Coetzee, Pancho Villa and Milan
Kundera, José Donoso and Marcelo Chiriboga, Ecuador's gift to the
Boom. Except that Urroz belongs to the constellation following the
Boom, or perhaps to the Crack, self-named so that others would not
name it themselves, to which also belong other authors discussed
here: Ignacio Padilla, Jorge Volpi and Pedro Ángel Palou.

None of them makes more explicit the theme I am dealing with
here than Urroz: there is no creation that is not built on tradition; and
no tradition that persists without creation. In *Friction*, Urroz allows
this literary reality to reach its most dangerous, concise, and secret relationship: the one between the character, Roberto Soto Gariglietti,
and the reader, you. You, meaning, the one who reads; the one holding the book entitled *Friction* in your hands; the one who gives life to
the fiction of *Friction* and to the *Friction* of fiction.

You, "hypocrite reader, my likeness, my brother," said Baudelaire
in order to say what is always known in poetic art but rarely said in
narrative art. I direct myself to *you*, reader; without *you*, I do not exist, the book becomes an object lying in wait for the next reader to
revive it, to save it from the volcano, to pick up Empedocles's sandal.

Eloy Urroz is also a critic of literature who has written about
literary form in the wake of two different writers: James Joyce and

D. H. Lawrence. Joyce: Jesuitical, Irish, uterine in his opposition to the religious phallus; Lawrence: phallic in opposition to the maternal Gynaecea, the son of *Sons and Lovers*, the son of Frieda Lawrence. Joyce—Catholic; Lawrence—Protestant. Both of them inconceivable without the tradition of the novel. A tradition which we like to trace back to Cervantes, declaring ourselves to be the sons and daughters of La Mancha, but which Urroz, doubtless a reader of Bakhtin, carries to the modern origin of fiction as a dissolution and a mixture of genres, a rejection of E. M. Forester's hypocritical reduction (the novel as simply argument and realistic characters) and a transgression of the Cervantean origin to a *beyond* that is an even greater *here*: Rabelais, and his great foundation novels *The Life of Gargantua and Pantagruel*, a series of five books composed between 1532 and 1564. It is important that Urroz thus reminds us of our novelistic origins, because without origin there is no destiny, and Rabelais is both origin and destiny if we consider that, against puritanical attempts to disarm the novel by dressing it in its transparent spoils, Rabelais writes a novel of religion, medicine, agriculture, language and dialects, carnival, and existence. Urroz's ability—not the least of his strengths—to engage this receptive amplitude central to the origin and destiny of the novel, is also shared by Padilla, Volpi, Palou, and Rivera Garza.

7.

In *Diablo guardián* (Guardian Devil), Xavier Velasco discredits official language. In Mexico, the PRI invented its own language, a public language crafted to disseminate nothing but falsehood, a language inherently incapable of telling the truth. But it broadcast its grandiose lies with a marmoreal rhetoric and an involuntary humor worthy of Cantinflas. To that Orwellian Newspeak, Velasco opposes an invasion of neologisms, disrespectful vocabulary, *leperadas*—literally "leper words," foul, uncouth remarks—and, above all, uncertainties.

The carnival of words in *Diablo guardián* fixes on the quotidian speech of a time period. Young women are classified as *borolas rarotongas* and *hermelindas*[8] but also, like Cortázar's ersatz *lunfardo*[9] in *Hop-*

8 *Borolas*: from Vargas's cartoon character, signifying abuse, anarchy, trickery, excess, imagination, fantasy, risk, disobedience, an immeasurable potential for enjoying life. *Rarotongas*: from *Rarotonga*, a sultry comic book jungle queen. *Hermelindas*: from another comic book character, the ironically named Hermelinda Linda, a fat leering hag neither *hermosa* (beautiful) nor *linda* (pretty).

9 *Lunfardo*: local slang of Buenos Aires; in the Southern Cone, the word refers to criminal, underworld slang.

scotch, Velasco gives the words a metaphysic and onomatopoeic value free of direct meanings. Velasco's bubbling verbal stew is rich with skewed Anglicisms—the popular refrain from the film *The Wizard of Oz*: "Ding dong the Wicked Witch is dead!" becomes *Ding dong the wicked bitch is wet*—to give us the picaresque guile of the nice middle class girl Violetta (with two t's: the second one crucifies her) who, when she realizes that her honorable mommy and daddy keep half of the money she has collected for the Red Cross, decides to rob them—*ladrón que roba a ladrón ha cien años de perdón*[10]—and then run away to spend it all in New York: "Por favor, Diosito, quiero ser puta de ciertopelo" ("Please, Dear Holy God, I want to be a true velvet-hair whore"). And her Walkman will be her university. This novel is the guardian devil of a little limping she-devil.

Diablo Guardián's first person narrator is the naughty girl, and her vocabulary is filled with popular speech measured by the middle class filter. The basis of popular speech is street slang, the most mutable in existence. The popular speech found in Lizardi's *The Mangy Parrot* today requires a dictionary to be understood; in my own lifetime, we have gone from *chicho* and *gacho* to *jambo* and *jodal* by way of *güey* and *la greña Pompadour*.[11] What I mean to explain is that the picaresque is essential to literature. *The epic* demands only one language: everyone understands one another, Hector and Achilles, the Trojan and the Greek.

The novel, by contrast, demands a plurality of languages. Anna Karenina does not understand her husband, nor Madame Bovary hers.

Don Quixote speaks the language of the chivalrous epic. Sancho Panza, that of the popular picaresque. Between the two of them, they create the modern novel, the Cervantean tradition.

Diversity of speech.

A re-processing of all the levels of language.

A mestizo language. Our language.

The language of Xavier Velasco and his guardian devils.

---

10 "The robber who robs the robber gets a hundred-year pardon."

11 *Chicho*: curl, ringlet, curler, roller; *gacho*: nasty, ugly, unlucky; *jambo*: bloke, geezer; *jodal*: a whole bunch; *güey*: lazy idiot; *greña*: a mop of hair.

18. The Post-Boom (2)

José Donoso's masterful oeuvre opened the door for a veritable constellation of Chilean novelists: Isabel Allende, Gonzalo Contreras, Arturo Fontaine, Antonio Skármeta, Sergio Missana, Marcela Serrano, Carlos Cerda, Diamela Eltit, Alberto Fuguet, Ariel Dorfman, and Carlos Franz. All of them preceded by, and presided over, by the deacon of the Chilean novel, Jorge Edwards.

Cervantes gathered together all genres—epic, picaresque, pastoral, Morisco—into a single one: the novel, and he gave it an unexpected turn: the novel of novels, the novel that knows it is a novel, as Don Quixote discovers in a printing shop where, precisely, Cervantes's novel is being printed.

I invoke this illustrious antecedent in order to consider Jorge Edwards's book *La muerte de Montaigne* (The Death of Montaigne), in which the Chilean writer brilliantly displays an array of genres to illustrate a single work: *La muerte de Montaigne*, a book of undefinable genre, somewhere between narration and reflection. But between one thing and another, Edwards unfolds the life of Michel de Montaigne, the history of France at the end of the sixteenth century, the politics of the great powers—the England of Elizabeth I, the Spain of Philip II, and, between them, the France of the Wars of Religion, and the Succession from the Valois (Henry III) to the Bourbons (Henry IV).

There is more: Montaigne's life has a space, one rigorously described by Edwards. A mansion which does not quite manage to become a castle. Its towers and its beams. Its trees and groves, wheat fields and vineyards. Its bees, henhouses, cows and calves; its donkeys. Montaigne has a loyal, taciturn wife. Also a possible mistress or, at least, a young female companion in his senescence: Montaigne is fifty-six years old, elderly in the sixteenth century; the young Marie de Gournay, barely twenty, young then and now. Is she an adoptive daughter, a secret lover, an erotic and untouchable presence? The mystery of life is the mystery of the novel and it permits Edwards, upon this backdrop of mystery, to make explicit the political age.

Henry III of Valois seems born for a novel. Effeminate, surrounded by young mignons and at the same time a flagellant as well as a friend of the witches' coven, and if more were needed, a voluptuary of the cassock and hooded torchlit processions. And yes, there is more. The portrait of the Queen Mother, Catherine de Medici and her lover, possessed of a capacity for intrigue which does not end in death: the queen's heart, the size of a loquat, in an urn. And her son Henry III, in the end murdered by a monk. And the Duke of Guise, called *Le Balafré* ("the scarred"), pretender to the throne, assassinated by order of Henry III.

This leaves only Henry IV, King of Navarre, who renounced Protestantism and became Catholic for political purposes ("Paris is worth a Mass"), who brought peace and monarchical authority to France. It would be this man, this Henry who recognizes, rewards Montaigne, who publicly embraces him, respects the private word of the writer in his tower, where he inaugurates a new genre against the genre of genres created by Cervantes: the novel. With Montaigne, the novel has a new face, the *Essay*, which means the attempt, the approximation, the open word, one without conclusion, because it is only that: an essay, an endeavor, something unfinished. Montaigne is clearly a great reader of Plutarch, Virgil, and Seneca. He transcends them in the sense of updating the genre of what is incomplete, the "open work" which gives its tone and tradition to an interminable genre, confirmed by Montaigne's many descendants, including, as Edwards suggests, Borges.

An interminable, open essay capable of wielding the "cold steel" (Edwards) of the classics but redolent of vineyards, smoked fish, belching, unwashed bodies, and unprotected sex. It matters and it matters not: the other face of the French Renaissance will be a masque and the lord of the masque is Rabelais, the gross, vital, all-embracing and excessive opposite of Montaigne. Would Montaigne be who he is without the tremendous contrast of *Gargantua* and *Pantagruel*? Or do the very excesses of Rabelais domesticate those of Montaigne and permit him to be who he is, without the need for Rabelaisian satisfaction?

And who is Montaigne, in the end? He is a writer who says: writing consists in not saying it all. Writing is a form of absence. Writing is a form of skepticism. Writing is an act of humor. Writing is the narrative of reflection. Writing is the art of digression. And for what reason does one write? "For readers." For one single reader: the father, the close friend, the married woman. "And some, for the ideal reader, an invention, one fiction more."

It is here that we realize Edwards, as he writes about Montaigne, is writing about himself. Not in an autobiographical way, of course, but as an approach to a model which is ours to the degree to which we know how to enrich it. And Edwards does it from a distant location: Chile, his native land. The remote province. The ultimate West. Yes, the homeland of Pablo Neruda. But also of Lucho Oyarzún, whose name I brazenly mention alongside Montaigne and Proust. "How can you allow yourself, Sir ... to confuse Lucho Oyarzún" with Proust and Montaigne? Because Jorge Edwards's writing "belongs to the same family, that of Montaigne, Proust, and Lucho Oyarzún." Because memory is "faster than writing," and includes Lucho Oyarzún as well as Carlucho Carrasco, José Donoso, Laurence Sterne and Machado de Assis. It includes the town of Zapallar and Edwards's lookout across the cold Pacific, rich with seafood, and the rocks of Isla Seca.

Few tombs remain in Zapallar. I am sure that Edwards has his reserved. And in it, in Chile, he will once again meet Montaigne and together, in the end, they will plan to go walking, traveling through changing countries, where they will be gracious pagans. Montaigne will hear Edwards say "Colorina," "Guagua," "se va a las pailas"[12] and he will understand this Chilean "caído de las nubes"—"fallen from the clouds."

To turn Chile into a country of novelists is quite a feat, considering that such "crazy geography," a long strip from the deserts of the tropics to the Antarctic, is a place where the great poets have flourished: Vicente Huidobro, Gabriela Mistral, Pablo Neruda and Nicanor Parra. For that reason, the Chilean novel descends from poetry and, thanks to this alliance, can reach the level, rare among us, of tragedy, meaning the capacity of seeing the world as a necessary but not fatal clash of values.

We love soap operas because they permit us the weepy indulgence of melodrama.

We like Hollywood westerns because it is easy to identify the "good guy" who wears the white hat, and the "bad guy" who wears the black hat. More difficult is to enter the gray terrain of doubt, which the Chilean writer Carlos Franz explores in *The Absent Sea*. In the novel, the hidden frailties of a military assassin for the Pinochet regime, stationed in northern Chile, are tragically revealed by a left-

---

12 These words together suggest a phrase like "Colorina, baby, it's all going to hell."

wing magistrate who returns from exile to confront the cruel man she loved, exposing them both, in order to find a modicum of humanity in contrition.

The woman's failure, however, conditions her daughter's experience of being reintegrated into Chile and a new life, and conditions, as well, the dynamic presence of a whole people. However, Franz's underlying warning is that there is no guaranteed happiness. The extremes of evil are manifest in the demonic part of the human being; what is good in the most luminous part of our being. But in the final act, what really counts is the tragic capacity to assume good and evil, transfiguring them into the modicum of equity and justice which corresponds to us. This is the importance of Franz's *The Absent Sea*.

Octavio Paz once said that originality was first an imitation. This idea would contradict the notion of "origin" as "beginning" or "existence without antecedent." By contrast, the word "originality," as defined by the Oxford English Dictionary, signifies thinking independently or creatively.

Carlos Franz's novel, *Almuerzo de Vampiros* (Vampire Lunch), recognizes some earlier themes and works. The book's cover shows us Dracula, the vampire par excellence, played by Bela Lugosi, in the act of sinking his fangs into the neck of some sleeping beauty. There is also a reference to Fritz Lang's film *M*. I believe that these are clever deceptions through which Franz distracts our attention in order to surprise us with some unexpected literary and political legerdemain. We are in *Flaubert*, a restaurant in Santiago, in the Chile of restored democracy, where the narrator is eating with a friend, Zósima. Suddenly, the narrator discovers, at another table, a man whom he thought was dead, *el maestrito*, the "little maestro," a kind of underworld jester whose mission was to entertain the criminals who prospered in the shadows of the Pinochet dictatorship, without actually belonging to it.

Is this squalid, deformed buffoonish little man, the *maestrito* of the gang composed of Lucio, Doc Fernández, young Vanesa and Maricaus (does her name suggest that she likes to eat *mariscos*—seafood)? This first enigma leads the narrator to recall his childhood during the years of tyranny when he was a mere hanger on to the band of ruffians. Now, a student by day and taxi driver at night, he wonders what he was doing in such company. He remembers his years as a young orphan on scholarship studying under the humanities professor Víctor Polli and the intellectual exaltation of those youthful days. But the implicit promise is broken, as is the life of the whole country. The narrator is sucked down to the underworld of crime and deceit, and the gigantic joke that envelops it all, giving Franz's novel a double character, both repugnant and creative, unhealthy and imaginative which, to be all this (and more), depends upon an extraordinary use of popular speech from Chile, one of the richest, most elusive and defensive in Latin America.

In this black comedy, Franz resorts to a language which is at once the expression and disguise of a purpose: to provoke hilarity, converting it all into *talla*,[13] that is, into an enormous joke, "a joke which will make us laugh, not only at ourselves. Which will make the whole country laugh. Which will turn this whole time period into a joke." Of course, *la talla* (size) has its origin in the wit of "broken" (*roto*) Chilean Spanish, first cousin to "poor, common" (*pelado*) Mexican Spanish, and the traditional provider of the speech which the narrator calls *cantinfleo* (empty, babbling chatter): the capacity for talking a lot without saying anything or saying a lot about things that are not talked about. It is the Mexican *relajo* (relaxation), which, like the Chilean "size," gives us the measure of ourselves.

In this sense, *Almuerzo con vampiros* is an extraordinary offering and transfiguration of Chilean speech, in which everything is verbally disguised, at times as dissimulation, at times as aggression, always as *talla*, pulling society's collective leg with a hilarious joke. *Fome* (boring, lethargic) and *siútico* (ridiculous, affected, corny, prissy) are originally Chilean words that are here linked with the sexual vocables that refer directly to the organ of masculine potency, turning it into "the word most commonly scrawled on the walls and toilet stalls of Chile": *Pico* (*polla* in Spain, *pito* in Mexico, *prick* in the U.S. and England), to the degree that in free elections, "*el pico* would be elected president of the republic."

The male sex organ ("finger without nail," "a lima-bean face"; in Mexico, *chile)* becomes a symbol of life and power, a private phantasm of public reality, just as the servile, ratlike *maestrito* is to the eminent professor of humanities. Few figures of human misery in our literature are comparable to this scrawny, squalid little man; a Rigoletto of the underworld, a fawning, flattering, servile, impotent *robachistes* (a "joke

---

13 *Talla*: size, height, stature; in Mexico: squabbling; in Central America: a fib or lie; in the Southern Cone: gossip, chit-chat, compliment; in the Andes: a beating.

thief"), the *maestrito* has perhaps usurped the persona of the *maestro*, the "maestro" or "teacher," just as the dictator has usurped the persona of "power."

Franz's novel proposes various enigmas whose solution depends—or not—on the reader's reading. Has the narrator confused a deformed lout with a humanist "who knew Latin"? Furthermore, is that grotesque figure saved, perhaps, thanks to his very vulgarity? In the final analysis, is ordinariness a form of survival in a now "defenseless" age, in the sense that nobody now defends it, except those who usurp it?

Carlos Franz does not offer easy solutions. He is not tender with the past. Nor with a present in which "only ambitions are rewarded" and the financial fortress "swallows it all." One need not ask too many questions, the narrator concludes: silence was the water of that age and "even when it was a miserable past, it is the only one we have."

I will not reveal the end of this beautiful, original novel. I only wish to admire Franz's great literary talent. His previous book, *The Absent Sea*, demonstrated that it is possible to create a *tragic* novel on a *melodramatic* continent. *Almuerzo con vampiros* is an unclassifiable book because as it imitates a literary tradition (*Dracula*) and a political reality (Pinochet), it creates absolutely unique, independent, and creative forms of narration.

El día de los muertos (The Day of the Dead), the novel by the Chilean writer Sergio Missana is divided into two parts. The first occurs in Chile on the eve of the 1973 military coup d'ètat that toppled the Allende presidency. The protagonists are Esteban (the narrator) and a radical group which Esteban approaches because he desires the young Valentina, the group's militant leftist, but also because he wishes to be accepted and loved. Otherwise he is ambivalent toward the group. He fears violence. Chaos pleases him. He desires, voluptuously, that the chaos intensify, that it be unleashed. He knows himself to be an intruder but he likes the welcome embrace of the clan. He believes himself "progressive" but "disconnected from passion." At the same time, he is on the right, "not from conviction, but by omission." He knows that "purity of conviction" is prohibited to him.

Meanwhile, the group "feeds on itself." Its members fear being separated. They fear losing what unites them. They need a framework for structure and support. Among them, Valentina possesses an "aura of restlessness." Esteban sees her as complicated, confused and, possibly, unhappy. Her relationships with men are phantasmal, prolific, "mere foreshortenings." Who is Esteban, the narrator, compared to Valentina? Is it enough for him to have her before him, to study her appearance, without saying a word? Or is Valentina simply an object of Esteban's greed, part of an oversized desire for acquisition?

Valentina looks at Esteban with rage, pity, scorn, and impatience. Esteban is fed up. He has become suspicious in everyone's eyes. He flees. The next day, the military coup overthrows the legitimate government of Salvador Allende.

Thirty years later, the novel takes place in exile, or rather, among the exiles. The protagonists are Gaspar, an itinerant Chilean, and Matilde, Esteban's stepdaughter. Matilde is a young woman who "moves among stigmas." She does not compromise. She does not adapt to her interlocutor. When she orders a coffee she gets it wrong. Her intonation is mistaken, her pauses inexact. The reason is that she wants to take things on her own terms. Gaspar sees in her an element of dignity, of pride, of tenacity, but does not know how to associate it with anything. In the end, he discovers that Matilde "had a vision, if not more complex or more profound, definitely more advanced." For her, action matters, acts and their consequences, not feelings or faith, "which are going to change and be forgotten, no matter what."

Like the previous relationship (Esteban-Valentina) this one (Gaspar-Matilde) remains in suspense. Only that the latter leads back to the former through a splendid "turn of the screw" by Missana. Gaspar reads Esteban's diary entry from September 4, 1973, which means that he discovers the novel prior to the one in which he, Gaspar, is the protagonist. He turns from being an actor into a reader of the novel which we already know, but he does not. It is a new triumph in the tradition of La Mancha. As in *Don Quixote*, the protagonist is transformed into reader, and thanks to that, he knows the destinies of the young actors from a single day in Chilean history: September 4, 1973.

The move from *El día de los muertos* (2007) to *Las muertes paralelas* (Parallel Deaths) (2010), was a bold leap forward for Sergio Missana. The former novel had an exact temporal and personal perimeter: the day of the military coup against Salvador Allende, a group of revolutionary friends, the detachment of the narrator who only belonged to the group because of his love for a woman, and several decades later, a reencounter in Paris, and a literary revelation: everything was already written beforehand.

In *Las muertes paralelas*, Sergio Missana begins with that same literary conundrum. Everything indicates that the narrator, Tomás Ugarte, is the novel's protagonist. He speaks in the first person. He occupies space, and maintains relationships with his family, wife, and friends. He dreams. He has a wife, Paula, who is leaving him. He has an occasional lover, Fernanda, who does not satisfy him and who puts him in danger. He has a cat, Lola, that—perhaps—is the messenger of an American millionairess, Phyllis, who accidentally leaves her fortune to anyone who attends her wake. The only one who shows up and signs the register is Tomás Ugarte. What the dead woman lacked in personal hygiene she made up for in cats.

Tomás returns to his job. The agency he works for "was fading fast from his memory, becoming unreal . . . everything there seems to have happened to someone else." Tomás has a dream. "He dreamed that he was an old woman." Except that the old woman, Inés, is not a dream. She is a real presence, a disturbing homeless woman whose fate, as it begins to get mixed up with his own, Tomás would like to avoid. He picks her up in the street and takes her to his apartment. She is a repugnant beggar: "her clothes were permeated with a foul stench of filth and excrement overshadowed by the early stages of decomposition."

Why does Tomás rescue her? Why does he take her from the streets into his house? Why has he dreamed about this old woman's fate—an atrocious death—and now wishes to save her, to avoid the future he dreamed for her? Nevertheless, Tomás knows that, "he had no right to interfere with her life, however sordid and miserable it might be." That life belonged to Inés, it was her only possession: a life of "dumpsters, turf wars and truces . . . her memory seemed trapped in a labyrinth." Now Tomás would like to "mold Inés into the adorable little old woman that she never was and was never going to be."

In a mysterious act of transposition, Tomás dresses the old woman in youthful clothes, as if he wanted to bring her closer to everything she is not by means of what Freud would call the desire to touch what is forbidden, to make contact with the taboo. Except that when someone (Tomás) has broken the taboo, he himself becomes taboo so as to not awaken his neighbors' forbidden desires. Tomás does not understand this. He believes that Inés can be redeemed. Inés knows better. She deceives Tomás. She escapes. She returns to the streets where five "antisocial" types who find her sleeping in an ATM vestibule, murder her by dousing her with gasoline, and setting her on fire.

Inés's destiny, dreamed by Tomás, is fulfilled, meaning that Tomás's dream is realized. He, the benefactor, understands that "he had no right to interfere in her life, however sordid and miserable it might be, it belonged to Inés, it was her only possession." Except that this rational explanation is accompanied by a suspicion: in trying to prevent Inés's future, does Tomás avoid, redirect, or cancel his own future? But, does one who engages the fate of others—although it be dreamed—have their own future?

There is a horrifying scene in which Tomás, at night, runs into some *rotos*[14]—rough, uncivilized characters—like the ones who burned Inés. He lays down next to one of them who emits an "abject stench, worse than an animal." The *roto* wants to "settle" a debt with Inés. He is unaware of Ines's debt to Tomás. Did Inés dream Tomás or did Tomás dream Inés? The indigents reveal the truth. They threaten him. They urinate on him. They call him a *huevón* a coward. But while they treat him badly, as they did Inés, they only killed her, not Tomás.

One begins to suspect: Did Tomás dream Inés or did Inés dream Tomás? Did Inés die, as in Tomás's dream, instead of Tomás? Did Tomás avoid a death similar to that of Inés at the hands of the "antisocial" thugs? Did Inés die in order to save Tomás from a comparable fate? Or is it Inés who, in order to save him, dreamed Tomás?

Tomás's encounter with the *rotos* who instead of killing him urinate on him is the encounter we all have—middle and upper classes, professionals and business people, intellectuals and housewives—with the vast Latin American underworld of misery and crime. Here the setting is Santiago de Chile. It could be Rio de Janeiro, Lima, Caracas, or Mexico City. Of course Missana does not explain this. He does something better: he gives life and opens the doors of a contagious fiction. He creates the secret link, through Inés, between the lives of Tomás and Ramiro and Osvaldo on a frozen night in the Andes, or Tomás's life fused with Aurelio, or all of them dwelling within Tomás, creating the "fiction" that is Tomás, the "campaign pitchman

14 *roto*: "broken"

. . . the efficient, paternal, hard-working, controlling, seductive boss." Were all of them Tomás? Or was Tomás all of them?

Missana gives a final turn of the screw in the concluding episode involving Matías and a filming session—that very Chilean return to the desert. I will not reveal the surprising ending of *Las muertes paralelas*. A burned out house. A sleepwalking girl. Credit cut off. The I.D. card: the loss of modern identity. And a question for Tomás that is both useless and necessary: "Was it possible that my own presence changed things . . . opening a series of new possibilities?" This is Sergio Missana's question. It is the question of literature.

But perhaps no one better represents the movement of Chile's political and social reality to its literary reality, and to the tensions, clashes, uncertainties, loyalties, and betrayals of a society in flux than Arturo Fontaine. And what does the novel do and say in Chilean society, and in all societies? I return to the Cervantean Foundation to celebrate the durability of the novelistic genre. On a daily basis we are told: "The novel is dead." Who killed it? Successively: radio, telephone, cinema, television, Mac, iPhone, the Internet, and Twitter. Nevertheless, following each technological assault, the Phoenix-novel arises to tell us what cannot be said in any other way.

I am approaching only one of the multiple meanings of Arturo Fontaine's novels—*Oír su voz* (Hear Their Voice), and *Cuando éramos inmortales* (When We Were Immortal). They are both passionate affirmations of the necessity of opposing an enemy word—its name is imagination, its name is language—to the verbiage which surrounds us. Imagination and language: in Fontaine's work, these two literary forces enter into conflict with a country which has been, simultaneously, both forge and combustion, a country of tremendous internal schisms, pains, sorrows, hopes, nostalgias, hatreds, and fanaticisms, which in the end are manifest in language and imagination.

In *Oír su voz*, Fontaine explores language as a necessity of power—there is no power without language—except for the fact that power tends to monopolize language: language is *its* language posing as *our* language.

Fontaine listens and allows another voice, or rather other voices, to be heard:

There is a society, the Chilean one.

There is business and there is love.

There are politics and there are passions.

Society, business, and politics tend toward a language of absolutes.

Literature relativizes them, installing itself, Fontaine tells us, between societal order and individual emotions.

In *Cuando éramos inmortales*, the author radically personalizes these tensions, incarnating them in a character—Emilio—whose name leads us to Rousseau and his double ethics: those of the one who educates and those of the one who teaches. The educated person requires education in order to escape from their original nature, not through the spontaneous tutoring of vice and error, but rather thanks to a teaching which empowers natural virtue—which includes making use of the vice of deception. *Cuando éramos inmortales* is in no way an exegesis of Rousseau's *Emile*. It is a literary creation that plays with tradition in order to convert both—creation and tradition—into problems.

Chile is a paradoxical country where the youngest, most vigorous democracy has coexisted alongside the oldest, proudest oligarchy. Both, in turn, coexist with an army trained on the Prussian model, which respected civic politics until the politics of the Cold War led it to dictatorship.

Using a novelist's weapons, which are letters, Fontaine goes to the heart of the matter. For all of its death rattles, an old order gives way to a new one. But, what does this really entail? Among other things, writing. But who is the writer? The writer is both a first and a third person who takes a close look at society and privacy, directing itself toward a reader who is the co-creator of the book. The book is a score which the reader brings to life. The reading is the sonority of the book.

Arturo Fontaine is possessed of a powerful Quixotesque *fervor*: he wants to put soap operas to flight or trust that there will at least appear a Cervantean soap opera to transform them, just as *Don Quixote* transformed the novels of chivalry. A glorious dedication whose defeat would nevertheless be a victory. Because the novel is, in itself, the victory of ambiguity. An ambiguity which proposes itself as word and imagination, language and memory, speech and purpose. Then, what good is a novel in the world of modern communication: the instantaneous communication of the communicated event?

In a totalitarian regime, says my friend Philip Roth, the novelist is taken to a concentration camp. In a democratic regime — he continues — he is taken to a television studio.

What is certain is that after each assault, political or technological, the Phoenix-novel rises again to tell us what cannot be said in any other way. Antonio Skármeta is the great novelist of this transition. Additionally, no one evokes Neruda so well as he does.

Word and imagination: Missana, Fontaine.

Language and memory: Franz, Dorfman.

Speech and purpose: Skármeta, Fuguet.

2.

With *Red April*, the young Peruvian novelist Santiago Roncagliolo has married the detective novel to the political novel. Roncagliolo's novel is a Pandora's Box. The protagonist is District Attorney Felix Chacaltana Saldívar, who likes to be addressed just so, by his full name and title. Until now, he has never broken the rules. From now on, he will know that death is the only form of life. I'll say no more, because this novel contains many secrets and to reveal one, the author tells us, is to reveal them all.

The crop of new Colombian novelists is remarkable because the enormous success of Gabriel García Márquez and *One Hundred Years of Solitude* has been taken up by the current generation in order to open previously unseen paths. It is as if Gabo, with *Hundred Years*, had completely exhausted the tradition of "magic realism," taking it to the peak, like the ship anchored on a mountain which cannot be climbed any higher. It is impossible to imitate García Márquez. To discover other paths is possible. To climb other mountains, necessary.

I barely sketch out the richness of contemporary Colombian fiction if I mention Laura Restrepo, William Ospina, Héctor Abad Faciolince, and Juan Carlos Botero. I will limit myself to two novels by two authors: *The Secret History of Costaguana* by Juan Gabriel Vásquez, and *El síndrome de Ulises* (The Ulysses Syndrome) by Santiago Gamboa.

Vásquez starts with an article of faith ("History is fiction") to tell the true history of the events which led to the breakup of Colombia and the construction of the Panama Canal. He then shifts to London and the writer Joseph Conrad, who with the information delivered to him by the Colombian José Altamirano, writes the novel *Nostromo*, set in the Republic of Costaguana (Colombia). Nostromo, the daring titular Italian expatriate, hides a treasure of silver on a deserted island. In Vásquez's story, Conrad's novel is born from the narration which Altamirano, the narrator of *Costaguana*, makes to Conrad, future narrator of *Nostromo*. But when Altamirano attempts to reclaim paternity of the events narrated: "You, Joseph Conrad, have robbed me," Conrad, with supreme arrogance, scorns historical origins and proclaims the sovereignty of novelistic destiny. The Panama Canal in exchange for a silver mine.

The secret and beauty of Juan Gabriel Vásquez's novel reside in the tension between two destinies and two writings, those of Conrad and Altamirano. Is the latter the author of some real experience, or scarcely the messenger of what has been narrated? What are the limits between fiction and reality, truth and lies? Or will Dostoyevsky always be right: the novel is the truth of the lie?

As much in *Costaguana* as in his previous book, *The Informers*, Vásquez confronts us with inevitable moral and historical disjunctions. He leads us to an infrequently visited territory: the effects of World War II in Latin America and the destiny of German communities in our countries. Unbridled haste led our governments, in order to "be in good standing" (once again) with Washington, to consider all Germans as "enemies," even those who opposed Hitler. Written into this larger conflict in *The Informers* is the only apparently minor conflict between families destroyed, destinies thwarted, and parents versus children. The Santero family, father and son, confront one another, primarily because of their "insufficient lives" as a response to a history that believes itself self-sufficient: good people over here, bad ones over there.

With great narrative intelligence, Vásquez shows us the gray be-

tween action and human conscience, where our capacity for com-
mitting errors, betrayal, and hiding, creates a chain of disloyalties
which condemns us to a world of insufficiencies. Friends and enemies, spouses and lovers, parents and children treat one another with
acrimony, silence, and blindness, while the novelist employs irony
and ellipsis to discover the characters' "strategies of protection" and
walk with them—not knowing them, accompanying them—to understand that the insufficient life can be, also, the life inherited.

Is the art of the novel the way of correcting what has been badly
said—what is wretched—about life; saying it, if not well, at least in
a different way? Whether continuous or successive, perhaps these histories—Altamirano's Panama and Conrad's Costaguana—contain
the key. Did "Panama" precede "Costaguana," as Altamirano claims
to Conrad? Or did Conrad's novel precede Vásquez's, permitting the
latter, in a certain way, to "re-write" Conrad's narration as a literary
fact that precedes and is preceded, is told and is anguished? I feel that,
in Vásquez, everyone contributes to dig "the big trench" of the Panama Canal, only to then be buried in it. Buried in history, whose final
voice is that of a crazed Colombian president who wanders through
the jungle exclaiming "Sovereignty!" "Colonialism!"

Fiction since Rabelais and Cervantes is one more way of questioning truth, while we strive to reach it through the paradox of a lie.
This lie can be called imagination. It can also be considered a parallel reality. It can be seen as a critical mirror of what passes for truth
in the world of convention. Certainly it constructs a second universe
of being, where Don Quixote and Heathcliff and Emma Bovary have
a greater reality, one no less important, than the crowd of citizens
whose paths we hurriedly cross in order to return to forget ourselves
in our daily lives.

Don Quixote or Emma Bovary effectively bring to light, and give
weight and presence to the virtue and vice—to the fugitive personal-
ities—which we encounter in daily life. What Ahab and Pedro Páramo and Effi Briest possess can also be the living memory of the great,
glorious, and mortal subjectivities of men and women whom we
forget, but whom our parents knew and our grandparents foresaw.
Who are they, and where did they go? Answer: they are in a novel.

With Cervantes, the novel establishes its *raison d'être* as a lie
that is the foundation of the truth. Because by means of fiction the

novelist puts reason to the test. Fiction invents what the world does not have, what the world has forgotten, what it hopes to obtain and perhaps can never reach. The novel is the Atheneum of our ancestors and the Congress of our descendants. In this way, fiction turns out to be a form of appropriating the world, something that confers on the world color, flavor, sense, dreams, vigils, perseverance, and even lazy repose which it demands in order to continue existing, with all the melancholy weight of our hopes and what we have forgotten.

I am, almost, describing the double movement—explosion and inclusion—of Santiago Gamboa's novel, *El síndrome de Ulises*. A superficial glance would find here antecedents like George Orwell's *Down and Out in Paris and London*, where the English writer (whose mother grew up in Burma, and whose father worked in the Opium Department of the British Indian Civil Service) deliberately descends to work in the English hops fields and as a dishwasher in the Hotel Crillon in Paris. Except that Orwell can return—and we know it—to his job at the newspaper and the radio while Gamboa's narrator—although fictional—is, in the novel, *condemned* to live in his chosen rat's warren of exile, and willpower alone will not serve to free him from the prison of incessant repetition. Because the anguish of this Colombian Ulysses consists in knowing that returning is forbidden him, not because of politics, family, or country, but because of the devouring demands of the journey, the adventure, the odyssey, of postponing the return home; not because something blocks him, but rather because there is nothing to prevent him, nothing except the internal logic—or irrationality—of the exile's situation, of living far from home, to burn through all the consequences of exile before returning home.

I don't recall having read a novel that penetrates, with such violence, the odyssey of the Latin American expatriate, confining him within a city—Paris—a neighborhood, a tiny room, the pestilent cellar of a Chinese restaurant, and the endless wandering nights of a compensatory, omnivorous, anthropophagic sexuality, beyond the limits of a Henry Miller who moves within the limits of the expatriate world: Gamboa, by contrast, creates for himself a voluntary exile, and in doing so rejects a way to go home, not through the masochism of banishment but rather by the immediate earthly hunger and the incarnation of the earth in that fugitive harem which gives its only heat to a cloudy, rainy wintry Paris.

A city whose only light shines forth from the bodies of Paula and Sabrina, Victoria and Yuyú and Susi and Saskia: inevitable encounters between the narrator's Hispanic language and the languages of Shem, son of Noah, the origin of language, which returns to speak in the voice of the woman in order to demonstrate that literature *is indeed* a human right.

3.

The relationship between the novel and history is given, on occasion, with the immediacy of current events. This is the case, for example, in Mariano Azuela's *The Underdogs* (1915) written from within the turbulence of the Mexican Revolution and, in a certain way, of Martín Luís Guzmán's *La sombra del caudillo* (The Shadow of the Dictator), practically contemporary with the events and characters of the Mexican political landscape of the time.

At other times, history only admits fiction thanks to perspective. The French Revolution has no instantaneous novelists. They would have to wait for Balzac and Stendhal. No one elevates the American Revolution to the level of fiction until the twentieth century when its best thematic works are written by Howard Fast: *The Unvanquished* and *Citizen Tom Paine*. Tolstoy writes about the events of the 1812 Napoleonic invasion of Russia half a century later in 1865. Stephen Crane writes the best novel of the American Civil War, *The Red Badge of Courage*, in 1895.

The nineteenth century in Mexico, so tumultuous and even chaotic, produced novels of its time and evocations of others: Riva Palacio, Rabassa, Payno. Two recent Mexican works offer us a renewed perspective, with great brio and imagination. In *Yankee Invasion* (2005) Ignacio Solares explores the experience of the war of 1847-1848 and the United States's occupation of Mexico City with a contrasted sense of lights and shadows, effects and defects. The story's "modernity" lies with the narrator relating the events several decades later, in his maturity and during *el Porfiriato*, the dictatorship of Porfirio Díaz, giving the work its requisite uncertainty: this is fiction, not "history." Since the novel is written by an author who is our contemporary (Solares), *Yankee Invasion* turns out to possess three levels of temporality: what was lived in 1848, what was remembered during the *Porfiriato*, and what is narrated today.

One of Mexico's most cultivated and reticent writers, Hernán Lara Zavala establishes from the outset the actuality of his narration thanks to a novelist (Lara Zavala himself?) who sits down to write the novel that we are reading: *Península Península*, whose theme is the Caste War of the Yucatan in 1847. Lara Zavala thus writes himself into the great tradition, the founding tradition of Cervantes, where Don Quixote's and Sancho Panza's novel coincides with current events of the time in Spain, the past evoked by the hidalgo's madness, the picaresque genre (Sancho) in dialogue with the epic (Quixote) and with the Moorish, Byzantine, amorous, and pastoral styles introduced to give the novel its charter of citizenship: generic diversity.

Lara Zavala's movement from his ironic actuality as narrator to the narrated content permits him to present the Caste War of the Yucatan with a variety of rhythms and themes that not only save the novel from any suspicion of didacticism but which enrich what we already knew with the treasure of what we can imagine. Here are not only the historical events and characters brought together, the governors Méndez and Barbachano, the Mayan leaders Pat and Chi, and the contrasting societies of the Creole elite and the indigenous communities. We also see the local merchants and the *gachupines*—the Spaniards—Doctor Fitzpatrick and his loyal (too loyal) dog Pompeyo. Also present are the clergy and the native acolytes and sacristans who assassinate them. We see José María Luis Mora's *Mexico and its Revolutions* in all of its chaotic simultaneity. The Yucatan, its barren white plains shining sorrowfully, becomes a protagonist. We see the sun, the laurel trees, the cool freshness; the leaden noontime, the muggy haze; and the herbs (damiana, rue, datura, yerba buena, mullein, etc.) evoked with a loving minuteness which reveals Lara Zavala's education in English literature, especially D. H. Lawrence's capacity for finding passion in nature.

Except that everything pulses with the menace of war and death. The author postpones them with magnificent moments of erotic passion (the novelist Turría and the widow Lorenza; the delightfully funny María and the town clerk Anastasio). Love is beleaguered by two forces which Lara Zavala handles with a master's touch. One is magic, the impalpable current of the supernatural present in the rites and exorcisms of the Yucatan peninsula, which serves Lorenza to think that her deceased husband, Genaro, still lives and haunts about her bedroom until discovering that the noise is made by a bat which stops fluttering as soon as she turns on the light. A bat? Or a vampire?

Because the magic of the earth contains the death of the earth. The rebel chieftain Chi is assassinated by his wife's lover, Anastasio. The rebellion loses (in every sense) its head, and the merchant who is presumed dead, Genaro, reappears to reclaim his married wife, only to be sent back to another death: anonymity and silence, like Balzac's Colonel Chabert, "dead in Eylau" without the right to resurrection.

On the peninsulas, at Campeche and Yucatan, Hernán Lara tells us, the news returns, swims, and drags along. It can also be novelized, as the author does here with a limpid prose, as transparent (in order to establish comparisons odious or amiable) as that of Martín Luis Guzmán.

A fragile enterprise, as Turrisa knows when the revolutionary fury burns the manuscript of her book and the author understands that "she will now no longer have the courage to rewrite her novel, which will only survive in her memory and imagination." Which are, fortunately, our own.

Ignacio Solares, the prominent Mexican novelist, playwright, critic, and cultural one-man-show, comes from the border state of Chihuahua. Perhaps this explains, to a certain extent, his fascination with northern Mexico and, especially, the universe — for it is such — of the border between Mexico and the United States.

Mexico has had a highly centralized cultural and political history. Since the reign of the Aztecs (to 1521) and then the Colonial period (1521 to 1810) and Independence (1810 to the present day), Mexico City has been the crown and magnet of Mexican life. A nation isolated within itself by a geography of volcanoes, mountain ranges, deserts and jungles, Mexico has always found a semblance of unity in the capital city, today a vast metropolis of more than twenty million people, reflecting the sudden increase from the country's total population of fifteen million in 1920.

The majority of Mexico's writers, whatever their regional origins, end up in Mexico City: government, art, education, and politics are all centered in what was previously known as *la región más transparente* — the place "where the air is clear." This does not mean that provincial Mexico has not had great works of fiction. Whether in the wake of the vast revolutionary movements (Azuela, Guzmán, Muñoz) or in the abiding truth of isolation, religion, and death (Rulfo, Yáñez, and the State of Jalisco), Mexico has seen itself in movement within Mexico, very rarely in its relationship with the world. The most outstanding novel of Mexico in the world is Fernando Del Paso's *News from the Empire*, the tragic tale of the failed empire of Maximilian and Carlota, told by the latter in a dream sequence of memory and madness.

The northern frontier and our relations with the United States have had few literary explorers. Solares is notable in this. Francisco Madero, the scion of the northern aristocracy and initiator of the Mexican Revolution, has attracted Solares both as fiction and theater. Pancho Villa, the bandit and revolutionary chieftain from Chihuahua, is central to Solares's tale — *Columbus* — about Villa's brief incursion into that New Mexico town in 1916.

In *Yankee Invasion* Solares takes on a major event, one mostly ignored by Mexican literature: the invasion of Mexico by United States forces in 1847, obeying the unwritten law of territorial expansion from the Atlantic to the Pacific. The young and disorganized Mexican Republic stood in the way and had to be dealt with in the name of "manifest destiny." The opposition to "President Polk's war" by figures such as Abraham Lincoln and Henry David Thoreau was fruitless. First, Texas achieved independence, and was then admitted into the Union. But to reach California and the American West, Mexico had to be defeated.

Yankee Invasion is the tale of a dramatic conflict. It is easy to describe it as offering a simplistic view of the powerful U.S.A. overcoming the weak Mexican Republic: Goliath beating David. It lends itself, thus, to a Manichaean tale of "Good Guys" and "Bad Guys" — but who were "the Good" and who "the Bad"? For as soon as we ponder the goodness and evil of the situation, we are obliged to shed some light on the latter, while withholding the shadows of the former.

This is the great virtue of *Yankee Invasion*. Solares plays with lights and shadows, effects and defects. He does so through a remarkable narrative structure. The narrator, Abelardo, is telling the story that he lived as a young man several decades later, when he is old, sick, cared for by his wife and his doctors but lucid in his memory of the dramatic days of his city: Mexico City, occupied by the forces of General Winfield Scott, the stars and stripes flying over the National Palace, and the contradictions that Solares does not shy away from. The American army brings a semblance of order to the defeated city.

Yet the defeated people themselves will not stay put. A famous contemporary print shows the Zócalo, Mexico City's central square, occupied by the United States Army, and the North American soldiers being harassed by an unforgiving population. Stones are about to be thrown and, sooner rather than later, the Americans understand that they cannot control a city as populous as Mexico City and a country with such a strong sense of identity, language, religion, sex, and cuisine, even if its politics are a sham, a rickety post-colonial structure that only a new revolution will fortify.

Thus it was. The United States left Mexico south of the Rio Grande to its own devices and took over the vast Southwest from Texas to California. And Mexico, chastened, fought its own civil war between liberals and conservatives. The latter lost: they betrayed the country by asking for foreign armed intervention, from Napoleon III of France. The liberals won. Led by Benito Juárez, they re-founded the Republic and let us find our own way.

Written from the precarious vantage point of the future immediate to the novel, yet written by Ignacio Solares, an author contemporaneous to ourselves, *Yankee Invasion* proffers a tacit invitation to see and be seen as subjects of history passing through the sieve of fiction. Solares thus gives us a very rich tale of history relived, the past as present, and the wholeness of experience as an act of the imagination directed not only at the past, but also at the future of the final warrior, the reader.

In founding the novel, Cervantes granted it the magnitude to be the genre of genres. Quixote and Sancho: the epic and the picaresque shake hands. Moorish novel: the Captive and Zoraida. A love story: Chrystostom and Marcela and, above all, Don Quixote's chivalric love for Dulcinea. The historical chronicle: the specter of Lepanto, the naval battle in Barcelona, captivity in Algiers. The social novel, from the lowest classes to the highest. The comic novel, the carnivalesque masquerade: Maritornes, the Doleful Duenna, Samson Carrasco. Novel of novels: the inserted tales of "ill-advised curiosity" and the wedding celebrations of Camacho.

What Milan Kundera calls "Cervantes's depreciated legacy" was starved to the point of anorexia by a demand for purity badly at odds with the genre's radical impurity. Henry James called the novel "a baggy monster" (himself, nonetheless, an author of extensive, bulky works), and a genre of extreme formal conclusions: in *Aspects of the Novel*, E. M. Forster put the canon of the novel on a strict diet, with no other resources than linear narration, clear argument, and coherent characters. From Joyce to the present moment—Gordimer, García Márquez, Goytisolo, Grass, Kundera himself—the modern novel has imposed upon itself the task of recovering Cervantes's lesson, giving back to the novel that characteristic which distinguishes it from all others: to be the genre of genres.

I make theses statements in order to approach more closely a Mexican book which incurs heresies against the Immaculate Conception, restoring a wide generic embrace to the novel. Fiction, history, memorial, politics, sociology, psychology, popular song, symphonic harmonization, and above (or below) all, poetry, in the primary sense of a union of contraries and a link between all things. The book I mean is *Tres lindas cubanas* (Three Lovely Cubans) by Gonzalo Celorio.

Celorio treads the nervous territories of family biography told through personal biography. In place of *ello* ("it") he uses a narrative *tú* (the familiar "you") written by *él* ("he") but which aspires to be *nosotros* ("we"). A similar plurality permits the writer two things: to give his family history a second-person distance while also granting it the imagination—which is not a lie—that permits him to invent what he did not live or did not know about his own ancestors.

Celorio also empowers the tension between the narrator's *tú* and the narrated *nosotros*, extending the relationship of the pronouns to an extraordinary discourse with another country—Cuba—which the Mexican Celorio feels to be *suyo* ("his") through love, blood, and words.

For example: did Celorio's father invent the "clip" whose registered trademark was stolen from him by some unscrupulous character? Who knows? Could the author's mother really carry out as many household chores as her son attributes to her on the unforgettable pages 126-127 in the Tusquets edition (Barcelona, 2006)? Possibly. What is certain is that his father and mother lived a life of "long-lasting, respectful, caring, and fruitful love." A migrant, biblical marriage: twelve children and six cities in twenty-eight years, twenty-two houses, three countries, and one constant: the matriarchy. But at a price: oblivion. We forget family chronology, customs, and the houses themselves. We try to recover the happiness that the family gave

us, but only if we don't forget the accidents and misfortunes that be-
fall every family.

There are tantrums. There is blackmail. There is misconduct.
There are scandals. There are unwelcome promiscuities. And there are
the separations imposed (or chosen) over time. An aunt from post-
revolutionary Havana departs for Miami, and dies alone in a con-
valescent home, unprotected by her own relatives who urged her to
leave the island. Another remains in Cuba, believes in the Revolution, but ends up losing, as in Cortázar's story "House Taken Over,"
the spaces which she must share with homeless strangers and their
relatives, a degradation of the traditional custom of a mother sharing
her house with her growing family under the maternal desire of having all her chickens in the same henhouse. Families, Celorio tells us,
impose values they do not always observe. Political powers, as well. If
Palou's nostalgia comes from the death of heroes, Celorio's is owing
to the extinction of the family and the consequential question: without a family, where do I find my roots, where my roof? This question, simultaneously anguished and lucid, runs throughout Celorio's
novel. The author is Mexican, by blood, speech, and culture. But in
reading his book, we notice that half of his blood, speech, and culture belong to Cuba, the homeland of Celorio's mother. There are af-
ternoons in which Celorio feels Cuban, that he could have been born
in Cuba, that he recognizes himself in "the eyes of Cubans, in their
gestures, in their words." And it is precisely this profound identification which permits him, at the same time, to be critical of the Cuban
Revolution with its sympathizers and critical of the critics of the very
same Revolution.

More than simply a contradiction, Celorio's attitude leads to a
certainty: writing does not resolve the conflict which motivates it. Because, is this not the very conflict of the Cuban population, debated
"as one single organism, between political compromise and individual liberty, between revolutionary orthodoxy and the heterodox
modalities of patriotism, between insularity and the call to be international?"

It is not strange that Gonzalo Celorio transcends conflict, without ever forgetting it, in what frames his own personality: the excellence of Cuban literature, domestic and abroad, from yesterday and
today. Here we read of Celorio's exciting relationship with the island's

living writers, a relationship which is a bet against the future. But we also see the presence of the past through two great evocations: José Lezama Lima and Dulce María Loynaz.

Celorio did not know Lezama, the devoted patron of open-air cafes and supremely loyal denizen of a library which covered the narrow walls of 122 Trocadero Street, obliging its corpulent owner to traverse the house sideways. By contrast, in Dulce María, Celorio finds an almost erotic relationship with the old woman, one which I fully share like a sin named *Aura*. And not because the aged woman is more vulnerable. The opposite is true. There are women to whom the years give a secret power and a weary attraction. The autobiography of Dulce María Loynaz permits Gonzalo Celorio to culminate his own history with the author's lesson: to say what you wish about yourself while hiding what you do not wish to be known.

19. Nélida Piñon in the Republic of Dreams

The planet, wrote Alfonso Reyes, had to give its all, rack its brains, be squeezed like an orange and wrung out like a sponge to create Brazil, a country that, contrary to what is commonly thought, was not invented at the beginning of the world, but a little bit later, and has been, ever since, an immense crucible in which the nation itself "is being forged."

At Mexico's most important publishing house, the Fondo de Cultura Económica or FCE, Pedro Henríquez Ureña created the Biblioteca Americana which introduced the Spanish language reading public to the enticing richness of Brazilian literature. Publications included José de Aléncar's *O Sertanejo*, Graça Aranha's *Canaan*, and the nineteenth century masterpiece of the Latin American novel, *The Posthumous Memoirs of Bras Cubas* by Machado de Assis, which I have previously discussed. These were followed by *The Devil to Pay in the Backlands* by João Guimarães Rosa, the greatest Brazilian novelist after Machado, not to mention Jorge Amado, Clarice Lispector, and Rubem Fonseca. But I include Nélida Piñon in this book because she is related more than any other Brazilian writer—she is of Galician origin—to the Latin American literary universe.

Juan Rulfo wrote the unsurpassed, and perhaps unsurpassable, Mexican novel: *Pedro Páramo*, a perfect work of self-contemplation which stands out like a stark black tree, its branches bare but for two shining fruits. The first is a golden sphere, the ultimate confluence of all the currents of previous Latin American fiction, a final recognition of our forebears and of ourselves. As in Mallarmé's great poem "The Tomb of Edgar Allan Poe," the subject is transformed forever by eternity into its true self. But eternity, wrote William Blake, is in love with the works of time, and the other fruit of Rulfo's tree is a silver prism which reflects the inseparable, mutated forms of tradition and creation, the mirrors of the encircling world, and the opening of the works of time passed on to the imagination of the time to come.

There are writers like Juan Rulfo, whose perfection is not a sign of finality, but rather of reinitiation. These writers bequeath to us universes that can be recreated and extended, inventing complete—though limitless—narrative regions: Rulfo's is called Comala: García Márquez's is Macondo; Onetti's is Santa María; Faulkner's is Yoknapatawpha; Cervantes's, at the beginning of all things, is La Mancha.

Nélida Piñon is a pilgrim, wise and smiling, though desperate, in search of another region, hers and everyone's, which she has baptized with a name that describes all the novels written in Ibero-America: *The Republic of Dreams*. Territory explored, plowed, and penetrated, jungle, ocean, and mineshaft, through a writing that ardently desires to find a territory which might be hers and ours, Iberian, Brazilian, Mexican, Portuguese, Spanish, Argentine, Chilean, Caribbean, Atlantic, mocking the Alexandrine bulls of Pope Borgia but unveiling Papa Borges's mirrors of Babel.

There is no sadder event, none less justifiable, in Latin America, than the persistence of a rigid Alexandrine demarcation between the two Ibero-Americas, between the Spanish speaking world and the world of Portuguese. By not knowing one another, Brazil and Spanish America each reduce the other. We are two sides of the same coin, head and tail, and to split that coin is to end up with only half of our being. Nélida Piñon seeks to repair that sad and unnecessary divorce. The writer's family origin is peninsular, Spanish and Galician; her individual destiny is American, Portuguese, and Brazilian, and in *The Republic of Dreams* the great writer weaves a bridge of ivy and mist, makes a journey of sails and orchids along the coasts of Galicia and Brazil, ironically inverting the usual terms of the European-American relationship.

If, as Edmundo O'Gorman said, the New World was invented by the imagination of the Old World, and that invention was a space for the Golden Age which Renaissance, mercantilist, absolutist, and religiously intolerant Europe needed, Nélida Piñon now converts Europe into a mythic age, gilded by the nostalgia of an American world despoiled of legendary justifications but not of human hopes. Nélida transforms Europe into the Golden Age of America, and America into the land of the quotidian, a land of work, struggle, and survival. The writer refuses to let the Old World evade its responsibilities, and prohibits the Europeans from inventing a New American World only to deposit its own sins into it, magnified. Nélida Piñon's republic of American dreams makes a gift of myths to the Europeans and forces us, the Americans, to live in the reality that we have made, thanks to, in spite of, with or without Europe. It does not matter, now that there is, since always and for ever, a New World culture, created by the arms and heads of Europeans, Africans, blacks, indigenous peoples and, above all, mestizos and mulattoes. Are these the signs of the future? Do we have the right, then, to our own dreams? As a novelist, Nélida roots us in the solid earth and tangible life of Brazil only in order to tell us that reality also includes dreams, because the dreams of the New World have failed. We have not reached the heights of our dreams. Only a new imagination, constant, interminable, always unfinished, can achieve them. Nélida has chosen the form of the novel in order to found the republic of our dreams, unfulfilled but unrenounceable, born from illusions lost and loves gained.

"I can understand God," says the writer, "with men it's more difficult." But Nélida Piñon's magic consists of allying imagination with compassion in order to give her characters, her writing, and her readers, "a skin the same temperature as her own." In her delightful novel, *Caetana's Sweet Song*, the male protagonist commits every folly in the world in order to reach his beloved Caetana, the erotic republic of his dreams. His dream fails, he never reaches Caetana, but he obtains something better, which is the company of the woman who followed him, understood him, and from imitating the man's desire so much, ended up becoming the desired woman.

Nélida Piñon's prodigious adventures occupy a moral climate imbued with the heat of carnal desire. For Nélida Piñon, a novel happens thanks to language, and language is an ethical phenomenon because it is a shared, social phenomenon upon which the novelist can confer all the folds and shadings, all the rhythms and colors, of his individual invention, but which will, in the end, return to the fountain from which it flowed—the collective life, the life of culture, the shared life—and thus enrich it.

Piñon seems to laugh and ask us if we have thought about what it means to carry inside ourselves the cadaver of a dead language, to drag along, on and on, the mortal remains of an unburied language? However, she also points out to us that we, these bearers of languages, are ungoverned creatures, and we have just emerged from the cavern; we are beings who have still not learned to explain all our feelings. Nélida Piñon's genius consists in conferring an errant, unburied language onto a race which emerges, blinded, from the caves, and demands of itself to explain itself, to give meaning to its voice, to its sensual attraction, to its civilized foundation, to its social composition, to its aesthetic liberty. One of Nélida's beautiful books is rightfully entitled *Fundador* (Founders). In it, a Brazilian cartographer, a true Zelig of the tropics, assumes all the forms, names, garments, and temperatures at hand to give form, virtue, and voice to a world, his world, his Brazil.

Rightly, too, Nélida Piñon has been an indispensable political figure in her land, as vice-president of the Brazilian Writers' Union during moments of authoritarian repression, when writers were persecuted, when the voice of Nélida rose up firm against censorship, but when, simultaneously, her imagination rose up with an even more powerful flight to write another great book, *Tebas do meu coração* (Thebes of My Heart), in which the writer identifies the fight against dictatorship, not so much as a struggle against oppression as one against fatality, routine, lack of imagination, ignorance, and the uncontrolled designation of things. To that end, she builds a boat to row on the land. A boat to row on the land: Nélida Piñon completes the circle of the Cervantean imagination. Her earthly boat is the wooden sister of Don Quixote's carpenter's horse, his *Clavileño* [15] Where does she row that boat? Where does that Pegasus fly? Through the lands of La Mancha, impure lands, infected by all the dreams and hopes from here and there, from Iberia and from America.

---

15 *Clavileño*: literally "nail the wood."

20. Juan Goytisolo: Persona Grata

When, in 1969, I published *La nueva novela hispanoamericana* (The New Latin American Novel), I included Juan Goytisolo in the list of authors discussed. The reproaches were not long in coming: what was a *"gachupín"*—a Spaniard—doing among our pure-blooded Latin American writers like Cortázar, García Márquez, Carpentier, and Vargas Llosa?

Well, he was doing two things: first, reminding us that we were neither pure-blooded nor, far less, pure, but rather fraternal and recognizable—Spanish and Spanish-American—in our impurity: impurity of language, impurity of blood, impurity of destiny. In *Marks of Identity*, and *Count Julian*, Goytisolo was already pointing out that Spain was not Spain without the Jewish and Muslim cultures that shaped language and history at the court of Alfonso the Wise, in the *Book of Good Love* by Juan Ruiz, the Archpriest of Hita, and in *La Celestina* by Fernando de Rojas. The expulsion of the Hebrew and Arabic cultures not only mutilated Spain but impoverished its colonies. It established a politics of exclusion and, even, the persecution of the other, of those who are different. As the great contemporary Spanish philosopher Emilio Lledó says so well, the lamentable trick belonging to the worst aspects of nationalism is the invention of the other as evil and inferior, so that we might not have to perceive our own misery.

The second thing (as the Archpriest of Hita would say) was to give us back a living language, experimental by necessity, by virtue uncertain, which in Spain stood opposed to the sum of complacencies of the fascist era: complacency with the landscape, with nostalgia, with folklore, with insularity, with populist romanticism, and with the supposed Spanish essence: nobility, honor, the sacred flame, and stubborn, surly realism—jealously reclaimed by inert tradition.

But was this not our problem, too? We Latin American writers had long been subjected to the traditions of property, of good taste and middling tone, of servile realism, of humble writing about local customs and manners, and the rejection of the supposedly black, mestizo, indigenous, and even Hispanic, barbarism in order to be, as soon as possible, Europeans, North Americans, civilized and universal.

No one arrives alone to literature. In Latin America, modern poetry, from Lugones and Huidobro to Neruda and Vallejo, opened the way to so many of our progenitors in the novel—Alejo Carpentier, Jorge Luis Borges, Miguel Ángel Asturias, Felisberto Hernández, Juan Carlos Onetti, Juan Rulfo—as in Spain, Valle Inclán and Cernuda opened the way for Goytisolo, and he for Valente, Sánchez Ferlosio, and Luis Martín Santos, all of them confirming that there is no creation that is not built on tradition, while tradition, in turn, demands new creation in order to stay alive. A whole past makes itself present in Goytisolo's novels, and in that rich heritage left behind by Ibn-Zaydún of Córdoba, the Archpriest of Hita, and *La Celestina*, Cervantes and Góngora, Francisco Delicado and María de Zayas. Goytisolo reminds us—we Spanish language writers in America— that we spring from a common trunk and that our branches, and sometimes our flowers, all belong to the same tree of literature. Old tree, strong tree. Because to the demands of times gone by—new language, old cultures—came to be added, in our times, a greater challenge. The recognition of the other. The embrace of him or her that is not like you or I.

In *Landscapes After the Battle*, Juan Goytisolo's extraordinary literary evolution, so rooted in what is best about Hispanic and Latin American culture, expands even more, to include the encounter with the other, that universal other, which is today the migrant worker, the living and uncomfortable accusation of a global order which consecrates the liberty of things but refuses the liberty of people; merchandise moves freely, without restraint, while workers are prohibited, pursued, harassed, humiliated, persecuted, and murdered. But without them, the great modern consumer societies would have no fruit, vegetables, transportation, hospitals, restaurants, nannies, or gardens. What they would have, as John Kenneth Galbraith has indicated regarding Mexican emigration into the U.S.A., is inflation, food scarcity, poor services, and very high prices. The migrant worker serves both the country he departs from and the one he arrives in. Only the laziest and stupidest of prejudices can consider them to be an economic burden or a racial infection.

In Goytisolo's work, the encounter with the other results from the narrated verbality. In *Landscapes After the Battle* technique and content are associated with one another because the authorial I, which is the character I, are united (merging into and supporting one another) in the narrator, who is the author-and-characters. Goytisolo obtains this polyphonic result through the crossing of pronouns, the crossing of verbal times, and the crossing of cultures. The mixture of form merges with that of the content. For Goytisolo, to mix is to Cervanticize, and to Cervanticize is to Islamicize and Judaize. It is to embrace anew what has been expelled and persecuted. It is to find anew the vocation of the inclusion and to transcend the malefic of exclusion.

Landscape is not lacking in humor: Africa begins on the boulevards of Paris and Goytisolo's comic urban hero detests the smell of vinegar. Why does he always end up in a cinema sitting next to someone who smells like vinegar? If he is a modern urban man, why doesn't he know how to change an automobile tire or properly slice a steak? Why, if he reads *Hola* magazine doesn't he know about the secret romance between Julio Iglesias and Margaret Thatcher?

The smile freezes on our lips when Juan Goytisolo, a writer of gravity and humor, a swift bird soaring on the wings of the mystical Arab poet Ibn Al-Farid and the Castilian Juan de la Cruz, is shot down by the hunters who defend sexual, racial, religious, and political intolerance. In 2000, he was in Sarajevo, defending the integrity of multicultural life against intolerance and ethnic cleansing. In his own Spain, however, he could not even go, with Sami Nair, to the launch of their book *El peaje de la vida* (The Tollbooth of Life) in the Andalusian town of El Ejido, where Maghreb immigrants have experienced the most brutal aggression. Goytisolo has been so vociferous in his denunciation of this violence that the local authorities have declared him *persona non grata*. The Don Quixote Prize awarded to Goytisolo in 2010 repaired—slightly—the inexcusable exclusion he experienced in his homeland.

Goytisolidarity, Goytisolitary. What can save Juan Goytisolo from tragedy? Since I first met him, in 1960, in the grand precincts of the Gallimard publishing house in Paris, I was surprised and subdued by the profundity of his gaze, his enormous hooded eyes which are blue but refuse to admit it: too many waves of pain, nostalgia, and melancholy cross them; dark clouds of holy rage, but also lightning flashes of humor. Perhaps it is that humor which preserves him from desperation. Goytisolo's eyes are movie screens, flashing images of our time: the Spanish Civil War, a mother killed in a bombing raid, the people's suffocation under Franco, the ragged exiles and migrations from the towns, neofascist threats and communist disillusions; the whole half century of our moral, political, and intellectual life, culminating in the Sacrifice of Sarajevo, the true end of the very brief twentieth century, which began in 1914, also in the martyred capital of Bosnia-Herzegovina. The generous illusions shared by Goytisolo and his generation overfly these terrible events. Illusions dispelled, however, Goytisolo became neither a renegade nor a reactionary of the opposite side. A reckless but lucid sailor of the great tide of our time—the coming and going of cultures, the movement of peoples, the contagion of languages, migration as the password of any new or possible humanism—Goytisolo no longer celebrates victories: he warns of new dangers, he remembers persistent problems which no capitalist triumphalism can sweep away. My wife Silvia says: "He always seems to be on the verge of departing." Departing or arriving, Goytisolo carries in his eyes the sum of the world's unresolved injustices and does not bow to the hymns of any group. He is a fleeting denizen of airports, but only so as to be a man rooted in his Paris of migrant neighborhoods, in his Barcelona of inescapable memories, in his Marrakech of fraternal souks. He is guilty, everywhere, of *lese-optimism*. But everywhere, he is also accused of that form of optimism which is the irreverent laugh, corrosive humor, the glove turned inside-out, the pyramid stood on its point. Orphan errant of Quevedo, Goytisolo's protagonist in *Marks of Identity* uses the most purely canonical books to trap and smash cockroaches between their pages.

Stepson of the Archpriest Juan Ruiz, in *Count Julian* the big bad wolf is an Arab fully prepared to rape Little White Riding Hood, chaste and pure. Rebel twin of Saint John of the Cross, in *Virtues of the Solitary Bird* he sets Arab and Christian texts, both sacred and profane, to fornicate amongst themselves. Tender and tenacious inhabitant of the Parisian Rue Sentier along with his extraordinary companion, Monique Lange, he traces some *Landscapes After the Battle* in which Africa begins, not in the Spanish Pyrenees, as some French perspectives might contend, but on the Parisian boulevards. But even the sensational, undesirable headlines make it there, the informative globalization which reveals to us the secret romance of Julio Iglesias and Margaret Thatcher. Will our only right to immortality be to appear photographed in *Hola* magazine? Goytisolo's humor is a mixture, a humor of contacts and contagion, of tradition as well as creation, both contaminated from the start, neither chaste nor pure. Against the happy robot of Postmodernity's mask of universal cheer, Goytisolo opposes, replaces, and superimposes the skin of cultures and their bright variety of colors. Like no one else, he does it in Spanish because our language is the one most impure, most mixed, least rooted and traditional in the world. To write in Spanish is to Cervanticize and to Cervanticize is to Islamicize and to Judaize. Today, it is also to Mexicanize, Chicanize, Cubanize, Puerto Ricanize, to insert the "Chile" pepper; to Argentinize, that is, to speak in *Plata*, the silver of the River Plate, el Río de la Plata. This is Goytisolo's invisible baggage, the paradox of nomadic rootedness; no wonder he was a very close friend of Jean Genet, another traveler without baggage whose coffin was confused with that of a migrant Moroccan worker.

Juan Goytisolo broke the narrow canons of Spanish narrative realism. His question, from *Count Julian* and *Marks of Identity*, is our own: Does an external, extra-subjective world whose objective facticity is more than enough for itself even need literature? Or stated in another way, what does literature give to the world? What does literature add to make itself indispensable in the world? Well, nothing more and nothing less than the reality that the world needed. Because if the world makes us, we also make the world. And a way of making the world is to create a verbalization of our surroundings, without which the very substance of literature—language and imagination—can be taken away from us, deformed, and manipulated. Which is to say: the fields of Castile have always existed. But on the day when Don Quixote de la Mancha galloped over them, lance in hand, a barber's basin on his head in place of a knight's helmet, Spain and the world could no longer be conceived without the imagination and language of Cervantes.

Among all the arts, literature is the most challenging because its material is the most current and popular of all: language, which belongs to everyone or no one. To convert the copper of language into the gold of literature requires an imaginative communion. Imagination assures the alchemy of the word, and imagination is nothing more than the mediation between physical sensation and mental perception.

Juan Goytisolo writes about Scheherazade, the mother of all narration, the midwife of imagination and language, the woman who saved her life by telling a story each night to the misogynist caliph in

order to postpone the destiny which, without the story, would condemn her to death the next morning. Jorge Semprún entitled his
memoir *Literature or Life*. Such is the name of all narratives from the
children of Scheherazade: to trade life for writing and writing in exchange for life. But with one condition: that the story never end.
Such is the secret of both Scheherazade and of literature itself. Never assume that the story is finished. Hand over to the reader the obligation and privilege of being the next narrator. Scheherazade. *The
Thousand and One Nights*. The story has not ended. Apart from the
intrinsic beauty of the great book of literary miscegenation—a work
that is Indo-Iranian, Arabic-Abyssinian, Arabic-Egyptian and, in the
end, Arabic-European—this is the contemporary message of Scheherazade's novel: the story has not ended. As the Spanish historian
Carmen Iglesias reminds us, whoever tells us differently, i.e. some
theory deviously interested in the end of the story—merely wants to
sell another story. Not our own. Theirs.

At the Madrid launch for Goytisolo's book *Telón de Boca* (The
Drop Curtain), the philosopher Emilio Lledó ventured to say that
this is a book—although the statement could be applied to Goytisolo's entire oeuvre—which vindicates liberty, equality, and love
against war, against oblivion, against ignorance, against malice,
against the mutilation and death of innocent lives. To Lledó's words
must be added those of Goytisolo himself, in opposition to another
abominable theory: Samuel Harrington's idea about the clash of civilizations. Goytisolo speaks for migrant Muslim workers in Europe as
we speak for migrant Mexican workers in the U.S.A., not as a threat
against racial purity and national unity which Harrington insidious-
ly suspects, but rather as subjects—I here cite Goytisolo—with "the
same rights enjoyed by European citizens."

Immigrants—Arabs in Europe, Mexicans in North America—
take nothing away from anyone: they give more than they receive. They
give their labor. And they give their culture to the only human civilization possible: that of the miscegenation which created Indo-Afro-Eu-
ropean America and Celtiberian, Phoenician, Greek, Roman, Arabic,
and Jewish Spain. This remains the unfinished tale of Scheherazade,
the nocturnal fable spinner: it is the tale of the encounter and mutual enrichment between cultures. It is the tale of inclusion and the
opposition to exclusion. It is the tale of the right to imagine, in op-

position to the prison of dogmas disguised as irrefutable truths. Scheherazade's story has not ended. It will be reborn each day under the light of works unfinished, liberties to conquer, and cultures to preserve and invigorate.

21. First Mexican Finale: Queens Quintile

I saw her for the first time costumed as a kitten at a dance in the Jockey Club in Mexico City. All white, blonde as she is, with a mask and sparkling jewels, she seemed like one of Jean Cocteau's gentle, lovely dreams. Like every good little kitten, she had whiskers that stuck out from her mask. But on her, the obligatory cat fur was not, like Frida Kahlo's wild mustache, a sign of aggression but rather an insinuation. With various antennae already pointing in multiple directions, it was an insinuation to the varied dimensions of a work that encompasses the short story, novel, chronicle, news report, and memory. Many years ago, we both made our publishing debut at the same time; mine with a book of stories, *The Masked Days*, hers the unique exercise in childhood innocence, *Lilus Kikus*. The irony and perversity of this, her first text, were not immediately perceived. Like one of those recurrent little girls of Balthus, like a Shirley Temple without the ringlets, Elena finally showed herself to be like an Alice in Testamentland Without ever abandoning her game of feigning astonishment in the face of an eccentricity that believes itself to be logical, or logic that believes itself eccentric, Elena gained gravity alongside grace. Her portraits of women famous and infamous, anonymous and celebrated, created a great biographical gallery of the feminine being in Mexico.

Elena has contributed, like other few writers, to give women a central, but not sacramental, role in our society. She has not excluded us men from loving and accompanying, and from being loved by and supported by women. But no one can obscure the fact that Elena Poniatowska has contributed in a powerful way to give women a unique place, showing the disadvantages, prejudices, and exclusions which surround them in our world still filled with machismo but which is every day more human. Not only feminist but human, inclusive. "Foolish men who accuse woman without reason": the motto of Sor Juana Inés de la Cruz is not only an echo in Sor Elena de la Cruz-y-Ficción. It is an embrace, a kind of inclusive compassion, "Foolish men, join my work, my struggle, my own foolishness." *Massacre in*

Mexico is her great, definitive chronicle of the cloudy twilight of the crime that also marked the sunset of the PRI's authoritarian regime in Mexico. From that terrible night of October 2, 1968 dates, perhaps, the transformation of the Princess Poniatowska—descendant of María Leszcynska, the second wife of Louis XV of France, of King Stanislaus I of Poland, and of Napoleon's heroic Marshall, Josef Poniatowski—into a tranquil, smiling passion flower for leftist causes. I do not always agree with her judgement. I always admire her conviction and her bravery. Fortunately, Mexican democracy today consists of legal agreements and disagreements, respectable and respected. The important thing about Elena is that her public positions neither diminish nor supplant her devotions at home: her love for her children, her loyalty to her friends, her dedication to her writing.

This study includes my reading of some biographies which turn fiction into journalism and journalism into biography. As I've been a friend of Elena for more years than I care, or am able, to recall, she seems to me now just as youthful as in our earliest years, as if she had the power to make and unmake genres, liberating herself (and liberating us) from generic narrowness. Where in *Here's To You, Jesusa!* does the journalism end and the fiction begin? Where does the fiction end and the biography begin in *Tinísima?*

Elena is a kind of new journalism unto herself, although she is also a new biographer and a new novelist. The French word for what we call a "novel" is *roman*. The Italians use the name *novela* for a brief work of prose, in contrast to the more extensive *romanzo*. Generic definitions do not suffice, however, to obscure the common ground between *roman, novela,* and *nouvelle,* on the one hand, and biography and journalism on the other. This point of encounter is the literary space—which is a way of being in the world. Thus the rigid formalities dissolve and we return to the modern Cervantean origin of narration: epic and picaresque, urban and bucolic, narration within narration, essay and poem, news and criticism.

DIAMONDS

Margo Glantz has many sides. She is a knowledgable critic of writers like Sor Juana de la Cruz and Bernal Díaz del Castillo. She is the tacit representative of an infrequently observed Latin American world: that of the Russian and Central European Jews exiled by the Nazi and Stalinist dictatorships, Ashkenazi Jews who came to Latin America seeking to be reunited with one another (let us here recall Spain's Sephardic legacy), a fact which also situates us in the conflagration of racist intolerance which led, in part, to the Second World War. We tend to overlook two crucial historical truths: the Sephardic Jews created the culture of professional work in Spain before 1492 and thus left us the language of the common people—Castilian— in place of the language of the elite — Latin. But in the aftermath of the Sephardic expulsion in 1492, Spain was slow to readopt the rules of work established by the Jews in Spain. For its part, the Ashkenazi migration brought the world of Central Europe to Mexico and Latin America. Both traditions, Sephardic and Ashkenazi, formed a receptive Latin American tradition. *The Family Tree* is Glantz's account of her own Jewish family experience.

In *The Wake*, Glantz follows the life of Nora García as if it were a psychoanalytic case study, in order to understand how a woman walks through life, in spite of how much she is beset by attempts to direct her steps. Glantz shows how Nora walks in designer shoes, revealing the author's obsession, not only with shoes but also with walking, of going from one place to another, with emigrating. There is, perhaps, a tacit emigrant in Glantz, a woman who must move from place to place, and for that she needs shoes.

Only that Glantz needs shoes to write, to move from syllable to syllable, from word to word, from page to page. These *migratory* books of Margo Glantz move from childhood to maturity, from the individual to society, from the family to the world. What is there behind these stories of human movement? In the first place, a testimony at once mythic, moral, and commercial. In order to walk one needs shoes, Adam and Eve went barefoot: there are no shoe stores in paradise. Expelled from the Garden of Eden they require footwear because now they know that "they were naked" (Genesis 3).

Glantz does something noteworthy: she puts on shoes to write, challenging the scriptures, saying that the earth will endure longer than heaven, if we have the courage to write it. Only then Glantz, as a Jewish girl, laughs at herself and the world and, before lying to the Catholic priest who hears her confession, writes: "I have fornicated." Then the novelist's world is filled with innocent apparitions—tamales, chocolate, nougat candy—and frightening specters—martyrs, witches, flagellants—to form a world of obsessive fictions redeemed by a smile.

CLUBS

When I began to write, in the 1950s, I had the impression that in Mexico and Latin America we lived under the tyranny of genres, particularly in Mexico. It was supposed that a beginning novelist was going to write a novel that was easily classifiable as a novel of the country, an Indian novel, a proletariat novel, a novel of the city, or a novel of the Revolution. This tyranny sometimes stirred me to rebellion, sometimes nostalgia, because I had the impression that the novel's modernity as established by Cervantes signified—for starters, immediately—a rupture, confusion, and the use of genres that would convert the novel into the genre of genres. The result was that this tyranny moved many of us, in Mexico and throughout Latin America, to try to escape from its pigeonholes and break the genres, and to aspire a little to that novelistic polyphony of which Hermann Broch speaks. Which is to say, the novel as a meeting of genres, which makes room for politics, science, cinematography, music, journalism. What remains, however, to unify? Once we have established that right to revolt against genre, what remains as the novel's possible unifying force? Georg Lukács tells us that it is the idea of displacement. All novels, regardless of theme or form, imply a displacement. In what sense? Not only in the sense of travel and movement, although it is notable that the first epics of classical antiquity include a trip away from home, the voyage to Troy, and a return trip, Odysseus's voyage home to Ithaca. The modern novel begins with Don Quixote's displacement, his movement beyond the idea of certainty, to the wide fields of uncertainty. And *Ulysses*, the modern novel par excellence, is nothing more than a displacement that unfolds during twenty-four hours, and throughout a city: Dublin. That's why Margo Glantz needs shoes: seven-league boots.

In *Vida con mi amigo* (Life with My Friend), Bárbara Jacobs invites us to all these displacements and some more. It is a displacement but through a conversation that is both warm and lucid at the same time. The displacement through space can occur, as I have just said, from Troy to Ithaca. It can be as vast as the territory of a nation. The North American novel consists of a constant displacement and movement westward, toward the Pacific. And there it stops. The Russian novel implies a displacement toward the East, which passes, at times unhappily, through Siberia. Virginia Woolf moves through space to the lighthouse and Thomas Mann towards the magic mountain, and Xavier de Maistre invites us to take a turn around his room. The displacement can occur in time, through the form of the historical novel, *War and Peace*; through a narration that creates its own history, as in the novels of William Faulkner. As a creation of its own novelistic time: the great example of Laurence Sterne's *Tristram Shandy*, which is, for Bárbara Jacobs, one of the most important novels of all. Finally, Proust's novel, *Remembrance of Things Past*. In Latin America, displacement has had particular significance in virtue of the immensity of our space. Following the epic of the discovery and conquest, we have struggled with space just as Jacob wrestled with the angel in Genesis. Bernal Díaz's chronicle of the Conquest is also, we recall, a search for lost time. In it, a blind man more than eighty years old, and from his place of exile in Guatemala, meticulously remembers, if it can be called such, the epic achievement of the Conquest of Mexico in all its detail of steeds, chargers, armor, and warriors. From the possibility of simply being devoured by space through displacement, which is the great drama of Rivera's *The Vortex* ("they were swallowed up by the jungle"), we move to a kind of marvelous equilibrium between time and space, which is what Gabriel García Márquez achieves in *One Hundred Years of Solitude*. But all these displacements, physical or imaginary, which I am considering, find a revelation, a modern compensation, in psychological displacement, as described by Freud. Displacement as substitution or as an exchange of the object of desire, displacement as sublimation, displacement as compromise of memory, displacement as the transfer of the sexual object to the social object, displacement as dream, as the function of the dream. The oneiric displacement, Freud tells us, in order to make what is characteristically sexual unrecognizable. All these forms of displacement are, tacitly or expressly, contained in Bárbara Jacobs's book, *Vida con mi amigo*. But although it contains all these levels of literary displacement, Jacobs's book is, first and foremost, a displacement in order to make recognizable the object of desire. Bárbara Jacobs moves, meaning that she writes to create recognition for both the figure of the book and the beloved; in her book they become synonymous. In the book's introduction she tells us:

> Throughout the years when I was writing *Vida con mi amigo*, I wondered what final form I might give it, whether a tale, which opens so many doors, or short essays, which tend to close them. As luck would have it, one day, through half-closed eyes, I saw that *Vida con mi amigo* had tone and form. But this displacement, this rupture of the genre, immediately inspired the need for some relocation in the form of a road trip. One rainy afternoon, equipped with some bottles of red wine, a blanket, and a series of books headed by Laurence Sterne, my friend and I took to the highway, setting out on our own sentimental journey. Not all trips are rambling, as are many conversations, but they share the fact that the denouement is unknown; one departs but does not know if they are going to arrive, nor to where, when, or how. For that reason, Dr. Samuel Johnson called one of his series of commentaries The Rambler, which is a vagabond, a wayfarer, and also a discursive talker. The opportunity par excellence which a travel book offers, my friend tells me, is that of rambling. Without a very refined sense of the essay, an author would spoil a travel book. All reading is a journey even if it is not about traveling. This book affirms, that writing is identical to a trip. It is a book of intelligent, but especially, amorous reading, in which to read is to imagine the beloved.

SPADES

In Carmen Boullosa's novel, *Duerme* (Sleep), the writer begins with a quote from Sor Juana Inés de la Cruz: "I thought that I was fleeing from myself, but oh, wretched me! I brought myself with me and so I brought along my own worst enemy." This quotation reminds me of one from the Italian tragedian Alfieri, in which he refers to the ingenious enemy that is one's own self, and to the concept, Hegelian, of course, of the enemy *I*. Sor Juana, Alfieri, Hegel. We are speaking of successive penetrations into alienation, an alienation which we judge to be a dimension inseparable from the modern one. Modernity is the place of alienation. But as she quotes Sor Juana, Carmen Boullosa reminds us that we have always lived separated from ourselves. She gives historical dimension to this alienation. A dimension of an alienation of roots, of birth, of origin, because the alienation in *Duerme* is, in the first place, a historical alienation. *Duerme* occurs at the dawn of the colony of Novo-Hispana, in the early days of Mexico after the conquest. It is, in fact, part of the unwritten chronicle of the Indies, that secret part not told by Bernal Díaz or Cicza de León, which belongs to the enormous *untold* and *unwritten* world of the American continent, that continent which, with an extraordinary success seemingly inconceivable to us today, the Peruvian writer Luis Alberto Sánchez once called "America, novel without novelists." Carmen Boullosa gives voice to that untold, unwritten chronicle by means of a stratagem which is nomination, the giving of names.

Alejo Carpentier told us that the American continent is a continent by baptism. All things are open to naming. From the first moment we had to know how to name this tree, that mountain, the cloud passing overhead, these clothes, this music, that face. In such a way that in order to speak of the origin of New Spain, of Mexico, Carmen Boullosa fully explores the theme of naming things, and above all, of naming people. The problem of the name lies within its very origin, as well as with literary criticism. When I consider the first work of literary criticism written in the Western world, in the ancient Mediterranean, I realize that, even before Aristotle's *Poetics*, was Plato's dialogue *Cratylus*, because in it Socrates sets forth the problem of the name, what a name means, what things we name. The debate, the dialogue which Socrates leads, consists of knowing basically if the name is intrinsic to things, if we name things because that is what things are, or if the name is simply a convention for naming things. Carmen Boullosa appropriates this radical question.

In *Duerme*, in this dawn of our country, of our civilization, of our continent, all the natives that appear are called Cosme, so that the master will not be confused. We see dialogues which proceed as follows: "My name is not Juana," to which the question is posed: "What, then, is your name?" And answered: "I'll tell you later." Or, "What is your name?" answered this way: "Guess my name, so that when you have it, I'll tell you that it's not mine." This anonymity, this ambiguity, this miscegenation and imaginative defense of integrity by pretending to have no name is a major stratagem of Boullosa's book.

Plato resolves his problem of names with a supremely Socratic conclusion: a name denies that the name be either intrinsic to things or purely conventional. A name, Socrates concludes, is simply a way of approaching the reality of things. It is nothing more than an approximation. For Carmen Boullosa, that essential approximation to understand her literary creation has, first, a historical path. It is the relationship between the Spanish and the indigenous. What we call or name the natives also signifies the act of naming, what one calls oneself, how we name ourselves, how we call them Indians and ourselves conquistadors, and how to name the community which results from the Conquest and from miscegenation. The Hispano-Indians are orphans, Carmen reminds us, they are orphans of a Spanish father and an Indian mother. To acquire a name is to stop being orphans, to stop being called Cosme in order to keep from confusing the master. It is to know the name instead of guessing it. It is to say the name right now and not just a little bit later. But this enormous awakening to a naming that is conscious, intelligent, and alert, has to pass through a historical period that can be very long, with very uncertain results, and with new surprise attacks against nominative identity, or against identity *tout court*.

For that reason Carmen Boullosa proposes another method to conquer and accelerate history, and this is the dream. To dream, in order to conquer or accelerate history. The dream as ellipsis of history. A country wakes up. It is mestizo Mexico, but only because another country, indigenous Mexico, sleeps. Carmen Boullosa, however, universalizes this indigenous dream. It is the price of not dying. It is the alternative to death. In this novel, Juliet's question, Juliet's famous question in Shakespeare: "What's in a name?" receives Hamlet's answer: "To die, to sleep—No more, and by a sleep to say we end the heartache, and the thousand natural shocks that flesh is heir to." And not only the heartaches of life, Carmen Boullosa tells us, but the heartaches of death as well. In order to avoid the Prince of Denmark's terrible fate, which is to dream and then awake in the "undiscovered country, from whose bourn no traveller returns"—death—Carmen Boullosa places sex between history and the dream. She has first introduced the dream between possible histories, she now introduces sex between history and the dream.

In mentioning Hamlet one must remember that it is a role that has sometimes been played by women. In the first cinematic version, a Danish version, it was very appropriately Asta Nielsen, the great Danish stage actress, who played Hamlet in a silent film while Sarah Bernhardt enjoyed the luxury of playing Hamlet and Ophelia on alternate nights; Hamlet one night, Ophelia the next. Here, in *Duerme*, Claire Fleury, the protagonist, dresses as a man in order to dream in a different way, in order to love in another way as well, and above all, perhaps, in order to alienate herself in another way, and to escape from the situations which threaten her.

Thus, Carmen Boullosa's novel saves itself from the danger of dreaming. Its mask is a moving light and a cascade of sand. But her dream is only a postponement of death, and the historical nightmare continues to grow around the sexual dream, the native temples fall, the Baroque cathedrals rise. Mexico wakes up because a novelist has summoned it.

QUEENS

There were times in which Ángeles Mastretta was celebrated for being a writer and for being a woman. As she is both, I feel that Mastretta today occupies her place as an author without compromising her feminine condition, but this is not what defines her work. Nothing new: three great novels of the nineteenth century, *Anna Karenina*, *Madame Bovary*, and *Effi Briest*, though written by men have, as their titles indicate, female protagonists. And although Flaubert supposedly said that "I am Madame Bovary," that only countersigns his authorial character. Thomas Hardy could as well have said "I am Tess D'Urbervilles." Just as George Eliot (who abandoned her birth name of Mary Ann Evans) could write *Adam Bede*. And Virginia Woolf, making use of a centuries-old story, could have Orlando switch from one sex to another.

Ángeles Mastretta, then, novelist before all else, woman of course, except that she is not only the author of feminist works, although they are indeed feminine. Her most famous is—and continues to be— *Tear This Heart Out* (1985), which is the story of Catalina Ascensio and her conservative upbringing in the Mexican city which is called

Puebla de Zaragoza by the liberals (in memory of the short-lived victory of the republican general Ignacio Zaragoza over Napoleon's Zouaves in 1862) and Puebla de los Ángeles by the conservatives. Catalina believes that she had found happiness at the side of a man, a soldier and politician, who rises during the Mexican Revolution. Catalina hopes for happiness only to lose it thanks to her husband's terrible corruption, and she is left wondering if she can find it alone.

Briefly stated, Mastretta's novel conceals a thousand (or one) Mexican novels: that of a country of "machos" dominated, from the start, by a woman. After the Virgin of Guadalupe, the mother is the most sacred personage in Mexican life. She is *la madre* (the mother), *la mamá* (the mom), *la mamacita* (both the mommy and the hot mama). *Mentar la madre*, meaning to "mention" someone's mother, is the supreme insult. *A toda madre*, literally "at full mother," signifies unsurpassable satisfaction. *Un desmadre* (an un-mothering) stands for excess, chaos, mayhem or a wild party. *Me vale madre* (it's worth a mother) is a way of expressing offensive indifference. But in the end, as one character asks in Fellini's film *Juliet of the Spirits*: "Who doesn't need their mother?"

It is natural, then, that this necessity, this primary and primitive passion, is the source for a whole barrage of insults and praise. What is less than *la madre*, an object of veneration, would be first, *la mujer* (the woman)—*la vieja* (the "old lady"), as used colloquially for mother in Mexico—while *la mujer* is the complete and total opposite of *la mamacita*. The woman (*la mujer*), like Catalina Ascensio, will be seduced; she will be the object of lies, deceit, injury, and every catastrophe sung in the boleros: *Pérfida* (traitress), *Canalla* (filthy slut), *Esclavo de tu amor* (slave to your love). She is the origin of *Amarga pesadumbre* (bitter nightmare), and the mistress of a *Veneno que fascina* (a fascinating poison). She sows *Odios y rencores* (Hatred and rancor). She is the gambler with the *Fichas negras* (the black chips) of perversity, the anguished pathway, the deceitful woman who "one night" stole my heart: *dile a tus ojos que no me miren, porque al mirarme me hacen sufrir* ("Tell your eyes not to stare at me, when they look at me they make me suffer").

This monstrous persona from the bolero is also the long-suffering spouse and, in the end, the little holy mother. All in one? Simultaneous, successive? Virgin or whore? Mother or lover? The history of

Mexico belies the facility of the cinema and the bolero. A woman was the greatest writer of colonial Mexico, Juana de Asbaje, Sor Juana Inés de la Cruz. Women promoted Mexican independence, Josefa Ortiz de Domínguez and Leona Vicario. Women were the protagonists celebrated in song by the Revolution: La Valentina, La Adelita. And women were an endless stream of professionals, politicians, writers, teachers, and of course, the owners of a domestic power which often, in order to be powerful, has to restrain itself.

I do not deny that machismo is a constant reference in Mexican life, constant and conspicuous: Jorge Negrete is its sovereign embodiment, Jalisco is its geographical location. Only that there is no native born Mexican *macho* who does not venerate his *mamacita* in equal measure to what he demands from his wife, who will in her turn be the *mamacita* of his children, who in their turn . . .

What Mastretta does is to show a piece of evidence and the falsity with which it is projected and which sustains it. Her question exceeds the topic of femininity to approach that of humanity. The writer asks us all, men, women: *be*, do not *pretend to be*. But never stop asking yourselves: Who are we? A question without an answer. The novel asks it, but does not answer it. Neither for women nor for men.

22. Second Mexican Finale: Three Jacks

1.

Una de dos (One of Two), by Daniel Sada, is a novel which could engage in a dialogue through a mirror with Carmen Boullosa's *Duerme*. If in *Duerme* the protagonist's two identities become one, in *Una de dos*, the same identity splits into two. Situated in a Mexico of deserts and small towns, in a Comala with neither tyrants nor televisions, Daniel Sada's novel maintains the mystery of isolation, of ancient occupations, of collective narration, a sum of stories, gossip, calumnies, and sermons. The twin protagonists, Constitución and Gloria Gamal, are saved from their sad, small town destiny, without ever departing from it, because they are two. Their duality enriches them, each one is mistress of the other, each one teaches the other, and what each one knows, the other twin, the sister, knows immediately. A nocturnal ghost, Sada tells us, takes charge of making them seem more and more alike while they sleep. At night, they are as identical as two drops of water. Their aunt encourages them to find boyfriends before it's too late, telling them: "Get married already, girls." But who or what were they going to marry if they're inseparable? Until one day, a certain Óscar steps down off one of those cramped buses crowded with travelers that Luis Buñuel depicted in his film *Mexican Bus Ride*, and falls in love with one of them. Then identity becomes a curse. The prodigious unhappiness of their inevitable likeness, says Sada, the sister, mirror, shadow, paradox or diabolical curse; this is what they turn into when one of them finds a lover. But as the two are one, they decide to share the gallant gent, who never suspects that he's dealing with two different women, but rather with one single woman, and for this reason, an ideal one. How would it be if the two of them got married to him? And if they had children, perfectly identical little children? Two wives that in reality are one? The ancient unity is touched by the devil. As Sada writes, the mirrors age in order to tarnish a bit, at the very least, the jovial specter of the future.

I will not reveal how this enigmatic Mexican novel ends, I only wish to add that the mystery of its tale is inseparable from a prose which hides and reveals at the same time, deforming it all with that

Hispanic aesthetic of which Valle Inclán spoke: the systematic deformation of all things. Daniel Sada's prose is sinuous, sinuous like
the highways of Mexico. There is, nevertheless, no other way of getting from A to Z. The sinuousness is animated by an unfailing verbal humor, always inventive, merging, hallucinatory, at times almost
a crazy marriage between Góngora and Cantinflas: "Work and more
work, everybody with their own individual belief, because even as she
was kissing her figurative boyfriend, Gloria forgot her own sister, so
that the memory of those magical moments served as a theme for her
dreams: the same was true for her sister, and Óscar, too, of course.
Whether it was eating, sleeping, or just banging away at something:
it was a lot of mental traveling." A neo-Baroque writer, Sada turns every word around, never accepting them at face value, he is suspicious
of them and puts them at the service of his theme, of hiding a twin
word, because each word hides, and twins, another word.

2.

The expression "nothing new under the sun" has an ironic application to literary creation. No, there is nothing "new." The Russian critic Vladimir Propp reduces the constant "themes" of the literary fable
to a sum of ten or twelve: running away from home, adventure in the
world, the partner and their vicissitudes, the return home (the prodigal son), etc. The result is that, if the themes are eternal, what varies
is the manner of telling them. Three great novels of the nineteenth
century—*Anna Karenina*, *Effie Briest*, and *Madame Bovary*—all deal
with the same matter, but no one would stop distinguishing them as
singular works due to their authorship, style, or intention.

Álvaro Enrigue's excellent novel *Vidas perpendiculares* (Perpendic-
ular Lives) belongs to a tradition—to many—and shows them all
off. The immediate situation hides the traditions which the author ac-
cesses. We are in Lagos de Moreno, in the state of Jalisco, where Don
Eusebio is a baker and married to Mercedes, mother of Jerónimo,
who will be the center of the story. In Lagos, people live their lives
"between Mass and the cows" with an implicit belief in "the Jaliscan
cultural hegemony." Captured in "the parameters of provincial militant Mexican Catholicism," Jerónimo speaks very little and passes for
being mentally retarded. In reality he possesses the gift of memory.

His secret is his memory. Jerónimo leads us in succession to his multiple "pasts." He has been a monk-hunting assassin, a pimp and ex-
ploiter of whores in the Spanish Naples of the seventeenth century. He
has been a young Greek woman in Palestine in the first century AD.
He has been a Hindu brahmin in some lost time. And he has been,
above all, an anonymous descendant of a nameless tribe at the dawn
of time.

It all brings to mind such celebrated antecedents as Virginia
Woolf's *Orlando*, where the title character travels through historical
time, changing sex in the distinct periods that go from a frozen London revived by the music of Handel, to Constantinople, to England
between the two World Wars. *Orlando* traces a process of change, in
the end, linear — from the past to the present — in which the historical times and the character's sex change.

In *Vidas perpendiculares*, by contrast, we do not travel from Jerónimo's past — or pasts — to his Jaliscan present. Jerónimo's pasts do not
follow one another. They only *happen*, one alongside the other, not in
progression, but rather in temporal simultaneity. This is not only the
difference, but rather Enrigue's great wager, and it is the novel's wager
in the wake of Joyce. To transcend successive narration by simultaneous narration. To give the novel the same instantaneity as painting, in
the way of Velázquez, who gives the immediate painting of *Las Meninas*, or Picasso, who breaks it down into its parts to go from the narrative to the event of narration: everything breaks down, everything
multiples. The frontal instantaneity of *Las Meninas* becomes the instantaneity of what we do not see although we guess it: the *behind*,
the *above*, the *below*, as well as the *sides* of the painting.

A similar aesthetic obeys multiple transformations that we associate with the information revolution of the twentieth century. In
science, Einstein and Heisenberg transform time and space in accordance with the observer's position and language: everything becomes
relative. In literary terms, this signifies that there is no reality without time and space — nor is there reality without the *language* of time
and space. I believe that this is important for reading *Vidas perpendiculares*, because Enrigue takes an extra step. His novel belongs more
to Max Planck's quantum universe than the relativist universe of Albert Einstein: a world of coexisting fields in constant interaction and
whose particles are created or destroyed in the same act.

Of course, this knowledge is not required to read and enjoy Enrigue's *Vidas perpendiculares*. The author's narrative talent transcends
its possible theoretical origins to deliver us the sense—better yet, the
senses—of each simultaneous epoch of the life of the young Jerónimo in Guadalajara, in a Jesuit school in the United States, and in a
Mexico City admirably and newly presented in its best moment (its
most desolate), and in his most desolate hour, "as sad as a Bolivian."

It is this immediacy which confers its presence on the past-present,
similar to Faulkner's evocation in *Intruder in the Dust*: "It's all now
you see. Yesterday won't be over until tomorrow and tomorrow began
ten thousand years ago." Enrigue penetrates through the senses—especially the sense of smell—in the concretion of his quantum fables.
In one of the most outstanding, Saul, before taking the road to Da-
mascus, is presented to us as a stunted, rickety man, vigorous and
sickly, "jealous and abstinent," insane for his "sentimental irregular-
ity" in the presence of the female Greek storyteller. The Neapolitan
monk-hunter and the Hindustani brahmins are all immersed in the
world of senses, they spit saliva, they clean their fingernails, and, not
being dead and mummified, they sweat.

I believe that Enrigue's narrative strategy comes to a head in the
pages of devastating power—storm, earthquake—in which the narrator has lost—or does not yet have—his identity, rather he is part
of the great prehistoric pack of wild dogs, the thundering herd at the
dawn of time, the first tribe that ran through the hills that belonged
to wolves, half animal, half man, following the leader with an instinct
at once obedient and ferocious, the one animal that consents to be
imitated. This segment gives *Vidas perpendiculares* its true originality,
which does not consist of reinventing the wheel, but rather in knowing itself to be part of a tradition which goes back to the origin of the
world, and the origin of the world is death.

Vidas perpendiculares depends to a high degree on the confidence
the author places in the reader, and which the reader gives the author.
Here the traditional capital letters disappear, the transitions from one
time to another are increasingly diluted until the Río Bravo and the
River Jordan coexist in the space of two passes of the iron over a
woman's skirt.

I will not relate the Mexican stories that nourish this work, because,
with retrospective fatality, Octavio del Río has to be killed. I prefer

to evoke the concluding sensuality, the dark and luminously playful humor, of a character—Tita—who Enrigue presents to us in two or three pages overflowing with creative display as a "coquettish, maternal, shrewish or skeptical" woman whose bracelets fly like sleigh bells, who has freckles on her breastbone and "the deepest pupils in the world."

3.

When I was born, in 1928, Mexico City had fewer than one million inhabitants. When I published my first novel, *Where the Air is Clear*, in 1958, the population had reached five million. When Juan Villoro published *El Testigo* (Witness) in 2004, the number of citizens had surpassed twenty million. I say this because, in a certain way, I was used to a Mexico City that was tighter, more compact and embraceable in its extremes, although never in its depths. From below, a city that is Nahuatl, colonial, nineteenth century, modern. Heading outwards, a city bordered by Azcapotzalco to the north, Cuatro Caminos and Magdalena Contreras to the west, Coyoacán to the south, and Lake Texcoco to the east. Today, Mexico has spilled beyond the Federal District to the State of Mexico, to the borders of Morelos, to Santa Fe.

In *El Testigo*, Juan Villoro has refused to let the space of the city be the space of his novel. Mexico City is here only a literary space— that of the novel *El Testigo*—complemented by the spaces that the city left behind or those that the city could not subdue. The novel's space is no longer constructed by extension or number. The novel is a city without limits, due to absences, due to nostalgias. Due to languages: *mamerto, Chómpiras, me vale sorbete* ("Chómpiras, you idiot, you're worthless").

Aware that Mexico City, D.F.—*el Distrito Federal*—has become uncontainable, Villoro thus opts to create a parceled city, more identifiable by what it is not than for what it is; more for its ways of deceiving itself than for the truths which it tells itself or which are told about it. Julio, the narrator, has returned from Europe with an Italian wife and two little daughters. If he ever thought that his absence would be forgiven, he was wrong. Mexico City awaits him loaded with everything that Julio had wanted to leave behind. The people from his past await him, disposed to deny him peace and throw his absence in his face: Félix Rovirosa and Constantino Portella, Gándara and Centollo, Orlando Barbosa and the women of yesterday, Nieves and Vlady Vay.

Also awaiting him are a broken country and the authority of disaster. The thousand ways of being offended that Mexicans have. The pending accounts of collective and personal life. The hard smiles of those who don't want to be noticed. The rancor, disappointment, and impotence. The eternal expectation of something that is never going to happen. The myth-deception of those who wanted "perfect socialism, free love, independent film, and poetry without a world or without any other world than that of poetry."

Abject prejudices—sometimes hidden but never forgotten—await him, from the world of privileges, sometimes privileges lost through circumstance, sometimes inherited at birth. To go to the toilet is to "hacer Juárez," that is, to "make (Benito) Juárez." Education becomes dangerous for the Indian. Juárez was an anticlerical Indian because they had educated him and the Indian has no rights, not even the right to get old: when the Indian's hair turns gray, the Spaniard passes away. Juárez had to die. Our Messiahs must be *insipid*

I point out this anti-indigenous racism because it is neither common nor admissible in the Mexican culture, where education of the indigenous is tantamount to insulting what is Spanish, creating the moral confusion in which we exalt the dead Indian but discriminate against the living one; we censure the Spanish conquest but we are who we are, and speak what we speak, thanks to Spain. How do we escape from such contradictions? There are more than enough pyramids and playas, notes Villoro, and their ease and accessibility, refuses our vocation for disaster. Democracy? To settle differences. Tranquility? Good for dying of boredom. History? Not reality but rather, barely, a poor remedy for reality.

What remains for us? Villoro makes a notable incursion to the world of the Mexican countryside. No longer is it, of course, the countryside of Yáñez or Rulfo, because the Mexican farmers and peasants have lost all their battles. Villoro recreates the great nostalgia for peasant *action*, not only in the Revolution of Zapata and Villa, but rather in that singular moment which was the Cristero War, the rebellion of domestic Catholics against the civil laws of the Revolution and, in particular, against the "atheist" governments of Obregón and Calles in the decade from 1920-1930. A desperate, heroic, senseless action, in Villoro's work the Cristero War is the historical symbol of a defeat for the land. The agrarian world of Mexico was despoiled, to the degree that today three quarters of Mexicans live in cities. The ultimate extravagance of the countryside was, perhaps, the Cristero war, and how the Cristero fighters aimed their rifles at clocks in order to stop a time that would not obey them. Defeated, they leapt from cliffs to their death in the canyons below, but left behind their shirts as evidence of their presence.

The province that Julio visits and Villoro evokes is a churchyard that cannot ignore its own death. Places, odors, memories, absences, speak of a mad war whose only leader was Christ and whose militants feared dying in their sleep, "without commending themselves to God," although, at times, they went to sleep with the noose around their neck. The Church, in the end, did not walk alongside the rebels.

The Mexican countryside only ended up with the "rancid splendor" granted it by a Zacatecan poet, Ramón López Velarde, whose short life (1880-1921) prevented him from seeing more than the reality of a passing movement but whose poetry rescued a world that, without it, would be lacking a soul. "The Catholic crossed by nostalgia and the dandy transgressor," as Villoro calls him, admitted all the "favorite quarrels" of Mexican culture: the provinces against the capital, rebellion against tradition, Mexico against the world, civilization against barbarism. Above all, the quarrel about women: blessed or cursed, "withered and faded, crazy or dead." A "Sad intimate reactionary" and yet, is there another poetic voice which takes notice of itself and its time, of us, of contradictions, more than López Velarde? Villoro rightly gives the poet a central place in his novel of desperation which is *El Testigo*. Perhaps the title's testimony belongs to López Velarde, because Villoro drags us down to all the things that repel him — "The horror, the horror," as Conrad's Kurtz would say in *Heart of Darkness* — in a shocking collision of the crimes of authorities and criminals who subject the protagonist Julio to a horror personified by the Commandant Ogarrio, with his large hand "saturated with rings," pockmarked complexion, thug's language, entrails for supper, cock like a cigar, and his sinister cohort, the Ferret.

The novelist makes us feel that, like Julio, all of us in any great

Latin American city, are exposed to the malign damage which Ogarrio and the Ferret, who also happen to be representatives of the law, have in store for us. Villoro leaves it to us to imagine what the representatives of crime will be like. Or is there no longer any difference? "Each person," specifies Villoro, "was assigned a certain amount of violence . . . a vaccine for living in Mexico City, el Distrito Federal."

In Bogotá, in Caracas, in Río de Janeiro,

in Lima, in Buenos Aires, in Mexico City,

in Santiago de Chile. Brave new world.

A Final Word

The reader holds in their hands a personal book. This is not a "history" of Ibero-American fiction. Some names, some works are missing. Some would say, on the other hand, that there are too many names, too many books. It has been my wish to subject myself to an irregular discipline which gives, for example, a place of origin to three works and three authors from our century of literary foundation in Spanish and Portuguese, Thomas More's *Utopia* (1516), Erasmus of Rotterdam's *In Praise of Folly* (1511) and Niccoló Machiavelli's *The Prince* (1513). From them I derive three constant themes in our narrative fiction: the *desire to be*, the *duty to be*, and what *can not* or *should not be*. The declinations of power *that is*, a Machiavellian theme, are found in a long list of novels that stretch from Valle-Inclán and Gallegos to Juan Rulfo, García Márquez, and Vargas Llosa. The imagination of the power which *must be* underlies the great utopian tradition of the American continent, be it revolutionary or democratic, but it does so with the warning of an ironic smile in Onetti or Cortázar. Lezama Lima describes the Baroque scaffolding—the cultural *plus ultra*—while the work of Jorge Luis Borges focuses on the *minus ultra* of the verbal imagination.

If Ibero-America has lacked political and economic continuity, it has known how to create a literary tradition, in spite of colonial and post-colonial prohibitions. Machado de Assis realizes this dynamic of humor in opposition to the solemnity of powers, a tradition carried on by practically all the authors studied in these pages. Especially in the most recent ones. Thus there is a bridge of continuity between the foundational writers, a long list from Borges to Carpentier, and another, parallel line of perturbation, humor, and personalization very much belonging to Cortázar and the current writers of our America. It is as if Cortázar himself had come back today and took notice of everything *unsaid* yesterday and that everything *unsaid* yesterday contained, in turn, what was necessary *to say* today. The happy and unhappy words of literature.

I will be rightly accused of showing preference for my own country, Mexico, and its writers. So be it. If I were Brazilian, I would dedicate much more space to such admirable writers as Euclides da Cunha, Jorge Amado, Guimarães Rosa, Clarice Lispector, Rubem

Fonseca, and the limitations of space oblige me to pass over, or barely mention, writers from Colombia, Peru, or Chile whom I admire as much as those studied herein. The reason is that these writers who are included, correspond more to the general speculative line of this book. And if the book abounds with Mexican writers it is because I know them better, I've read them more, and *¡qué chingados!* there's no place like Mexico.

Seriously, this is a book about the great power of the novel, including the *potential* novel which has yet to be written. What I mean is: there was one world before the publication of *Don Quixote* in 1605, and afterwards, another one, forever different. The Cervantean reference — the novel of La Mancha, that is *manchada* (stained, impure) — is indispensable in order to speak about fiction, of the immediate past, of today, of tomorrow. Nonetheless there are many important post-*Quixote* references, as well as the Dickensian, Proustian, Faulknerian, and Joycean novels. Good and valid ones. Each period goes about naming the world and in the process names itself and its works.

Why? First, because the notions of time and space which inform any novel change as the concept of the world changes, from Galileo to Newton to Einstein, each one accompanied — cause? effect? — by works — music, literature, philosophy, architecture — resembling the way that the world conceives of itself. But however this may be, however times and spaces change, there will be dissatisfaction, there will be diversity, and there will be words. Novels will be written, and no *technical* or *amusing* novelty will change this vital necessity and pleasure, which comes before any and all ideological or technocratic framework. Thus arise the strength, the disturbance, and the pleasure which is called the "novel."

Rome, July 2011